TREND FOLLOWING
WITH
MANAGED FUTURES

Founded in 1807, John Wiley & Sons is the oldest independent publishing company in the United States. With offices in North America, Europe, Australia and Asia, Wiley is globally committed to developing and marketing print and electronic products and services for our customers' professional and personal knowledge and understanding.

The Wiley Trading series features books by traders who have survived the market's ever changing temperament and have prospered—some by reinventing systems, others by getting back to basics. Whether a novice trader, professional or somewhere in-between, these books will provide the advice and strategies needed to prosper today and well into the future.

For more on this series, visit our Web site at www.WileyTrading.com.

TREND FOLLOWING WITH MANAGED FUTURES

The Search for Crisis Alpha

Alex Greyserman
Kathryn Kaminski

WILEY

CONTENTS

FOREWORD

It is a rare pleasure and honor for an academic to be asked to write a foreword for a book coauthored by one of his charges, not unlike a parent seeing a child off to college and onto a successful career of her own. However, unlike parenthood, my experience with Katy Kaminski was considerably less challenging because she first showed up at my office more than a decade ago already well-trained in mathematics, statistics, and operations research, and an eager student of finance. Like most MIT students I've had the privilege of advising over the years, Katy did most of the driving; my role was largely to stay out of her way and cheer her on from the stands.

This book—coauthored with Alex Greyserman, a seasoned Wall Street veteran and PhD in statistics—is a fascinating and timely examination of an investment strategy that, for too long, has dwelt in the shadows of the financial industry. Trend following has received a bad rap among mainstream investors and portfolio managers for a number of reasons. Perhaps the most obvious is the natural preference for originality in any creative endeavor, whether it be in the arts or the sciences—why would you want to follow the crowd when you can do something unique?

This instinctive aversion to copycats belies the surprising frequency of copycat strategies found in nature, including herding behavior among most animal species, mimicking abilities such as the color shifting of chameleons, and the high-fidelity nature of DNA replication across eons of time. Among Homo sapiens, trends have also been documented in the spread of technologies such as fire, stone tools, agriculture, and industrialization, not to mention hemlines, low-carb diets, and apps. In the narrow context of financial investments, trends are all too familiar to brokers, financial advisors, and others responsible for marketing new products such as global tactical asset allocation overlays, 130/30 funds, and risk-parity strategies. As certain investment products come into or fall out of favor, trends in asset prices are created by the flow of funds into and out of these products.

But despite the many reasons for trends to exist and persist, there still seems to be an almost religious aversion to trend following investment strategies among certain investors. I believe there are three primary sources for this aversion. The first is the efficient markets hypothesis—if trend following really works, everyone would do it, and then wouldn't it stop working? The second is the fact that early trend following strategies were associated with technical analysis or "charting," which finance academics equate with voodoo and astrology. And the third is the lack of transparency surrounding trend following strategies, which makes it hard for investors to understand how and when they generate value, why they offer unique diversification benefits, and under what conditions they are likely to underperform more traditional investments.

The first point can be addressed by observing that even if prices do fully reflect all available information instantaneously and costless, trends can still exist if an asset carries a positive risk premium. After all, what is a risk premium but a positive expected excess return, which implies an upward-trending price series! Trend following strategies exploit such risk premia, but are one level more sophisticated than traditional buy-and-hold strategies because they acknowledge that risk premia are time-varying and when trends break, stop-loss policies are used to reduce downside risk. But markets are not always and everywhere efficient, as many academics and industry professionals now recognize—investors adapt to changing economic conditions, and trends and reversals are commonplace in adaptive markets.

The second point is an unfortunate aspect of heritage that trend followers can't easily escape, but rather than suffer silently from guilt by association, practitioners can differentiate themselves by articulating a deeper narrative for trend following strategies. And the third point can be addressed by deriving the many investment implications of this deeper narrative such as benchmarking, portfolio construction, style analysis, and performance attribution. This is exactly what Greyserman and Kaminski have done in this exciting volume.

Trend following strategies may never achieve the popularity that passive equity index funds enjoy, but that's probably a good thing—if they did, they might not be as great a source of diversification as they are now. But until then, every serious investor should read this book!

Andrew W. Lo
Cambridge, Massachusetts
March 2014

I was born in the former Soviet Union and came to the United States when I was 12 years old. After studying math, statistics, and engineering, I reached a fork in the road 25 years ago. Having worked at a slow-paced engineering job for a year, I remembered taking an elective course in graduate school at Columbia called "Operations Research in Finance" and wondered what the world of finance was all about. In 1989, I went on an interview with Larry Hite in Millburn, New Jersey. Larry was one of the early pioneers of trend following systems. At that time Larry was running the largest CTA in the world, called Mint, with nearly $1 billion under management. The job description was entry level programming and data analysis. During the interview, when I asked Larry what he does, Larry told me that he wins because he "knows what he doesn't know." He also told me that he thinks "not being hindered by higher education" gives him an edge. Having just come from said "higher education" I had no idea what he was talking about. But I knew one fact . . . Larry offered me a salary several thousand dollars a year higher than I was earning in engineering, and on that basis, I decided to take the plunge. Larry Hite has been my mentor since my entry into the finance world. His lack of formal quantitative education is his main asset . . . he asks questions and pushes the envelope from an outside-the-box mind-set better than most quants.

Over the past 25 years I've experienced lots of ups and downs in the CTA industry. A number of times the industry has been declared dead for various reasons, and an equal number of times it has survived and grown. The trials and tribulations of constructing systematic trading strategies is a wild ride. Certain models sometimes work and sometimes don't. The Holy Grail does not exist. Prudent risk management and survival is the name of the game. The markets often seemingly move in a way to make the largest number of people lose the most amount of money. These are necessary forces of adaptation and evolution. As Keynes famously said, "Markets can remain irrational longer than you can remain solvent."

Financial modeling often involves avoiding complexity in favor of simplicity and practical compromise. The "buy side" is dominated not by highly rigorous math or miraculous discoveries, but rather by a mix of analytical and financial understanding, sensible risk management, and a general sense of "humbleness" in the pursuit of an "edge." I have taught in the mathematical finance program at Columbia University for the past 12 years. My main challenge and goal every term has been to take a room full of high-IQ math geniuses, who have rarely been wrong in doing anything, and teach them some humility when facing the realities of the investment world. We cover various materials and math formulas, but at the end of the day, my goal is partially psychological . . . I want the students to understand that they can be wrong, or that the markets can prove them wrong, or that sometimes models can lose money and you simply don't know why, and that rule number one of being successful in the investment world is to lose any emotional attachment to one's superior IQ or sense of infallibility. If, at the end of the term, even a small percentage of the students come out with the understanding and ability to deal with failure as part of the process, I think I have done my job.

First and foremost, I want to thank my family. My parents sacrificed a lot to enable me to pursue the full scope of opportunities in the United States. My wife Elaine drove with me to the aforementioned interview with Larry Hite. As Yogi Berra once said, "When you come to a fork in the road, take it." We took the fork into the world of finance, and she has provided enduring support and encouragement for more than 25 years. My children, Jacquie, Max, Dean, and Reed, provide the daily inspiration to work hard (four college degrees are not cheap).

I want to thank the team at ISAM for encouraging me to pursue this project. Stanley Fink, Larry Hite, Roy Sher, Alex Lowe, Darren Upton, Jack Weiner, and Riva Waller have been supportive colleagues (and part-time editors) for a long time.

Alex Greyserman

■ ■ ■

When I was eleven, I did my first science project on nerve conduction and temperature. Given that my mother is a savvy financial planner and father is an expert clinical neurologist, it comes as no surprise that my path has led me from mathematics, to electrical engineering, to operations research, and finally into the world of quantitative finance with a twist of behavioral and neurofinance. I grew up in Nashville, Tennessee, but my passion for math and science led me to MIT. I was fascinated by signal processing and systems engineering—who doesn't want to build an MP3 player or write code for satellite phones? After several years enthralled by Fourier transforms, studying engineering physics in French at École Polytechnique, and time modeling subordinated debt contracts for a quantitative modeling team at Société Générale, I was drawn to quantitative finance, pursuing a doctorate in operations research at MIT Sloan. I was overjoyed at the opportunity to work with Andrew Lo, one of finance's top quantitative gurus. He asked me why stop loss rules stop losses and what value simple rules and heuristics have in investments. Everyone used these rules; there must be some reason behind them.

When people say go right, I generally go left. I wanted to study heuristics and simple rules because, given what my father taught me about human cognition, expected utility theory was clearly fantastical nonsense. I spent several incredible years working with Andrew Lo learning everything he could teach me about finance. Andrew taught me to continue to ask questions, to challenge ideas, to never be afraid to try a new angle to attack a difficult problem and to stick to my guns (for example—it's okay that I think utility theory is fantastical nonsense). Over the years, Andrew has been my advisor, my mentor, my friend, and eventually my colleague. I am forever grateful that he set me out on the journey to understand the use of heuristics and rules in investment management. Given that trend following is essentially a set of investment heuristics and simple rules, it is no surprise that I have been thoroughly obsessed with understanding how and why it works for years.

First and foremost, I want to thank my family: my husband, two daughters, parents, and extended American and Swedish families. My husband, Pierre, has continually supported me and encouraged me to take on this insanely big project. My darlings Ellinor and Hailie are the light of my life. I thank my parents for opening up so many doors for me and setting high expectations for success. My brother Matt has been my rock for longer than I can remember. I am forever grateful for my humble superstar mentor, advisor, and friend Andrew Lo. Without your tutelage and support, I would never have achieved so much and learned to think outside of any box. I am thankful for my fellow finance lady friends: Mila Getmansky-Sherman, Jasmina Hasanhodzic, and Maria Strömqvist. My many fellow students and professors at MIT opened new doors and allowed me to see things from new perspectives. I am also grateful for my friends for keeping me closer to the ground: Ann,

Benedicte, Emily, Juliane, Lucile, Lynn, Margret, Maria, Nebibe, Sumita, Susan, Svetlana, and Tanya.

My past colleagues at RPM were a significant part of my journey into managed futures. John Sjödin has been a friend, confidant, and sounding board for my many ideas. I am thankful for my supportive colleagues at the Swedish House of Finance and my friends in the Swedish financial industry. My boss, friend, and colleague Pehr Wissen has been a great source of support on this journey. My passion for teaching has always been greatly supported by my many students from the Stockholm School of Economics (SSE), MIT Sloan School of Management, and the Swedish Royal Institute of Technology (KTH).

Kathryn Kaminski

■ ■ ■

We both have a mutual friend at the CME Group, Randy Warsager. Randy has been a tremendous industry advocate and friend to many. Randy introduced us based on our common research interests. When we met for the first time the challenge was obvious: We had to write an all-inclusive academic textbook on trend following. In addition to our mutual backgrounds in signal processing turned to finance, we both also have an innate desire to bring simplicity to complexity. Our mutual challenge was to turn the world of trend following from a world of geeks and financial folklore into the serious objective discipline that it really is.

First and foremost, we would like to thank the incredible team at ISAM. Lian Yan has been an integral part of this research and played a significant role in the creation of this book. We would also like to thank Noelle Sisco for her keen attention to detail and support. Jack Weiner carefully read and commented on the entire book. We also thank the supporting quantitative analyst team: Chris Bridges and Patrick Luckett.

We thank our industry friends and fellow trend following fans: RPM, Efficient Capital, Abbey Capital, Lighthouse Partners, Hermes, Newedge, and the CME Group. Our mutual relationship with the CME Group, fueled by the enthusiastic efforts of Randy Warsager, led us to meet and create this book. As a fellow believer in research, Newedge has been particularly helpful in supporting this project. We thank James Skeggs for his detailed review of this book. We would like to thank the many bright and insightful colleagues in industry and academia: Ingemar Bergdahl, Svante Bergström, Ranjan Bhaduri, Eric Bundonis, Galen Burghardt, Andreas Clenow, John Connolly, Adam Duncan, Tony Gannon, Joel Handy, Eric Hoh, Per Ivarsson, Ernest Jaffarian, Grant Jaffarian, Greg Jones, Martin Källström, Hossein Kazemi,

Larry Kissko, John Labuszewski, Andrew Lo, Mark Melin, Alexander Mende, Sean McGould, Romule Nohasiarisoa, Petter Odhnoff, Kelly Perkins, Blu Putnam, Ed Robertiello, Tarek Rizk, John Sjödin, James Skeggs, Chris Solarz, Mikael Stenbom, and Brian Wells. We are especially grateful for those of you who took a look at our work, provided feedback, or helped give us insights to create this book.

Alex Greyserman, PhD, and Kathryn Kaminski, PhD

Trend following is one of the classic investment styles. "Find a trend and follow it" is a common adage that has been passed on throughout the centuries. The concept of trend following is simple. When there is a trend, follow it; when things move against you or when the trend isn't really there, cut your losses. Despite the simplicity of the concept, the strategy has roused substantial criticism among neo-classical economists. For decades, trend following has been shunned as the black sheep of investment styles. In the classroom, in research, and even in the popular press, many have preached the word of efficient markets, touted the value of the equity premium, and asserted the importance of buying and holding for the long term. Figure I.1 presents the performance for trend following and equity markets. Figure I.2 presents the drawdown profile for trend following and equity markets. Over the past two decades, equity markets have experienced rather severe boom and bust cycles. Although trend followers follow trends across markets, the approach is seemingly uncorrelated with this dramatic boom and bust cycle. The drawdown profile for equity markets is akin to a high-speed roller-coaster ride. Although there are many benefits to long-term investing, this simple example demonstrates that the ride may be a bumpy one. In comparison, trend followers have a rather persistent

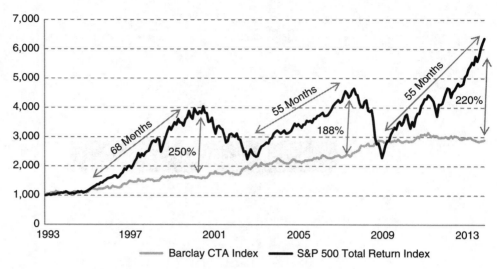

FIGURE I.1 The cumulative performance for trend following (using the Barclay CTA index) and equity markets (using the S&P 500 Total Return Index). The sample period is 1993 to 2013. *Data source*: Bloomberg.

drawdown profile. Despite a history of criticism, there is clearly something to following the trend.[1]

The rather stable performance of trend following over a turbulent period for equity markets gives rise to several questions. What would happen if the trend following index had the same volatility? Or even more interesting—what would happen if equity markets and trend following were combined 50/50?

Figure I.3 plots the cumulative performance for equity markets, trend following at the same volatility, and a 50/50 combination of the two. The combination of trend following and equity markets seems to provide the most stable return series over time. Table I.1 lists the performance statistics for equity markets, trend following, and a 50/50 combination of the two. Both equity markets and trend following have similar Sharpe ratios, but an equal combination of the two increases the Sharpe ratio for equity markets by 66 percent. The maximum drawdown for the combined portfolio reduces the maximum drawdown for equity markets from 51 percent to 22 percent. Despite the simplicity of this example, there is clearly something unique and complementary to a trend following approach that deserves further analysis and inspection.

---

[1] Market efficiency, equity premiums, and buy and hold are all important notions in finance. The point to be made here is that they do not negate the value of trend following. In fact, trend following is a natural complement to these concepts. The goal of this book is to demonstrate and motivate this point.

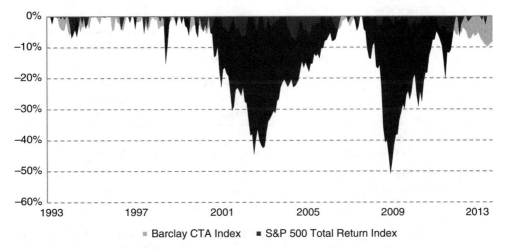

FIGURE I.2   The drawdown profile for trend following (using the Barclay CTA Index) and equity markets (using the S&P 500 Total Return Index). The sample period is 1993 to 2013.
Data source: Bloomberg.

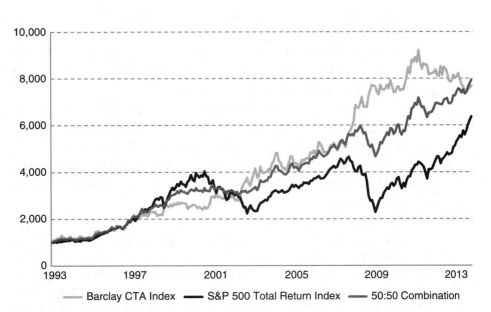

FIGURE I.3   The cumulative performance for equity markets (S&P 500 Total Return Index), trend following with the same volatility as equity markets (Barclay CTA Index), and 50/50 equities and trend following (S&P 500 Total Return Index, Barclay CTA Index). The sample period is 1993 to 2013.
Data source: Bloomberg.

TABLE I.1 Performance statistics for equity markets (S&P 500 Total Return Index), trend following at equity volatility (Barclay CTA Index), and a 50/50 combination of equity markets and trend following (S&P 500 Total Return Index, Barclay CTA Index). The sample period is 1993 to 2013.

	Barclay CTA Index (at equity volatility)	S&P 500 Total Return Index	50:50 Combination
Average Return (annual)	10.19%	9.22%	10.37%
Standard Deviation (annual)	14.94%	14.94%	10.10%
Sharpe Ratio (annual)	0.68	0.62	1.03
Max Drawdown	19.53%	50.95%	21.89%

Modern-day trend following strategies are about systematically finding trends in market prices, riding them, and getting out before they revert. For this type of momentum strategy, there is both an art and a science to execution. The science of modern systematic trend following is facilitated by computational power and trading automation. Subjective (or discretionary) rules of thumb and heuristics have been replaced by structured systems of trading rules creating autonomous trading systems, the notorious "black boxes." A modern systematic trend following system has become more like a finely tuned and engineered machine. These machines adjust their outputs (trading positions) as a function of price movements (inputs). Each system includes internal components (risk management systems) to regulate stressors and shocks.[2] The design of these systems is structurally simple, efficient, and transparent. Simplicity and robustness is essential, as these trading systems manage hundreds to thousands of positions simultaneously.

The art of modern day trend following is in signal processing and trading execution. Trend followers use signals to determine when a trend is beginning or ending. These signals must be quantified, processed, and combined with other signals. Creating a connection between the signal processing and the corresponding trading execution for implementation is a skill that requires eloquence, experience, and a fine attention to detail.[3]

---

[2] A cellular phone (or any mobile device) provides a good, practical example. Mobile devices have structured methodology for processing external inputs from a user. The functionality of a mobile device is organized by a network of systems coupled together with rules and instructions. These rules and instructions are initiated by external inputs. External inputs are processed, and an action takes place if the proper parameters of that action create a sequence of actions by the device. If there are actions that stress the system, there are internal blocks similar to circuit breakers and controls that deal with external inputs that are not within the bands acceptable for the device.

[3] Returning to the analogy of a mobile phone, the structure and operation system of a mobile device must be functional. The art is in the external user interface and the eloquence in which it processes external inputs.

As with any comprehensive and arduous endeavor, this book begins with *history* by taking a philosophical and historical look at the concept of trend following over the centuries. The remainder of this book has the noble goal of demystifying both the *art* and the *science* of trend following from the perspective of the end user, the institutional investor.

■ A Foreword for the Remainder of the Book

The book begins by telling *the tale of trend following* throughout the ages. A multi-centennial view of the strategy from a historical perspective sets the stage for the deeper more detailed analysis of modern systematic trend following in the remainder of the book. The book is divided into six core sections:

I. Historical Perspectives

Using a unique 800-year dataset, trend following is examined from a multi-century perspective.

II. Introduction to Trend Following Basics

The goal of this section is to explain trend following system construction and the mechanics of trading in futures markets. Futures markets, futures trading, and the managed futures industry are reviewed. The basic building blocks of a modern systematic trend following system are discussed.

III. Theoretical Foundations

This section provides theoretical motivation for understanding why trend following works. The Adaptive Markets Hypothesis (AMH) is introduced and applied to derive and clarify the concept of crisis alpha. The concepts of divergent and convergent risk-taking strategies are introduced. This section explains the concept of market divergence and its role in trend following performance. Given that trend following is applied in futures markets, the role of interest rates and the roll yield are also discussed.

IV. Trend Following as an Alternative Asset Class

Trend following is discussed as an alternative asset class. The key properties of trend following returns are discussed, including performance measures, crisis alpha, crisis beta, drawdowns, correlation, and volatility. The concept of hidden and unhidden risks, leverage risk with dynamic leveraging, and macro environments are explained.

V. Benchmarking and Style Analysis

This section discusses return dispersion, benchmarking, and style analysis. The idiosyncratic effects of parameter selection are linked to return dispersion in trend following. A divergent trend following index and three construction style factors are introduced. The divergent trend following index and style factors are used to demonstrate the applications of return based style analysis. Performance attribution, monitoring, appropriate benchmarking, manager selection, and manager allocation are applications of style analysis.

VI. Trend Following in an Investment Portfolio

This section discusses trend following from the investor's perspective and advanced topics based on common themes earlier in the book. Topics include the role of equity markets in crisis alpha, the role of mark-to-market on inter-manager correlation, aspects of size, liquidity, and capacity, as well as the move from pure trend following to multistrategy. Finally dynamic allocation, or the question of when to invest in trend following, is discussed.

TREND FOLLOWING
WITH
MANAGED FUTURES

PART I

HISTORICAL
PERSPECTIVES

CHAPTER 1

A Multicentennial View of Trend Following

Cut short your losses, and let your profits run on.
—David Ricardo, legendary political economist
Source: The Great Metropolis, 1838

Trend following is one of the classic investment styles. This chapter tells the *tale of trend following* throughout the centuries. Before delving into the highly detailed analysis in subsequent chapters, it is interesting to discuss the paradigm of trend following from a qualitative historical perspective. Although data-intensive, this approach is by no means a bulletproof rigorous academic exercise. As with any long-term historical study, this analysis is fraught with assumptions, questions of data reliability, and other biases. Despite all of these concerns, history shapes our perspectives; history is arguably highly subjective, yet it provides contextual relevance.

This chapter examines a simple characterization of trend following using roughly 800 years of financial data. Despite this rather naive characterization and albeit crude set of financial data throughout the centuries, the performance of "cutting your losses, and letting your profits run on" is robust enough to garner our attention. The goal of this chapter is not to quote *t*-statistics and make resolute assumptions based on historical data. The goal is to ask the question of whether the legendary David

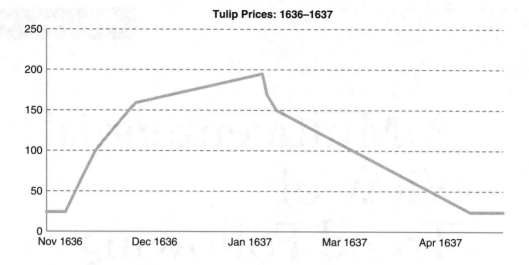

FIGURE 1.1   A standard price index for tulip bulb prices.
Source: Thompson (2007).

Ricardo, the famous turtle traders, and many successful trend followers throughout history are simply a matter of overembellished folklore or whether they may have had a point.

In recent times, trend following has garnered substantial attention for deftly performing during a period of extreme market distress. Trend following managers boasted returns of 15 to 80 percent during the abysmal period following the credit crisis and infamous Lehmann debacle. Many have wondered if this performance is simply a fluke or if the strategy would have performed so well in other difficult periods in markets. For example, how would a trend follower have performed during past crises like those experienced in the Great Depression, the 1600s, or even the 1200s?

Given that this chapter engages in a historical discussion of trend following, it seems only fitting to begin with a rather controversial and relatively spectacular historical event, the Dutch Tulip Bubble of the early 1600s. Historical prices for tulips are plotted in Figure 1.1. One common type of trend following strategy is a channel breakout strategy. A channel breakout signal takes a long (short) position when a signal breaks out of a certain upper (lower) boundary for a range of values. Using a simple channel breakout signal,[1] a trend following investor might have entered

TREND FOLLOWING WITH MANAGED FUTURES

---

[1] Breakout strategies and other components for building trend following systems are discussed in Chapter 3.

a long position before November 25th, 1636 and would have exited the trade (by selling tulip bulbs and eventually short selling if that was even possible) around February 9th, 1637. A trend following investor simply "follows the trend" and cuts losses when the trend seems to disappear. In the case of tulips, a trend following investor might have ridden the bubble upward and sold when prices started to fall. This approach would have led to a sizeable return rather than a handful of flower bulbs and economic ruin. Although it is one rather esoteric example, the tulip bulb example demonstrates that there may be something robust or fundamental about the performance of a dynamic strategy like trend following over the long run. It is important to note that in this example, as in most financial markets, the **exit decision** seems to be more important than the entry. The importance of *cutting your losses and taking profits* seems to drive performance. This is a concept that is revisited often throughout the course of this book.

Trend following strategies adapt with financial markets. They find opportunities when market prices create trends due to many fundamental, technical, and behavioral reasons. As a group, trend followers profit from market divergence, riding trends in market prices, and cutting their losses across markets. Examples of drivers that may create trends in markets include risk transfer (or economic rents being transferred from hedgers to speculators), the process of information dissemination, and behavioral biases (euphoria, panic, etc.). Despite the wide range of explanations, the underlying reasons behind market divergence are *of little consequence* to a trend follower. They seek simply to be there when opportunity arises. Throughout history, opportunities do arise. The robust performance of trend following over the past 800 years helps to historically motivate this point.[2]

■ The Tale of Trend Following: A Historical Study

Although almost two centuries have passed since the advice of legendary political economist David Ricardo, the same core principles of trend following have garnered significant attention in modern times. Using a unique dataset dating back roughly 800 years, the performance of trend following can be examined across a wide array of economic environments documenting low correlation with traditional asset classes, positive skewness, and robust performance during crisis periods.[3]

---

[2] Chapters 4 and 5 of this book discuss theories of adaptive markets, dynamic risk taking, and the role of divergence.

[3] In Chapters 7 through 10, the modern version of systematic trend following is examined as an alternative asset class.

The performance of trend following has been discussed extensively in the applied and academic literature (see Moskowitz, Ooi, and Pedersen 2012).[4] Despite this, most of the data series that are examined are typically limited to actual track records over several decades or futures/cash data from the past century. In this chapter, an 800-year dataset is examined to extend and confirm previous studies.[5] To examine trend following over the long haul, monthly returns of 84 markets in equity, fixed income, foreign exchange, and commodity markets are used as they became available from the 1200s through to 2013.[6] There are several assumptions and approximations that are made to allow for a long-term analysis of trend following. For simplicity, an outline of assumptions and approximations as well as a list of included markets is included in the appendix.

Market behavior has varied substantially throughout the ages. To correctly construct a representative dataset through history, it is important to be particularly mindful of dramatic economic developments. This means that the dataset should, as closely as possible, represent investment returns that could have actually been investable. For a specific example, from the early seventeenth century to the 1930s, the United Kingdom (U.K.), the United States (U.S.), and other major countries were committed to the gold standard. During this period, the price of gold was essentially fixed. As a result, gold must be removed from the sample of investable markets during this particular time period. As a second example, during most of the nineteenth century, capital gains represented an insignificant portion of equity returns. On average, U.S. investors in the nineteenth century received only a 0.7 percent annualized capital gain, but a 5.8 percent dividend per annum (see Figure 1.2). In fact, up to the 1950s, stocks consistently paid a higher dividend yield than corporate bonds.[7] As a consequence, total return indices must be used to represent equity market returns over time.

Using return data collected from as far back as 1223, a representative trend following system can be built for a period spanning roughly 800 years.[8] A representative

---

[4] Moskowitz, Ooi, and Pedersen (2012) document a phenomenon they dub "time series momentum." They show that a multiasset **momentum** portfolio earns a positive premium. Time series momentum is different from the classic cross-sectional momentum of Jegadeesh and Titman (1993) and the vast academic literature that follows it.

[5] The authors note that the analysis in this chapter is meant to tell the "tale of trend following." This chapter provides a historical perspective on the concept of trend following. It is not meant to be replaced by a more rigorous analysis seen in modern academic papers or the detailed analysis later in this book. With any long-term analysis, there are many issues related to tradability, trading constraints such as short sales constraints, reliability of long-term data series, and other concerns.

[6] The data sources are Reuters, Bloomberg, and Global Financial Data.

[7] See also "The GFD Guide to Total Returns" (Taylor).

[8] Using 12-month rolling returns, a trend signal is constructed at the end of each month. A particular market (for example, corn) enters a long (short) position when its return is positive (negative) during the past 12 months. Position sizing is based on equal risk allocation between markets. This concept will be developed further in Chapter 3.

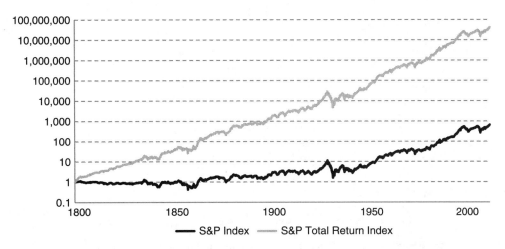

FIGURE 1.2 A historical plot of the S&P 500 Index and S&P 500 Total Return Index from 1800 to 2013 in log scale.

trend following system represents the performance of "following the trend" throughout the centuries in whatever markets might be available. Although certain commodity markets, such as rice, date all the way back to around 1000 AD, the analysis begins in 1223 when there are at least a handful of available markets. At any point in time, to calculate whether a trend exists, the portfolio consists only of the markets that have at least a 12-month history. The trend following portfolio is assumed to be allowed to go both long and short. Monthly data is used for the analysis. Based on a set of simple liquidity constraints, the portfolio is constructed of available markets. Figure 1.3

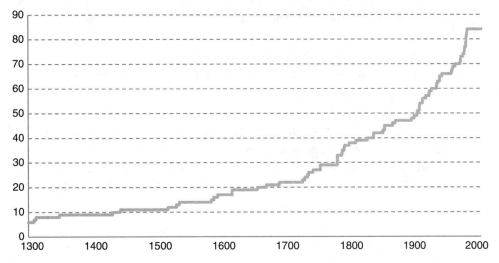

FIGURE 1.3 The number of included markets in the representative trend following program from 1300 to 2013.

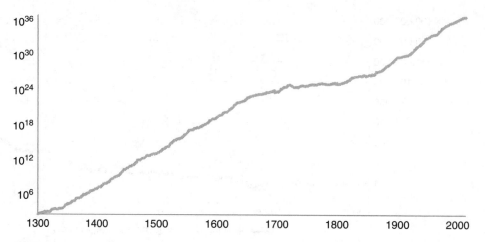

FIGURE 1.4 Cumulative (log) performance of the representative trend following portfolio from 1300 to 2013.

depicts the number of markets in the portfolio over time. The growth of futures markets has facilitated trend followers by making more markets available for trading.

■ Return Characteristics over the Centuries

Trend following requires dynamic allocation of capital to both long and short trends across many different assets over time. Figure 1.4 plots the log scale performance of a trend following strategy for roughly 800 years. Over the entire historical period from the 1300s to 2013, the representative trend following system generates an annual return of 13 percent, with an annualized volatility of 11 percent. This results in a Sharpe ratio of 1.16.[9]

Many finance experts have argued for the reduction of risks in the long run or that one should just simply buy-and-hold. Trend following strategies dynamically adjust positions according to trends, making them the counter to a buy-and-hold long-only strategy. The difference between these two can give insight into the value added of active management across asset classes. Position sizes for both trend following and a buy-and-hold strategy are rebalanced on a monthly basis to achieve equal risk. In contrast with the buy-and-hold, the trend following system is free

[9] Sharpe ratios are calculated assuming that the risk-free rate is zero. This assumption is made because risk-free lending rates are not available for the entire dataset.

TABLE 1.1	Performance statistics for buy-and-hold and trend following portfolios from 1223 to 2013.	
	Buy-and-Hold Portfolio	**Trend Following Portfolio**
Average Return (annual)	4.8%	13.0%
Standard Deviation (annual)	10.3%	11.2%
Sharpe Ratio	0.47	1.16

to go short.[10] For comparison, the buy-and-hold portfolio represents a diversified long-only portfolio consisting of equities, bonds, and commodities.[11] Table 1.1 displays performance statistics for the long-only buy-and-hold portfolio and the representative trend following portfolio. In terms of Sharpe ratio, the total performance of trend following over the past 800 years is far superior. This suggests that there may be a premium to active management and directional flexibility in allowing short positions. Given the spectacular outperformance of trend following over a long-only buy-and-hold portfolio, it is only natural to take a closer look at various factors that may impact this performance. The role of interest rates, inflation, market divergence, and financial bubbles and crisis are examined in closer detail in the following sections.

Interest Rate Regime Dependence

Because interest rates affect market participants' ability to borrow and lend as well as the time value of money, they are an important factor to examine for dynamic strategies. As interest rate regimes change, they can impact dynamic strategies in a plethora of ways. Interest rates are currently historically low, but interest rate regimes have varied substantially across history. Figure 1.5 plots government bond yields over the past 700 years. In this section, interest rate regimes are discussed from a 700-year perspective.[12]

Since around 1300 AD, the median long-term bond yield has averaged around 5.8 percent. Despite the intuitive/fundamental importance of interest rate regimes, the correlation between the level of interest rates and trend following returns is

---

[10] Short selling is simple with futures contracts, but historically short selling would have been difficult or even impossible during many periods in history.

[11] FX markets are not included in the traditional buy-and-hold portfolio. For the buy-and-hold portfolio, monthly rebalancing is done to maintain equal risk with the corresponding trend following portfolio.

[12] In Chapters 6 and 10, interest rates are discussed in a more recent context.

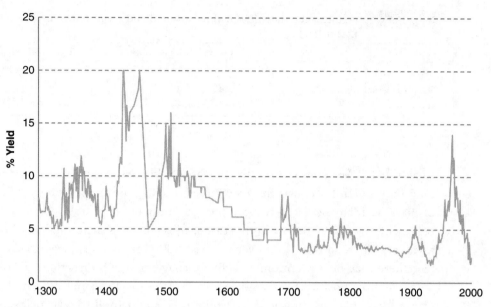

FIGURE 1.5 The GFD long-term government bond yield index from 1300 to 2013.
Source: Global Financial Data.

only 0.14. To see if different regimes have an impact on trend following performance, interest rate levels can be divided into high and low. A high interest rate regime can be defined by a year where the average yield is above the median, and a low-interest rate regime can be defined by a year where the average yield is below the median. Across both high- and low-interest rate regimes, on average, trend following performs better during high-interest rate regimes. This can be seen in Table 1.2.

In practice, it is not only the level of interest rates but also the relative movements in interest rates that impacts markets. To evaluate the impact of changes in interest rate, the yield differential from year-end to year-end can be computed. If the change over a time period is positive (negative), the year is defined as a rising (falling) interest rate year. The correlation between the change in yield and trend following returns is close to zero, suggesting that the difference in trend following performance, during periods of either rising or falling interest rates, does not seem to be significant.

TABLE 1.2 Performance of trend following over different interest rate regimes from 1300 to 2013.

	High IR	Low IR	Rising IR	Falling IR
Average Return (annual)	15.5%	10.6%	11.9%	14.4%
Standard Deviation (annual)	9.9%	12.2%	11.2%	11.1%
Sharpe Ratio	1.56	0.86	1.06	1.30

Inflationary Environments

Having examined the impact of interest rate environments, it is also interesting to discuss inflation. Since both the buy-and-hold and trend following strategies allocate capital across asset classes, including commodities and currencies (buy-and-hold has only commodities), the inflationary environment may play an important role over time. Even outside this long-term historical study, in current times, threats of new, high-inflationary environments are rather pertinent. In light of the current *stimulative monetary policies* undertaken across the globe since the financial crisis of 2008, it may be reasonable to anticipate that these policies may eventually lead to higher inflation globally.

To examine the impact of different inflationary environments, using consumer price index and producer price index for the United States and the United Kingdom starting in 1720, a composite inflation rate index can be constructed. This composite inflation index is plotted in Figure 1.6.

From 1720 to 2013, the composite inflation rate is above 5 percent more than 25 percent of the time and above 10 percent more than 13 percent of the time. Inflation can be divided into *low* (less than 5 percent), *medium* (between 5 percent and 10 percent), and *high* (above 10 percent). Performance can then be examined across different inflationary environments. Despite the large differences in inflationary environments, trend following performs roughly the same across all three types of inflationary environments: low, medium, and high. Table 1.3 summarizes the performance of trend following across different inflationary regimes. The robust performance for trend following across these inflationary regimes suggests that the strategy seems to be able to adapt to different inflationary regimes.

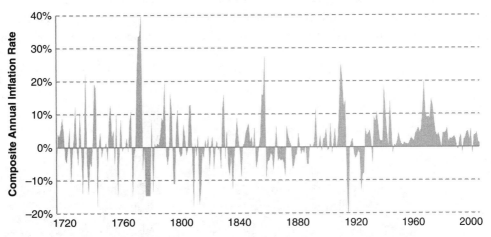

FIGURE 1.6   A composite annual inflation rate for the United States and the United Kingdom from 1720 to 2013.
Source: Global Financial Data.

TABLE 1.3 Performance for trend following in different inflationary environments during the period from 1720 to 2013.

	Inflation <5%	5%< Inflation <10%	Inflation >10%
Average Return (annual)	10.4%	10.1%	14.9%
Standard Deviation (annual)	12.0%	9.90%	14.6%
Sharpe Ratio	0.87	1.02	1.02

Financial Bubbles and Crisis

As an illustrative example, the Dutch Tulip Bubble of the 1600s was briefly discussed in the chapter introduction. Over the centuries, numerous financial crises (or market bubbles) have plagued financial markets. Based on its global impact and severity, the 1929 Wall Street Crash (the notorious Black Monday of October 28, 1929) is another good example. Figure 1.7 plots the two-year period surrounding this date. Black Monday is the spectacular day when the Dow Jones Industrial index lost 13 percent.

Figure 1.8 plots the cumulative performance of the representative trend following system over the same period from Figure 1.7. During the month of October 1929, a month where the Dow Jones lost approximately half of its value, the representative trend following system had a slightly positive return. Even more astonishing during the two years pre- and post-crash, trend following earned a roughly 90 percent return with much of this return coming post-crash during the start of the Great Depression.

The positive performance of trend following during crisis periods is not specific to the 1929 Wall Street Crash or the performance during the Dutch Tulip mania. In fact, the strategy seems to perform well during most of the difficult periods throughout history. Taking a closer look at negative performance periods for both fixed income and equity markets, the average performance for trend following is plotted in Figure 1.9. In this figure, the conditional average returns for trend following are positive for months when the equity index experienced negative performance. For

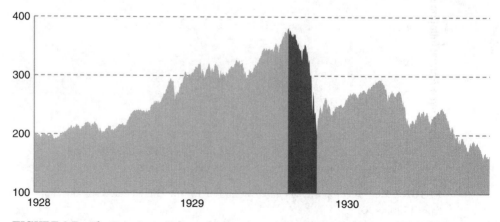

FIGURE 1.7 The Dow Jones Industrial Index during the 1929 Wall Street Crash (Black Monday). *Source:* Global Financial Data.

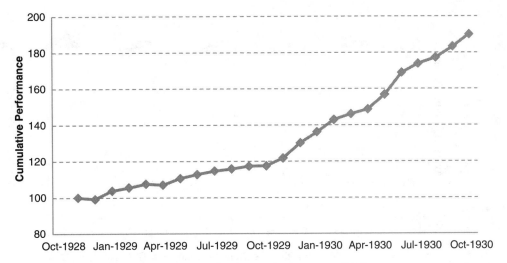

FIGURE 1.8 Cumulative performance for the representative trend following system pre and post the 1929 Wall Street Crash (Black Monday). The data period is October 1928 to October 1930.

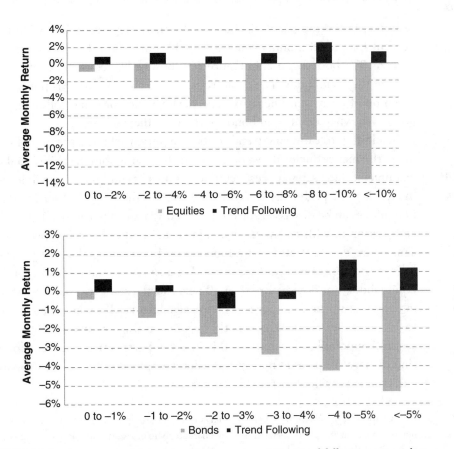

FIGURE 1.9 Average monthly returns for the representative trend following system during down periods in equity and bond portfolios.

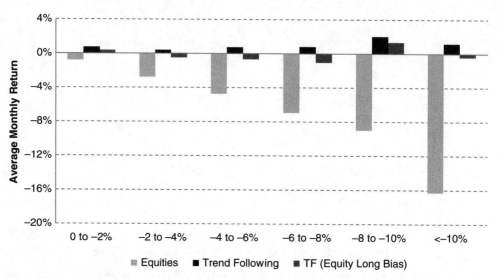

FIGURE 1.10 Average monthly returns for trend following when the equity index is down. Conditional performance is plotted for both with and without a long bias to the equity sector.

example, in the top panel of Figure 1.9, the average trend following return is 0.2 percent for the 98 months when the equity portfolio return is between −4 and −6 percent. The bottom panel in Figure 1.9 shows a less consistent pattern with reference to the bond index. The mean return for trend following is positive for months when bond returns are negative. The performance of trend following seems to be good even when equity and bonds perform at their worst.[13]

In addition to capturing trends outside equity markets, a portion of trend following performance during down periods can also come from the ability to short sell. For example, if short sales are restricted in equities, trend following will have a long bias in equities, the performance (with and without the long bias) during down months in equities can be discussed for the past 300 years of the dataset. Figure 1.10 plots a comparison of with-and-without long bias to equities for down periods in equities. This figure demonstrates that a long equity bias reduces the performance of trend following during down equity months. For a concrete example, for months when the equity index was down more than 10 percent, the standard (balanced) trend following system returned 1.2 percent on average historically, while the system restricted to long equities returned a slightly negative average return. Slightly negative may seem disappointing, but putting this into the perspective of a pure long portfolio, slightly negative pales in magnitude when compared with the unfortunate long only equity investor who lost roughly 14 percent.

---

[13] In Chapter 4, the concept of adaptive markets and crisis alpha are explained at length. Crisis alpha, performance during crisis periods, is a key characteristic of trend following. This concept is discussed throughout the rest of this book.

Market Divergence

Markets move and adapt over time. Periods when markets move the most dramatically (or periods of elevated market divergence) are those that provide "trends" suitable for trend following strategies. At the monthly level, the simplest way to demonstrate this is to divide performance into quintiles (five equal buckets). These buckets represent the worst equity return performance (1) to the best equity performance (5). Figure 1.11 and Figure 1.12 plot the conditional performance of trend following for each of the five quintiles. Figure 1.11 plots the past 100 years of the dataset divided into two subperiods: 1913 to 1962 and 1963 to 2013. Figure 1.12 divides these two periods into two further 25-year subperiods: 1913–1937, 1938–1962, 1963–1987, and 1988–2013. These figures demonstrate a phenomenon practitioners often call the "CTA smile." Trend following returns tend to perform well during moments when market divergence is the largest. For example in the four 25-year time periods, the first period, which includes the Great Depression and the 1929 Wall Street Crash, exhibits the well-known "CTA smile": the best performance is during the best and worst moments for equities. The period after the Great Depression is a period when the best periods for equities were the best for a trend following strategy. The third time period also exhibits the smile. Finally, the past 25 years, a time period including the credit crisis and the tech bubble and other crises, is a time period when the most opportunities have come during the worst periods for equity markets. The convex performance (performance on both extremes)

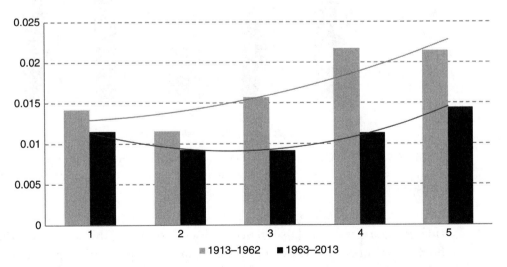

FIGURE 1.11 The "CTA Smile": Quintile analysis of trend following for 1913–1962 and 1963–2013. Returns are sorted by quintiles of equity performance from 1 (worst) to 5 (best).

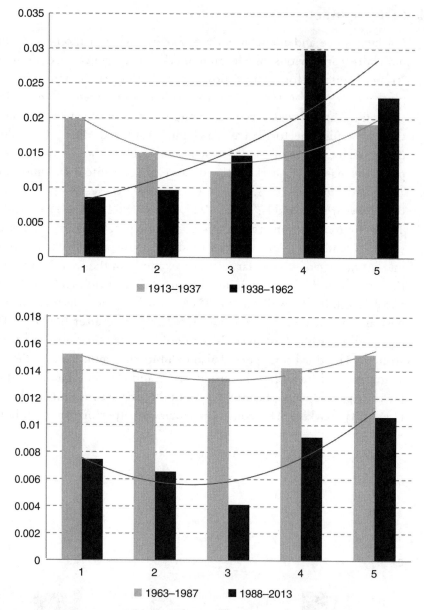

FIGURE 1.12 The "CTA Smile": Quintile analysis of trend following for 1913–1937, 1938–1962, 1963–1987, and 1988–2013. Returns are sorted by quintiles of equity performance from 1 (worst) to 5 (best).

of trend following demonstrates the role of divergence or dislocation in markets (for good or for bad). Divergence is discussed at length in Chapter 5 of this book. This concept helps to motivate an index based on divergent risk taking principles, setting the scene for benchmarking and style analysis from a modern perspective in Chapters 12 and 13.

Because the "CTA smile" demonstrates a convex relationship between trend following and equity markets, it is not surprising that many investors label trend following as "long volatility." Although trend followers perform well at the extremes, not all volatility is created equal. If volatility increased and there were trends across markets, trend followers are long volatility. If volatility increases and there are no trends, trend followers may be flat or even look like short volatility.[14] Put more simply, trend following is long market divergence. Market divergence and volatility are related but they are by no means the same. Market divergence will be explained in further detail in Chapter 5.[15]

■ Risk Characteristics over the Centuries

The principle of "let profits run and cut short your losses" enables trend following to achieve a desirable risk profile with more small losses as opposed to large drawdowns.[16] In statistical terms, trend following returns exhibit positive skewness. Over the roughly 800-year period, the skewness for monthly returns is 0.30. Positive skewness indicates that the chance for left tail risk or large drawdowns in trend following is relatively small. This characteristic is somewhat unique to trend following. Most asset classes and strategies exhibit negative skewness.[17]

In addition to positive skewness for the same roughly 800-year period, trend following has low correlation with traditional asset classes. To quantify the relationship between trend following and the traditional asset classes, a simple equity index and a simple bond index can be constructed by averaging the monthly returns of several global equity indices and bond markets.[18] The overall correlation between the monthly returns of the representative trend following system and the equity index is 0.05, and 0.09 with the bond index. Given that these correlations are a proxy for the relationship between trend following with bond and equity markets, it is not surprising that the betas for trend following with both equity and fixed income are generally extremely low.

---

[14] For further discussion of this topic from a behavioral finance perspective, see Kaminski (2012).

[15] Market divergence takes into account the price trend and volatility. Volatility takes into account only relative price movements. See Chapter 5.

[16] The concept of divergent risk taking is explained in Chapter 5.

[17] Positive skewness for trend following is discussed directly in Chapter 7.

[18] The equity index is the average of monthly total returns of FTSE 100 index, S&P 500 index, CAC 40 index, and the Japanese Nikkei 225 index, and the bond index is constructed by the average monthly returns of U.S. 10-Year Treasury Note, French 10-Year Bond, and the Japanese 10-Year Bond and GFD long-term government bond index. Before the existence of these several individual stock indexes or bond markets, the returns of equivalent markets were used to extend the data. The equity index starts in 1693. The bond index starts in 1300.

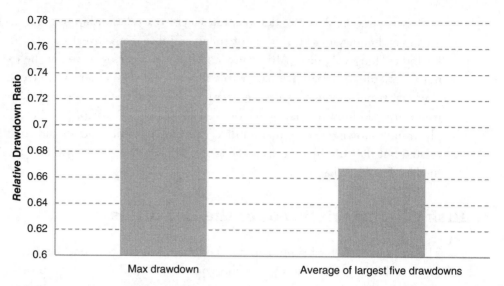

FIGURE 1.13 The maximum and average of the largest five relative drawdowns as a percentage for trend following relative to the buy-and-hold portfolio. The maximum drawdown of trend following is 75 percent of the magnitude of the maximum drawdown for the buy-and-hold portfolio.

Outside of skewness and correlation, drawdown is another important concern for most trend following investors. Figure 1.13 plots the maximum drawdown and the average of the five largest drawdowns for the representative trend following system relative to the corresponding largest drawdowns of the buy-and-hold portfolio. Drawdowns for trend following are significantly lower relative to the buy-and-hold portfolio. The maximum drawdown for trend following is approximately 25 percent lower than the maximum drawdown of the buy-and-hold portfolio. The average of the top five drawdowns for trend following is roughly a third lower than the average of the top five drawdowns for buy-and-hold.

As shown in Figure 1.14, the drawdown durations for trend following are also substantially shorter than those experienced by the buy-and-hold portfolio. During the past 700 years, when compared to the buy-and-hold portfolio, the duration of the longest drawdown and the average duration of the longest five drawdowns are 90 percent and 80 percent shorter, respectively. The superior drawdown profile of trend following is related to the positive skewness of returns and the negative serial correlation.[19] Issues related to drawdown in trend following portfolios will be discussed further in Chapter 8, and again from a portfolio perspective in Part VI of the book.

[19] For a more detailed theoretical analysis of drawdown, see Bailey and Prado (2013).

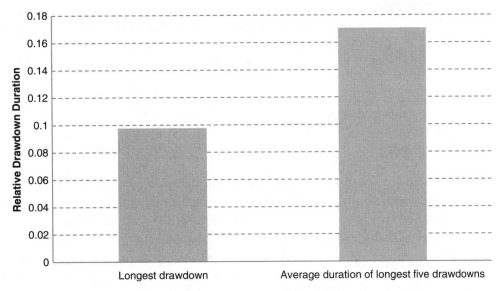

FIGURE 1.14 The relative size of the longest duration and average duration of the longest five drawdowns for trend following relative to the buy-and-hold portfolio. The longest drawdown duration is less than 10 percent of the length of the longest drawdown length for the buy-and-hold drawdown.

■ Portfolio Benefits over the Centuries

The previous sections discussed the return and risk characteristics of trend following over the centuries. Over an extensive 800-year period, trend following portfolios exhibit robust performance with a Sharpe ratio of 1.16. The strategy has low correlation with traditional asset classes, interest rate regimes, and inflation. In addition, performance during crisis periods is positive across the entire sample. A rough look across quintiles in equity markets demonstrates that divergence in market prices is a driver of trend following performance. The strategy also exhibits positive skewness and smaller drawdowns than buy-and-hold strategies. All of these characteristics make trend following a good candidate to diversify traditional portfolios.

During the period beginning in the 1690s up until 2013, the equity index achieves a reasonably high Sharpe ratio of 0.7.[20] For an even longer period beginning in the 1300s up until 2013, the bond index also has a positive Sharpe ratio. Despite the fact that both indices are positive, the Sharpe ratio for trend following is still much higher than a combined buy-and-hold strategy. This suggests that adding some trend following may improve upon a buy-and-hold strategy. Table 1.4 displays the portfolio benefits created by combining the buy-and-hold portfolio (incorporating either the equity or

[20]The equity index is the same index from the previous section.

TABLE 1.4 Performance for the equity index, bond index, trend following, and combined portfolios. The sample period is 1695–2013 for the equity index and 1300–2013 for the bond index.

	Equity and Trend Following: 1695–2013			Bond and Trend Following: 1300–2013		
	Equity	TF	Equity+TF	Bond	TF	Bond+TF
Average Return (annual)	7.85%	10.74%	9.68%	6.57%	12.97%	7.74%
Standard Deviation (annual)	11.28%	12.91%	8.81%	7.31%	11.21%	5.44%
Sharpe Ratio	0.7	0.83	1.1	0.9	1.16	1.42

bond indices) with an equal allocation to the representative trend following portfolio.[21] The start dates for this analysis correspond to the first availability of data for equity and bond markets. In an equal risk allocated portfolio, the performance improvement (over both the traditional equity and bond portfolios) is relatively substantial.

Adding trend following to a traditional equity or bond portfolio improves the Sharpe ratio of both indices. To examine this from the perspective of a traditional investment portfolio, trend following can be added to a typical 60/40 equity bond portfolio. For example, a combined portfolio can be constructed such that it consists of 80 percent of a traditional 60/40 portfolio and 20 percent trend following. In this case, this translates to 48 percent of equities, 32 percent of bonds, and 20 percent of trend following.[22] Figure 1.15 plots the performance in terms of Sharpe ratio for

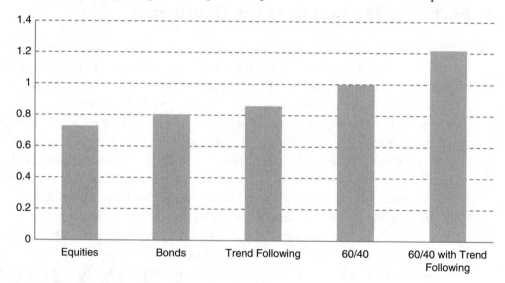

FIGURE 1.15 Sharpe ratios for individual asset classes including equity and combinations of the three asset classes from 1695 to 2013.

---

[21] When trend following is combined with the equity or bond portfolio, the trend following strategy is levered to the same volatility as the equity or bond portfolio.

[22] Before combining them, the different asset classes are normalized to the same volatility.

the individual portfolios, the trend following portfolio, the 60/40 portfolio, and the combined 60/40 and trend following portfolio. During the period of 1695 to 2013, a 20 percent allocation to trend following is able to boost the Sharpe ratio of a 60/40 portfolio from 1.0 to 1.2.

■ Summary

The use of trend following as an alternative investment strategy has certainly grown over the past 30 years. Using roughly 800 years of market data, trend following can be viewed from a long-term perspective. Over the centuries, empirically, trend following has provided distinctly positive returns, a high Sharpe ratio, as well as low correlation with traditional asset classes, inflation, and interest rate regimes. The strategy provides consistently positive performance during crisis periods and the performance seems to be linked to divergence across markets. From a portfolio perspective, the combination of trend following with traditional portfolios such as a 60/40 portfolio significantly improves risk adjusted performance.

■ Appendix: Included Markets and Relevant Assumptions

Sector	Market	Sector	Market
Commodities	Aluminum	Commodities	Hops
	Brent Crude Oil		Iron Ore
	Butter		Lean Hogs
	Cheese		Live Cattle
	Coal		Malt
	Cocoa, NY		Manufactured Iron
	Cocoa, London		Natural Gas
	Coffee		Nickel
	Copper		Oat
	Corn		Orange Juice
	Cotton		Platinum
	Crude Oil		Rice
	Feeder Cattle		Rye
	French Gold Coin Mintage in Livres Tournois		Silver
			Soybeans
	French Silver Coin Mintage in Livres Tournois		Soyameal
			Soyaoil
	Gas Oil-Petroleum		Sugar #11
	Gold		Sugar, White
	Heating Oil		Tobacco

(*Continued*)

Sector	Market	Sector	Market
Commodities	Wheat	Currencies	Canadian Dollars per British Pound
	Wheat, Hard Red Winter		CHF/USD
	Wood		Dutch Guilders per British Pound
	Wool		EUR/USD (DEM/USD)
	Zinc		GBP/USD
Bonds	Bankers Acceptance Canada		Hamburg Mark for Paris Francs
	Canadian 10-Year Bond		Hamburg Mark for Vienna Crowns
	Euro-BUND		JPY/USD
	Eurodollar		Portugal Escudo per US Dollar
	France 10-Year Bond		Swedish Krona per British Pound
	Gilts		
	Japanese Bond	Equities	Australian SPI200 Index
	Long-Term Government Bond		CAC 40
	Netherlands 10-Year Bond		DAX Index
	Short Sterling		E-Mini Nasdaq 100 Index
	UK Consolidated		E-Mini Russell 2000 Index
	U.S. 10-year T-Note		E-Mini S&P 500 Index
	U.S. 2-year T-Note		FTSE 100 Index
	U.S. 30-year T-Note		Hang Seng
	U.S. 5-year T-Note		Italy All Index
	Venice Prestiti		Nikkei
			Singapore MSCI Index
Currencies	AUD/USD		Taiwan MSCI Index
	CAD/USD		Tokyo Stock Exchange Index

Assumptions and Approximations

There are several assumptions and approximations, which are made to allow for a long-term analysis of trend following. For simplicity, these are listed below.

1. Futures Prices First: When available, futures market returns are used.
2. Equity and Fixed Income: Prior to the availability of futures data, index returns are used for both equity and fixed income markets. Total returns are constructed using the appropriate short-term interest rates.
3. FX: For currency markets, spot price returns are adjusted by the interest rates differential of the two relevant currencies. When interest rates are not available, spot returns for currencies are used without adjustment.

4. Commodities: For commodities in the absence of futures price data, cash market returns are used.
5. Excess Cash Return: The interest earned on collateral and cash returns are excluded from this analysis.

■ Further Reading and References

Bailey, D., and M. Prado. "Drawdown-Based Stop-Outs and the 'Triple Penance' Rule." Working paper, 2013.

Grant, J. *The Great Metropolis*. Philadelphia: E. L. Carey & A. Hart, 1838.

Greyserman, A. "The Multi-Centennial View of Trend Following." ISAM white paper, 2012.

Jegadeesh, N., and S. Titman. "Returns to Buying Winners and Selling Losers: Implications for Stock Market Efficiency." *Journal of Finance* 48, no. 1 (1993): 65–91.

Kaminski, K. "Managed Futures and Volatility: Decoupling a 'Convex' Relationship with Volatility Cycles." CME Market Education Group, May 2012.

Moskowitz, T., T. Ooi, and L. Pedersen. "Time Series Momentum." *Journal of Financial Economics*, no. 104 (2012).

Taylor, B. "The GFD Guide to Total Returns on Stocks, Bonds, and Bills." Global Financial Data working document, www.globalfinancialdata.com/articles/total_return_guide.doc.

Thompson, Earl. "The Tulipmania: Fact or Artifact?" *Public Choice* 130, nos. 1–2 (2007): 99–114.

PART II

TREND FOLLOWING BASICS

CHAPTER 2

Review of Futures Markets and Futures Trading

This book is focused on demystifying both the art and the science of trend following from the perspective of the end user, the institutional investor. This chapter is an introduction to the background necessary for understanding the basics of futures markets, futures trading, and the managed futures industry. Due to ease of trade and relatively high level of liquidity, trend following systems trade in futures markets and interbank forward markets worldwide. As a result, an understanding of the key characteristics of forwards and futures contracts and futures markets is essential. These markets offer exposure to a wide selection of asset classes including equities, currencies, hard and soft commodities, and fixed income. The use of derivatives allows for access to leverage and central clearing structures alleviate counterparty risks.

■ Forward and Futures Contract Fundamentals

Even prior to the use of currency exchanges and modern banking systems, people have been trading commodities. Agricultural products have been bought and sold throughout the centuries under systems of exchange, future promises, and barter. A **forward contract** is an agreement between two counterparties (the buyer and the seller) to exchange a certain good or commodity (the underlying) for a determined price (the forward price) agreed on at the beginning of the contract (agreement time) and delivered at maturity (at settlement). The concept of a

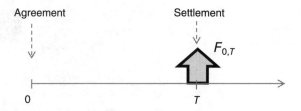

FIGURE 2.1 A schematic of the cash flows for a forward contract.

forward market emerged as people began to create contracts to deliver a product in the future for a price determined at the current time. The use of forward contracts allowed people to plan for the future, to contract at prespecified prices, and to hedge against future uncertainty in prices or exchange rates between goods. Forward contracts carry two very important and nonnegligible risks: counterparty risk and liquidity risk.

Figure 2.1 presents a schematic for the cash flows of a forward contract. At the beginning of a forward contract (at the agreement time 0), there is an agreement between two parties to exchange the commodity or good for a price ($F_{0,T}$) to be delivered at time T (the settlement time). There are two counterparties in this bilateral transaction, the seller who delivers the commodity or good and the purchaser who commits to purchase the commodity or good in the future at time (T). The value of the contract for the seller and purchaser at the settlement time (T) (maturity) depends on the future value of the spot market for the commodity or good, denoted by (S_T).

For an example, imagine a corn producer who wants to sell 10,000 bushels of corn at \$4.50 per bushel in three months. If a distributor wants to purchase 10,000 bushels of corn for \$4.50 per bushel in three months, the distributor and the corn producer can enter into a forward contract. The purchase price for the corn is locked in at time 0, but corn is bought in the future for that price. It is highly likely that the price of corn may be different in three months. This may be due to seasonal factors, the balance between supply and demand, and many other factors. When the three-month period is complete, the distributor will take delivery of 10,000 bushels of corn and pay \$4.50 per bushel. If the price of corn goes up, for example to \$6 per bushel, the purchaser will be glad to have contracted to purchase the corn at \$4.50

TABLE 2.1 A summary of value at agreement time 0 and settlement time T for a forward contract.

Counterparty	Value at Time 0	Value at Time T
Seller (ensures delivery)	0	$F_{0,T} - S_T$
Purchaser (takes delivery)	0	$S_T - F_{0,T}$

while the seller may be disappointed to sell corn below the spot market price of $6. On the other hand, if the price of corn goes down to $3, the seller will be happy and the distributor will be disappointed. In forward contracts, unless the spot price ends up at the same price as the originally agreed upon price there is always one counterparty who profits and one who loses relative to the spot price. This leads to the first core issue with forward contracts: **counterparty risk**. If spot prices move far away from the agreed on delivery prices, there is significant concern that one side of the contract may not fulfill his or her side of the obligation. If one of the counterparties defaults on the obligation, the other counterparty will be forced to take delivery or sell on the spot market, most likely, at unfavorable prices. In this case, both counterparties are very dependent on the other counterparty fulfilling their side of the contract creating substantial counterparty risk. This is a common concern in bilateral contracts.

Another issue of concern is **liquidity risk**. Forward contracts are often highly specific. Each contract fits a mutual coincidence of wants between two individual counterparties. If the contract is overly specific, it may be substantially difficult or impossible to find another counterparty to take over the contract. For example, returning to the distributor who takes delivery of 10,000 bushels of corn in three months, if after one month the distributor decides to stop creating a product that includes this particular type of corn, this may lead to problems. The distributor will need to find a way to get out of their contract or find another party who may take over the contract if possible. If the distributor simply takes delivery of corn, he or she will depend on reselling the corn on the spot market at delivery. Transferring contracts can create legal challenges and thus additional costs. As a result, bilateral forward contracts, especially those with nonstandard terms, may be very illiquid. This creates challenges if business conditions change.

A Review of Futures Markets

Dating back prior to medieval times, forward contracts were an innovation that facilitated the purchase and sale of goods in the future. The specific bilateral structure of these types of contracts contains a significant amount of counterparty risk and issues concerning specificity and illiquidity. Futures contracts are a modern financial innovation that came about in 1848 with the opening of the Chicago Board of Trade. At the CBOT, farmers came to trade goods and to ensure the future value of their goods. Shortly after the opening of the CBOT, the first futures contracts were traded in agricultural products such as corn.

Futures contracts are designed to alleviate the core issues of traditional forward contracts: counterparty risks and illiquidity. A **futures contract** is a forward-like contract with a value that depends on the future value of a good or commodity (the underlying). Futures contracts are standardized, transferable, and exchange traded. Contracts are traded in standard units where the current contract value is contingent on the future value of the specific underlying. As opposed to a forward contract, futures contract holders take a position (long or short) in a specified amount of underlying with a specific delivery or maturity. For each futures contract holder, their counterparty is the clearinghouse. By pooling the funds of all contract holders, the clearinghouse serves as the counterparty to all position holders. To cover fluctuations in prices of the underlying on a daily basis, all participants who maintain a futures contract (long or short) must maintain a margin account. A margin account is a buffer fund, which protects the clearinghouse against fluctuations in prices. The current price for future delivery price of the underlying moves each day, and at the end of the day all positions are marked-to-market prices. For example, suppose yesterday you took one short position in 10,000 bushels of corn to sell corn in three months at $4.50. The total notional exposure would be $45,000. If today the price to sell in three months goes down to $4.40, from the perspective of the short position this would be a profitable position. At the end of each trading day, all positions in corn are marked-to-market prices and funds are redistributed across market participants via margin accounts. In this case, participants who took the short position receive funds from participants who were holding long positions. Funds are transferred across market participants through central clearinghouses and the market essentially starts again the next day. This mechanism of marking-to-market allows prices to follow the current market prices for future delivery. More specifically, returning to bilateral forward contracts, at the end of the contract the spot price and the agreement price can be very different. In futures markets, the futures price will slowly converge to the spot price as maturity approaches.

> The current futures price is the price today for delivery of the underlying asset at a prespecified date in the future.

Futures contracts are derivatives contracts. They derive their value from the value of a specified underlying asset. Each contract has delivery and classification specifics, a standard **contract size**, and a fixed maturity. Typically, futures contracts tend to be shorter in maturity. When a futures contract price is plotted over time, this is called the **futures curve**. The state of the futures curve can be either in **contango** or **backwardation**. Contango occurs when a futures contract price is above the expected future spot price.[1] In this situation, it is often suggested that hedgers are willing to pay more for something in the future as opposed to what they should expect to pay. For example, it may be the case that hedging out risks for the price

---

[1] To make things more confusing, contango can also be defined as occurring when a futures contract price is above the spot price. This approach does not take into account the time value of money.

of oil in three months is valuable for companies who need to use the oil for their operations. They may be willing to pay more for the oil in the future to guarantee the price (as opposed to waiting to see what the spot price may become in the future). Backwardation is the opposite of contango; in this case, the futures price is below the expected future spot price (and sometimes the current spot price). In this situation, hedgers are willing to sell for prices below the expected spot prices. Returning to the example of oil, that may be the case if there is a net surplus of producers hoping to hedge the sale of oil. They may be willing to sell oil futures contracts to lock in sale prices even at a slight loss or haircut on the price. Backwardation is common for commodities but not for equity markets. In practice, there are still instances where the futures curve for certain commodities is in contango. For example, for commodities that have larger storage costs, this results in a more difficult **cost of carry** resulting in contango.[2] In other words, there are many situations where people will pay a premium to lock in the price of a commodity that is less fungible over time.

Core Attributes of Futures Contracts

There are many features of futures contracts that have caused them to become widely used for both speculation and hedging. First, futures contracts do not exhibit the traditional asymmetry between long and short contracts as seen in traditional markets such as equities or options markets. For example, short selling equities (selling options) is much more complicated than buying equities (buying options). This is not the case for futures markets. Futures markets allow for long and short positions in a wide range of underlying assets including currencies, fixed income, equity indices, commodities, and energy. Although delivery is possible in most futures contracts, it is quite rare (only roughly 1 percent of the contracts are actually delivered).

To take a position in a futures contract, all investors must post collateral for the positions in the form of margin and maintain their **margin account** with a clearinghouse broker. The clearinghouse works as the counterparty for all investors and on a daily basis marks all contracts to market, settling up the losses and gains between pools of investors using the collateral that each investor has in their margin account. Due to daily marking-to-market, the required margin for futures contracts usually runs around 1 to 15 percent for both long and short positions.[3]

---

[2] This effect is often referred to in the academic literature as *convenience yield*—the propensity to consume inventory now. When this occurs some holders will consume inventory later, leading to lower current prices and contango.

[3] Using the Eurodollar contract as an example, the margin for a $1 million face value Eurodollar futures contract often goes down as low as $625. This corresponds to roughly 625 basis points. *Source:* CME Group.

TABLE 2.2	The features of futures markets.

Features of Futures Markets	
Transparent	Standardized contracts
Minimal counterparty/credit risk	Daily marking-to-market, pooling of investment profits and losses for redistribution via clearinghouse brokers
Highly liquid	Ease of access and use, low requirements for collateral, lack of asymmetry between long and short positions, standardization of contracts, reduced counterparty risk

Collateral requirements for positions in traditional markets are significantly higher and often asymmetrically higher for short positions. For example, based on Regulation T in the United States, 150 percent margin is required for short equity positions whereas only 50 percent margin is required for long equity positions.

Since futures contracts depend on the underlying asset's value at a future date in time, futures prices are highly correlated with their corresponding underlying assets. This correlation makes them excellent vehicles for taking directional positions in various asset classes and hedging. The clearinghouse mechanisms of futures markets, daily pooling and redistribution of funds, lower collateral constraints, and transparency and standardization of contracts create a market that is extremely liquid and relatively void of both the counterparty risk and asymmetries between long and short positions common in traditional markets. These characteristics are summarized in Table 2.2.

Hedging and Speculation

Forward contracts allow market participants to hedge against future changes in the price of a good or commodity. The structure of futures contracts allows for more flexibility, extending possibilities for hedging and speculation. Futures market participants are often divided into two categories: **hedgers** and **speculators**. These categories are divided based on their underlying objectives for taking a position. Hedgers are focused on hedging an underlying exposure and using derivatives to adjust for risks in their portfolios or business strategies. For example, a company such as Southwest Airlines may take long positions in oil futures contracts to hedge against the risk of rising prices in oil. By hedging future cash flows with offsetting futures contracts, Southwest can offset underlying business risks and stabilize cash flows over the long run. Long run cash flow stability allows a nonfinancial company, such as Southwest Airlines, to better plan production and distribution processes. A speculator is someone who speculates taking a view on the direction of future prices.

Historically, the relationship between speculators and hedgers has been widely discussed. Hedgers need speculators to take the other side of trades and to offset an imbalance between hedging demand on either the long or short side. Using oil as an example again, oil producers also need to hedge against the future selling price of oil. Companies, which are the consumers of oil, use futures to control their risk in their operating costs, while oil producers use futures contracts to control their revenue streams. If there is an offset in the net hedging position long or short, this means that there are more hedgers on either the long or short side. Speculators come in to offset imbalance. If there is an offset in the balance net hedging demand, prices will reflect this imbalance. The offset in demand will create a **hedging premium** for taking the less desirable position. A speculator would take this position with the understanding that, in the long run, prices should correct to the appropriate fundamental value.

Trading Specifics of Futures Contracts

A futures contract is a position whose value is contingent on the value of an underlying asset or good in the future. This means that the holders of futures contracts do not really buy or sell an asset; they take a position.[4] These positions are maintained with collateral via the use of margin accounts. Margin accounts are similar to a buffer account to absorb the losses and accumulate gains in futures positions. Margin account structures are dictated by both the brokers who act as a direct liaison to the exchange and the exchanges that dictate rules on margin limits and contributions. A futures trader will create an account with a futures broker who in turn has an account and relationship with the exchange. The exchange determines the initial margin required to establish a position. Initial margin is often 10 to 15 percent of the notional value of the underlying. For example, if the price of corn is $4.30 per bushel and a contract is standardized at 5,000 bushels per contract. In this case the initial margin is $2,150. At the end of each trading day, the value of the contract is **marked-to-market** and trading losses and gains are realized via the transfer of funds between participants' margin accounts.[5] For demonstrative purposes, suppose that a long position was initiated at a price of $4.30 in corn with initial margin $2,150. If a long position in corn closes at $4.20 the following day, the account will lose $500 and that value will be distributed to market participants who hold a short position in corn. When a margin account gets below a certain threshold it is often called the **maintenance margin**, as defined by the exchange or broker. The participant will be required to post additional margin to maintain the position. This event is

---

[4] Delivery occurs in often less than 1 percent of futures contracts. To take delivery, market participants must submit their intent to deliver to the exchange. It is common folklore that 300,000 pounds of cattle may just be delivered on your doorstep.

[5] To use an analogy in gambling, futures trading is similar to betting at the horse track. When you engage in a forward contract, you buy the actual horse. In futures markets, you take a position (or view) on the outcome of an underlying horse. For each race, accounts are settled and it is not possible to take a position unless you have money (collateral) on the table.

called a **margin call**, where historically market participants will receive a phone call from their broker asking them to post further margin. Other features of margin accounts include the use of **variation margin**. When futures prices move in directions against a particular position, variation margin is the additional cash added to offset these adverse price moves. Initial margin can be posted in the form of Treasury bills (as opposed to cash) while variation margin is generally added in cash.

Given the particular structure of futures trading, initial margin is generally a reflection of the close-to-close risk for the particular market in question. This is why it is interesting from the perspective of a futures trader to look closer at the margin to equity. **Margin to equity ratio** represents the amount of capital posted in margin accounts. For example, if $100,000 of the total capital of $1,000,000 is allocated to a margin account, the margin to equity ratio is 10 percent. Margin to equity is explained in further detail in Chapter 9.

Futures orders are divided into several types of orders. A simple **market order** is an order that is marked to be carried out immediately at the best available price.[6] **Limit orders** are orders that are filled when the market price hits a specific limit or price. As soon as a limit order has been filled, the order is marked to be executed immediately at the best available price. **Stop loss orders** are orders to sell at a pre-specified price. A stop loss limit order is a stop loss order that becomes a limit order as soon as a certain limit has been reached. There are many other types of orders for trading execution.

■ Review of the Managed Futures Industry

Managed futures, commonly associated with commodity trading advisors (or CTAs) is a subclass of alternative investment strategies, which take positions and trade primarily in futures markets, forward markets, options and other liquid derivatives and structured products. Using highly liquid mark-to-market contracts, they generally follow directional strategies in a wide range of asset classes including fixed income, currencies, equity indices, soft commodities, energy, and metals. They apply leverage either directly via margin or indirectly via the use of derivatives products such as options. Another key feature these managers often exploit is the ability to go long or short with relative ease, a feature that makes futures markets a good candidate for these types of strategies. The managed futures industry is also an industry with a long history of regulation. Focusing on the United States, the Commodity Futures

---

[6] For electronic trading platforms (for example, CME Globex®), a simple market order may not be possible as orders generally need to be entered with certain price constraints similar to a limit order. *Source:* CME Group.

TABLE 2.3	A summary of characteristics of the managed futures industry.
Managed futures funds invest in futures markets via professional money managers (CTAs)	
Directional	Systematically exploit directional moves in futures markets prices—upward or downward
Globally diversified	Trade both long and short contracts in FX, interest rates, stock indices, energy, metals, and soft commodities in regulated and interbank forward markets worldwide
Regulated	Typically authorized and regulated by financial supervisory authorities such as the CFTC and NFA in the United States

Trading Commission (CFTC) was established in 1974 and CTAs have been regulated by both the CFTC and National Futures Association (NFA). Table 2.3 lists a summary of the key characteristics of the managed futures industry.

Managed Futures Strategies

There are many types of managed futures strategies; the most common type and the focus of this book is systematic trend following. In general, managed futures strategies can be either systematic or discretionary. **Systematic** means that a manager uses technical signals and a trading system to implement positions in a systematic fashion. Systematic trading systems are fully automated trading systems. **Discretionary** strategies are strategies that use some level of manager discretion. The amount of discretion can vary from one strategy to another. Within the class of systematic trading strategies, there are several core types:

- Medium/long-term trend following

- Short-term trading

- Relative value and nontrend

- Fundamental trading

Fundamental managers use fundamental information to determine mispricings. Core inputs to their systems are economic data and they often use economic models to value the assets they trade. Medium/long-term trend followers use signals from historical prices and other data sequences to determine when trends occur. Short-term trading strategies focus on shorter term trends and faster data/price information. They are sometimes also divided into short-term trend following and countertrend (or contrarian). A **contrarian strategy** trades against the trend, seeking to profit from a reversal in prices. Relative value and nontrend strategies focus on finding relative mispricings between different assets across markets or across time.

Historically, medium/long-term trend following is the core strategy in managed futures. There are several reasons for this. Core issues for dynamic trading strategies are transaction costs, capacity, and slippage. Medium-term trend following strategies focus on longer term trends in prices; they do not adjust their positions as quickly or as often as shorter term programs. Fewer transactions incur less transactions costs over the long run. A larger position will also be easier to move over the long run and there are fewer concerns of moving market prices with size or capacity constraints. Fundamental trading strategies or global macro strategies can be a good complement to trend following strategies but they rely on the realignment of value of underlying securities. If all economic models suggest something is undervalued, the core problem is that the fundamental strategy will not profit until the market realizes and agrees that an underlying asset is undervalued and corrects.

Growth in the Managed Futures Industry

In parallel with the tremendous growth of the futures markets, the managed futures industry has grown tremendously in the past 30 years. According to data from BarclayHedge, as shown in Figure 2.2, from 1980 to 2013 the number of unique trading managed futures programs has increased by 40-fold. Assets under management (AUM) skyrocketed to roughly $330 billion by the end of 2013. In fact, as seen in Figure 2.3, the increase in AUM has been roughly linear since 2002.

It is important to demonstrate that the managed futures industry has grown hand in hand with futures markets. The change in scale and size of the managed futures industry appears to be less dramatic when the significant increase of aggregated trading volumes in futures markets is taken into account. Figure 2.4 shows the relative trading volume plotted together with AUM from 2000 to 2013. Relative trading volume is expressed as a multiple of trading volume in 2000.

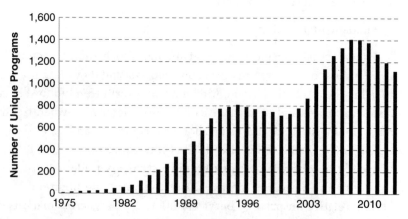

FIGURE 2.2 The number of unique Managed Futures programs from 1975 to 2013. *Data source:* BarclayHedge.

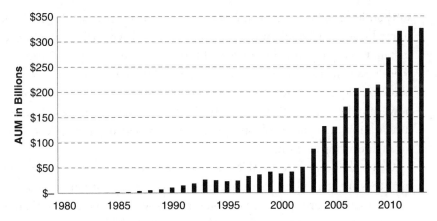

FIGURE 2.3 Assets under management in Managed Futures from 1980 to 2013.
Data source: BarclayHedge.

The average trading volume relative to 2000 is computed using only markets that started trading prior to January 1, 2000. The relative AUM in managed futures is also expressed as a multiplier of the AUM in 2000 where the AUM in 2000 is 1. From this chart, it is noteworthy that the volume growth of these older futures markets *alone* has kept pace with the AUM increase in managed futures. Since the 1990s a

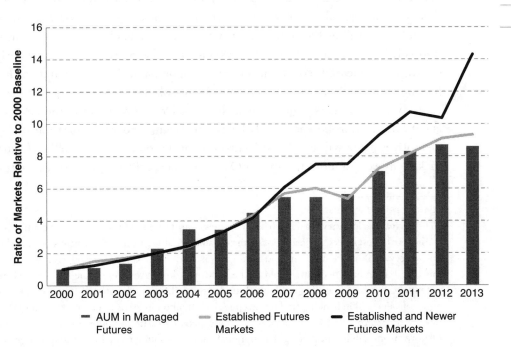

FIGURE 2.4 Average relative trading volume for both established and newer markets and assets under management relative to the level in 2000 for the Managed Futures industry from 2000 to 2013. Newer markets consist of 10 markets, which started trading after January 1, 2000.

substantial number of new futures markets, many that are highly liquid, have also started trading. Growth in trading volumes may have enabled the futures markets to sustain the rapid growth in managed futures. During the past decade, the growth of these newer markets is even more substantial than what is shown for relatively older markets. Figure 2.4 plots the trading volume growth of a small sampling of relatively newer markets, those that started trading after 2000.[7] It is clear from this graph that futurization may play a role in the future of managed futures. This topic is discussed in the following section.

Given the large rise in AUM in managed futures, it is not surprising that many investors are starting to have concerns regarding capacity in the industry. Their concern is that as more speculative capital rushes into these markets, there will be fewer opportunities to exploit as competition increases. This topic is addressed in the discussion of size and capacity in Chapter 15.

■ Futurization

The world of derivatives is ripe with change. Prior to the credit crisis, the derivatives game was played on two very different fields: over-the-counter (OTC) via dealer networks and exchange traded (ETD) via centralized clearinghouses.[8] Although in theory the nature of derivatives contracts should be roughly the same, in application the rules, as well as the structural way these contracts changed hands, varied substantially. The mess that unfolded in 2008 led to a sharp review of the way derivatives contracts are cleared, collateralized, and change hands. In an attempt to "level the playing field" on both sides and create a more cohesive and less disjointed approach to derivatives markets, legislation such as the Dodd-Frank Act in the United States and EMIR in Europe spearhead the restructuring and reorganization of how the derivatives game will be played.[9] This reorganization has led to further futurization making more and more traditional OTC contracts shift toward futures contracts.

---

[7] Based on 11 newer markets.

[8] The derivatives industry is a $700 trillion business. Most of these OTC derivatives contracts are held by the few largest banks. A closer look at these banks, or at least the top tier banks by size, shows that only a very small percentage (around 4 percent) is held in exchange-traded derivatives. Reasons for this distribution have been attributed to the previously lower costs in trading off the exchanges and potential difficulties in dealing with block trades on exchanges. The core of the action, in both total notional value and in banking trading revenues ($17 trillion in 2012 to be exact), is in OTC interest rate swaps. *Source:* OCC Q4 Report 2012. These statistics relate to notional value. The numbers for turnover paint a different picture. The notional value of volume traded in futures is larger than that traded in the OTC derivatives markets. For further details see the BIS Triennial Survey.

[9] John E. Parsons from MIT discussed this analogy and futurization in his blog: Betting the business, financial risk management for nonfinancial firms. See bettingthebusiness.com.

Futurization is the migration of traditional dealer-based bilateral contracts into similar standardized "futures-style" contracts that are centrally cleared and exchange traded. This idea is by no means novel. In fact, this is exactly why futures contracts came about; to mimic bilateral OTC forward contracts. The futures market structure is meant to address counterparty risks, lack of transparency, and lack of transferability ("nonfungible" structure) of bilateral OTC contracts. An aggregated exchange-traded structure allows for collateral reductions, multilateral position netting, and risk mitigation across pools of counterparties. The new wave of futurization of swaps and other OTC derivatives is occurring to adhere to some of the same issues. By mandating centralized clearing, OTC derivatives are already moving a step closer to futures contracts. As regulatory demands begin to stretch the limits of OTC contracts, this is creating further incentives for futurization, which may allow users to circumvent some of these issues. (See Figure 2.5.)

Drivers of Futurization

New regulation aims to tighten control regarding reporting, registration, and mandatory central clearing of many, especially vanilla OTC contracts.[10] Central clearing of most derivatives contracts is done through central counterparties (CCPs) allowing for aggregation of information for reporting, multilateral position netting, and cross validation. The share of derivatives that are not centrally cleared will become low[11] and regulatory costs in the form of increased reporting, operating, and collateral are set to impact all users of OTC derivatives products.

To handle the large demand for central clearing of OTC products, large exchanges have extended their mandate to operate as central counterparties (CCPs). New players are also entering the swaps markets by registering as swap execution facilities (SEFs),[12] creating competition for swap dealers. Transaction costs, operational efficiency, and collateral management should bring down differences between OTC

---

[10] Title VII of the Dodd-Frank Act focuses specifically on swaps, and in the United States there is a legal distinction between swaps and futures. In the EU, EMIR attempts to deal with counterparty risks and transparency in a more pluralistic manner by creating a list of all derivatives that must be centrally cleared as well as which derivatives should have mandatory trading. The list includes the standard options, swaps, futures, cash settled commodity derivatives and other exotics. Implementation in the EU will be phased in over the next few years.

[11] Those that are not cleared will be possible via exception or with collateral constraints above the five-day margin requirement for vanilla OTC swaps. Implementation in Europe is still in process and discussion.

[12] In the EU, these include multilateral trading facilities (MTFs) and organized trading facilities (OTFs).

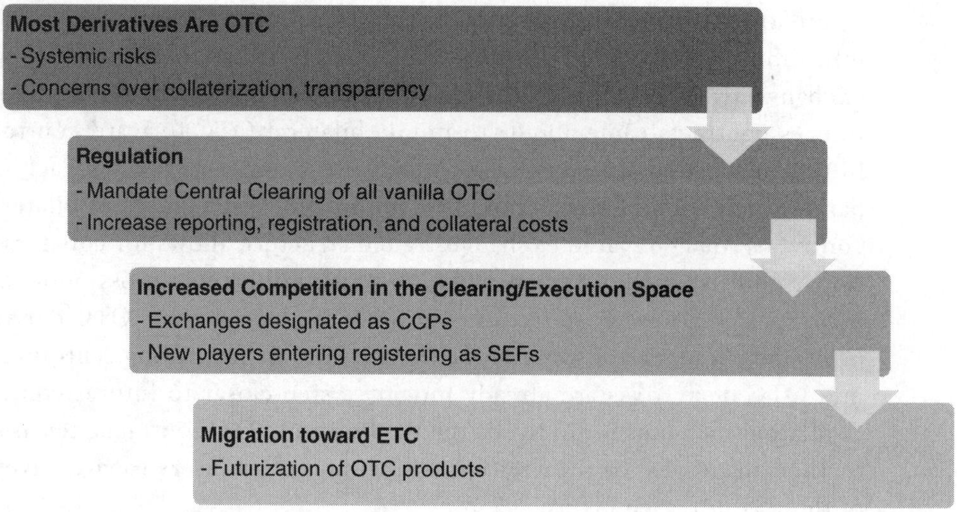

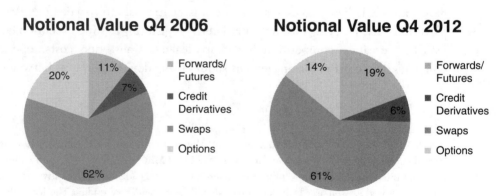

Most Derivatives Are OTC
- Systemic risks
- Concerns over collaterization, transparency

Regulation
- Mandate Central Clearing of all vanilla OTC
- Increase reporting, registration, and collateral costs

Increased Competition in the Clearing/Execution Space
- Exchanges designated as CCPs
- New players entering registering as SEFs

Migration toward ETC
- Futurization of OTC products

FIGURE 2.5 A schematic of the path to futurization of the OTC derivative space.

and exchange traded. Despite this move, there are still plenty of adjustments to be made and room for growth.[13] For example, in 2012, 60 percent of all derivatives in the United States were swaps. There is a migration toward exchange-traded products but it is happening gradually. For another example, in only six years in the United States (from 2006 to 2012), futures/forward contracts, which are mostly exchange-traded contracts, have climbed in derivatives markets from 11 percent to 19 percent of total outstanding notional value. (See Figure 2.6.)

Notional Value Q4 2006

- Forwards/Futures — 11%
- Credit Derivatives — 7%
- Options — 20%
- Swaps — 62%

Notional Value Q4 2012

- Forwards/Futures — 19%
- Credit Derivatives — 6%
- Options — 14%
- Swaps — 61%

FIGURE 2.6 A comparison of the percentage of notional value across U.S. derivative markets in 2006 and 2012.
Data source: OCC Q4 Report 2012.

[13]This is especially true in Europe where implementation is delayed until 2014 or later.

Swap Futures

Swap futures (or futurized swaps) are new, exchange-traded variants of swap contracts, which are meant to mimic swaps. To use an analogy, futures are to forwards as swap futures are to swaps. To appease users of swaps, these new futures contracts are an attempt to keep some of the customizable features of swaps while maintaining some of the advantages of a centralized exchange. Exchanges will allow for more flexibility on delivery options.[14] Exchanges will also allow for more flexibility on block trades. Exceptions and modifications will make swap futures fit somewhere in the gray zone between traditional swaps and traditional futures contracts. The key advantages of swap futures include transparency, lower collateral requirements, possibly reduced registration requirements, and ease of trade when highly liquid. The key disadvantages may include lack of customization, delivery limitations, concerns for block trades, and the potential for liquidity issues. A simplified comparison of contracts is presented in Table 2.4.

TABLE 2.4   **A dual comparison of futures versus forwards and swaps versus futurized swaps. Futures are to forwards as swap futures are to swaps.**

	Futures	Forwards	Swap Futures	Swaps
Trade via	Exchange traded	OTC** (U.S.: Exceptions, EU: Exception for physical delivery)	Exchange traded with exceptions	OTC* (U.S.: SEFs, EU: MTFs and OTFs)
Clearing	Cleared	Depends	Centrally cleared with exceptions	Most cleared** with exceptions
Delivery	Rare, ~2%	Most delivery	May depend, contract dependent	Most delivery
Transparency	Standardized	Customized	Standardized with some flexibility	Customized, more standardized*
Collateralization	Daily margin required for collateral	Depends	1–2 days margin required for collateral	5 days required for collateral (may vary as well)
Counterparty Risks	Low	Moderate (varied)	Low	Low,* moderate (for bilateral, uncleared contracts)

*This characteristic will be in effect post implementation of Title VII of the Dodd-Frank Act and EMIR.
**There are some exceptions for forward rate agreements and FX. Physical delivery and some customized swaps may also be exempted. These exceptions, including blocks and exchange for physical (EFPs), also exist for other futures contracts as well.

---

[14] For example, in the United States, deliverable swap futures were launched in 2012. These are futures contracts that provide delivery of an OTC swap at maturity. The advantages of these contracts are that during the life of the future, the contract, as a futures contract, is eligible for much less stringent collateral and margin requirements than the delivered OTC swap contract.

The Pros and the Cons of Futurization

There are some concerns about the applicability of futurization in a market that is focused on customization. General concerns are related to regulatory arbitrage, systemic risk, and potential issues with lack of customization and usability. Opponents with concerns regarding regulatory arbitrage cite concerns related to the asymmetries in fees and collateral across similar contracts.[15] Their concerns are that markets driven by regulatory arbitrage may have unclear consequences. Cross-border issues and difference in regulation across the globe may complicate things even further. Systemic risk is another key issue. In a post–Dodd-Frank and EMIR world, with mandatory clearing and contract migration onto exchanges, large central counterparties (CCPs) are designated as systemically important entities or entities that are "too big to fail." Critics of this structure are weary of vertically integrated clearing and execution. In addition, new users of futures also have concerns about potential basis risk and liquidity issues with new products that may not be adequately customizable. Issues related to block trading, flexibility, and increased delivery options are of high priority.

Proponents of futurization cite the long and successful history of futures markets, the benefits of more migration to futures, and the potential for cost reduction and flexibility in new futures products. Futures markets have a long-standing relationship with regulation. They were designed with a keen focus on transparency, transferability, reduction of counterparty risk, optimized collateral costs, and risk mitigation. Yet, it is important to emphasize that futures gain much of their success in numbers. Illiquid futures contracts are not as popular and have added liquidity risks especially with contracts that are marked to market so frequently. Proponents of futurization suggest that increased volumes in futures markets may help diversify product offerings. For example, one positive sign has been the relatively eventless move of more than half of the $18 trillion daily notional energy trading from swaps into futures in the fall of 2012 (see Leising, 2013). Increased volumes may help make room for new contracts, which can better mimic longer dated swap contracts. Consistent with anecdotal comments from energy traders who switched to futures, cost reduction, lower collateral requirements, efficiency, and flexibility are the commonly cited advantages for using futures. Lastly, similar to how futurization of forwards created futures, proponents of futurization can argue that the current wave of futurization in OTC derivatives is simply a natural development of modern financial markets. Consistent with futurization of the past, this wave will help level the playing field and increase flexibility.

---

[15] This is even more evident in the United States, where collateral and margin requirements for swaps are treated differently than futures. In the EU, these distinctions are less clear as EMIR focuses on a contract by contract basis.

The derivatives industry is a $700 trillion business. Regulatory forces and demographics in this industry are migrating contracts from dealer networks onto exchanges spawning a new wave of futurization. The push toward transparency and transferability has already begun. Yesterday's challenges may be addressed, but the perils and challenges that lie ahead in derivatives markets remain unclear. Despite many opposing views, it does remain evident that the future of derivatives markets is futurization. From the perspective of managed futures strategies, this means that volumes in futures markets should be expected to increase.

■ Summary

Trend following is one of the most classic investment styles. Modern day trend followers use trading systems that allow them to take positions in trends across a wide array of asset classes. Trend following systems require both an art and science in their design. Futures contracts are transparent, liquid contracts with relatively low counterparty risk. Their structure allows for both ease in trade and ease in access to leverage via margin accounts. Traditionally, futures market participants have been divided into hedgers who protect against price moves and speculators who take positions in them. Given the structure of futures contracts, futures markets provide the ideal location for implementing a diversified trend following strategy. Trend followers speculate on the direction of a trend using futures contracts.

The managed futures industry is made up of professional money managers who take speculative positions in futures markets. Trend following is perhaps the most popular managed futures strategy. The managed futures industry has grown substantially in the past 30 years. Trading volumes in futures markets has also grown hand in hand with the managed futures industry. The role of futures contracts in the derivatives industry is growing. By requiring transparency, collateral management, and central clearing, recent regulatory trends have created a push for further futurization in the financial industry. Futurization can lead to even further increases in volumes of futures contracts and a blurring of the lines between OTC and ETD contracts going forward.

■ Further Reading and References

Acworth, W. "Futurization: Market Participants Clash." *Futures Industry* 23, no. 2 (March 2013): 36–40.

Casa, T., M. Rechsteiner, and A. Lehmann. "De-Mystifying Managed Futures: Why First Class Research and Innovation Are Key to Stay Ahead of the Game." White paper, Man Investments, 2010.

Hull, J. *Options, Futures, and Other Derivatives*. 6th ed. Upper Saddle River, NJ: Pearson Prentice-Hall, 2011.

Kaminski, K. "Diversifying Risk with Crisis Alpha." *Futures Magazine*, February 1, 2011.

Kaminski, K. "In Search of Crisis Alpha: A Short Guide to Investing in Managed Futures." CME Group white paper, April 2011.

Kaminski, K. "Thought Leadership: Riding the Next Wave of Futurization." *Institutional Insights*, June 2013.

Kaminski, K. "The Next Wave of Futurization." *Alternative Investment Analyst Review* 2, no. 3 (2013).

Kurbanov, R. "Swap Futurization—The Emergence of a New Business Model or Avoiding Regulation and Retaining the Status Quo?" *DerivSource*, February 13, 2013.

Leising, M. "Energy Swaps Migrating to Futures as Dodd-Frank Rules Take Hold." *Futures Magazine*, January 24, 2013.

Litan, R. "Futurization of Swaps: A Clever Innovation Raises Novel Policy Issues for Regulators." Bloomberg Government, BGOV Analysis, January 14, 2013.

Parsons, J. "3 Points on the Futurization of Swaps." *Betting the Business* (blog), January 31, 2013.

Rodriguez-Valladares, M. "Futures and Futurization: Full Steam Ahead on Dodd-Frank" MRV Associates, November 19, 2012.

CHAPTER 3

Systematic Trend Following Basics

This chapter is dedicated to taking a closer look at the basic building blocks in a systematic trend following system. The modern approach to trend following has taken the shape of a finely tuned, automated and engineered machine. These trading systems automate trades across a wide range of asset classes. Technological advances and developments in the futures markets have allowed for this transition. The modernization of trend following has increased the efficacy of implementing the strategy but at the cost of increased competition.

A typical trend following system is comprised of the following four core decisions:

1. When to enter a position.
2. How large a position to take on.
3. How to get out of positions.
4. How much risk to allocate to different sectors and markets.

Given these four core decisions, a trend following system is a dynamic system that processes price data inputs, generates trading signals, and outputs automated executable trading decisions. The first section in this chapter addresses the building blocks of a simple trend following system. It is important to understand how the main components come together to create a trading system from both the aggregate and individual trade level. The second section looks at a trend following system from the outside and explains several metrics and methods for classifying trend following systems. This chapter's main objective is to give a detailed overview in order to provide the baseline for trend following systems from an investment management perspective for the remainder of this book.

FIGURE 3.1 A schematic of trend following from data acquisition to position allocation.

A **trend following system** is a system that takes data inputs, processes the information in this data, and systematizes trading decisions. Figure 3.1 presents a flow diagram for the concept of trend following. A trend following system can simultaneously take into account large amounts of data, process it, create trading signals, calculate and allocate risks, as well as determine position sizes, stops, and limits.

Inside a trend following system, there are several components that are integrated into portfolio construction. These include data processing, signal generation, position sizing, market allocation, and trading execution. Each of these components is described in further detail in Figure 3.2.

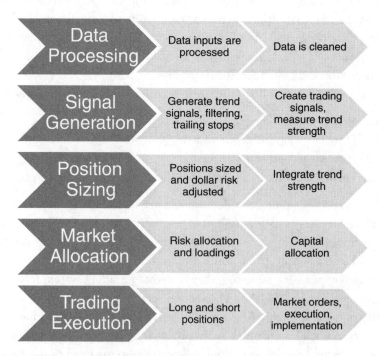

FIGURE 3.2 The five components of a trend following system.

■ The Basic Building Blocks of a Trend Following System

There are many different ways to build a trend following system. Despite this, at their core, these systems are based on using price data to determine when to go long or short. This action is coupled with a method for allocating dollar risk or capital to different markets as well as methods for trade execution. In this section, given the wide range in how these methods are applied, an approach similar to Greyserman, Kaminski, Lo, and Yan (2014) is explained with a few additional clarifications.[1] Starting from the top down, how these components come together will be explained.

Data Processing

Data inputs for a trend following system are generally simple price and volume data with information on the size and value of each contract. It is also important to note that for a typical medium/long-term futures strategy, the aspect of rolling forward contracts must be taken into consideration. More specifically, positions will need to be rolled from expiring contracts to newer ones. The rolling aspect of futures contracts will create gaps in the price series requiring adjustments in price data series. Since trend following decisions are focused on difference in price as opposed to absolute prices, trend signals can be calculated on what are often called **continuous price series**. Continuous price series are created by removing the gaps in price series. This is done to offset the price difference (spread) between the two contracts with different expiration dates. Price series adjustment makes both data processing and eventually signal generation possible.

Position Sizing

Trend following systems allocate capital across many different asset classes taking long and short positions across markets. They do this by systematically allocating risk or capital to individual markets. Position sizing must take into account the volatility of a particular market. The nominal position (v) in a particular market, long or short, is equal to a **sizing function** times the **total adjusted dollar risk** times the nominal value of one contract. This can be written as:

$$v = s \times \left(\frac{\theta \times c}{\sigma_K(\Delta P) \times PV} \right) \times (PV \times P)$$

---

[1] The purpose of this section is to summarize the approach. For further details regarding implementation and design of a simple trend following system, see Clenow (2013).

The sizing function (s) is a number between -1 and 1 ($s \in [-1,1]$). It determines the size and direction of a contract based on trading signals and trend strength. The sizing function and trend strength will be discussed in further detail later in this section. The total adjusted dollar risk allocated is equal to the **allocated dollar risk** divided by the **futures contract dollar risk**. The allocated dollar risk is simply the risk loading (θ) times the allocated capital (c) per market. The futures contract dollar risk is the realized dollar risk ($\sigma_K(\Delta P)$ of each contract price over a lookback window of time (K) times the point value(PV)).[2] The nominal value of one contract is equal to the point value (multiplier) times the contract price.

An example, such as a long position in corn, can further clarify this equation. Suppose that future contracts for corn have a realized dollar risk ($\sigma_K^{Corn}(\Delta P) \times PV = \$7,000$), the risk loading is 0.02, capital allocated is \$1,000,000, the contract size (point value) is 50, and a typical price of \$430. If the sizing of the position was simply 1 ($s = 1$), the nominal position is \$61,427.57 long in corn. For comparison, corn contracts can be compared with a typical oil contract. For example, suppose that crude oil futures have a realized dollar risk of ($\sigma_K^{oil}(\Delta P) \times PV = \$24,000$), the risk loading is 0.02, the capital allocation is \$1,000,000, the point value is 1,000, and the typical price is \$95. Again with $s = 1$, this would constitute a long position of \$79,166.67 to oil.[3] The relative sizing is quite important. Total risk of the trend following system can be geared upwards or downwards by changing the risk loading. For example, if the risk loading for each contract is doubled to 0.04, the positions would also double for each market with \$122,857.14 in corn and \$158,333.33 in oil for the same allocated capital.

This section provides only one characterization for position sizing based on dollar risk. There are many ways that this can be done. For example, as opposed to dollar risk, position sizing can also depend on average trading range (ATR) for each individual market.[4] Average trading ranges are a simple way to incorporate actual trading volatility and volumes as opposed to using realized volatility. **Trading range (TR)** is an estimate of the range that an individual market trades over in a given day. It is defined as the maximum of the high (H) for a day or the previous closing price (C_{t-1}) minus the minimum of the low (L) for the day or the previous closing price (C_{t-1}). The **average trading range (ATR)** is an average of the trading range over a given window (n) of time. For example, this window could be 100 days or 50 days depending on the speed of trading.

---

[2] The point value is a multiplier that is used for the size of futures contracts.

[3] It is important to point out here that the total notional exposure is not the same as capital allocated. The total capital allocated will also depend on each future's contract margin requirements as set by the futures exchange. These requirements are also typically a function of past volatility and trading ranges.

[4] This approach is discussed at length in Clenow (2013).

The nominal position (v), as a function of average trading range (ATR_n) for each individual market, can be characterized by the following expression:

$$v(ATR) = s \times \left(\frac{\theta \times c}{ATR_n \times PV} \right) \times (PV \times P)$$

where

$$TR_t = \max(H, C_{t-1}) - \min(L, C_{t-1})$$

$$ATR_n(t) = \frac{1}{n} \sum_{i=0}^{n-1} TR_{t-i}$$

Signal Generation and Aggregation

Position sizing depends on risk allocation and the sizing function (s). The sizing function is built on trading signals that depend on underlying trend signals. **Trend signals** are the basic signals for defining long or short trends. **Trading signals** require the aggregation and sometimes filtering of simple trend signals.[5] Across the industry, there are two core simple strategies that often provide the basis for a trend signal. The first type of strategy is a **moving average strategy** and the second is a **breakout strategy**. A moving average is simply a rolling average value of the price. A simple moving average strategy has a long signal when the price is above the moving average and a short signal when it is below. Figure 3.3 plots an example of a simple 20-day

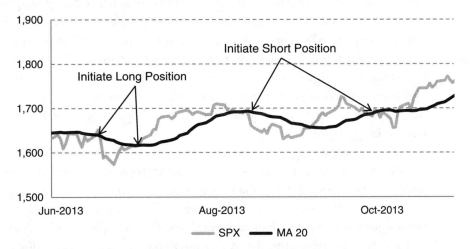

FIGURE 3.3 An example of a 20-day moving average signal on the SPX from June 2013 to December 2013. The trend signal will be long when the price crosses above the 20-day moving average and be short when the price crosses below the 20-day moving average.

---

[5] In practice, trend signals are often a binary 0 or 1 signal. Trading signals may be binary or nonbinary. Trend strength may be binary or nonbinary. This is shown in an example later in this chapter.

moving average for the SPX from June 2013 to December 2013. This example also shows several entry points for a long and short signal. A **moving average crossover strategy** uses moving averages across different windows coupled with crossover rules to determine when trend signals are long or short. For example, the simple case is both a fast moving average and a slow moving average. More explicitly, a 150-day moving average of the price could be the slow moving average and a 50-day moving average of the price could be the fast moving average. A moving average crossover strategy has a long trend signal when the fast-moving average is greater than the slow one and a short trend signal when the fast-moving average is below the short one. One key issue with a simple application of this strategy is that trend signals based on moving averages may change sign often. This can result in unwanted trading and the associated trading costs. At the core, trend signals based on moving averages follow the trends as they evolve.

A breakout strategy creates a positive or negative trend signal when the price breaks out of a range of values. These ranges of values are often called **resistance and support levels**. Resistance and support levels can be defined using many different techniques including past prices, trading range, and other indicators. However, very often these levels are simply the high and low prices over a given lookback window. A breakout strategy has a positive trend signal when the price goes above the resistance level and a negative trend signal when the price goes below the support level. Trading signals based on breakout trend signals are designed so that the position exits when either an opposite breakout trend signal occurs or when a **trailing stop** is reached. A trailing stop is a stopping rule that depends on the recent path of the price such that the stop "trails" the price. It is important to remember that trading signals are aggregated and filtered versions of the underlying trend signals. Compared with moving average trend signals, depending on specific parameter implementation, the trend signals for a breakout strategy may change more dramatically over time. Despite this fact, both the moving average and breakout trend signals produce highly correlated systems in aggregate.

Both a moving average and a breakout strategy define a set of rules to create trend signals. These trend signals can be filtered and aggregated to define trading signals. A trading signal is a signal that defines the position in a particular market long or short.[6] In practice, trading signals are often combined sets of breakout or moving average trend signals with various lookback windows. For example, simple moving average signals can be aggregated to determine position sizing. This issue is discussed in the next section.

---

[6] For clarification, trading signals can simply be raw trend signals or filtered versions and combined versions of trend signals. Trend strength is determined by the aggregation of trading signals. If trading signals are all the raw trend signals, the term trading signal is redundant.

Signal Aggregation and Links to Position Sizing

One important issue to address is the role of **trend strength**. Trend strength is defined as the measured strength of a trend. It is a quantitative measure of the level of conviction of the trend. Trend strength is typically measured at the total signal level by aggregating trading signals across various lookback windows. There are many methodologies that can link trend strength to position sizing. For example, using a pool of moving average trend signals, trend strength can simply be the differential between the numbers of positive crossovers and negative crossovers in a prespecified set of lookback windows. Likewise, for the breakout signal, trend strength can be the difference between the numbers of immediately previous positive breakouts and negative breakouts, which occurred during a set of lookback windows prior to the current time period. Position size is often an explicit function of trend strength. For demonstrative purposes, Figure 3.4 plots a set of examples of how trend strength can be linked to position sizing.

The first example (A) is a simple binary approach. This example switches from long to short positions across one threshold at zero. Example (B) uses a buffer around zero. Here, weak signals only switch once trend strength is large enough in absolute terms. Example (C) is a linear allocation to trend strength. Example (D) and Example (E) are nonlinear approaches. Example (F) is an example of linear position sizing with profit taking. Figure 3.4 clearly demonstrates that there are many different approaches for linking trend strength to position sizing. For each example in Figure 3.4, trend strength (TS) ranges from -10 to 10. Returning to the equation for the nominal position, for each of these cases the sizing function can be written as a function of normalized trend strength. For the examples in Figure 3.4, the sizing function would simply be trend strength divided by 10 (i.e., $s = TS/10$).

Market Allocation

Market allocation is the process with which both risk and capital is allocated across various futures markets. The process of allocation comes from both capital allocation schemes and risk adjustments and loadings. From the equation for the nominal position, there are two avenues where market allocation can be adjusted based on risk. Risks are adjusted by both the risk loading and by the volatility adjustment for risk per contract. Returning to the equation, the nominal position (v) for each particular market is equal to the sizing function times the total adjusted dollar risk times the nominal value of one contract. This can be written as:

$$v = s \times \left(\frac{\theta \times c}{\sigma_K(\Delta P) \times PV} \right) \times (PV \times P)$$

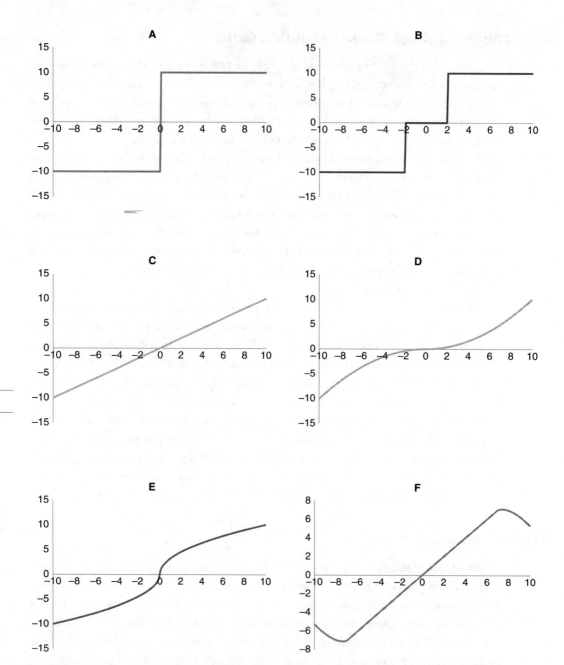

FIGURE 3.4 Examples of the linking position sizing to trend strength. The x-axis is trend strength and the y-axis is the sizing function. In this example, trend strength varies from −10 to 10 and the sizing function varies from −10 to 10. In order to scale positions to −1 to 1, a simple normalization by 10 must be applied to use the nominal position equation where s = TS/10.

Taking a closer look at this equation, there are several simplifications. First, in the simple case the risk loading (θ) can be set to be equal for all markets. The risk loading is often quoted in basis points, for example, 0.02 for each market. The risk loading is set up in this way to allow for simple gearing of trend following systems. Correlation can also be taken into account in this structure. More specifically, if the risk loading is 2 bps risk per market and the trading system trades 50 markets. In aggregate, correlation can be taken into account using a scalar (K). For the example, with 50 markets, the total risk is $100K$. Based on the correlation structure of underlying markets, K is a scalar between 0 and 1. Similar to a system without correlation included, this framework allows for simple gearing of total risk via adjusting the risk loadings for each market. In the simple case where the risk loadings are the same in the case of correlation, the total risk can easily be scaled from $100K$ bps at risk to $400K$ bps (assuming related risk and regulatory constraints are still within the appropriate limits). In a similar manner, trend following systems can also easily be designed to adjust risk loadings across different individual markets or market regimes. For the case of risk as defined by volatility, it is important to remember that the position sizing already takes past volatility into account by adjusting for dollar risk.

Capital allocated can also vary from market to market. In the equation for nominal position (v), capital allocation is denoted by (c). In the simplest case, capital allocation can be equal dollar risk weighted (EDR). This means that the capital for an individual market is equal to the total capital (c_T) divided by the number of traded markets (N).

$$c^{EDR} = \frac{c_T}{N}$$

There is a wide range of methodologies for implementing capital allocation. Several of these methods fit easily into the simple structure proposed in this section. Others may require more complicated or new structures to implement them. The main ways to allocate risk include equal dollar risk allocation (EDR), equal risk contribution (ERC), and market capacity weighting (MCW).[7]

- **Equal dollar risk allocation (EDR)** is a strategy that allocates the same amount of dollar risk to each market. This approach, similar to the $1/N$ approach, does not consider the correlation between markets.

- **Equal risk contribution (ERC)** is a strategy that allocates risk based on the risk contribution of each market taking correlation into account. This approach is similar to risk parity.

---

[7] For a more detailed description of these methods and several others see "Quantcraft" (2013).

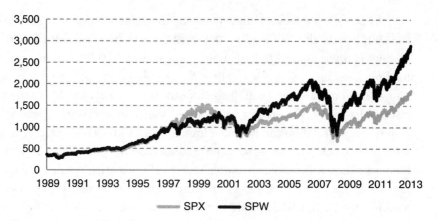

FIGURE 3.5 The equally weighted S&P 500 index (SPW) and the value weighted S&P 500 index (SPX) from 1989 to 2013.

- **Market capacity weighting (MCW)** is an approach where capital is allocated as a function of individual market capacity. In futures markets, a market capacity weighting will depend on the market size as measured by both volume and daily price volatility.

Equal dollar risk allocation (EDR) and market capacity weighting (MCW) are discussed here in further detail.[8] These two approaches mirror the typical capital allocation approaches in equity markets: more notably equal weighted versus value weighted. Research on equal weighted indices in equities tends to suggest that they have historically outperformed value weighted. The performance of the S&P 500 index for both equal and value weighted is plotted since 1989 in Figure 3.5. Despite the historical outperformance of equal weighted allocation in equity markets, there are still skeptics that suggest that survivorship bias and varying risks may also explain some of this outperformance. Trend following allocation can also be divided into EDR and MCW. Here, market capacity is defined as the average daily volume multiplied by the dollar volatility of each market. This metric is a risk-based liquidity measure of market capacity. In a trend following system, the market capacity (or value) weighted approach will allocate more capital to larger, more liquid markets similar to a value weighted equity index. Similar to an equal weighted equity index, the equal dollar risk allocation approach will allocate more risk to smaller and less liquid markets.

Similar to equal weighted versus value weighted in equities, trend following strategies with equal risk allocation outperform market capacity weighted over the longer run.[9] A fund with large assets under management cannot allocate capital to

[8] In the formula for the nominal position (v), capital allocation (c) will be equal capital for each market for equal dollar risk (EDR) and scaled by market capacity weighting (MCW).
[9] A market size factor is discussed in Chapter 12.

markets with lower open interest and volumes. They are more likely to follow an allocation scheme closer to a market capacity weighted scheme. For example, in simple experiments, the market capacity based scheme allocates more than 60 percent of capital in equity index futures and bond futures, while the agricultural sector receives only a 5 percent allocation. This highly imbalanced allocation makes the portfolio concentrated primarily on the financials sectors. This reduces the diversification benefits that can be provided by other markets. This topic is discussed in further detail in Chapter 15.

Sector Allocation and Allocation Constraints

Most trend following systems have their own slant or objective. In particular, a trend following system can have either a sector bias or a sector directional bias. A **sector bias** occurs when a particular sector has a higher risk weighting than others. The simplest example of this is a large fund with a financial sector bias. Smaller futures markets such as commodities have considerable liquidity constraints due to their size and volumes. Given this for larger funds, a financial sector bias is inevitable. A sector bias can often simply be obtained by adjusting risk loadings or capital allocations in certain markets. A **sector directional bias** is when a trading system is specifically designed to have a slant toward long or short positions in a particular market sector. The most common of this is an equity long bias. A sector directional bias is often applied at the trading signal level. Positions are filtered to favor long positions over short positions. In the extreme case, only long positions are included in the portfolio. For this case, only long trading signals are included and short signals are filtered out. Figure 3.6 presents an example schematic for an

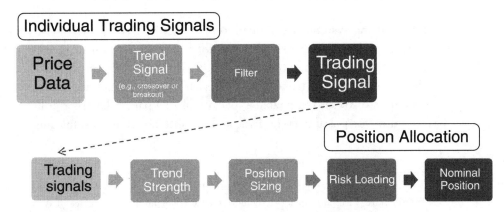

FIGURE 3.6   An example schematic of an integrated trend following system.

integrated trend following system. Sector bias can be added at the risk loading or capital allocation stage. A sector directional bias can be added at the filtering stage for individual trend signals.

Trading Execution

The final component of a trend following system is trading execution. Implementation approaches for turning trading signals into actual positions can vary from one system to another. However, it is important to note that for most medium- to long-term trend following systems execution is not urgent. More specifically, the level of alpha decay is not significant. **Alpha decay** is the speed that performance degrades as you delay execution. In the long-term perspective, alpha decay is much less important for trend following than many other hedge fund strategies.[10] As a result, the more important consideration for execution for trend following systems is costs rather than the execution speed. Trend following orders can be executed in a rather passive manner. For example, orders can be executed during liquid periods on the following trading day using time weighted average price (TWAP) strategies.[11] Some systems may also sample prices throughout the liquid periods of the day to generate signals and split daily orders into several intraday orders.

Trend following strategies are generally executed via simple market orders. Stop loss orders and more complicated limit orders are less commonly used. Trend following systems use stopping rules but they are often at the trading signal level as opposed to at the execution level. For example, a trading system may use a trailing stop to adjust a breakout trend signal but implement positions using simple market orders intraday.

■ Strategy Classification and Core Differentiators

Trend following systems are similar to finely tuned trading machines. From "outside the black box," investors often do not have access to all of the fine details of how a strategy is implemented. As a result, they must rely on several metrics that can help classify how a trend following system is constructed. These metrics can help an investor to set reasonable expectations of a particular trend following strategy, monitor for possible style drift, and ask intelligent and useful questions when

---

[10] The concept of trend leakage and importance of the entry decisions is discussed in Chapter 5.

[11] A TWAP strategy executes orders to achieve the time weighted average price (TWAP).

TABLE 3.1	Core factors that differentiate trend following systems and common metrics for comparison.
Core Factors That Differentiate Trend Following Systems	**Metrics to Measure These Factors**
Target risk (leverage)	Normalize risks of return streams
Capital allocation	Equal dollar risk weighted versus market capacity weighted
System speed (holding period)	Lookback window size: Medium or long term
Directional bias	Long equity bias versus no equity bias

evaluating manager performance. This section provides a short review of common differentiators among trend following programs and common metrics for measuring these differentiators.

Returning back to the basics set out in the first part of this chapter, a trend following system is composed of four key elements: signal generation and filtering, position sizing, risk allocation, and trading execution. Within each of these elements, there are many permutations of parameters, techniques, and approaches, which can be applied. The level of degrees of freedom is large and perhaps intractable from the perspective of the investor. As a result, this section focuses on the core characteristics that differentiate these systems. These core characteristics include risk targets, capital allocation, holding horizon, and directional bias. Table 3.1 lists these core factors and common metrics, which can help measure these factors. In this section, these characteristics are introduced to provide further detail on how they can be measured. These core characteristics will give rise to a division of trend following systems into different categories. The division of trend following strategies into different classes will motivate the creation of broader style factors facilitating performance evaluation, benchmarking, and style analysis. These topics are detailed at length in Part V of this book.

Target Risk and Leverage

A **risk target** is the total amount of risk allocated to a trend following strategy. From one trend following strategy to another, the risk target will vary depending on the preferences of the manager. In futures trading, risk targets are approximately linear. This means that trend following programs with different risk targets can be taken into account by normalizing all the returns to a common level of risk. Normalization must be performed before any comparison is made between strategies.

Risk targets are often stipulated by trend following programs in their investment mandates. Yet, ex-post they are often measured by realized volatility. In practice, one concern can be adjusting for programs that change their risk target over time. For example, many large trend followers have tended to bring their volatility targets as they increase in assets under management. This causes simple risk normalization to become more complicated to apply. In this case, it may be appropriate to divide the return series into different sub periods.

Capital Allocation

Capital allocation is a second core differentiator of portfolio performance. As discussed in the previous section, there are many approaches to allocate capital across markets. For simplicity, this section focuses on the two well-accepted methodologies from the previous section: EDR and MCW. These classifications mirror the typical classifications for allocation in equity markets, more notably value weighted versus equal weighted. Here, market capacity is defined as the average daily volume multiplied by the dollar volatility of each market. This metric is a risk-based liquidity measure of that market. In a trend following system, the market capacity (or value) weighted approach will allocate more capital to larger more liquid markets similar to a value weighted equity index. Similar to an equal weighted equity index, the equal dollar risk allocation approach will allocate more risk to smaller and less liquid markets. Key differences in equal risk weighted versus market capacity weighted is that a market capacity weighting may allocate more than 60 percent of the capital to financial sectors with sectors like the agricultural sector receiving only around 5 percent of the capital. A trend following program with large assets under management will be constrained to capital allocations more similar to market capacity weighted. The implications of less liquid markets and the role of the market size on a trend following program is discussed in further detail in Chapter 15.

Holding Period

The **average holding period** is the average amount of time a trade is held. Holding periods depend mostly on signal generation and trading execution but they may also depend on position allocation and risk allocation. Trading signals determine when positions should be entered and exited. Signal generation can include many different parameter choices increasing complexity. A simple metric to consider is the length of the lookback windows, which are used for identifying entry and exit parameters. A **lookback window** is the length of time used for calculations necessary for signal generation. For example, a 100-day moving average signal uses a 100-day lookback period to calculate the moving average.

Risk control mechanisms can also have an impact on holding periods. This is especially true in the case where trailing stops are used to control risks. For example, a trend following system with looser stops or no stops in their trend signals will have longer holding periods than ones with tighter stops. Position sizing and risk allocation may also have an impact on holding periods. Depending on the method used to perform market allocation and position sizing, there are many parameters that can affect how long positions are held. For example, in the position sizing formula, the lookback window for ATR can affect how positions are adjusted based on the recent trading volatility as proxied by trading ranges. If this window is shorter, position sizing will be more focused on shorter term volatility meaning that in an equal dollar risk allocation, markets with larger trading activity will be toned down possibly reducing holding periods over the long run. With a larger lookback window, shorter periods of larger trading activity will be toned down less quickly resulting in longer holding periods. Given this discussion, there are several parameters contributing to the average holding period. In particular, the size of lookback windows for signal generation, the use of stopping rules in trading signals, and the lookback windows for risk allocation can give some insight into average holding periods.

Directional Bias

The default for a trend following program might, in theory, be agnostic to long and short bias. As explained in the discussion of the building blocks of trend following systems, some managers intentionally impose either a sector bias or sector directional bias. The most common types of sector bias are equity sector bias or financial sector bias. Equity sector bias may be chosen to help follow the uptrends in equity markets more explicitly or for other reasons. Financial sector bias may be a choice or may be simply driven by liquidity constraints. Sector bias can most easily be imposed at the position allocation level. Sector directional bias is a bit more complicated. Many managers explicitly state their **average sector allocations,** or the amount of capital allocated to a particular sector. If this is not stated explicitly, it can be inferred approximately from the disclosure of sector performance or risks.

A sector directional bias can be imposed at the trading signal level using trend filters or at the risk level depending on how the market allocation is determined. To determine sector directional bias from the outside looking in is also more complex than sector allocation. A directional bias may not be stated by a manager but it may result as a function of the signals that they use to generate positions. For example, if a trend following system applies a filter that favors long positions over shorts or if a market itself favors longs to shorts, this results in a directional bias. In principle, a directional bias is not a bad thing. Many markets have an inherent bias in one way or the other. For example, many trend following systems may seem to have a long bias because they have selected long positions in fixed income more often than short. If one takes a step back, this is to be expected as the longer term trend in bonds for an extended period of time has been long as rates have drifted close to zero. Sector directional bias creates dispersion in returns among systems and changes some of the statistical properties of the strategy. For example, trend following programs with a large equity long bias can exhibit negative skewness similar to equity market returns. **Skewness** of returns is one method of measuring the level of equity bias in a trend following system.[12]

■ Partitioning Trend Following Systems

Three of the core characteristics that differentiate trend following systems include capital allocation, directional bias, and holding horizon. These three characteristics can be combined to create eight unique trading systems. Capital allocation is divided into equal dollar risk weighted and market capacity weighted. Trading speeds are divided between medium and long term. A medium- versus a long-term holding horizon is achieved by choosing different lengths of lookback windows for signals.[13] Equity directional bias is divided into long equity bias or no explicit equity bias. The equity bias is achieved by overweighting long positions and underweighting short positions. Each trend following system is characterized by three core characteristics of the system design. Given the possible choices for capital allocation, holding horizon, and trading speed, trend following strategies can be partitioned into eight trading systems. The division of these strategies is detailed in Table 3.2.

TABLE 3.2 Eight systems for trend following along three dimensions: equity bias, capital allocation, and holding horizon. Here, "No Long Horizon" indicates a median horizon.

	Equity Long Bias	Market Capacity Weighted	Long Horizon
1	No	No	No
2	Yes	No	No
3	No	Yes	No
4	No	No	Yes
5	Yes	Yes	No
6	No	Yes	Yes
7	Yes	No	Yes
8	Yes	Yes	Yes

---

[12] Several other statistics are discussed later in this book including return dispersion and benchmarking for trend following systems.

[13] The classification between medium and long term is quite arbitrary. In this book, medium represents an average holding period of shorter than 100 trading days and long represents an average holding period of longer than 100 days.

System 1 is defined as a pure trend following system. System 1 is medium term as most CTAs have been over time, the system has equal dollar risk weighting for all markets, and the system has no equity bias. This system will be denoted as **pure trend following** for the remainder of this book. By definition, a pure trend following system is the most agnostic system that can be constructed. A pure trend following system is a trading system that is designed with no particular bias in liquidity, risk allocation, or sector. The partitioning of trend following strategies allows for a discussion of the performance of trend following and motivates the construction of benchmarks and style factors later in this book.

■ Summary

Trend following systems are finely tuned, automated trading systems. These systems may seem like a "black box" to some, but a closer look at the building blocks, which make up a trend following system, provides a baseline for understanding how these strategies are constructed. Trend following systems are made up of several components: data processing, signal generation, position sizing, market allocation, and trading execution. Each of these components are coupled together to systematically determine trends and allocate capital across markets. By reviewing the basic components, a closer look at several core differentiators in trend following systems can be connected to the mechanics inside a trend following system. Using these core differentiators, trend following systems can be partitioned into eight subsystems. An understanding of the basics of trend following systems and core metrics to differentiate between systems provides the baseline for understanding them.

■ Further Reading and References

Alverez, M., M. Beceren, C. Davies, S. Mesomeris, and C. Natividade. "Quantcraft: Colours of the Trend." Deutsche Bank Markets Research, September 2013.

Clenow, A. *Following the Trend*. Hoboken, NJ: John Wiley & Sons, 2013.

Greyserman, A., K. Kaminski, A. Lo, and L. Yan. "Style Analysis in Systematic Trend Following." Working paper, 2014.

Kissko, L., and T. Sanzin. "Shedding Light on the Black Box." Strategy Insight white paper, Hermes BPK Parters, 2012.

PART III

THEORETICAL FOUNDATIONS

CHAPTER 4

Adaptive Markets and Trend Following

Financial theorists and practitioners both agree that the classic efficient markets hypothesis (EMH) may often fall short of explaining certain aspects of dynamic trading strategies. The core issue with efficient market theory comes from the fact that it presents a somewhat static view of the behavior of markets. On the other hand, behavioral finance suggests that we systematically deviate from what most economists label rational expectations. In reality, markets are adaptive and market conditions continue to evolve over time as a function of the market environment and the composition and level of competition present in financial markets. The **adaptive markets hypothesis (AMH)** is a framework for explaining how markets behave using principles from evolutionary biology. In an adaptive markets framework, it is precisely the market players that are best able to adapt, which by the forces of natural selection are able to compete and survive to continue competing in highly competitive and dynamic financial markets.

In this chapter, as proposed by Andrew Lo (2004, 2005, 2006, 2012), the AMH is introduced to provide more detail into how to understand dynamic trading strategies. Using this framework, it is much easier to understand dynamic strategies, such as trend following, and the role of adaptation in success and survival over the long run. A discussion of the evolutionary origin of human behavior, when faced with sequential choices over time, leads to the definition of **speculative risk premiums** and speculative opportunities in financial markets. With an adaptive markets view, as opposed to a traditional efficient markets view, the competitive advantage and adaptive properties of trend following explain why the strategy works well during periods of market divergence and in particular during financial crisis. Financial crisis represents a time when market divergence, potential imbalances between supply and demand, and general price dislocation are often at their greatest. Put in traditional efficient market terms, these are often transitory moments where market efficiency may be put to the test.

To put crisis alpha and speculative risk premiums into an empirical perspective, the performance of trend following can be decomposed into three components: the risk-free rate, a speculative risk premium, and crisis alpha. The risk-free rate is the positive carry of collateral. The speculative risk premium is driven by skill at capturing premiums, such as hedging premiums, outside of crisis. Crisis alpha is driven by trend following's ability to adapt and remain competitive during periods of market stress. Using common industry benchmarks, crisis alpha has provided a substantial portion of return for CTAs during the period of 2000 to 2013. Speculative risk premiums outside of crisis at the index level have been relatively low during this period. To provide further insight and perspective on the recent performance of trend following, the decomposition is also applied to 200 years of data from Chapter 1's multicentennial analysis. The longer term perspective demonstrates that crisis alpha has always driven some of but not always most of trend following performance especially during recent times, from 2000 to 2013.

■ The Adaptive Market Hypothesis

The classic efficient markets hypothesis (EMH) is a framework for understanding how market prices behave. In its strongest form, it declares that all relevant information is incorporated into prices. Even in its weakest form, the EMH implies that all historical price information cannot be used to make profitable investments. Given that trend following is a method for systematically investing across asset classes following trends in historical prices, it is in direct conflict with even the weakest form of EMH. It comes, therefore, as no surprise that the strategy has often been somewhat ignored by academics and viewed with skepticism by most academically trained practitioners. In fact, until only recently, the strategy was often classified in the ranks of what some call "Voodoo" finance strategies such as technical analysis. Yet, recently, as more and more academics and practitioners have begun to discuss limitations of the EMH view of markets, trend following has started to be discussed in a more positive light.

The main problem with the EMH is that it is not dynamic, and given this framework, strategies such as trend following may seem counterintuitive. In 2004, Andrew

Lo from MIT suggested an alternative to efficient market theory, which allows for a more dynamic and adaptive view of market behavior. The AMH is an approach for understanding how markets evolve, how opportunities occur, and how market players succeed or fail based on principles of evolutionary biology.[1] This theory was put forth by Lo in 2004 and it attempts to reconcile the key issues related to the traditional EMH.[2] According to the AMH, concepts central in evolutionary biology govern market dynamics via the forces of competition, mutation, reproduction, and natural selection.

> Prices reflect as much information as dictated by the combination of environmental conditions and the number and nature of "species" in the economy, or . . . ecology. Species are defined as distinct groups of market participants: ex: pension funds, retail investors, hedge funds. (Lo 2004)

According to the AMH, profit opportunities exist when more resources are present and competition is lower. As competition increases, by natural selection, the players, who have competitive advantage over others, survive and adapt. Those who are not able to adapt disappear, reducing competition, starting the evolutionary cycle all over again. The waxing and waning of the hedge fund styles is an excellent example of this phenomenon at work. Figure 4.1 demonstrates the cycle of natural selection where the forces of competition and adaptation determine who succeeds and fails.

When markets are viewed as ecologies, it is easy to see that both market efficiency and behavioral finance are justifiable theories. First, when competition is high, prices will be very efficient. When competition is low, prices may be less efficient, also consistent with EMH. Second, according to the AMH, markets are seen as ecologies made up of species. Just as in evolutionary biology, financial species survive based on the principles of natural selection. Neuroscientists, psychologists, and behavioral experts agree that humans adapt heuristics or simple rules to make decisions. If humans use heuristics to make decisions and they adapt them to survive, behavioral biases are simply a natural consequence of human heuristic-based decision making.

---

[1] In other papers, Lo and Mueller (2010) discuss how economists often suffer from "physics envy or a false sense of mathematical precision." They discuss how finance is often governed by partially irreducible uncertainty. Put more simply, finance is not as quantifiable as physics. The famous physicist Richard Feynman is often quoted as saying "Imagine how much harder physics would be if electrons had feelings!"

[2] The advantage of the AMH is that it is consistent with both the EMH and theories of behavioral finance.

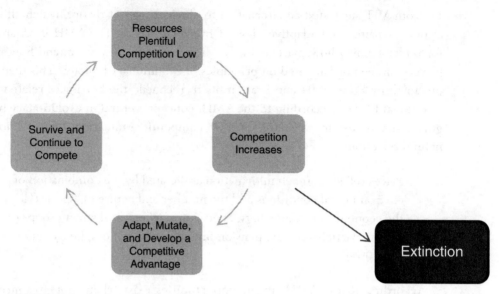

FIGURE 4.1 A schematic of natural selection with opportunities and competition.

For example, if one turns to fear and greed, they are two primal human emotions that are known to drive behavioral bias.[3] Despite some of the mishaps of our behavioral based heuristics, it is precisely these heuristics that have helped humans to survive over the ages.[4] There is a growing body of literature in the field of neuroscience, neuroeconomics (or even neurofinance), and psychology that supports the fact that heuristics (not utility optimization) are at the core of human decision making. Put simply, humans use heuristics that they adapt over time with experience. It is no surprise that from time to time, these simple heuristics can cause us to make financial

---

[3] From an evolutionary perspective, "Fear is the hardwired fire alarm for the brain" (Lo 2011). Fear of taking losses or fear of regret may lead investors to exhibit the disposition effect. Fear of losing out or pure greed can cause investors to follow the herd leading to financial bubbles. For further information regarding emotion in financial decision making: see Shull, Celiano, and Menaker, 2014.

[4] To cite a particularly comical example, Lee and Schwarz (2012) wrote a paper with a subtitle "The Embodiment of Social Suspicion and Fishy Smells." In their research, they demonstrated that investors take 25 percent less risk when they smell fish. This study demonstrates how visceral response even affects our financial decisions. When we smell something funny, such as rotten fish, a simple behavioral heuristic tells us to reduce risk. Another example, Dijksterhuis and Nordgren (2006) present a framework that demonstrates how unconscious thought may outperform in complex situations. Yet, another example, Bossaerts, Bruguier, and Quartz (2010) demonstrate how people, who use Theory of Mind (TOM), an understanding of how others are thinking or, as they put it, "the human capacity to discern malicious or benevolent intent," outperform strategies using probabilistic reasoning. For a more detailed overview of recent literature in this area, see Shull, Celiano, and Menaker, 2014.

decisions inconsistent with what might be considered rational decision making.[5] A closer look at what factors affect a heuristic's ability to adapt to changing financial environments will provide more insights into why and when heuristic approaches such as trend following may work. The next section dives deeper into factors that affect adaptation.

Factors That Affect Adaptation

For trading strategies, in particular dynamic trading strategies, the key to survival in highly competitive financial markets is adaptation. **Adaptation** is an evolutionary process whereby a species, or group of market participants, are able to adapt to changes in the market environment. The most extreme example of a drastic change in market environment occurs during a financial crisis. Given the industry-wide long bias toward equities, equity market crisis is a scenario when the most market participants are impacted and when market efficiency is often put to the test.

In the complex network of markets and market players, which make up the modern financial environment, there are many factors that affect a market player's ability to adapt to changes in the market environment. These factors can be divided into three categories: institutional restrictions, market functionality, and behavioral biases. These three categories can also be subdivided into several specific factors that directly affect adaptation. Table 4.1 lists each of these factors and subfactors

TABLE 4.1 Specific factors that affect adaptation and illustrative examples.

Specific Factors That Affect Adaptation	Examples
Institutional restrictions	Systemized drawdown limits
	Systemized risk limits (e.g., Basel III)
	Allocation constraints
	Asset class and market restrictions
	Margin and collateral constraints
Market functionality	Liquidity
	Counterparty risk
	Asymmetry between long and short
Behavioral biases	Long equity bias
	Loss aversion
	Anchoring
	Herding

---

[5] Brennan and Lo (2011) and Brennan and Lo (2012) discuss the origin of behavior. Using a binary choice model, they can explain a wide range of commonly discussed heuristics including probability matching, risk foraging, risk aversion, and others.

with examples, and the following sections provide some background for how each one of these factors affects adaptation.

Institutional Restrictions   Given the nature and construction of the financial industry, all market players are subject to varying levels of institutionalized regulation and frictions. These constraints include systematized drawdown limits or policies, systemized risk limits (including VaR policies such as those in Basel II and soon Basel III and Solvency II), allocation constraints (such as long only policies for mutual funds), asset class and market restrictions (such as restrictions on commodities or derivative contracts), and margin or collateral constraints. Drawdown limits refer to policies based on cutting losses with stop-limits to get out of positions following certain predetermined drawdowns. Systemized risk limits refer to policies that cut positions when risk limits are hit. These limits are defined by VaR and other volatility based measures. Allocation constraints are specific mandated constraints, which restrict allocation. No short sales is the most classic example of this type of constraint, which is valid for most mutual funds. Asset specific or market specific constraints refer to mandates that restrict trading in certain types of contracts such as commodities for pension funds or derivative markets for some mutual funds. Margin and collateral constraints also vary based on both the type of player, type of market, and type of contract.

The level of strictness of these factors varies significantly among market players from the tightest regulation in the case of pension funds and retail based investors to the loosest regulation in the case of hedge funds. Even for the case of hedge funds, drawdown, risk limits, and margin limits still apply although much less stringent than for other retail and institutional investors.

Market Functionality   All markets are not created equal. Market functionality varies substantially across all financial markets based in most cases by their design, their construction, the players that trade in them, and the specific contracts that are traded there. The key factors related to market functionality that affect a market player's ability to adapt are liquidity, counterparty risk, and asymmetry between long and short positions. Liquidity is a factor that is affected by the level of standardization of contracts, the level of transparency in contracts, the role of counterparty risk in that market, the diversity of market participants trading in that market, and the market depth. Although counterparty risk also affects liquidity, it is also important enough to be considered a factor in its own right. The level of counterparty risk varies substantially from market to market. Over-the-counter (OTC) contracts are an example of contracts that have an elevated dependence on counterparty risk. Chapter 2 provided a discussion of forward and futures contracts. When compared with bilateral forward contracts, futures contracts, by construction and due to the clearinghouse structure, have much lower counterparty risk. In general based on their design, exchange-traded contracts are exposed to less counterparty risk. Asymmetry between long and short positions is also something that varies substantially from market to market and, for institutional reasons, from one market participant to another. Using short sales as an example, equity markets short sales require 50 percent margin and are restricted to only certain subclasses of investors; private equity short sales are not feasible, yet in futures markets short sales have the same restrictions as long positions.

Behavioral Biases: Financial Darwinism?   Behavioral finance experts have documented a plethora of behavioral biases, which cause investors to react in ways that might be at odds with rational economic decision making. It is documented that, for various periods of time, investors or even classes of investors can behave in ways linked to human behavior and emotion.[6] For this exact reason, behavioral biases can also be a driving factor, which can hinder a market player's ability to adapt. Several key behavioral biases include "home" bias to a particular financial market (usually equity markets), loss aversion, overreaction, and herding behavior. There are many other behavioral biases that have been documented, but these biases are the most relevant for adaptation during a market crisis. Just as investors have a home bias for equities in their nearest and most familiar market, market players also have a home bias in the types of markets they trade. In most cases, this bias is toward equity and fixed income markets (pension funds), or toward fixed income markets (fixed income arbitrage hedge funds) or futures markets (CTAs). Home bias is important because most players will have difficulty changing their allocation to other markets when opportunities dry up in markets they are familiar with or accustomed to. Loss aversion and prospect theory explain that investors value opportunities in relative terms and that they asymmetrically are more disappointed by losses than they are pleased with gains. Loss aversion implies that investors are more likely to have stronger behavioral reactions in the case of large losses.[7] Herding is characterized when individuals act together in collective irrationality. Herding has often been blamed for market bubbles and crashes. In some contexts, herding may be rationally motivated, but in certain scenarios the tendency to herd can have devastating consequences.

The previous subsections provide a summary of factors that affect adaptation for all market participants. It is clear that each market participant will be affected by these factors in various levels of severity. Whether these factors are important will

---

[6] See Shull, Celiano, and Menaker 2014.

[7] Knutson and Kuhnen (2005) document that losses and gains that are processed by different parts of the brain and the response patterns of individuals can be linked to their actual portfolio decisions.

depend on what happens in the market environment. During an equity crisis event, several of these factors may be important for explaining why particular market participants survive, adapt, and outperform other market players. Using the concept of adaptation and an adaptive markets perspective, the next step is to look more closely at why a strategy such as trend following may be able to find opportunity during crisis periods.

Crisis Alpha Opportunities

Most investment strategies are susceptible to suffering devastating losses during an equity market crisis. Given this, for almost any investor, the key to finding true diversification is in finding an investment that is able to deliver performance during these turbulent periods. The painful losses of the credit crisis reinforced to investors the importance of understanding why a particular investment strategy makes sense. For any new or current investor in trend following, it is well known that these strategies tend to perform well when equity markets take losses, making them an excellent candidate for diversifying a portfolio. By taking a closer look into what really happens during equity market crisis events (often called tail risk events), this section can help to explain why trend following strategies can deliver crisis alpha opportunities for their investors. **Crisis alpha opportunities** are profits that are gained by exploiting the persistent trends that occur across markets during times of crisis.

For an investment strategy to be profitable, there must be an underlying fundamental reason for the existence of a profit opportunity that the strategy can exploit. Given that trend followers trade exclusively in the most liquid, efficient, and credit protected markets, their profitability must rely on those characteristics in order to obtain a competitive edge.[8] Trend following strategies will not profit from credit exposures or illiquidity, which are commonly cited risks and opportunities for most hedge fund strategies.[9] In fact, since trend following strategies rely on the most efficient type of trading vehicles, they must profit from persistent trends in markets, which, given that markets are efficient, should not, under ordinary circumstances, exist. The next logical step is to examine unordinary circumstances where it may be feasible for market efficiency to break down and persistent trends to occur even in the most efficient of markets. Given that the vast majority of investors are systematically long biased to equity markets and that we may be susceptible to behavioral

---

[8] See Chapter 2 for a discussion of the key characteristics of futures contracts. Futures contracts are transparent, highly liquid, and regulated with reduced counterparty risks due to clearinghouse mechanisms. Futures markets also allow trend following strategies to take directional positions both long and short across a wide range of asset classes.

[9] Hidden risks are discussed in further detail in Chapter 9.

biases especially, or perhaps only, when we lose money, it is clear that equity market crisis is the market scenario where predictable behavior and, as a consequence, persistent trends will be the most likely. Later in Chapter 5, market divergence is discussed in more detail. Equity market crisis are precisely the moments when market divergence is at extreme levels.

By examining what happens during equity market crisis, trend following strategies, based purely on the design and construction of the strategy, will enable it to deliver **crisis alpha**.

Equity Market Crisis and Crisis Alpha

For both behavioral and institutional reasons, market crisis represents a time when market participants become synchronized in their actions creating trends in markets. It is only the select (few) most adaptable market players who are able to take advantage of these "crisis alpha" opportunities.

When equity markets go down, the vast majority of investors are long biased to equity, including hedge funds, and they realize losses. Given loss aversion, losses represent periods when investors are more likely to be governed by behavioral bias and emotional based decision making. When this is coupled with the widespread use of institutionalized drawdown, leverage, and risk limits that are all triggered by losses, increased volatility, and increased correlation, given an investment community that is fundamentally long biased, equity losses will force or drive large groups of investors into action. When large groups of investors are forced into action, liquidity disappears, credit issues come to the forefront, fundamental valuation becomes less relevant, and persistent trends occur across all markets while investors fervently attempt to change their positions desperately seeking liquidity. Figure 4.2 displays a schematic of what happens during an equity market crisis.

Systematic trend following strategies trade across a wide range of asset classes primarily in futures; they do not exhibit a long bias to equity. Futures markets are extremely liquid and credit solvent and they remain more liquid and credit solvent than other markets during times of crisis. Although trend followers are also subject to institutionalized drawdown, risk and loss limits, trading primarily in futures guarantees they will be less affected by the reduced liquidity and credit solvency issues that accompany market crisis events. Given their lack of long bias to equities and systematic trading style, they will also be less susceptible to the behavioral effects that also accompany market crisis. Putting all of this together, trend following strategies are adaptable, liquid, systematic, and void of long equity bias making them less susceptible to the trap that almost all investors fall into during an equity crisis. Following the onset of a market crisis, a trend following strategy will be one of the select (few) strategies that are able to adapt to take advantage of the persistent trends

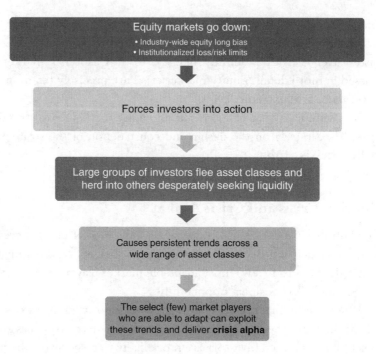

FIGURE 4.2   A schematic of the equity market crisis.

across the wide range of asset classes they trade in. This feature allows the strategy to be one of the few to deliver crisis alpha. It is important to also note that trend followers are not timing the onset of an equity markets crisis. They profit from a wide range of opportunities across asset classes following the onset of a market crisis. This includes currencies, bonds, short rates, soft commodities, energies, metals, and equity indices. The characteristics of systematic trend following and their implications during equity market crisis are summarized below in Table 4.2.

TABLE 4.2   The characteristics of trend following and their implications during equity crisis periods.

Characteristics of Trend Following	Implications during Equity Crisis Periods
Highly liquid, adaptable strategies based exclusively in futures with minimal credit exposure	Less susceptible to the illiquidity and credit traps that most investors experience during equity market crisis
Systematic trading strategies, lack of long equity bias	Less susceptible to behavioral biases and emotional based decision making triggered by experiencing losses
Active across a wide range of asset classes in futures	Poised to profit from trends across a wide range of asset classes

■ A Framework for Speculative Risk Taking

This section returns to the adaptive markets hypothesis (AMH) and discusses a framework for understanding a general class of speculative risk-taking strategies. Once this framework is explained, it can be used to examine the specific case of trend following and its signature crisis alpha. The AMH provides a general framework for understanding how opportunities occur and markets evolve. According to Lo (2012) some of the important practical implications of an adaptive view on markets include:

1. **Time varying risk premiums:** The trade-off between risk and return is not stable over time (risk premiums are time varying).
2. **Market efficiency is a relative concept:** Market efficiency should be measured and discussed in relative terms as opposed to absolute terms. Market efficiency is a continuum; it is not simply efficient or inefficient.
3. **Adaptation for success and survival:** It is necessary to use adaptable investment approaches to handle changes in the market environment.
4. **The inevitable degradation of alpha:** With time what once was alpha, eventually, due to innovation and competition becomes beta. Persistent alpha opportunities are not possible; fleeting alpha opportunities may be possible. For a schematic of this effect see Figure 4.3.

The Origin of Behavior

Before moving forward, a detour into the world of evolutionary finance, decision making theory, and neurofinance seems necessary. Unlike the classic EMH, the

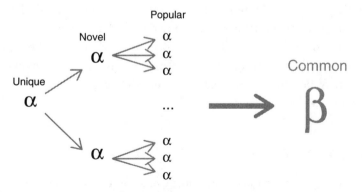

FIGURE 4.3 A schematic of the eventual degradation of alpha.
Source: Lo (2012).

AMH leaves room for some human considerations. The world of behavioral finance has long been viewed with disdain by neoclassical economists. In recent work by Brennan and Lo (2011, 2012), they approach the field of finance from a new angle. Instead of asking what investors should decide and optimizing their decision, they ask which behaviors are optimal from a survival perspective. The key difference in their work on the origin of behavior is that they view life as a sequence of decisions. Each day is a new risk situation and new decision. In real life, people do not make discrete static decisions. They choose things with a frequency. For a simple example, consider the purchase of a morning coffee. Although some people buy a coffee from the same place every day, many times our coffee selection looks like a random process with a certain frequency. For example, one person may go to Dunkin Donuts 60 percent of the time and Starbucks 40 percent of the time. In reality, humans are programmed to like variety and we make stochastic decisions in the face of risk. In the case of binary decisions, people often engage in a process which is called probability matching (this concept is discussed in further detail in Chapter 12). This means that people tend to select things at the same frequency as they expect them to occur. Using a simple sequential binary choice model, Brennan and Lo (2011) demonstrate that probability matching (and dynamic decisions over time) are population optimal. This means that behaviors like probability matching are built-in heuristics. These heuristics allow us to adapt and survive as a species (not necessarily always as an individual) over time. Brennan and Lo (2011) examine a wide range of "behavioral biases and heuristics" and derive how they link to survival and decision making over time. Their work provides an evolutionary perspective on our behavior and motivation for why people behave the way that they do.

To further push the understanding of bounded rationality and the concept of human intelligence, Brennan and Lo (2012) take their framework to the next level to explain both bounded rationality and how it is possible for certain market participants with "intelligence" adopt better "behaviors" than others over time. Although mathematically complex, this result in combination with the adaptive markets hypothesis confirms that over time there may be "smart investors" who are more effective at adapting to changes in the market environment. These investors may be able to outperform others over certain periods of time and under certain scenarios.

Speculative Risk Taking

Following a detour into evolutionary finance, this section returns to the act of speculation and the use of so-called intelligent trading strategies. First, two simplifying assumptions are made based on the AMH.

A1: (AMH holds). Market prices are a function of the market environment, level of competition, and composition of market players in a given market ecology. Supply, demand, risk appetite, and competition drive market prices.

A2: (Risk-free lending and no transaction costs). Markets are frictionless, there are no transaction costs and all collateral earns the full collateral yield at the risk-free rate.

Given these two assumptions, prices may, from time to time, take time to adapt to changes in the market environment. Risk appetite and preferences will also vary across time as market participants adjust to new scenarios and environments.[10] In this case, price discrepancies in supply and demand create the possibility for **speculative opportunities**. In the case where supply and demand takes time to correct prices immediately, this results in a speculative risk premium. Turning to a practical example, momentum strategies profit from this speculative premium. This concept mirrors the recent work by Moskowitz, Ooi, and Pedersen (2012), which documents the existence of time series momentum effects in futures markets. Using one characterization of momentum and a specific set of parameters, their work demonstrates that time series momentum strategies provide positive risk premiums over time. It is important to note that these "speculative risk premiums" do not come from one asset class but from the opportunistic application of momentum strategies across all asset classes.

The return of a speculative strategy (r_t) in futures markets can be characterized by

$$r_t = \pi_{sp} + r_f$$

where $E[r_t] = E[\pi_{sp}] + r_f$ and π_{sp} is a speculative risk premium (positive or negative). The volatility (σ) represents the volatility of the particular speculative trading strategy. The risk-free rate contribution comes from the collateral yield on margin in futures positions.[11] The Sharpe ratio of a speculative trading strategy is then characterized by

$$Shp\ (r_t) = \frac{E[\pi_{sp}]}{\sigma}$$

---

[10] For example, Hasanhodzic and Lo (2012) discuss that leverage does not drive the relationship between equity markets and volatility. They suggest that risk is dependent on past experiences. As we gain experience and the environment changes, our preferences for risk vary as well.

[11] Application of the risk-free rate may not be relevant in strategies that do not earn collateral yield.

Using trend following as an example, some trend following strategies have averaged Sharpe ratios of 0.5 to 0.7 over long time horizons. Using a simple back of the envelope calculation, if the average volatility of a trend following program is 10 percent, this means that the speculative risk premium is roughly 5 to 7 percent depending on the time frame. If assumption A2 is relaxed, adding market frictions and transaction costs, the collateral yield may fall below the risk-free rate and trading activity itself will decrease the expected return of a trend following strategy.

It is important to reiterate that for an investment strategy to be profitable there must be an underlying reason for the existence of a profit opportunity, which the strategy can exploit. Speculative strategies that are smart or adaptive enough to consistently exploit opportunities as markets change will earn speculative risk premiums. The most classic example of this is the hedging premium. In commodity markets, speculative traders are said to earn a hedging premium when hedging demand exceeds supply on either the short or long side. Alpha, on the other hand, is a transitory and rare beast. Alpha opportunities are fleeting opportunities that are in excess of a simple speculative risk premium. It is possible to examine two simple examples for demonstrative purposes. First, short bias funds provide negative speculative risk premiums over time, yet in certain scenarios, market crisis, they earn a substantial speculative risk premium. On the other hand, trend following strategies, during most normal market scenarios, earn speculative risk premiums when there is an offset in supply and demand or risk appetite. In extreme scenarios, they adapt to capture crisis alpha. This is explained in further detail in the next section.

■ A Closer Look at Crisis Alpha

> Given that trend following strategies trade exclusively in the most liquid, efficient, and credit protected markets, their profitability must rely on those characteristics in order to obtain a competitive edge.

Taking the framework for speculative risk taking one step further, a speculative risk premium is earned by taking speculative bets across asset classes based on the dynamic allocation of capital. Under normal scenarios, there may be fewer opportunities to profit from an offset between supply and demand. Instead, a closer look at the extreme scenario of financial crisis provides a unique situation in financial markets. In this situation, market supply and demand is often highly asymmetric due to natural selection. Competition may be extremely low and market efficiency may be put to the test. To borrow some terminology from the adaptive markets hypothesis, the market ecology will be in what evolutionary biologists call a moment of

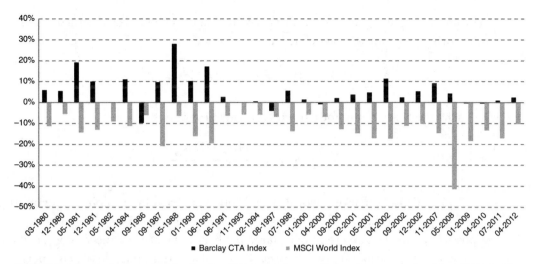

FIGURE 4.4 Performance of the Barclay CTA Index during all drawdown periods of the MSCI World TR Gross Index. Dates reflect starting point of all drawdowns greater than 5 percent.
Source: Bloomberg.

punctured equilibrium.[12] In these moments, certain species will thrive and be adaptable enough to take advantage of crisis alpha opportunities. Figure 4.4 plots the performance of trend following strategies during all of the past large drawdown periods in the S&P 500 since 1980. In this graph, clearly under most circumstances, trend following strategies seem to provide substantial returns during equity crisis periods.

Given this, as a speculative risk-taking strategy, the return of a trend following system can be partitioned into crisis alpha, a speculative risk premium (for noncrisis periods), and the risk-free rate (positive carry from collateral). The speculative risk premium represents the risk premium obtained by speculative positions across various futures markets outside of crisis. Crisis alpha are the profits earned during an extreme financial market event. In this case, the return of trend following strategies can be characterized by

$$r_t = \alpha_c + \pi_{sp} + r_f$$

where α_c is the crisis alpha contribution, π_{sp} is the speculative risk premium outside of crisis, and the risk-free rate, which represents collateral yield contribution of a

---

[12] Punctured equilibrium is a theory that the evolution of species is relatively stable over long periods of time with short periods where there is rapid change and mutation.

future trading program. Given this characterization, the expected return of a trend following program will be defined as

$$E[r_t] = E[\alpha_c] + E[\pi_{sp}] + r_f$$

And the Sharpe ratio for a trend following program is

$$Shp\ (r_t) = \frac{E[\alpha_c] + E[\pi_{sp}]}{\sigma}$$

In an adaptive markets world, trend followers earn crisis alpha opportunities by being one of the few that can adapt to a financial crisis. This adaptation is made possible by the lack of credit exposure, highly liquid nature of the strategy, and the existence of positions across all asset classes. In addition, outside of crisis periods, trend following strategies can profit from temporary dislocations in market prices or divergence where speculative pressure helps to realign price discrepancies, which may be due to moderate rifts between supply and demand. Outside of crisis the speculative risk premium may be more relevant in less liquid and newer markets.[13] If the expected crisis alpha contribution were 3 percent over time, given a volatility of 10 percent in a trend following program and a Sharpe ratio of 0.5, this implies that the speculative risk premium would be much smaller at only 2 percent (this number is backed out from the Sharpe ratio). The key benefit of dividing trend following performance into these three components comes from the fact that the speculative risk premium should be expected to moderate as, outside of periods of crisis, speculative trading is highly competitive in futures markets. Another important point to highlight is that each trading system will provide a different crisis alpha and speculative risk premium. The characteristics of these two drivers of trend following performance depend intimately on the construction and style of the strategy. This topic is something that will be discussed and developed throughout the course of this book.

Given the EMH and frictionless markets, trend followers can only deliver the risk-free rate with considerable noise. Adding transaction costs, their returns would be less than the risk-free rate. Given the AMH and frictionless markets, trend following strategies deliver the risk-free rate and a speculative risk premium. Taking this one step further, trend following systems deliver crisis alpha, a speculative risk premium, and the risk-free rate. The decomposition of trend following performance is displayed graphically in Figure 4.5.

---

[13] This concept is explored later in Chapter 12 on style analysis and style factors.

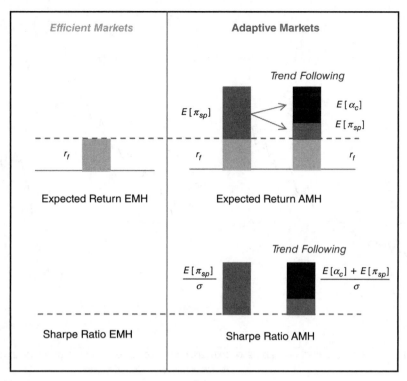

FIGURE 4.5 A schematic for the return and Sharpe ratio for speculative risk-taking strategies and trend following as an example. Both the EMH and AMH are combined with an assumption that there are no market frictions and no transaction costs.

Empirical Decomposition of Trend Following Returns

Under the assumptions of the AMH, trend following strategies deliver crisis alpha, speculative risk premiums, and collateral yield. Given this, trend following performance can be divided into these three components. To achieve this first, a crisis period must be defined in a simple manner. A **crisis period** can be defined as a sequence of negative returns, which represents a drawdown below some threshold. In the following example, −5 percent is used as a threshold. The results in this section are relatively robust to modifications in the definition of a crisis period. Figure 4.6 highlights the largest crisis periods in equity markets from 1993 to 2013 where the MSCI World Total Return Index is used as a proxy for equity markets.

By comparing the performance of a trend following strategy with the same trend following strategy where the performance during crisis events is replaced by an investment in Treasury bills, the performance can be divided into three components.

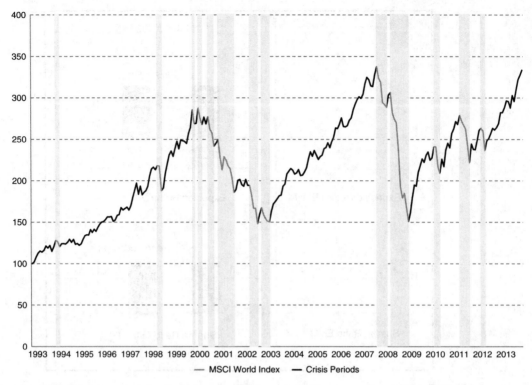

FIGURE 4.6 The MSCI World Index and Crisis Periods from January 1993 to December 2013.
Source: Bloomberg.

Using the Dow Jones Credit Suisse Managed Futures Index from 1993 to 2013, the Newedge CTA Index from 2000 to 2013, and the Newedge Sub-Trend Index from 2000 to 2013, performance of these common industry indices can be decomposed by crisis alpha, a speculative risk premium, and the risk-free rate. In this case, the 30-day Treasury bill is used as a proxy for the risk-free rate.[14] The strategy with crisis periods removed and replaced by the Treasury bill represents the strategy performance without crisis. Figure 4.7, Figure 4.8, and Figure 4.9 plot the performance of the Dow Jones Credit Suisse Managed Futures Index, the Newedge CTA Index and the Newedge Sub-Trend Index over time with and without crisis performance. Following these graphs, the decomposition of trend following return is presented for each of these indices in Figure 4.10. Over the entire sample period from 1993 to 2013, equity crisis periods make up roughly 20 to 25 percent of the investment horizon, but they are responsible for often more than half of the total trend following

---

[14] For a rough estimate, collateral yield is often roughly 50 percent the Treasury bill rate as a proxy for positive carry.

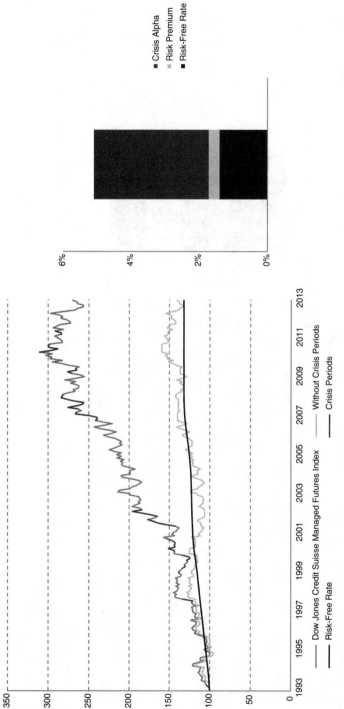

FIGURE 4.7 Crisis alpha decomposition of the Dow Jones Credit Suisse Managed Futures Index from 1993 to 2013. The risk-free rate is the total return on the 30-day Treasury bill.

Sources: Bloomberg, CRSP.

ADAPTIVE MARKETS AND TREND FOLLOWING

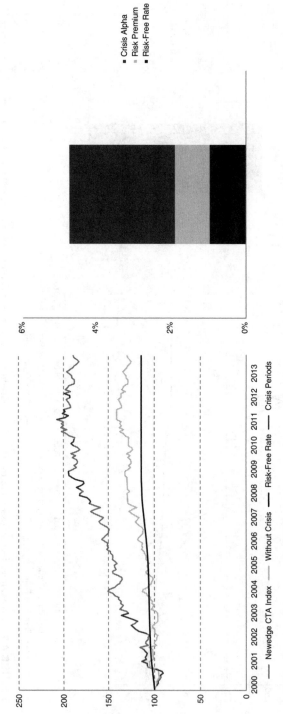

FIGURE 4.8 Crisis alpha decomposition of the Newedge CTA Index from 2000 to 2013. The risk-free rate is the total return on the 30-day Treasury bill.

Sources: Bloomberg, CRSP.

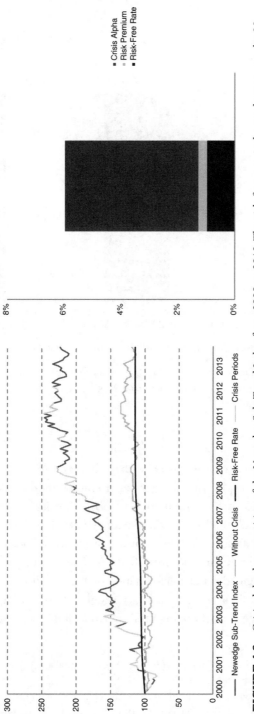

FIGURE 4.9 Crisis alpha decomposition of the Newedge Sub-Trend Index from 2000 to 2013. The risk-free rate is the total return on the 30-day Treasury bill.

Sources: Bloomberg, CRSP.

ADAPTIVE MARKETS AND TREND FOLLOWING

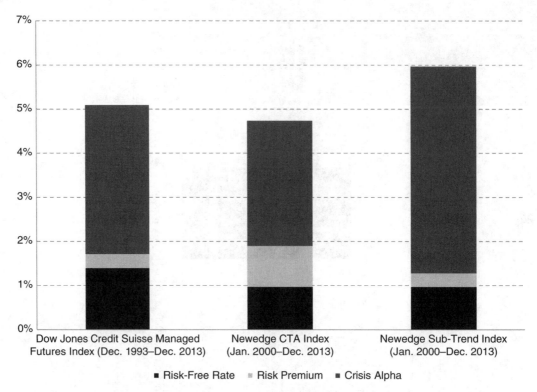

■ Risk-Free Rate   ■ Risk Premium   ■ Crisis Alpha

FIGURE 4.10 Crisis Alpha Decomposition of the DJCS Managed Futures Index from 1993 to 2013, Newedge CTA Index and Newedge Sub-Trend Index from 2000 to 2013. The risk-free rate is the total return on the 30-day Treasury bill.
Source: Bloomberg, CRSP.

return. This is not too surprising as crises have been quite frequent during the past 20 years in history. Despite this, longer term studies tend to demonstrate similar results with larger risk premium but always a positive crisis alpha.[15]

In recent times, a closer look at the performance of commonly used trend following and Managed Futures indices shows that crisis periods have been the main driver of performance during the past 20 years. The speculative risk premium has been relatively low and the net performance of trend following has been roughly the same as the rate of return on short-term debt.[16] For example in Figure 4.11, the annualized average return during crisis periods and noncrisis periods is plotted

---

[15] For another example see Kaminski (2011), AQR Capital's "A Century of Evidence on Trend-Following" by Hurst, Ooi, and Pedersen (2012).

[16] For the crisis alpha decomposition in this section, the collateral yield or interest earned on capital for trend following is set to half the return of the 30-day T-bill rate. This is chosen as a proxy for interest earned as full collateralization is often not possible.

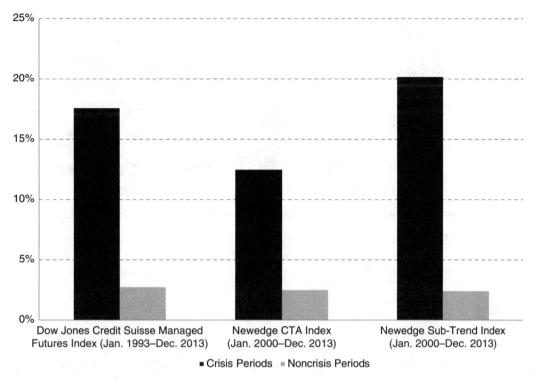

■ Crisis Periods　■ Noncrisis Periods

FIGURE 4.11 Annualized return of the DJCS Managed Futures Index, Newedge CTA Index, and Newedge Sub-Trend Index during crisis periods and noncrisis periods.
Source: Bloomberg.

for each CTA index. This subtle analysis demonstrates that crisis alpha is at the core of trend following strategic advantage in a portfolio. In Figure 4.10, the crisis alpha contribution in the Newedge CTA index is smaller than the Newedge Sub-Trend Index. This is because trend following strategies, as opposed to a more diversified set of strategies perform best during crisis periods. The Newedge CTA Index has a higher speculative risk premium outside of crisis periods as well. In the next chapter, this observation can be connected to risk-taking approaches. The analysis in this section further demonstrates how trend following is connected to dislocation periods (or market divergence) in financial markets. In recent times most of the market divergence has occurred during periods of financial crisis and stock market bubbles.

A Multicentennial View of Crisis Alpha

Despite the compelling role of crisis alpha in most available studies, many other studies have looked at trend following performance over much longer time periods. Hurst, Ooi, and Pedersen (2012) present a 100-year review of trend following. To

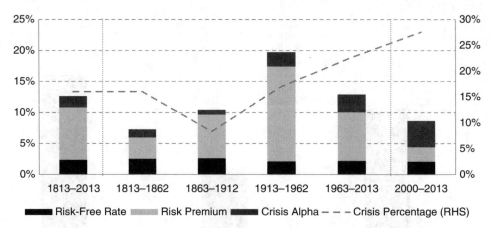

FIGURE 4.12 Crisis Alpha Decomposition from 1813–2013, corresponding 50-year subperiods, and the recent period of 2000–2013. Crisis periods are periods less than –5 percent with negative returns for the Equity index from Chapter 1. The risk-free rate is assumed to be 50 percent of the yield on the bond index from Chapter 1. Crisis Percentage is quoted as number of crisis months over total months in a time period.

reconnect with the analysis in Chapter 1, a closer look at crisis alpha over the past two centuries may help put the recent performance of trend following into perspective and set the stage for a deeper discussion of market divergence in Chapter 5. Taking the simple trend following system from Chapter 1 and the respective equity index, the crisis alpha decomposition for this simple approach can be examined over a 200-year period, respective subperiods, and the most recent time period (for comparison with the last section using industry indices). Figure 4.12 plots the crisis alpha decomposition for 1813 to 2013, four 50-year subperiods, and roughly the same period as examined with the Newedge CTA Index (2000–2013). This decomposition is plotted against the percentage of crisis periods to put the time period into perspective. Figure 4.13 plots crisis alpha versus the percentage of crisis periods. It is clear from both of these figures that the crisis alpha contribution is positive and somewhat linearly related to the amount of crisis in a given period. On average, if there is crisis, trend following seems to take advantage of it. It is also notable that the most recent time period exhibits both the highest percentage of crisis periods and the highest crisis alpha contribution. It is also noticeable that the speculative risk premium varies substantially from time period to time period. This indicates that during certain periods there are trends outside of crisis during some periods more than others. Perhaps it is important to note that in this case crisis alpha is defined only by equity markets. If there are speculative risk opportunities unrelated to equity markets, this will be visible in the speculative risk premium. For example, during the third subperiod of 1913 to 1962, trend following seemed to perform remarkably well during the long

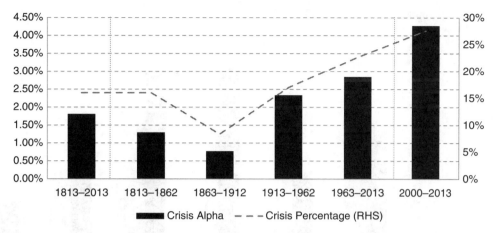

FIGURE 4.13 Crisis Alpha and Crisis Percentage from 1813 to 2013, 50-year subperiods, and the recent period of 2000–2013.

recovery after the Great Depression. This analysis is in no means a substitute for a deeper more quantitative study, but it provides a historical perspective on the fervor for crisis alpha that has raised many questions for investors over the past 15 years.

Taking a closer look at crisis periods and noncrisis periods, the conditional performance of returns during crisis periods and noncrisis periods is plotted in Figure 4.14. This figure shows that the conditional performance during crisis also follows the crisis percentage. More interesting, the conditional performance of trend following

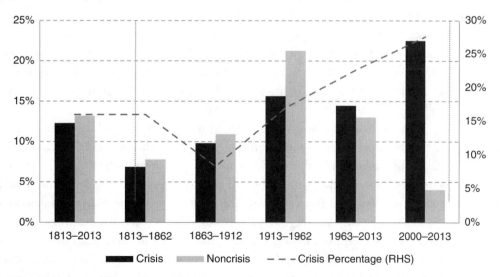

FIGURE 4.14 Conditional performance during crisis periods and noncrisis periods from 1813 to 2013.

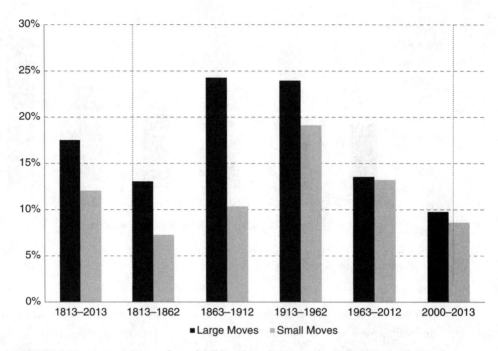

FIGURE 4.15 A comparison of trend following performance during both large and small moves in equities. Large (small) moves are defined as when the Equity index from Chapter 1 is greater than (less than) 3 percent. The entire time period 1813–2013, 50-year subperiods, and the most recent period of 2000–2013 are plotted.

outside of crisis has been higher during noncrisis for all time periods except the most recent 50 years. This seems to be driven mostly by the large difference in performance over the past 13 years. As this study is more qualitative and descriptive, it is not possible to make any predictions as to why, but a longer term analysis may avoid the potential of treating the recent past as a point statistic to explain trend following in a narrow perspective. Chapter 5 will provide a risk-based understanding trend following to complement this perspective.

Trend following strategies seem to do well during periods of divergence in markets. This chapter has focused on one particular, extreme event: financial crisis in equity markets. Crisis alpha is one core driver of trend following performance. Yet, given Figure 4.12 and Figure 4.14, it is clear that speculative risk premiums and other forces may also be at work. To begin this analysis, and to provide a foreshadowing to a discussion of market divergence, the conditional performance of trend following for large moves in equity markets (greater than 3 percent) and small moves (less than 3 percent) is plotted in Figure 4.15. Consistent with the discussion in this section, this figure demonstrates the opportunistic nature of trend following during large equity moves, positive or negative. During the past 13 years, large negative equity moves have been positive for trend following where large positive equity moves have not. During the period of 1863 to 1912, the opposite is true; large positive equity moves were positive for trend following and less so for large negative equity moves (the risk premium is much larger than crisis alpha). Figure 4.15 demonstrates that it is indeed possible that performance comes from market moves (or market divergence). This point leads directly to the discussion in Chapter 5.

■ Summary

According to the adaptive markets hypothesis, the forces of natural selection, the combination of species and level of competition in a market and the ability to mutate, adapt, and compete dictates who succeeds or fails in financial markets. Using this perspective, trend following strategies are one of the few strategies that seem able to find crisis alpha opportunities consistently over time. They do this by being liquid, low credit risk, and relatively void of behavioral bias. During periods of crisis they adapt to take of opportunities as they may arise. Returning to the AMH, a speculative risk premium was discussed. For the case of trend following, this premium is composed of the risk-free rate, a risk premium outside of crisis, and crisis alpha. Common industry indices can be decomposed empirically into: the risk-free rate (for positive carry), a noncrisis speculative risk premium, and crisis alpha. The contribution of crisis alpha during recent periods in markets is substantial. To put this into a longer term perspective, 200 years of data on trend following and equity markets is examined demonstrating that the crisis alpha decomposition is highly time period dependent. Crisis alpha is consistently positive and positively correlated with the prevalence of crisis, or crisis percentage. Speculative risk premiums are also a driver of total performance but they vary substantially. Finally, a look at trend following performance for both large and small moves in equity markets demonstrates that trend following strategies depend on market divergence.

■ Further Readings and References

Bossaerts, P., A. Bruguier, and S. Quartz. "Exploring the Nature of Trader Intuition." *Journal of Finance* 65 (2010): 1703–1723.

Brennan, T., and A. Lo. "The Origin of Behavior." *Quarterly Journal of Finance* 1 (2011): 55–108.

Brennan, T., and A. Lo. "An Evolutionary Model of Bounded Rationality and Intelligence." *PLOS One*, 7 (2012).

Dijksterhuis, B., and L. Nordgren. "A Theory of Unconscious Thought." *Perspectives on Psychological Science* 1, no. 2 (June 2006): 95–109.

Hasanhodzic, J., and A. Lo. "Black's Leverage Effect Is Not Due to Leverage." Working paper, 2012.

Hurst, B., Y. Ooi, and L. Pedersen. "A Century of Evidence on Trend-Following." AQR Capital white paper, 2012.

Kaminski, K. "Diversify Risk with Crisis Alpha." *Futures Magazine*, February 1, 2011.

Kaminski, K. "In Search of Crisis Alpha: A Short Guide to Investing in Managed Futures." CME Market Education Group, 2011.

Kaminski, K. "Regulators' Unintentional Effect on Markets." *SFO*, July 2011.

Kaminski, K. "Understanding the Performance of CTAs during Market Crisis in the Context of the Adaptive Markets Hypothesis." RPM working paper, November 2010.

Kaminski, K., and A. Lo. "Managed Futures and Adaptive Markets." Working paper, 2011.

Kaminski, K., and A. Mende. "Crisis Alpha and Risks in Alternative Investment Strategies." CME Market Education Group, 2011.

Knutson, B., and C. M. Kuhnen. "The Neural Basis of Financial Risk Taking." *Neuron* 47, no. 5 (2005): 763–770.

Lee, S., and N. Schwarz. "Bidirectionality, Mediation, and Moderation of Metaphorical Effects: The Embodiment of Social Suspicion and Fishy Smells." *Journal of Personality and Social Psychology* 103, no. 5 (2012): 737–749.

Lo, A. "The Adaptive Markets Hypothesis: Market Efficiency from an Evolutionary Perspective." *Journal of Portfolio Management* 30 (2004): 15–29.

Lo, A. "Adaptive Markets and the New World Order," *Financial Analysts Journal* 68 (2012): 18–29.

Lo, A. "Fear, Greed, and Financial Crises: A Cognitive Neurosciences Perspective." In *Handbook of Systemic Risk*, edited by J.-P. Fouque and J. A. Langsam, 622–662. New York: Cambridge University Press, 2011.

Lo, A. "Reconciling Efficient Markets with Behavioral Finance: The Adaptive Markets Hypothesis." *Journal of Investment Consulting* 7 (2005): 21–44.

Lo, A. "Survival of the Richest." *Harvard Business Review*, March 2006.

Lo, A., and M. Mueller. "WARNING!: Physics Envy May Be Hazardous to Your Wealth." *Journal of Investment Management* 8 (2010): 13–63.

Moskowitz, T., Y. Ooi, and L. Pedersen. "Time Series Momentum." *Journal of Financial Economics* 104 (2012): 228–250.

Shull, D. K., K. Celiano, and A. Menaker. "The Surprising World of Trader's Psychology." In *Investor Behavior: The Psychology of Financial Planning and Investing*, edited by B. Baker and V. Ricciardi (pp. 477–493). Hoboken, NJ: John Wiley & Sons, 2014.

CHAPTER 5

Divergence and the Tradability of Trend

Risk taking is at the core of human experience. When dealing with and processing risk, we use a variety of strategies and techniques to help us handle the risks we face. At the core, our risk-taking strategy is dependent on our belief in the structure of financial markets, also called our *financial worldview*. When this is taken into account, risk-taking strategies can be divided into **convergent** and **divergent**. These two approaches encompass the two basic of types of risk taking. In this chapter, the basic tenets of risk and uncertainty are reviewed to explain how and when our particular financial worldview may lead us to use both convergent and divergent strategies. Convergent and divergent risk-taking strategies can be easily connected to the adaptive markets hypothesis allowing for a clearer understanding of their use over time. Trend following is a divergent risk-taking strategy, which profits from market **divergence**. Market divergence is discussed and a simple portfolio level measure the market divergence index (MDI) is defined. Empirically, both market divergence and the speed of market divergence are stationary over time. These empirical results suggest that market divergence is a normal phenomenon in financial markets. Finally, the role of predictability and tradability of trend following strategies are examined to show how both predictability and tradability vary over time.

■ Risk versus Uncertainty

As individuals, in both finance and in our personal lives, we are constantly engaged in some form of risk taking. Risk taking is simply a conglomeration of decision rules, risk tolerance, and their corresponding actions. This varies from what we decide to

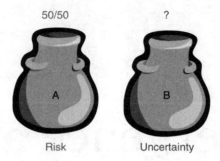

Risk   Uncertainty

FIGURE 5.1 A schematic of risk versus uncertainty.

eat for lunch to when to go bearish in equities. In finance, both impending and past risks are often described with the term *volatility*. Volatility represents the range of expected possibilities looking forward and the range experienced looking backwards (impending future volatility versus realized volatility). The distinction between past and future is very important as these two types of volatility are two very different beasts.

By definition, volatility is often defined as the *risk* or *uncertainty* regarding a position in an underlying security or asset. The higher the volatility is the greater the range of values that the underlying may experience. **Risk** is defined as the chance that things will not turn out as you expect. **Uncertainty**, perhaps more ominous, is the situation where the consequences, extent or magnitude of circumstances, conditions or events is unknown. (See Figure 5.1.) To explain this concept, imagine there is a large urn with 100 balls: 50 red and 50 black. If you select the correct color that is drawn from the urn you win $10,000 and the game is not repeatable. Think for a minute—how much you would pay to play this game? In general, most people who are rather risk-neutral treat this like the roulette wheel and would pay $5,000, but those who do not like the chance of losing $5,000 are a bit more risk-averse and willing to pay less than $5,000. Ironically, in a casino most people are willing to pay more than $5,000 for a game like this.

Now again imagine a new urn, Urn B, where there are red and black balls but the distribution of these balls is unknown. How much would you pay to play with Urn B? More or less than Urn A? In practice, we all dislike Urn B much more than Urn A; given this we are willing to pay less to play with Urn B than with Urn A. Behavioral finance experts call this uncertainty aversion.[1] Urn A is an example of risk while Urn B is an example of uncertainty. The important parallel to make in

---

[1] The concept of uncertainty, otherwise called "Knightian Uncertainty," was introduced by Knight (1921). This concept eventually led to a literature in behavioral finance called uncertainty aversion and ambiguity aversion.

this situation is that our conceptions of volatility in financial markets are often about uncertainty, and frankly uncertainty makes us uncomfortable.[2] Whether financial markets are about risk or uncertainty depends intrinsically on what is knowable and what remains intrinsically unknown. For us to distinguish when we are dealing with risk or uncertainty (the knowable and the unknown), we depend on our intrinsic belief in our own structural knowledge of financial assets.

Convergence versus Divergence

As individuals, when we engage in risk taking, our behavior (or choice of risk-taking method) depends inherently on our level of conviction in our own structural knowledge concerning impending risks. The extent to which we believe that we are facing uncertainty or risk dictates our behavior and choices. Put more simply, it depends whether we express a strong fundamental conviction or whether we profess our blatant ignorance to the structure of impending risks. Our views determine which type of risk-taking decisions we employ. Given that risk taking is at the core of human experience, it is necessary to take a closer look at risk-taking approaches and how they impact our financial performance and expectations.

In a seminal article on this topic, Mark Rzepczynski (1999) outlined how two very different worldviews impact the style of risk taking.[3] The two types of risk taking are divided based on our underlying frame of reference: convergent and divergent. Convergent risk takers believe that the world is well structured, stable, and somewhat dependable. Divergent risk takers profess their own ignorance to the true structure of potential risks/benefits with some level of skepticism for what is or is not dependable. To explain this point, it is easier to first use an example.

Examples of Convergent and Divergent Risk Taking

Imagine two simple strategies: Strategy C for convergent and strategy D for divergent. Each strategy is applied to a simple game of chance, which is played consecutively over

---

[2] As briefly discussed in Chapter 4, Lo and Mueller (2010) explain that finance is a field that is of partially reducible uncertainty. This means that there are always components that can never be quantified causing mathematical models to systematically fail from time to time. They explain that on the risk to uncertainty spectrum, finance, psychology, and economics lie in the middle between physics and mathematics on the reducible uncertainty or risk side and religion on the purely unquantifiable irreducible uncertainty side. The key contribution of their work is to provide a taxonomy and deeper look into the subtle differences between risk and uncertainty in finance.

[3] Reviews risk taking from the trading perspective: Rzepczynski (1999).

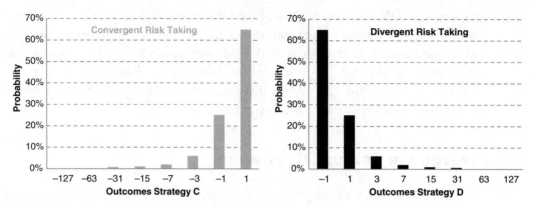

FIGURE 5.2 An example of Strategy C and Strategy D in a simple simulation.

time.[4] Starting with strategy C, each time you win you take your money and start a new subsequent game. When you lose, you keep playing the same game until you win again then start a new game. This game doubles up on losers and takes profit on winners. Strategy C believes in the profits and takes them but reconfirms its conviction by doubling up with losses. A strategy like this will have many small gains with the occasional catastrophic loss. A person who uses a strategy C believes in the system, trusting that in the long run they will win. When they are shown to be incorrect, they simply wait until things get better again to reconfirm their beliefs.

Turning to strategy D, in this strategy each time you lose you quit, cut your losses and start a new game. When you start to win instead of quitting, you double your bet. This strategy has little faith in positions that are losing and tries to follow the prevailing run when they seem to have found a string of luck. In each particular game, strategy D has little faith in a losing position. Strategy D faces many small losses with occasional huge wins.

When the distributions of convergent strategy C and divergent strategy D are compared, strategy C is comfortable with winning, almost expecting things to go as they suppose. Strategy D is rather skeptical taking lots of risks but never investing too much in any particular game. These two approaches are mirror images in their outcomes. The convergent strategy has many small gains and catastrophic losses and the divergent strategy has many small losses and euphoric wins. When a few simple assumptions regarding the underlying game are made, the distribution of an example of these two strategies is shown in Figure 5.2. These two extreme, yet simple, examples show that convergent strategies have negative skewness while divergent strategies have positive skewness.

---

[4] No assumptions are made regarding the distribution of the game allowing for generality.

Reflection on Convergent, Divergent

For many activities in life, in general, our behavior and decision making over time is based on applying both convergent and divergent risk-taking approaches (and combinations of the two). For example, when you cross the street, you are taking a convergent risk. In most cases, you get to the other side earning a small gain. In the rare catastrophic event that you are run over by a passing vehicle, the consequences are disastrous. In this example, we tend to believe that crossing the street is generally safe.[5] Using social networking as another example, successful social networkers often use divergent risk-taking strategies. They talk to as many people as possible quickly and often stealthily cutting their losses with those of less interest. Powerful social networkers understand that they never know how many people it could take to hit the key contract persons, which lead to new business deals. Social networkers who use convergent risk-taking strategies only speak to the people they know and already consider interesting, developing those relationships but creating few new ones. There are many fields where divergent risk taking is the name of the game. Entrepreneurs, venture capitalists, and researchers try lots of different ideas and approaches until they actually find one that is the big winner.[6]

Returning to a simple financial example, investment in equities is something that most investors believe in. They believe in both the existence of an equity risk premium over the long run driven by fundamental value and the efficiency of financial markets. In the convergent/divergent framework, "investing" in equity markets is a convergent risk-taking activity. In distribution, this is also true. Equity returns are positive in expectation, yet negatively skewed with fat left tails. For a financial example of divergent risk taking, the obvious example is trend following. Trend followers do not believe in anything but opportunity. They profess their ignorance to the fundamental structure of market prices, guessing that on occasion markets may be driven by so-called Keynesian animal spirits leading to periods of opportunity. When they see a trend they follow it, they give no consideration to fundamentals.[7] In fact, the distribution of trend following is positive in expectation with positive skewness. Table 5.1 presents Rzepczynski's (1999) division of financial worldviews for convergent and divergent risk taking.

---

[5] In the United Kingdom, it is common for tourists crossing the street to look right instead of left. They are taking substantial risks without even considering it.

[6] This is a process that Nassim Taleb labels as *tinkering*. In his book *Antifragile* (2012), he discusses how tinkering leads to most important discoveries.

[7] In practice, most trend following strategies often have greater than a 50 percent failure rate of positions. This means that most trades may lose money but the ones that win seem to outweigh the smaller losses over time.

TABLE 5.1	Rzepczynski (1999) convergent versus divergent financial worldviews.	
Convergent	**Divergent**
Stationary, stable world	Nonstationary
World is knowable and static; structural knowledge	World is uncertain and dynamic; structural ignorance
Market participants generally form rational expectations; errors are random	Market participants form rational beliefs but may make mistakes and have biases
Markets adjust relatively to new information	Learning takes time; slower adjustment to information
Divergences from equilibrium are short lived	Divergence exists and may be dramatic from time to time
Fundamentals do not change dramatically in the short run	Fundamental changes are often unanticipated

Convergent trading systems generally focus on many smaller gains with the occasional extreme loss. Divergent trading approaches focus on smaller losses with the occasional extreme gains. Convergent strategies have concave payoff functions with negative skewness. Divergent strategies have convex payoff functions with positive skewness. Convergent strategies exhibit negative convexity and sometimes the occasional negative black swans. Divergent strategies exhibit positive convexity and the occasional positive black swans. Convexity means that the input or initial risk is magnified by a factor much larger than the input. **Positive convexity** is when you place a small amount at risk (or even as a sunk cost) and the output may be significantly larger than the input. A lottery is the simplest example of something that has positive convexity. The winners of a lottery receive amounts that are a vast multitude of times larger than the lottery ticket price. This property makes lotteries very interesting (and also thrilling) to people who enjoy divergent risk taking. One problem with lotteries is that they also have negative expected return. **Negative convexity** with occasional black swans are investments where most of the time it earns small gains but on rare occasions it ends up with a gigantic loss. For all investors who invested in equities and experienced the Lehman debacle, an equity market crisis is a negative convexity event for an equity investor. Rzepczynski (1999) classifies the trading and return behavior for both convergent and divergent risk-taking strategies. This classification is listed in Table 5.2.

Most investment strategies can also be classified by convergent and divergent risk-taking approaches. For example with equity markets, a long position in equities could be considered a structural belief in the equity risk premium or a belief in mean reversion. Across different equity strategies, growth could be classified as more divergent than value. Particularly in the long run, growth companies are

TABLE 5.2 Rzepczynski (1999) convergent versus divergent—trading/return behavior.

Convergent	Divergent
Strong sense of fair value	No prediction of fair value
Arbitrage trading, value trading, contrarian	Trend following, momentum
Negative Convexity	Positive Convexity
Profits made from reversion to the mean or long-term risk premiums	Profits made from the extremes, the mean fleeting events
Concave payoffs	Convex payoffs
Negatives skewness	Positive skewness

exceptionally difficult to model or forecast using fundamental models.[8] In relative terms, value strategies are convergent since it may be possible to calculate the intrinsic value of value companies (allowing for a particular view and conviction in the valuation). In the private equity space, larger leveraged buy-outs (LBOs) restructuring projects are closer to convergent risk taking as mature companies are easier to value. On the other hand, venture capitalists engage in divergent risk taking. They typically invest small amounts in a large pool of companies hoping to find the next superstar (as opposed to several prudent investments in comparison with their mature LBO counterparts). Another set of intuitive examples is short and long volatility strategies. Long volatility strategies are often plagued by negative carry during stable time periods with unlimited returns during unstable time periods. Short volatility strategies earn small positive premiums over time but they occasionally blow up. Long (and short) volatility strategies are an investment (liability) in future volatility. Future volatility depends on both risk (the convergent part) and uncertainty (the divergent part). Reflecting back onto Chapter 4, the volatility premium is another example of a speculative risk premium.[9] Rzepczynski (1999) provided the following distinction between several common trading styles. This is presented in Table 5.3.

Connections to the Adaptive Markets Hypothesis

Risk taking and the actions taken in response to risk are directly linked to our belief structure and financial worldview. As a result, this may lead us to change the way we

---

[8] Future cash flows for growth companies are often uncertain. This makes the application of discounted cash flow models or other fundamental models for asset valuation more complex.

[9] For example, despite the fact that they often exhibit negative carry for short periods, over the long run, long volatility strategies seem to exhibit positive skewness and a positive premium over certain time periods. Long volatility strategies are similar to insurance. In the same vein, short volatility strategies may also provide a speculative risk premium when the "insurance" price for long volatility exposure is too high.

TABLE 5.3	Rzepczynski (1999) convergent versus divergent trading by strategy type.	
Asset Class	**Convergent**	**Divergent**
Equity	Value, contrarian, arbitrage (pairs trading)	Momentum, growth
Fixed Income	Arbitrage, credit valuation	Interest rate directional
Hedge Funds	Arbitrage (fixed income, convertible) long short equity, sector funds, currency arbitrage	Managed futures, trend following, technical analysis

invest especially across time. This begs the question, what does it mean to invest? What is speculation and what is investment or does this even matter? By definition, an investment is an asset or item that is purchased with the hope that it will appreciate in the future. If our views are polarized, for example if we think that markets are either efficient or infected by irrational exuberance, this leads to either convergent or divergent (but not both). In 2013, the Nobel Prize was awarded to empirical asset pricing researchers with two very different worldviews: one view is the EMH and the other is behavioral finance.[10] If both of these views are important, both styles of risk taking are important for success and performance in financial markets.

If markets are efficient, convergent strategies may be prudent in assets that maintain a core fundamental structure. For example, in this context, long-term investment in equities without cutting your losses makes sense over certain periods of time. On the other hand, we must also profess our ignorance to the true structure of financial markets yielding to the "animal spirits" of the market. In this case, divergent risk-taking strategies that respond well to the unknown and the uncertain. The optimal combination will depend of course on the state of the financial markets and the players who participate in them. The best overall strategy will be to combine some of both risk-taking approaches.[11] To summarize, convergent risk taking allows us to compete and maintain value over time while exposing us to hidden risks (the so-called black swans) whereas divergent risk taking allows us to adapt, innovate, and hopefully survive during periods of market distress.

The adaptive markets hypothesis dictates that prices are determined by the combination of market players in the market ecology, the level of resources available, and the ability of players to adapt and compete for them. Resources and competition vary over time as the environment changes. Returning to the concept of risk taking

---

[10] In 2013, the Nobel Prize was given to Eugene Fama, Lars Peter Hansen, and Robert Shiller for their work in the area of empirical asset pricing. Fama is most well-known for his work on efficient markets while Robert Shiller is one of the pioneers in the world of behavioral finance.

[11] As an example, Chung, Rosenberg, and Tomeo (2004) discuss how to allocate capital using a convergent and divergent approach in hedge fund portfolios. Their article shows, both conceptually and empirically, how this can be done in practice.

in financial markets, convergent risk taking will be appropriate during certain periods and divergent during others. In certain periods, a combination of the two may also make sense. Convergent risk taking is appropriate to remain competitive when the market is relatively stable and knowable. On the other hand, divergent risk taking can allow for the rare big successes, which sometimes outweigh the losses they incur over time. Convergent risks allow us to remain successful over time and competitive, yet they can subject us to catastrophic losses, the black swans that plague financial systems and investments. Divergent strategies allow us to innovate, adapt, and create value from chaos and disorder.[12]

Measuring Convergence and Divergence

Just as with risks in our personal lives, sometimes convergent risk taking makes sense, sometimes divergent risk taking makes sense. The payouts are very different and they provide very different utility to an individual. It is also natural that when one approach or the other is successful will depend directly on how knowable or unknowable the risk structure of an asset class is. For example, returning to risk and uncertainty, the level of risk or uncertainty that governs an assets behavior may indicate the potential success of either convergent or divergent risk-taking strategies. More specifically, divergent strategies often thrive on uncertainty. As with adaptive markets, this relationship is time varying. Over time, the performance of both types of risk taking varies from period to period. Using an equity example, value strategies have sometimes outperformed growth and vice versa. Value being convergent and growth being divergent. In order to measure the amount of divergence in a particular market, the market can be decomposed by the **risk to uncertainty ratio** (RUR). In simple terms, this ratio can be measured with volatility, meaning the amount of explained volatility divided by the uncertain volatility.

$$\text{RUR} = \frac{\text{explained volatility}}{\text{unexplained volatility}} = \frac{\text{explained volatility}}{\text{total volatility} - \text{explained volatility}}$$

Explained volatility is the amount of volatility that can be ascribed to fair value and fundamental models. Explained volatility represents the level of risk that is "knowable." **Unexplained volatility** is the amount of volatility that is attributed to unexplainable factors.

---

[12] This concept parallels Nassim Taleb's book *Antifragile* (2012). He discusses how volatility and stress can make systems stronger. In this context, a convergent risk-taking approach can be more robust over time if some divergent is mixed with convergent. Pure divergent approaches are subject to underperformance during stable periods but they react well to stress. Convergent strategies perform well when things are stable but they are intrinsically fragile.

Given the RUR ratio, individual asset classes can be examined to determine how much volatility is explained and unexplained. When the risk to uncertainty ratio is high, convergent risk-taking strategies are often more appropriate and vice versa. For example, in currencies fundamental models explain very little of total price volatility. In fact, technical analysis is a common tool in currency trading. Even in equities, there is a phenomenon called *excessive volatility*, which is a commonly cited behavioral finance market anomaly. These phenomena show that equity price volatility is much larger than what fundamental models would predict. From a convergent/divergent view, this means that uncertainty is included in equity volatility. Commodity markets also have a low risk to uncertainty ratio, which implies that it is more difficult to take convergent risks as fundamental models are less reliable.

Linking Uncertainty to Liquidity and Credit Risks

Credit risk is the risk associated with a counterparty not being able to repay their obligation or fulfill their side of a contract or position. Credit risk relies on the behavior of individuals. Networks of relationships are complex. In general, it is somewhat complicated to understand how people will react in stressed situations. Liquidity risk stems from a lack of marketability or that an investment cannot be bought or sold quickly enough to prevent or minimize a loss. In general, liquidity is complicated to measure and it seems to be moderately unpredictable. Liquidity can be there one minute but when the balance of supply disappears, liquidity can disappear altogether. For the party who needs liquidity this creates a serious cause for concern (there is substantial uncertainty).

Despite many attempts in academic research to characterize the behavior of credit and liquidity risks, these risks still remain hard to predict and relatively unknown. They often come in shocks and they can spread in ways that are difficult to model or control. Research may have helped us to make these risks more knowable yet still they remain relatively elusive and unknowable. Convergent risk takers may consider these risks to be knowable. They will feel comfortable taking these risks on over time, exposing themselves to possibly devastating losses when these risks turn out to be more serious than previously assumed.

How Does Trend Following Fit In?

Trend following strategies are divergent risk takers. Similar to strategy D, trend followers take many small positions across many markets. They quickly cut losses as they incur and build positions in those that are not cut. Trend following performance over time exhibits positive skewness, **positive convexity**, and often less than a 50 percent success rate in their positions. Trend followers profit during market divergence and generate crisis alpha when there are extreme disruptions

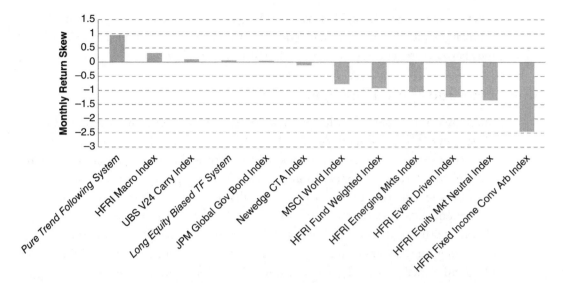

FIGURE 5.3 Monthly return skewness for pure trend following (Pure Trend Following System) and a variety of other strategies.

in markets.[13] From a risk perspective, these strategies take a divergent view on market prices across assets. To be fair, despite being divergent risk takers in price, trend followers are convergent risk takers when it comes to liquidity and credit. They avoid counterparty and liquidity risk and do not take on positions that might directly profit from divergence in counterparty quality or liquidity. They may profit from the effects of these risks on prices but they are not taking these risks as their structural view is that these are too unpredictable. These issues also hinder their ability to cut losses and adapt to a price trend. To explain this more clearly, another divergent risk-taking approach is venture capital (as opposed to LBO in private equity). In this type of divergent risk-taking strategy, the strategy takes small stakes (limiting the losses) in many different entrepreneurs hoping for one that will be the next big superstar. This type of strategy depends on the people one invests in (counterparty risk) and the ability to sell and capture the value of a new idea (liquidity risk). For example, in Figure 5.3 the return skewness for trend following and other alternative investment strategies are plotted. Trend following is the strategy with the largest positive skewness suggesting it is more divergent than other strategies.

This explanation reinforces the fact that risk taking depends on the financial worldview of a risk taker. It is possible to mix between financial worldviews where markets oscillate between knowable and unknowable. This depends on the type of

---

[13] The moments of punctured equilibria are discussed in Chapter 4.

risk that one is considering. Just as most things in life, risk taking is contextual. Trend following strategies profess their ignorance to the structure of market prices,[14] yet they have the structural view that credit risks and liquidity risks are not worth taking.

Momentum and Market Divergence

Many investors label trend following strategies as momentum strategies. In fact, Moskowitz, Ooi, and Pedersen (2012) document the phenomenon they label time series momentum. Time series momentum is different than cross-sectional momentum. Cross-sectional momentum is driven by price moves between different assets in the cross section for a particular asset class. Time series momentum is momentum across time across asset classes. Time series momentum is a simple characterization of trend following. There is one key problem with the concept of momentum. Momentum is the effect not the cause. Similar to Moskowitz, Ooi, and Pedersen (2012), most empirical studies of momentum simply suggest a huge list of causes for momentum. These include a wide range of explanations from behavioral bias to market frictions. From an adaptive markets perspective, momentum is simply caused by slow or prolonged periods of market divergence. Just as in evolutionary biology, financial systems are made up of people and computers run by people. Pasquariello (2014) presents empirical evidence for the existence of market **dislocation**, which is somewhat similar to momentum. Market dislocation is defined as periods when prices deviate from simple no arbitrage relationships. Both market dislocation and momentum are the effect of prolonged market divergence.[15] Table 5.4 presents a summary of the definition of divergence, dislocation, and momentum. Both the corresponding biological definition and the financial interpretation are presented to provide parallel connections with evolutionary biology.

Empirical Evidence of Divergent Risk Taking in Trend Following

The previous sections discussed how trend following is a divergent risk-taking strategy qualitatively. Since this concept is used throughout the remainder of this book and to develop style analysis in Chapter 12, the principles and approaches in pure trend following and their corresponding empirical qualifications are listed in Table 5.5.

---

[14] In late 2013, *The Economist* ran an article discussing the periods of tough performance for trend following post-2008. The article cited quantitative managers as relatively "sanguine." Trend followers do not believe they can predict markets; they believe they can only design systems that systematically allocate risk.

[15] Just as with biological systems, most changes are not dramatic enough to destabilize the system.

TABLE 5.4 Definitions of divergence, dislocation, and momentum.

Term	Biological Definition	Financial Interpretation	Causes
Divergence	The evolutionary tendency or process by which animals or plants that are descended from a common ancestor evolve into different forms when living under different conditions	The process that market participants and groups of market species evolve and adapt to new market conditions	Shifts in risk appetite, offsets in supply and demand, behavioral bias, sentiment, crisis and market frictions, systemic risks
Dislocation	The act of displacing or the state of being displaced; disruption from the norm or steady state	Prices move away from no arbitrage relationships	Slow or prolonged divergence
Momentum	Force or speed of movement for a physical object or course of events	Prices moving in one direction continue to do so for some period of time	Slow or prolonged divergence

TABLE 5.5 Summary of the principles and characteristics of trend following, which make the strategy a divergent risk-taking strategy.

Principles and Approaches in Pure Trend Following	Implementation and Empirical Evidence
No fundamental view on macro[16]	Positions are based only on past information in prices
No asset class bias	Allocate risk across a wide range of asset classes
Systematic loss taking	No discretion in position taking, losses are taken when trends move adverse to signals
Worst performance with many small losses	The winning ratio for trades is typically less than 50%, drawdowns are highly negatively correlated with the winning ratio[17]
Best performance, less often big wins (positive convexity)	The magnitude of wins measured in PnL is directly related to best performance
Positive skewness, convexity	Positive skewness statistically, convexity in return profile (fat right tails as opposed to left fat tails)
Profits from market divergence	Performance is highly correlated with market divergence[18]

---

[16] From an economist's perspective, a trend following approach may be rational as long as prices are governed by partially irreducible uncertainty (see Lo and Mueller 2010).

[17] To be discussed in Chapter 9.

[18] In the following sections, a measure for market divergence will be discussed. Using this measure trend following performance has a correlation of roughly 0.75 with simple market divergence measures.

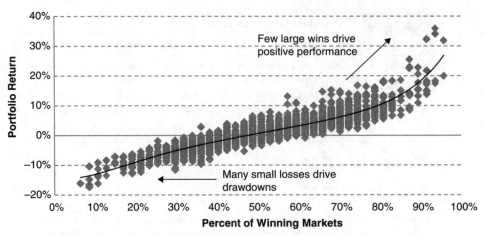

FIGURE 5.4   A scatter plot between the portfolio return and winning percentage. (This graph uses a 22-day rolling window for a representative pure trend following system.)

First and foremost, trend followers do not have a fundamental view on macro effects. In the purest form, they also have no bias toward one asset class or another, or even to long or short. The decisions are based purely on the trend signals and trend strength in price data. Using a systematic approach, trend following systems spread risk across many asset classes and systematically cut losses when prices move against their signals. When it comes to performance, the worst performance comes from many small and additive losses. Empirically, the winning ratio of trades is less than 50 percent and much higher correlated to drawdown depth. In contrast, the best performance comes from both many wins and large wins. Empirically, both the number of winning trades and the magnitude of winning trades to losing are related to the best performance. Figure 5.4 plots the relationship between the percentage of winning trades and trend following performance. This graph demonstrates the convex payout profile of trend following. The final and most important point is that trend following is long market divergence. The concept of market divergence will be examined in further detail for the remainder of this chapter.

■ Measuring Market Divergence at the Portfolio Level

Divergent risk-taking strategies thrive in environments driven by extreme levels of **market divergence**.[19] As trend followers follow trends, market divergence (not simply volatility) drives performance. Since market divergence may be a new

---

[19] This definition is related to the concept of "antifragility" presented by Nassim Taleb in his 2012 book, *Antifragile*. Using terminology from his book, divergent risk-taking strategies are antifragile and convergent risk-taking strategies are fragile.

concept for some, it is necessary to provide a simple definition and a few examples. Similar to how volatility can be measured by standard deviation, market divergence can also be measured empirically.[20] In Figure 5.5 several price trends are plotted, first with a clean price trend and then with low noise and high noise in the price series. On the left-hand side, a long 100-day trend is plotted and, for comparison, a shorter and steeper 20-day trend during the 100-day period is plotted. The level for both trends is the same; a $10 increase in price.

To measure the level of divergence for a particular price series, it is necessary to examine the signal to noise ratio. The **signal to noise ratio** is a ratio between the trend and individual price changes over a specific period. For any specific day, at time (t), the signal to noise ratio SNR_t for a particular price series with lookback period (n) can be calculated mathematically using the following formula:

$$SNR_t(n) = \frac{\left| P_t - P_{t-n} \right|}{\sum_{k=0}^{n-1} \left| P_{t-k} - P_{t-k-1} \right|}$$

where (P_t) is the price at time (t) and (n) is the lookback window for the signal, or the signal observation period. For medium- to long-term trend followers, this is typically chosen at roughly 100 days. Returning to Figure 5.5, the 100-day SNR is given for each individual price series. The perfect price trends have a signal to noise ratio of 1. A higher SNR indicates a higher quality of the trend, or higher price divergence for that individual market. Notice that as noise (or volatility) enters into price trends, SNR become lower as the trend is much harder to discern. For example, the SNR for the noisy and very noisy linear price trends are 0.1728 and 0.0314 respectively. The first noisy price trend would be interesting for a trend follower but the second would be deemed too volatile. This simple example explains how trend followers have a complex relationship with volatility. Adding volatility to a price series reduces the attractiveness of a price trend. On the other hand, when there are trends in prices, price series exhibit higher volatility. This is sometimes called directional volatility.[21] The right-hand side of Figure 5.5 plots a shorter trend with the same increase in the price over a 100-day period. In terms of level, these two price moves are the same, yet the second price trend would be less desirable from a 100-day perspective. Notice that the SNR for the noisy linear price trend is 0.1728 versus

---

[20] It is important to remind the reader that volatility as a concept represents risk and uncertainty. Standard deviation is just a simple metric that is well accepted to "represent" risk. In reality risk is much more complex than standard deviation, market divergence is also more complex than its simple MDI measure.

[21] Chapter 8 explains more explicitly how changes in volatility are more important for trend following strategies.

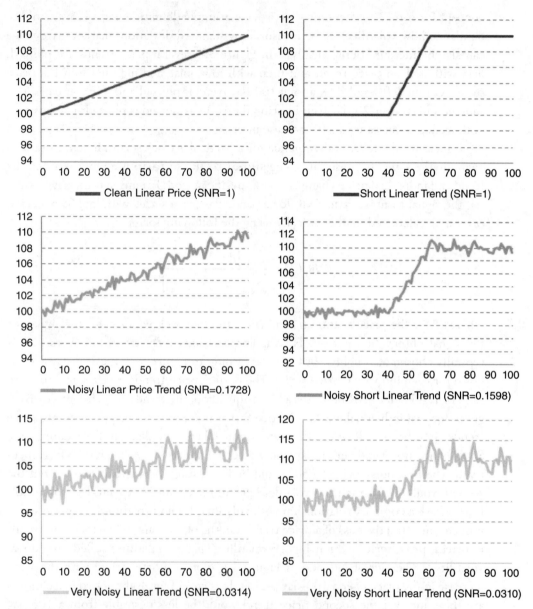

FIGURE 5.5 Examples of price trends with and without noise. 100-day SNR are calculated for each 100-day example. The noisy series have a return volatility of 10 percent and the very noisy price series have a volatility of 40 percent.

0.1598 for the short-term price trend. The same noise series is used in this example to make the SNRs comparable. When the annualized volatility is 40 percent, both the very noisy linear and short-term price trends are relatively useless.

The SNR can be calculated for each individual market. The next step is to look at the aggregate level of "trendiness" in markets at the portfolio level. For each individual market (i), for simplicity the total level of market divergence (or "trendiness") can be calculated as the average signal to noise ratio. This quantity can be defined as the **market divergence index (MDI)** for a given signal observation period (n).[22]

$$MDI_t(n) = \frac{1}{M} \sum_{i=1}^{M} SNR_t^i(n)$$

where (SNR_t^i) is the signal to noise ratio for an individual market (i), (n) is the signal observation window, and (M) is the number of included markets. The MDI is a simple aggregate measure of "trendiness" in prices taking into account the level of volatility (or noise) in the price series.[23] When the MDI is higher, this corresponds to a market environment with higher trendiness across markets in a portfolio.

Market Divergence and Trend Following Performance

Given that trend following strategies follow trends, the higher the MDI the higher the profitability of a trend following program. Figure 5.6 plots the 100-day MDI and the rolling 100-day returns of a representative pure trend following system from 2001 to 2013. The trend following system includes all asset classes: commodities, equity indexes, fixed income, and currencies. The correlation between the 100-day MDI and the rolling 100-day return for a trend following program is 0.74. This high correlation demonstrates the direct link between market divergence and trend following performance.

The MDI also tends to be positively skewed with fat right tails. These extreme events represent periods when markets diverge dramatically. For example in Figure 5.6, the Lehman crisis, the Flash Crash, and other key events coincide with peak values for the MDI. Figure 5.7 shows a plot of a histogram for the 100-day MDI over the same period as Figure 5.6. During this period, for this particular portfolio, the MDI has a mean of 0.11 and a standard deviation of 0.03. The distribution is positively skewed, consistent with the return distribution for a trend following system. It is also interesting to understand how the performance of a trend following system depends on market divergence. Figure 5.7 plots the conditional performance

---

[22] There are many different variants of the MDI indicator. For example, in this book, an absolute value indicator is used. It is also possible to measure the signal to noise ratio with a ratio of squares or square roots. It is also possible to weight the markets (instead of simple averages) for a specific portfolio. For example, the use of squares will increase the impact of extreme moves on the total index. The design and use of an MDI indicator will depend on the circumstance with which it is applied.

[23] The MDI is related to the Random Walk Indicator (RWI). See http://tradingsim.com/blog/random-walk-index/ for an example. The calculation details are different for the RWI. Here, the MDI is calculated at the portfolio level only.

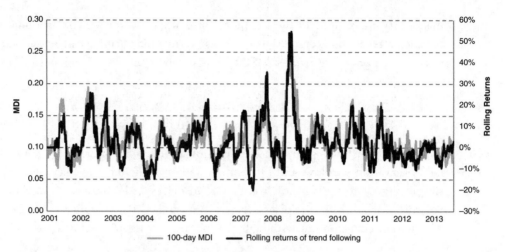

FIGURE 5.6 The MDI with the rolling 100-day returns of a representative pure trend following system over a 10-year period from 2001 to 2013.

of the 100-day rolling return for the trend following system as a function of the market divergence (MDI). To interpret this plot, in this case when the MDI is above at 0.10, the performance of trend following over the previous 100 days is expected to be positive.[24] The relationship between market divergence and trend following is roughly linear.

TREND FOLLOWING WITH MANAGED FUTURES

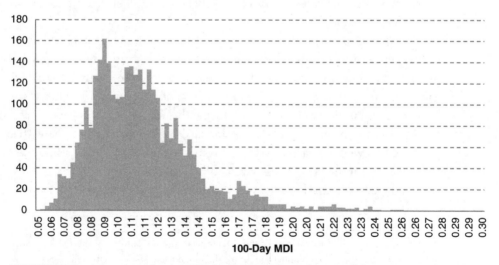

FIGURE 5.7 A histogram for the MDI from 2001 to 2013 for a portfolio consisting of commodities, equity indexes, fixed income, and FX. The horizontal axis is the MDI value and the vertical axis is the number of samples in each bin of the MDI value.

---

[24] 0.1 is an appropriate threshold for this specific portfolio. The threshold will be determined by the characteristics of a particular portfolio.

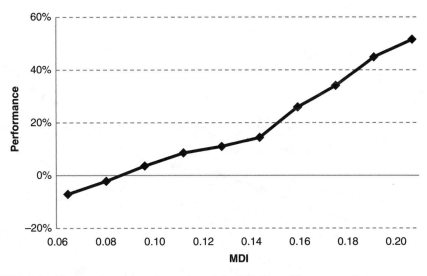

FIGURE 5.8 The conditional performance of the 100-day rolling return for a representative pure trend following program as a function of the MDI. The horizontal axis is the MDI value, and the vertical axis is the conditional mean of the 100-day return for each corresponding MDI value.

Reconnecting to Crisis Alpha and Divergent Risk Taking

In Figure 5.8, it is important to notice that the performance of trend following is linear until market divergence becomes extreme. Extreme levels of divergence occur during crisis periods; the conditional performance of trend following is the strongest during this time period. In the example from Figure 5.8, when the MDI increase from 0.10 to 0.18 the performance doubles for periods of extreme market divergence. The performance is roughly scaled by a factor of 10. Using this example, a move of 0.03 in the MDI corresponds to a 30 percent increase in expected return. Moderate MDI represents periods when trend following earns a speculative risk premium outside of crisis periods. The extreme levels of the MDI link directly to crisis alpha.

Divergent risk takers take lots of small risks over time and ride the winners. Returning to Figure 5.8, it is important to remember that each of these points is not equally likely. Figure 5.9 demonstrates the link between conditional performance, frequency, and the crisis alpha decomposition from Chapter 4. The lower return periods are much more likely. In fact, trend following strategies have positive returns on roughly a third or more of their trades. Remembering that in this example, the mean value of the MDI is 0.11, the conditional performance of trend following portfolios is close to zero for the average MDI value

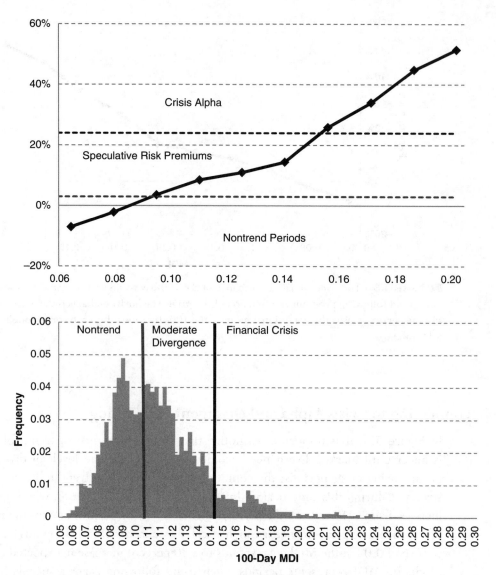

FIGURE 5.9 Connecting market divergence to crisis alpha.

and negative for MDI values below the average MDI value. When market divergence is high, many of a trend follower's position will be winners. An analysis of market divergence and the connection between trend following performance and market divergence further motivates denoting trend following as a divergent risk-taking strategy.

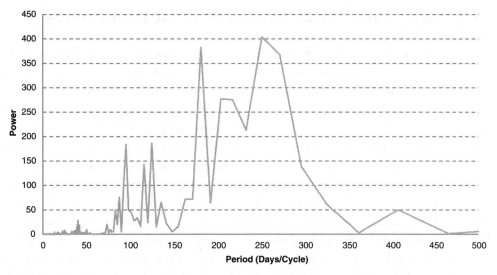

FIGURE 5.10 The periodogram of the 100-day MDI from Figure 5.6. The periodogram depicts the power of each frequency component for the MDI. Very low frequency components were removed from the chart.

The Velocity of the Market Divergence

If markets are truly efficient (in the EMH sense), the MDI will still be positive but trends will look much more like an even faster version of the short price trend on the right-hand side of Figure 5.5.[25] If instead market price adapts as the market environment changes, there may be periods of adjustment with trends that are not instantaneous creating tradable trends. To examine the speed of divergence, the velocity of the MDI can be examined. To examine the speed of the MDI, this section reverts to a classic tool in signal processing, the Fourier transform. A Fourier transform simply transforms a signal from the time domain into the frequency domain. Put into less complex terms, a Fourier transform gives a representation of the frequencies (akin to speeds) that a time series travels.[26] Figure 5.10 plots the periodogram of the MDI. The y-axis depicts the power of each frequency (or speed). To estimate the average speed of the MDI, a power-weighted average of the frequencies (or periods) can be calculated to estimate the average velocity of the MDI. For the particular trend following program in this section, the power-weighted average period is roughly 14 months. This estimate indicates that favorable and unfavorable market environments alternate approximately every half year. The Fourier transform is revisited again in Chapter 14.

[25] For example, under the EMH, all information will be incorporated into prices instantaneously. This can create jumps in prices at the point the information becomes available.

[26] Mathematically, for any function $f(t)$, in this case the MDI, the Fourier transform $F(k)$ can be calculated as follows: $F(k) = \int_{-\infty}^{\infty} f(x)e^{-2\pi i k x}\, dx$.

■ Testing the Stationarity of Market Divergence

The adaptive markets hypothesis states that markets adapt and adjust to changes in the financial environment. As the environment changes, competition spikes among market players, shocks disrupt the market environment, and other factors change markets dynamically. Prices will reflect the current environment and the distribution of and level of competition between market participants. Similar to a biological system, shocks will move the system to a new equilibrium. The process of adaptation will create an occasional divergence in prices. Put simply, changing environmental conditions and imbalances in the distribution of market players can create divergence as prices move to adjust for this. If markets adapt and this process is not instantaneous, as it typically isn't for biological systems, there will be short periods of adaptation resulting in market divergence. Again similar to a biological system, the period of adjustment will depend on the severity of the shock and how much it destabilizes a system.[27] If it is in fact true that markets are adaptive, both convergence and divergence are a core part of financial markets. Because of the efficient markets hypothesis and traditional theories in economics, the role of convergence is widely accepted. The role of divergence has often been contested; as a result the behavior of market divergence can be tested to see if it is a transitory property of prices over time. The market divergence index (MDI) is examined empirically to test its stationarity. Despite significant changes in the CTA industry, tremendous growth in the futures markets, and a wide array of economic environments, market divergence is a stable property of markets.[28]

 Market divergence is a stable characteristic of functioning financial markets.

A Test for the Stationarity of Market Divergence

The market divergence index (MDI) is a measure of market divergence. Empirically, statistical tests for stationarity can determine how stable market divergence has been over time. Given the long history of agricultural futures contracts, the analysis in this

---

[27] Take the simple example of heart rate: When you run for a bus, your heart rate goes up. After you get on the bus your heart rate will slowly calm down. Take an example of running to save your child in front of a moving bus: Your heart rate will increase, adrenalin will pump through your veins, and you will most likely shake for a few minutes following the experience. Both include a shock to the environment, but one shock destabilizes your circulatory system more severely.

[28] Technically, in a historical empirical study, market divergence cannot be shown to reject the hypothesis that it is nonstationary.

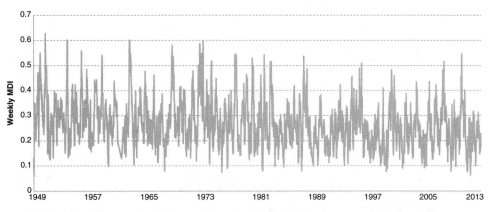

FIGURE 5.11 The MDI from 1949 to 2013 for the portfolio of six agriculture markets.

section is based on six agriculture markets with substantial price histories.[29] Beginning in June 1949, Figure 5.11 plots the 100-day MDI for the agricultural trend following portfolio. To assess the null hypothesis that this MDI time series is stationary, the Kwiatkowski, Phillips, Schmidt, and Shin (1992), further denoted as the KPSS, test can be applied. The KPSS test requires one important input argument: the number of autocovariance lags that are included in the Newey-West (1987) estimator for long run variance. During the past 30 years, the CTA Industry has grown to a mature industry, growth in futures markets has been exponential, and the federal funds rate varied substantially. Over a range of economic environments, even with a small number of lags, the KPSS test cannot reject the null hypothesis that the MDI is nonstationary at the significance level of 5 percent. For the entire period from 1949 to 2011, with a large lag, the KPSS test still fails to reject at the significance level of 0.5.[30] To put these results into context, market divergence is stationary. This implies that occasional "trendiness" in markets is a stable characteristic of markets over the long run.

Stationarity of the Velocity of Market Divergence

It is not only the existence of a trend but the speed of trends that are important. A closer look at the velocity of trends can give further insight into how fast these

---

[29] Weekly cash prices of the agriculture markets are used to calculate the MDI for a time period as early as 1949. Empirically, the cash-price-based MDI and the futures-based MDI are highly correlated. In this sample, the correlation is above 0.85. If daily price changes are assumed to follow a random walk, the MDI based on weekly price change is simply 2.2 times of the MDI based on daily price changes. It is important to point out that the price changes are in the denominator of the signal to noise (SNR) calculation.

[30] For consistency of the Newey-West (1987) estimator, the number of lags must grow as the sample size increases.

FIGURE 5.12 The velocity of the MDI, represented by the power-weighted average period, from 1949 to 2013 for the portfolio of eight agriculture markets.

trends occur. The KPSS test can also be applied to the velocity (as defined by the Fourier transform) of the MDI. The Fourier transform is applied over 20-year rolling windows and the power-weighted average period for the MDI is calculated.[31] The power-weighted average periods are for the agricultural portfolio is shown in Figure 5.12. On average, the MDI has a 19-month cycle since the 1970s. Despite huge shifts and changes in the CTA industry as well as explosive growth in futures markets, the speed of trends (or the velocity of the MDI as represented by the power-weighted average period here) is not impacted significantly. When the KPSS test is applied to the velocity time series, it cannot reject at the significance level of 0.05. This implies that since the 1970s the velocity of the MDI is stationary. As a further robustness test, market divergence (trendiness) can also be compared with the federal funds rate as a proxy for the overall economic environment. The correlation between the MDI and the 100-day rolling average of the federal funds rate is 0.03 in this sample.[32]

In this section, empirical evidence over several decades demonstrates that market divergence (via MDI) has been a stationary characteristic of markets. Favorable (higher MDI) and unfavorable (lower MDI) market environments for trend following appear to be statistically similar across a wide range of market environments and distributions of market players involved. A closer look at the velocity of market divergence (via the Fourier Transform of the MDI) demonstrates that even the speed of adaption between favorable and unfavorable market environments is quite stable since the 1970s.

---

[31] Note that the weekly MDI is used here: for example, 20 years of data consists of 1,040 samples.

[32] The *p*-value for this correlation is 0.09 since the 1960s.

■ The Tradability of Trend

Trend following has had its fair share of skeptics. Some of the main concerns relate to the argument that trends may exist in historical data, but that does not necessarily imply that they are actually tradable. Other questions are related to data snooping and return predictability. Four important questions include:

1. How important are the parameters for entry and exit?
2. How important is position management?
3. How much do historical results depend on parameter selection and specification?
4. Are trends a self-fulfilling process?

In this section, these concerns are examined in further detail.

Trend Leakage: A Focus on the Entry

Imagine a perfect world when the future trend is known. In historical data series, the future trend is known. The entry decision can be examined more closely to determine when trends leak out. A trading system can be said to detect a trend when the sign of the trend is the same as the future trend. In practical terms, **trend leakage** can be simply calculated as the difference between the percentage of positions that have the same sign as the future trend and the percentage of positions that have the opposite sign of the futures trend. The measurement of trend leakage will depend on (a) the future **trend size** and (b) the **lookahead window** for finding future trends. The trend size can be measured by price movements where price movements are grouped by scalar multiples of price volatility. The look-ahead window is the observation window for a future trend.

When trend leakage is high, trend following signals seem to be picking up some information regarding the trend in their entry decisions. If trend leakage is negative, the entry signals are indicating the wrong positions more often than not. For a range of both future trend sizes (price movements as a multiple of volatility) and lookahead windows, Figure 5.13 plots both the ratio of days when the trend positions are the same sign and the opposite sign of the future trend.[33] In this figure, lookahead windows range from 20 to 180 days and price movements range from 10 times (10x) to 18 times (18x) volatility. The difference between these two ratios defines the total trend leakage. Even with a simple breakout trend following system, Figure 5.13 demonstrates that there is trend leakage when moves are large

---

[33] The figure is based on a breakout system for a portfolio consisting of equity indexes, commodities, fixed income, and FX from 2003 to 2013.

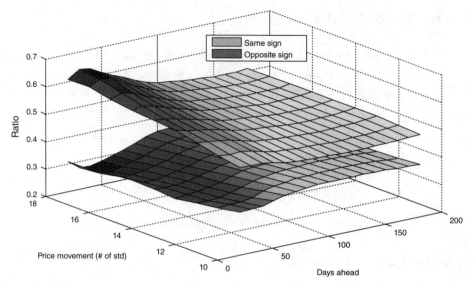

FIGURE 5.13   Trend leakage: The vertical axis shows the rate of days when a trend following system's positions are the same as or different from the direction of a large price movement (*x* standard deviations away) in a certain period in the future (*n* days ahead).

for a wide range of lookahead windows. In practical terms, this suggests that in extreme cases, trends leak out into prices. If there is trend leakage, this implies that occasionally information is disseminated slowly enough to be captured in historical prices. If the EMH holds, trend leakage should be zero. If markets are adaptive, there will be temporary periods where trend leakage occurs as markets adapt over time. Extreme shocks and large moves should destabilize markets more than ordinary events. Figure 5.14 plots the average trend leakage as a function of price trend (price movements as a scalar multiple of volatility). The relationship between trend leakage and the size of a future trend is roughly linear. This demonstrates that the larger the future trend, the more likely it is for a trend following system to pick it up with their entry signals.

Stationarity of Trend Leakage

In the previous section, trend leakage is measured by the difference between the rates of positions with the same sign and opposite sign of a future trend. Despite the statistical evidence for trend leakage for large price moves, it is also interesting to examine how often trend leakage occurs and whether it has decreased as markets seemingly become more efficient or competitive in time. Similar to the stationarity tests for market divergence, trend leakage can also be tested for stationarity. To allow for longer price series, trend leakage is calculated for a portfolio of agricultural

FIGURE 5.14 Trend leakage as a function of the future trend size. Trend size is measured by price movements, which are a scalar multiple of volatility.

markets.[34] The average level of trend leakage is calculated across all included markets. Using one-year rolling windows, the level of trend leakage can be sorted by trend size and the length of lookahead period for the future trend.[35] Figure 5.15 plots the average level of trend leakage for this portfolio since June 1982. When the KPSS test is applied to the time series for the level of trend leakage, the null hypothesis cannot be rejected for a significance level of 0.05. This implies that it is not possible to claim that the level of trend leakage over the past three decades is nonstationary. This empirical evidence demonstrates the **tradability** of entry signals for trend following systems. The possibility that a trend following system can enter a position early enough to capture a large price movement is statistically similar over time. Given the tremendous changes in the CTA industry, wide range of economic environments, and profound technological advances in market infrastructure and trading, it is rather remarkable trends still seem to continue to sporadically leak out.

A Focus on the Exit: The Random Entry System

A central principle for trend following is "let the profits run and cut the losses." An *agnostic* divergent risk-taking system, with a rather naive entry approach, is a **random entry system**. A random entry system will enter a long or short position

---

[34] The portfolio consists of more markets than the MDI analysis in the previous section. All of the markets have futures price data starting in the late 1970s.

[35] Trend size is defined as 10 to 18 standard deviations of daily price changes, and the lookahead window or number of days in the future trend period varies from 20 to 180 days.

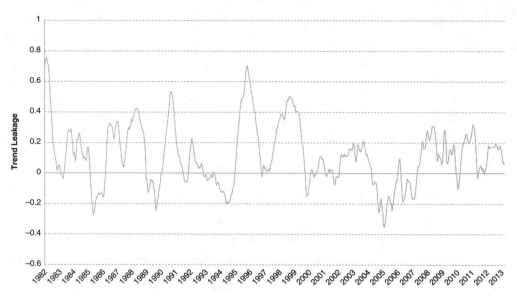

FIGURE 5.15 Average one-year rolling trend leakage for a portfolio of agriculture markets since 1982.

with equal probability and exits from an existing position only when a trailing stop is reached. A trailing stop is a rule that follows historical prices over time.[36] This type of system has minimal dependence on any entry signal. Although rather simple, in comparative terms, a random entry system provides a unique way to evaluate the role of the exit decision.[37] The tightness of the trailing stop, or loss tolerance, is the main parameter in this type of system. The loss tolerance can be measured as a scalar multiple of the past price volatility. For a given loss tolerance as a scalar multiple of the past standard return volatility and a specified lookback size for estimating the past return volatility, a large pool of random traders (or random entry system) is simulated for a given parameter set. For each set of parameterizations, a large number of random implementations of the system are conducted. Figure 5.16 shows the **average winning trade rate** and **average PnL ratio** between winning and losing trades. The winning trade rate is 36 percent and the PnL ratio is 1.6. Despite the entry independence, these estimates appear to be relatively stable over several decades of data. They are also typical for a trend following system. Empirically, for both time series, the KPSS test cannot reject the null hypothesis for a significance level of 0.05. This statistical evidence implies that the exit decision for

---

[36] Trailing stops are discussed in further detail in Chapter 12.

[37] For example, when a random entry system is compared with simple 12-month momentum strategy, it is unclear why 12 months is important and whether the performance is driven by the exit or the entry of that signal.

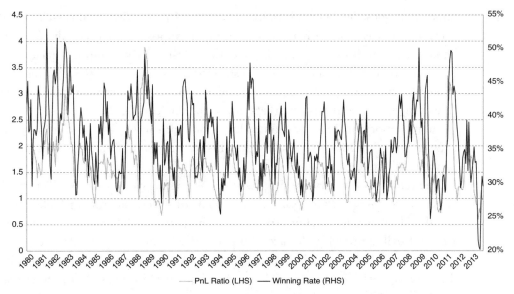

FIGURE 5.16 The average winning trade rate and average PnL ratio between winning and losing trades for the random entry system from 1980 to 2013.

trend following and the corresponding effect on position management has not fundamentally changed over time. The effect of cutting losses does not diminish over a long sample period. If trends are simply a self-fulfilling prophecy, it would be expected that the mechanism for exiting positions (cutting losses) would deteriorate over time. Additional evidence against this is that the observed slippage (the difference between execution price and signal price) is in fact decreasing.[38]

■ The Importance of Entry versus Exit

Chapter 3 discussed the construction of trend following systems. A typical trend following system is comprised of the following four core decisions:

1. When to enter a position (*Entry*).
2. When to exit a position (*Exit*).
3. How large of a position to take on.
4. How much risk and capital to allocate to sectors and markets.

The last two points relate to position sizing and capital allocation. These points are discussed throughout many later chapters in this book. This section asks a simple, yet

---

[38] Independent analysis confirms decreasing slippage, but an example using public slippage data is available in a published report by Man Investments (2010).

important, question: Which is more important, *Entry* or *Exit*?[39] In certain contexts, it can be the case that either one or the other is most crucial. For the case of less liquid securities, for example real estate, the entrance may be more crucial. Another example could be certain types of distressed securities strategies or even activist strategies; the timing of the entrance may be more important than the exit. For the case of highly liquid futures markets, it may be unclear if either *Entry* or *Exit* should be more important. The question of Entry or Exit can be discussed using a simple experiment. Consider two trading systems: (A) a random entry system and (B) a "crystal ball" system.

The random entry system was discussed in the previous section. A "crystal ball" system is seemingly clairvoyant. At the point of entry, the system looks one year ahead and takes a long (short) position if the price is higher (lower). Over time, a crystal ball approach will have 100 percent winning rate on all trades. Despite a perfect win rate on trades, the system may have substantial drawdowns during the holding period of one year. For example, if it were possible to know that oil would close $20 higher in one year, from now until one year from now the price of oil could move up and down in many different directions. The mark-to-market net asset value (NAV) of the crystal ball system still contains substantial volatility as positions are not managed. As the foresight power of the crystal ball system decreases, volatility will progressively make drawdowns larger and deteriorate performance. Even when the probability of foresight is relatively high, the system will be essentially useless from a risk adjusted performance perspective. While the system would be conceptually correct 100 percent of the time, for all practical purposes it may not even have sufficient capital to withstand margin calls on losing positions along the way.

In reality, trend following systems use an array of exit rules to determine how to exit and adjust positions. Exit rules such as trailing stops are essentially an implicit *risk management* tool for trend following systems. A simple experiment can demonstrate the importance of this type of risk management (via exit rules). Consider a "crystal ball" system with (*x* percent) forecasting accuracy. Forecasting accuracy of (*x* percent) means that *x* percent of the time the system has knowledge of price in one year's time.

The initial "crystal ball" system has no risk management overlay as positions are not adjusted and trailing stops are not applied. As the forecasting accuracy of the crystal ball system is reduced, the performance of the system should also decrease. It is interesting to see how adding exit rules, or risk management, might impact performance of a forecasting based system. Figure 5.16 plots the Sharpe ratio and maximum drawdowns as a function of the forecasting accuracy (*x* percent) for a "crystal ball" system both with and without risk management (via the addition of exit

---

[39] This analysis was first suggested by Larry Hite in the early days of Mint.

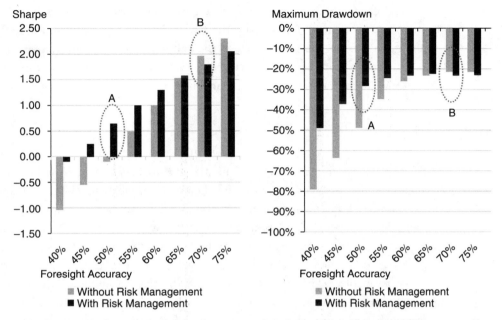

FIGURE 5.17 Sharpe ratio (left) and maximum drawdown (right) for a crystal ball system with foresight accuracy (*x* percent) both with and without risk management via trailing stops. Estimates are generated via Monte Carlo simulation using monthly risk of 5 percent.

rules). This figure demonstrates that if risk management approaches (via exit rules) are added to the "crystal ball" system, it improves performance even if forecasting accuracy deteriorates. When forecasting accuracy is high (and margin constraints are ignored), there is less need for risk management via exiting rules.

For example, a crystal ball system with forecasting accuracy of 50 percent should have a Sharpe ratio close to zero as the chance they are right or wrong is 50/50.[40] This point is labeled Point A in Figure 5.17. Interestingly enough when risk management (via exit rules) is added, a crystal ball system with 50 percent forecasting accuracy has a Sharpe ratio over 0.5. For the same case, the drawdown decreases from 50 percent to less than 30 percent by adding risk management. In this example, up until 70 percent forecasting accuracy (Point B), risk management (via exit rules) improves the performance of a crystal ball system.

The random entry system from the previous section is the mirror opposite of a crystal ball system. The system is somewhat *trend seeking* as opposed to trend following. There is no forecast in a random entry system. The act of stopping at trailing stops (exit rules) drives the performance of a random entry system. In the

---

[40] In theory, for this case the Sharpe ratio should be exactly zero. Estimates in aggregate are typically nonzero due to noise in data and estimation.

previous section, the random entry system was shown to have moderate positive performance over time. Comparing the crystal ball system and the random entry system demonstrates the importance of the exit in trend following systems. The exit of and the sizing of the positions are much more important than the timing of the entry. To the certain relative degree, that timing of the entry *almost doesn't matter*.

■ Summary

Risk taking is a dynamic process of sequential decisions. When taking risks, our frame of reference and our financial worldview dictate our underlying behavior. Conceptually, dynamic risk taking approaches can be divided into two core approaches: convergent and divergent. Convergent strategies are applied when we have some level of conviction in the structure of impending risks. Divergent strategies are applied when we profess our ignorance to the underlying structure of impending risks. If markets are adaptive, convergent and divergent approaches will be successful in very different market environments. Trend following is a divergent risk-taking strategy. Given this, market divergence drives trend following performance. The market divergence index (MDI) is introduced as a simple measure of divergence at the portfolio level. Despite tremendous changes over time, market divergence is a stable part of functioning financial markets. Finally, the tradability of trend following strategies is discussed from both the entry and exit perspective. Trend leakage is highly variable yet stable in aggregate over time. A closer look at trend leakage suggests that brief periods with extreme moves seem to leak out to prices consistent with an adaptive market view. The random entry system provides a simple link to divergent risk-taking approaches discussed in the first part of this chapter. A random entry system demonstrates that much of trend following performance can be explained by the exit decision. Comparing the random entry system with a clairvoyant crystal ball system demonstrates how risk management (via exit decisions) is more important than forecasting in trend following.

■ Further Reading and References

Casa, T., A. Lehmann, and M. Rechsteiner. "De-Mystifying Managed Futures: Why First Class Research and Innovation Are Key to Stay Ahead of the Game." Man Investments white paper, 2010.

Chung, S., M. Rosenberg, and J. Tomeo. "Hedge Fund of Fund Allocations Using a Convergent and Divergent Approach." *The Journal of Alternative Investments* (Summer 2004).

"Computer Says No," *The Economist,* November 30, 2013.

Greyserman, A. "Trend Following: Empirical Evidence of the Stationarity of Trendiness," ISAM white paper, February 2012.

Hite, L. and S. Feldman. "Game Theory Applications." *The Commodity Journal* (May-June 1972).

Knight, F. H. *Risk, Uncertainty, and Profit*. Library of Economics and Liberty. Originally published 1921. Retrieved May 21, 2014 from www.econlib.org/library/Knight/knRUP.html.

Kwiatkowski, D., P. C. B. Phillips, P. Schmidt, and Y. Shin. "Testing the Null Hypothesis of Stationarity against the Alternative of a Unit Root." *Journal of Econometrics* 54 (1992): 159–178.

Lo, A. "The Adaptive Markets Hypothesis: Market Efficiency from an Evolutionary Perspective," *Journal of Portfolio Management* 30 (2004), 15–29.

Lo, A. "Reconciling Efficient Markets with Behavioral Finance: The Adaptive Markets Hypothesis." *Journal of Investment Consulting* 7 (2005): 21–44.

Lo, A. "Survival of the Richest." *Harvard Business Review*, March 2006.

Lo, A., and M. Mueller. "WARNING!: Physics Envy May Be Hazardous to Your Wealth." *Journal of Investment Management* 8 (2010): 13–63.

Moskowitz, T., Y. Ooi, and L. Pedersen. "Time Series Momentum." *Journal of Financial Economics* 104 (2012): 228–250.

Newey, W., and K. West. "A Simple Positive Semidefinite, Heteroskedasticity and Autocorrelation Consistent Covariance Matrix." *Econometrica* 55 (1987): 703–708.

Pasquariello, P. "Financial Market Dislocations." *Review of Financial Studies*. Published electronically February 12, 2014.

Rzepczynski, M., "Market Vision and Investment Styles: Convergent versus Divergent Trading," *Journal of Alternative Investments* (Winter 1999).

Taleb, N. *Antifragile: Things That Gain from Disorder*. New York: Random House, 2012.

CHAPTER 6

The Role of Interest Rates and the Roll Yield

Chapter 2 presented a review of futures markets, futures trading, and the managed futures industry. Given this introduction, it is clear that issues related to trading on margin, the impact of collateral, and the associated costs of borrowing across markets can clearly impact trend following. In addition, trends in interest rates can also drive trend following performance over time. Just as equity crisis can cause market divergence, moves in interest rates can also cause market divergence. In recent times, markets have been plagued by a historically low interest rate environment. Given the success of trend following during the long period of decline in interest rates since the 1970s, it is only natural that some investors are concerned about how trend following would cope with rising interest rates.

The potential impact of interest rates comes from two main sources: (1) **collateral yield** and (2) *trends in futures prices* (especially bond futures). (See Figure 6.1.) Collateral yield is the return that is earned for collateralized positions via margin accounts. Futures strategies trade on margin; some or even most of the invested cash is typically invested in short dated government debt such as U.S. Treasury bills. If **invested capital** includes noncollateral investments, it is also called *earned interest* on cash management or the cash return. During periods when interest rates are high, for example in the 1980s, the interest income generated by this cash investment can be quite significant. In this case, collateral yield (and earned interest) provides a positive carry for a managed futures strategy similar to the crisis alpha decomposition in Chapter 4.

FIGURE 6.1 The two main sources of interest rate impact on trend following.

The second source of impact on trend following is more obvious, the existence of trends in bond futures may create opportunities. Despite the fact that price trends in bond futures clearly affect trend following, this relationship is less obvious analytically, as it may be more complicated to evaluate and analyze. There are two main mechanisms with which interest rates can affect futures prices or, more precisely, price changes. The first is explicit changes in interest rates. As interest rates change, this directly results in price changes for the bonds that represent the underlying for futures contracts. For example, if the interest rate increases, the corresponding bond prices decrease and futures prices decrease in tandem. The second mechanism is via the level of interest rates across time. This is an important factor for the **roll yield** of futures making it an important driver in futures price changes. Finally, because all futures depend on discounting future values, the time value of money and associated costs of borrowing across markets affects all auxiliary futures market prices (outside of simply bond futures). For example, price changes in FX, short-term interest rates, and equity futures will also shift as interest rates shift. For simplicity in this chapter, the main focus is on the bond and commodity sectors.

■ Collateral Yield

In the current interest rate environment, earned interest and collateral yields are relatively insignificant due to the historically low interest rates. However, when interest rates were high, for example, in the 1980s, interest income generated by cash investments was rather substantial. Figure 6.2 plots the yield for the three-month U.S.

FIGURE 6.2 Three-month U.S. Treasury bill yields since 1980.
Data source: Global Financial Data.

Treasury bill beginning in 1980. Interest rates have been in a sustained downward trend since the 1980s.

Collateral yield (and/or cash return) provides managed futures strategies with positive carry from cash management. As a result, including the collateral yield improves both total return and Sharpe ratios as well as decreases drawdowns. Mathematically, the impact on the Sharpe ratio can be calculated by simply adding fixed interest income to a return series with a given Sharpe ratio.[1] In Table 6.1, for return series with Sharpe ratios of 0.75 and 1.0 with an annual volatility from 10 percent to 20 percent, even a 2 percent T-bill yield is able to improve the Sharpe ratio by more than 20 percent.[2]

TABLE 6.1 The impact of adding interest income via cash management to the Sharpe ratio. The rate ranges from 2 percent to 8 percent, and volatility ranges from 10 percent to 20 percent.

	Sharpe = 0.75				Sharpe = 1.0		
	2%	5%	8%		2%	5%	8%
10%	0.93	1.20	1.47	10%	1.18	1.45	1.72
15%	0.87	1.05	1.23	15%	1.12	1.30	1.48
20%	0.84	0.98	1.11	20%	1.09	1.23	1.36

[1] For simplicity, all Sharpe ratios are calculated with a reference risk-free rate of zero.

[2] The interest income is set to 90 percent of the three-month T-bill. To simplify calculations, interest income is also assumed to have zero correlation with the trend following return series and to have zero volatility for the Sharpe ratio calculation.

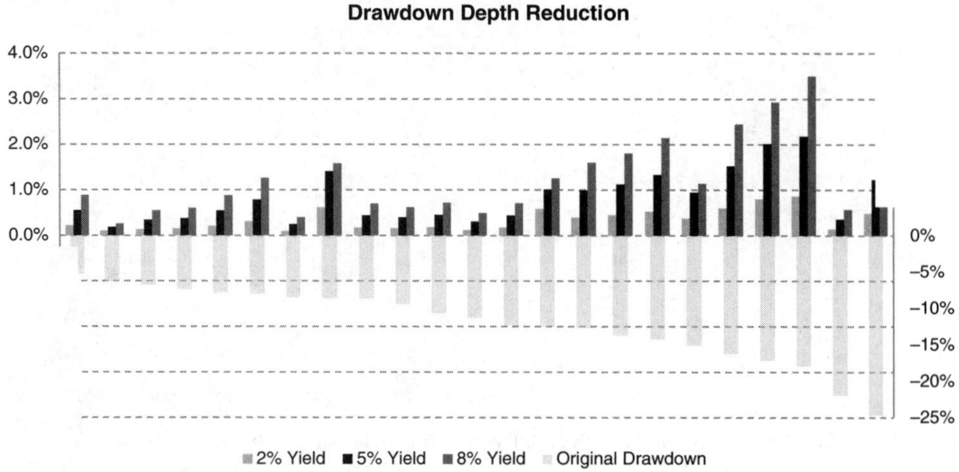

Drawdown Depth Reduction

■ 2% Yield ■ 5% Yield ■ 8% Yield □ Original Drawdown

FIGURE 6.3 The impact of adding interest income from cash management on drawdown depth. The interest rate ranges from 2 percent to 8 percent. The original drawdown depth is plotted on the right-hand side.

As collateral yield and added interest from cash management provide positive carry, they can also help decrease drawdown depth and duration over time. To evaluate the impact of cash return on drawdowns, a collateral yield can be added to a return series for a representative-pure trend following system without collateral yield (not net performance) over the past 20 years.[3] For drawdown periods that last at least three months, interest income is added to the original return series and the maximum drawdown depth and length are recalculated for the same periods.[4] As shown in Figure 6.3, the maximum drawdown can be reduced by as much as 350 bps if the T-bill yield ever reaches 8 percent. Figure 6.4 displays the impact on drawdown length. The reduction of drawdown length is quite substantial when the T-bill yield rises only to 2 percent. For a numerical example, one of the drawdown periods with a roughly five-month drawdown would be shortened to less than three months.

---

[3] The representative-pure trend following system trades a diversified set of equity index, commodity, fixed income, and FX markets.

[4] For each of these drawdown periods, the return series with the added interest income is compared to the starting equity to calculate the maximum drawdown in each period. The maximum drawdown length is the maximum number of days between two consecutive days with at least the same level as the starting equity in the drawdown period.

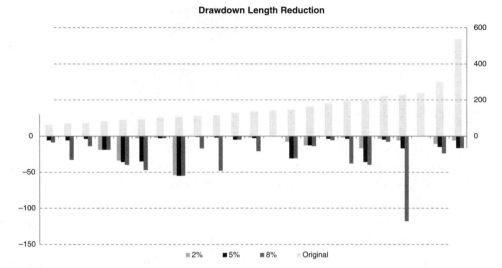

FIGURE 6.4 The impact of adding interest income from cash management on drawdown length (days). The interest rate ranges from 2 percent to 8 percent. The original drawdown length is on the right-hand side.

■ Decomposition into Roll Yield and Spot

Trend following signals depend on changes in futures prices over time. For a futures contract with price $(F_{0,T})$ at time 0 with maturity (T), the theoretical price of a futures contract can be written as follows:

$$F_{0,T} = S_0(1 + r_{f,T} + \hat{y})^T$$

Where (S_0) is the spot price of the underlying, $(r_{f,T})$ is the corresponding interest rate (often denoted by the risk-free rate) over the time period to the maturity (T), $(\hat{y})$ is the **net convenience yield** including storage costs and benefits for different maturities over time. For bonds this would be the impact of coupons. For commodities, this concept is somewhat more complex. Convenience yields between commodities are often said to depend on the underlying balance between supply and demand over the course of time. Bond futures will have deducted interest income as futures contracts do not earn coupon payments. This deduction is part of the net convenience yield for a bond future. For commodities, in addition to interest rates, the convenience yield will create differences in futures prices across time and over the futures curve. The convenience yield and interest rate make up part of what is called the roll yield. The roll yield is the average difference between near and far dated futures prices. If the roll yield is positive, this means that nearer contracts are priced higher than farther contracts, adjusted for the number of days in between contracts. If this is the case, a roll strategy can simply roll short-term contracts forward to earn

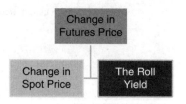

FIGURE 6.5 A schematic for the relationship between futures prices, spot prices, and the roll yield.

the roll yield as spot prices increase toward a higher spot price. This strategy works when markets are in backwardation but suffers losses when markets are in contango.[5]

Given this explanation, it is clear that the change of a futures contract's price can be decomposed into the spot price change and the roll yield. Both changes in the spot price and the roll yield impact futures prices. The interplay between the changes in the spot price and changes in the roll yield determines the total price trendiness. As explained in Chapter 5, trendiness in markets corresponds directly to profitability in trend following. Figure 6.5 presents a schematic for the relationship between the futures price change, the spot price change, and the roll yield.

For clarification purposes, the roll yield ($Roll(t)$) can be roughly defined by the following equation:

$$Roll(t) = \frac{(F_{t,T_n} - F_{t,T_f})}{T_f - T_n}$$

where F_{t,T_n} and F_{t,T_f} are the near and far contract futures prices at time t. (T_n) and (T_f) are their corresponding maturities. In this case, the roll yield is the price difference between the near and far contracts normalized by the number of days between the expiration dates of the pair of contracts. Because prices for far contracts are often less reliable, five-day moving averages can be used to smooth the time series. Once the roll yield is known, the spot price change is then equal to the total price change minus the roll yield. Figure 6.6 presents a decomposition of cumulative returns based on the total futures price changes, the roll yield, and spot prices for corn futures contracts.

Based on this decomposition, the total trend following performance can be decomposed into two components: the spot price change and roll yield. Table 6.2 demonstrates this decomposition using a representative-pure trend following system. The difference between the performance of total futures price and spot price is the contribution of the roll yield. In this table, it is clear that the roll yield is responsible for the majority of performance in the bond and commodity sectors. Spot price changes are the primary source for performance in equity indices, currencies (FX), and short-term interest rates (STIR). In net, roughly more than a third of trend following performance comes from the roll yield.

---

[5] In contango (backwardation) the futures curve is downward (upward) sloping.

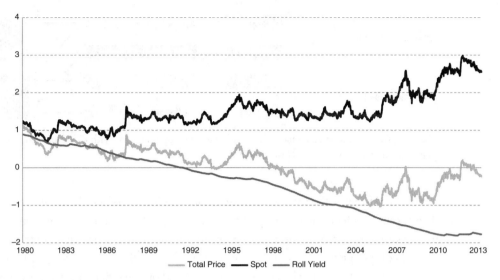

FIGURE 6.6 Cumulative returns based on the total price, roll yield, and spot price for futures contracts in corn.

Data source: Bloomberg.

Interest Rates and the Roll Yield for Bond Futures

Many factors affect the price changes. For the case of bond futures, spot price changes are affected by changes in the level of interest rates. The roll yield is primarily affected by changes in the yield curve. When interest rates rise, spot price can be expected to decrease. In addition, when the slope of the yield curve increases, the roll yield will also increase. Figure 6.7 presents several scenarios for interest rate change and the yield curve slope.

TABLE 6.2 The total futures price and spot price only performance for a representative-pure trend following system.

		Sharpe Ratio	Monthly Return (%)	Monthly Risk (%)
All	Futures	0.74	1.01	4.65
	Spot	0.46	0.63	4.64
Bonds	Futures	0.51	1.45	9.64
	Spot	0.21	0.60	9.63
STIR	Futures	1.12	2.95	8.90
	Spot	0.98	2.57	8.88
Equity	Futures	0.08	0.20	8.08
	Spot	0.09	0.21	8.08
Commodity	Futures	0.73	1.00	4.60
	Spot	0.35	0.47	4.59
FX	Futures	0.39	0.93	8.10
	Spot	0.28	0.66	8.10

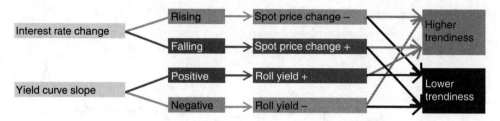

FIGURE 6.7 Interest rate change and yield curve slope scenarios with different outcomes as related to the trendiness of total futures prices.

For bond futures, the total price change is a combination of the change in the spot price change plus the change in the roll yield. When the signs for spot price change and roll yield are the same, this is a more desirable environment for futures prices to form trends. When the signs of spot price change and roll yield are different, they can work against each other. In this situation, trends are less likely to occur. Based on the schematic in Figure 6.5, when the interest rates rise, a yield curve with a positive slope is the most detrimental for total price trendiness. In this case, the negative spot price change offsets the positive roll yield. The net effect would most likely be reduced trends in futures prices.

Given the current low interest rate environment, scenarios for rising interest rates are of particular interest for investors in trend following. The relationship between interest rate changes and roll yield can be evaluated empirically using historical data. Data for both the three-month U.S. Treasury Bills and one-year yields is available since 1959 (Source: Bloomberg). The difference between the one-year yield and three-month yield (one-year minus three-month) can be used as a proxy for the roll yield. To measure interest rate change, the monthly or annual change in the federal funds rate can be used.

Figure 6.8 displays scatter plots for the roll yield (average difference between the one-year and three-month yields) and interest rate change (the federal funds rate change) over the same period both monthly and annual. There does not appear to be a clear relationship between the yield difference (proxy for the roll yield) and the changes in interests in a dataset spanning over 50 years. In fact, for both the monthly and annual averages, the correlation between the roll yield and interest rate change is close to zero. This empirical finding shows that, in comparison with the falling interest rate environment, a rising interest rate environment is not more likely associated with a yield curve working against the spot price change. In other words, it appears that there is no obvious statistical evidence, which supports the hypothesis that the roll yield is more likely to reduce the trendiness caused by the spot price change in a rising interest rate environment.

Market Divergence and the Roll Yield

The analysis of the relationship between the spot price change and roll yield in the previous section indicates that a rising interest rate environment does not negatively

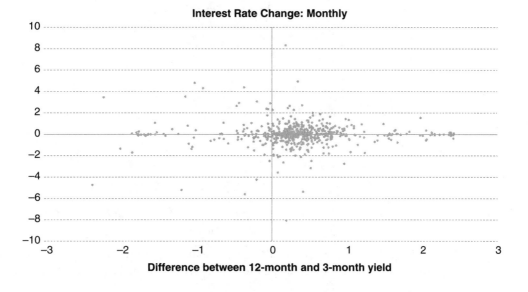

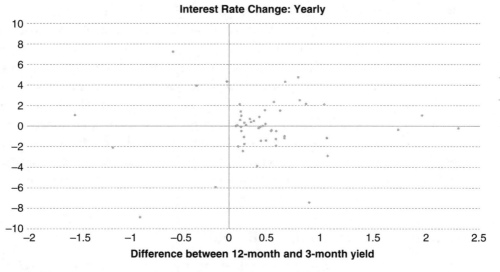

FIGURE 6.8 Scatter plots for the roll yield (the average difference between the one-year and three-month yields) and interest rate change (the federal funds rate change). The left panel plots monthly averages while the right panel plots annual averages.

impact the trendiness of a positively sloped yield curve. Next, the relationship between the interest rate change and the roll yield with market divergence via the market divergence index (MDI) is discussed. MDI was introduced in Chapter 5 as a simple measure of price trendiness calculated using actual futures price data. The 30-year U.S. Treasury bond was one of the first bond futures contracts to start trading. As a result, it can be used to analyze the MDI over a relatively long time series starting in 1980.

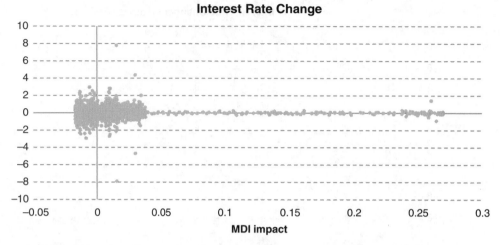

FIGURE 6.9 A scatter plot for the MDI impact (for the 30-year U.S. Treasury bond) of the roll yield and the interest rate change (average federal funds rate change) during the same period.

To evaluate the impact of the roll yield on the market divergence (MDI), the difference between the MDI based on the changes of total futures price and the spot price can be calculated. The spot price change is derived by deducting the roll yield from the total price change. Figure 6.9 displays a scatter plot between the MDI impact of the roll yield and the interest rate change (average federal funds rate change) during the same time period. On average, the MDI impact of roll yield is positive. More importantly, there is no apparent relationship between the MDI impact and the interest rate change. More specifically, in a rising interest rate environment, the roll yield does not reduce overall trendiness. The correlation between the MDI impact of roll yield and interest rate change is relatively insignificant.

Commodity Markets and the Roll Yield

Most of the analysis in the previous sections has focused on bond futures. This section turns to the case of commodity futures. Table 6.2 demonstrates that roughly half of the performance for trend following in commodities comes from the roll yield. Since performance is driven by market divergence, it is also interesting to examine how market divergence is affected by interest rates in the commodity sector. This question can also be addressed by examining the MDI with spot price changes and the roll yield. Rising and falling interest rates have a symmetric effect on spot price changes, that is, interest rates rise and spot prices decrease as well as interest rates fall and spot prices increase. The impact on the roll yield is less obvious. As a result, an empirical analysis may provide further insight. Theoretically, higher roll yields should increase trendiness since the difference between nearer and farther futures

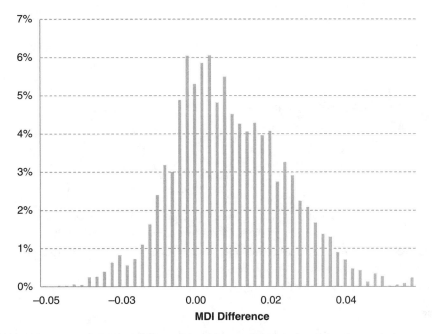

FIGURE 6.10 A histogram for differences in the MDI using futures prices instead of spot prices for the commodity sector.

contracts is larger. Empirically, higher roll yield is associated with greater market divergence (higher MDI) in the commodity sector. Figure 6.10 plots a histogram of changes to the MDI when using futures prices compared to spot prices; both the mean and median are positive. This suggests that commodity futures prices should be positively impacted relative to changes in spot prices.

The relationship between contribution of the roll yield and the contribution of interest rate changes is important to discuss. Figure 6.11 shows the two-year rolling

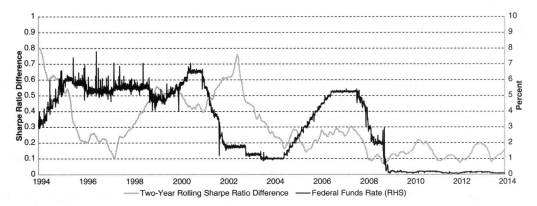

FIGURE 6.11 Two-year rolling Sharpe ratio difference between the total return and spot-price-based return (the roll yield contribution) for the commodity sector with the federal funds rate.
Data source: Global Financial Data.

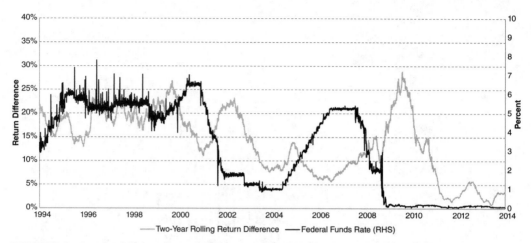

FIGURE 6.12 The difference between the two-year rolling total return and spot-price-based return for the commodity sector with the federal funds rate.

Data source: Global Financial Data.

Sharpe ratio difference between the total return and spot-price-based return, that is, the roll yield contribution, for the commodity sector. Figure 6.12 plots the two-year rolling return difference. The Federal Funds rate is plotted in both Figure 6.11 and Figure 6.12. In general, whether risk adjusted or not, the roll yield appears to contribute more to the total performance when interest rates are higher. The correlation between the rolling Sharpe ratio difference and the moving average of the Federal Funds rate over the same rolling window is 0.66. This suggests that a higher interest rate level often improves trend following performance in the commodity sector. This improved performance manifests itself in the roll yield.

■ Summary

Futures trading maintains a complex but important relationship with interest rates. For trend following strategies this impact comes in two forms: the collateral yield (and/or cash returns) and trends in futures prices. This chapter first discussed the impact of collateral yield and interest income. Interest income creates positive carry for trend following strategies. This positive carry increases total returns and Sharpe ratios while decreasing drawdown depth and duration. These effects are directly related to the level of interest rates. The second way that interest rates have an impact on trend following is by creating trends in futures prices. Although intuitively this impact is more obvious, it is less obvious analytically. The level of interest rates affects spot prices and the slope of the yield curve affects the roll yield. Across all sectors, bonds and commodities are the most significantly affected by the roll yield and changes in interest rates. Especially for commodities, the total futures price change can be attributed to changes in the spot price and changes in the roll yield. For commodity futures, when interest rates are higher or rising, the roll yield plays a larger role in trend following performance.

■ Further Reading and References

Greyserman, A. "Rising Interest Rates and Roll Yield." ISAM White paper, 2013.

PART IV

TREND FOLLOWING AS AN ALTERNATIVE ASSET CLASS

CHAPTER 7

Properties of Trend Following Returns

Trend following strategies are dynamic risk-taking strategies that profit from market divergence by systematically allocating capital across markets over a wide range of asset classes. Given their complementary approach to risk taking, a trend following approach can be a natural complement to many traditional investment strategies. To understand how trend following performs over time, this chapter discusses several key statistical properties of trend following returns. First, two divergence-focused performance measures, crisis alpha and crisis beta, which can be used to measure the complementary properties of trend following return are explained. Second, several key statistical properties of trend following returns are reviewed including total returns, crisis performance, correlation with equities, and skewness. These statistics represent different ways of understanding how trend following performs across time. A review of these statistics across pure trend following and other variants of trend following provides a view into how different approaches for system design can affect these statistical properties.

■ Trend Following as an Alternative Asset Class

A traditional asset is an economic resource, something that can be owned or maintain value. An asset class is defined as a group of securities or assets that have similar characteristics. An alternative asset class is defined as a set of assets outside the traditional asset classes of equity and bonds. Trend following is usually labeled as following a momentum strategy. This is correct but the problem is that the use of the term momentum is descriptive not causal. More specifically, divergence is the cause, momentum is the effect. Momentum is prolonged persistence in market prices. From an adaptive markets perspective, market divergence (as a concept, not a mathematical equation), is a situation that causes momentum in prices. With this perspective, trend following is a strategy that is generally long market divergence. Many convergent investment strategies, such as a long investment in the equity risk premium, are short market divergence.

Divergence can be compared with volatility, another alternative asset class. Volatility, as a concept not a mathematical equation, is a measure or manifestation of how we, as market participants, deal with and value uncertainty. As market participants take action by buying or selling assets as well as buying or selling contracts, which depend on future volatility, they incorporate their views on/or perception of future uncertainty. Returning to equity markets, past prices tell us what our valuation was, whereas future value is about our perceptions of value going forward. In the same vein, past volatility or realized volatility tells us about the risks we have faced while future volatility is about our perceptions of the unknown future that lies ahead of us. In the case of divergence, past trends in markets tell us about realized momentum, where future divergence is about the potential for structural shifts and shocks in the complex ecologies, which make up financial markets. Table 7.1 presents a summary of two traditional asset classes including equity and fixed income with two alternative asset classes of volatility and divergence. From this perspective, volatility and divergence represent different but related concepts. Uncertainty is the situation where the consequences, extent, or magnitude of circumstances is unknown. The past is not uncertain, yet the future contains both risk and uncertainty. For market divergence, just like the evolutionary history of Homo sapiens, the past trends are known. The future level of divergence in a market ecology is governed by the magnitude and occurrence of structural shifts and shocks to the market environment. As a result, it is not surprising that the level of market divergence is related to the changes in volatility (or changes in the level of uncertainty and risk).

Chapters 4 and 5 introduced the concept of adaptive markets and divergence. This chapter focuses on aspects of trend following as an alternative asset class. Based on their divergent risk-taking approach, trend following strategies are long market divergence. Given this unique profile, two specific measures, which help to capture the unique characteristics of this alternative asset class, are discussed in this section. These metrics are crisis alpha and crisis beta.

| TABLE 7.1 | A summary of two traditional asset classes of equity and fixed income with two alternative asset classes of volatility and divergence: Parts of this discussion are highlighted in Kaminski (2012b).[1] | | |

Traditional and Alternative Asset Classes	Past	Future
Equity	Past prices represent the *realized value* of corporations.	Future expectations for value
Fixed Income	Past values represent the *realized return* on money over different horizons.	Future expectations for the return on money over different horizons
Volatility	Realized volatility represents the *realized risk* faced in markets.	Future expectations for level of risk and uncertainty going forward
Divergence	Past trends represent the *realized momentum* in markets.	Future expectations for the level of divergence going forward

Measurement Perspectives	Past Measurement	Forecasting the Future
Equity	Past prices	Valuation models
Fixed Income	Past returns	Interest rate models
Volatility	Standard deviation	Implied volatility, volatility models
Divergence	Signal to noise ratio, market divergence (MDI), market dislocation	Systemic risk models, measures of fragility[2]

■ Crisis Alpha

In Chapter 4, the adaptive markets hypothesis (AMH) was used as a framework to explain why trend following strategies can deliver crisis alpha. Crisis alpha opportunities are profits that are gained by exploiting the persistent trends that occur across markets during times of crisis. Crisis alpha is an important performance metric for an institutional investor. This is because crisis alpha measures a strategy's performance during periods of market stress or divergence, a period where most investment strategies have difficulties. In this framework, trend following performance can be decomposed into three core components: crisis alpha, a speculative risk premium, and the risk-free rate. These three components can be estimated ex-post similar to a measure of the equity risk premium. A simple decomposition of monthly returns is applied to several common industry indices. In this analysis, it became clear that crisis performance plays an important role in the overall performance of

---

[1] Kaminski (2012b) explains how to conceptually view volatility as an alternative asset class.

[2] Many researchers have examined forward-looking measures for determining when a financial system is fragile. This concept is not addressed in detail in this book. For example, Lo and Zhou (2012) discuss a wide range of systemic risk measures. They find that several hedge fund based indicators have some predictable power in determining the level of systemic risk.

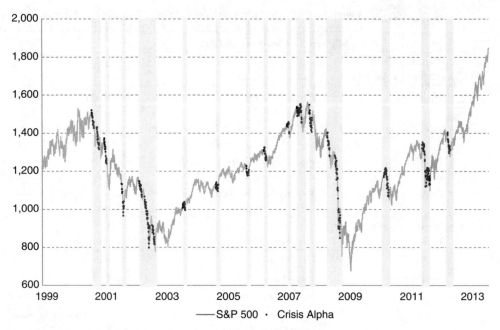

FIGURE 7.1   The S&P 500 index. The crisis periods as defined by increases in the VIX are highlighted by the shaded bars.

trend following over time. Crisis is a period of time when market divergence, as measured by the market divergence index (MDI), is the highest.

The key issue with measuring crisis alpha is in defining the crisis periods. In Chapter 4, crisis alpha is defined using strings of negative returns, which are below some threshold. This method is appropriate for longer term historical studies and for calculating longer term risk premiums. The threshold still remains somewhat subjective. Because changes in volatility and divergence are related, an alternative approach is to use extreme changes in volatility to represent crisis periods.[3] For example, the VIX can be used to define crisis periods systematically. Any month with a move in the VIX that is greater than 20 percent at the end of last month is identified as a crisis month. Using market volatility, by the VIX index, to define market crisis events is a commonly used technique. Several academic papers use volatility based definitions for crisis periods.[4] Figure 7.1 presents the S&P 500 index where the VIX-defined crisis periods are highlighted by the shaded bars.

---

[3] In Chapter 8, the relationship between trend following and market volatility is discussed in more detail. It is the change in volatility that can impact trend following performance. Position sizing is volatility weighted but this weighting is a lagged estimate of volatility. Changes in volatility affect the vega neutrality of trend following positions.

[4] For example, (Vayanos 2004) and (Brunnermeier and Pedersen 2009). In a white paper, Kaminski (2012a) describes how trend following strategies are long changes in volatility when volatility is part of a negative volatility cycle.

From Figure 7.1, it is clear that the VIX-based definition of crisis periods corresponds to periods with large negative returns for the S&P 500. There are three core issues with the VIX-based approach. First, given that the VIX is based on equity volatility, it is less applicable for other asset classes such as commodities or fixed income. To measure volatility for other asset classes, it is necessary to back out implied volatility from options prices. This is a rather cumbersome computational process. Second, similar to the returns-based definition of crisis alpha, over shorter periods if there is no crisis in a particular sample period this can pose problems. This point highlights the fact that crisis alpha, as a general measure, is meant to be used as a stress test over longer historical periods. Crisis alpha is not meant to be used for short-term tactical asset allocation decisions. Third, crisis alpha based on the VIX is somewhat less intuitive for an investor. This definition may incorrectly imply that trend following is a long volatility strategy, which is not exactly true. The correlation of trend following with volatility is generally around 10 to 20 percent depending on the sample period.

Crisis Alpha Across Asset Classes

Trend following strategies are adaptive, opportunistic investment strategies that thrive on market divergence and the corresponding momentum in prices. In general, price momentum is not confined to equity markets. The main difference is that historically, given our industry-wide bias to equity markets and the auxiliary effects of capital constrained companies, market divergence across all asset classes is often the most pronounced during equity crisis.[5] For example, during several of the past markets crises market divergence occurred in all asset classes: fixed income, commodities, real estate, and energy markets. Put simply, when equity markets fall, typically all markets move significantly in some way or another.

During periods of market divergence driven by shocks outside of equity market crisis, the concept is roughly the same. The core difference is that outside of financial crisis, momentum tends to be less pervasive across all markets. Returning to the AMH, given a market environment where there is divergence of any type, it is still the market players who are most adaptive and capable to take advantage of opportunities that outperform. Given this, it is straightforward to expand the crisis alpha concept to bond and commodity crisis periods. In addition to the global equity index, two commonly used global bond and diversified commodity indices can also be used to define crisis periods. For each index, the corresponding asset

---

[5] There is an industry-wide long bias to equity markets. Market participants tend to anchor their expectations based on equity markets.

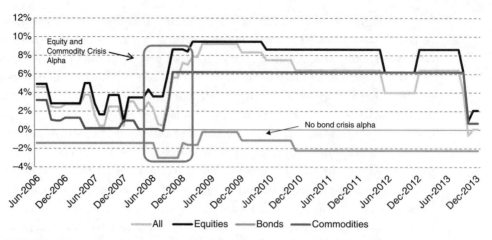

FIGURE 7.2 Rolling windows of crisis alpha. Crisis months are defined when each corresponding index is below its rolling five-year mean and two times its standard deviation.

class specific crisis alpha can be calculated. The **sector specific crisis alpha** for a strategy is defined as the return difference between the return series and the return series with the monthly returns replaced by the three-month T-bill rate during crisis periods. The approach is similar to the approach in global equities in Chapter 4. Crisis periods are defined as the months when the index return is lower than a specific threshold. In this case, the threshold is based on a function of the rolling past average return and standard deviation for consistency across the asset classes. For this discussion, three widely used indices with a long history are chosen as benchmarks for the equity, bond, and commodity sectors: MSCI World Index, JPM Global Bond Index, and the CRB Commodity Index.[6]

Figure 7.2 and Figure 7.3 plot the rolling level of **commodity crisis alpha**, **bond crisis alpha**, **equity crisis alpha**, and the average of the three (crisis all). Each of these three figures uses a different rule for the crisis period definition. The value of crisis alpha is plotting in rolling windows. This means that crisis alpha is measured over a lookback window of five years and the value is plotted over time. Both of these graphs have one commonality; they both catch the credit crisis. Plotting rolling windows shows how crisis alpha is accumulated over time. Figure 7.2 uses the five-year rolling average minus twice the standard deviation for the five-year rolling window as the threshold for a crisis period. Note that in the first figure, the definition of crisis alpha is rather restrictive. There are few months that would qualify

---

[6] CRB is the Thomson Reuters/Jefferies CRB Index. CRB stands for Commodity Research Bureau. The index is designed to represent dynamic trends in commodity markets.

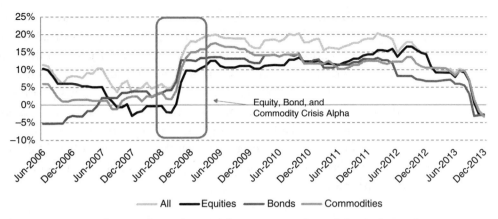

FIGURE 7.3 Rolling windows of crisis alpha. Crisis periods are defined when each corresponding index is negative.

as a crisis month. In this case, the rolling value of crisis alpha changes infrequently, focusing on the left tail of the distribution. For the case of bonds with this restrictive definition, there seems to be little crisis alpha during the sample period based on the crisis period definition. For the second graph, the definition of a crisis month is rather loose, as any negative month. In this case, a large portion of the included months impact the crisis alpha value. These two figures demonstrate the sensitivity of crisis alpha to the definition of a crisis period.

■ Crisis Beta

Whether it is commodities, equities, or bonds, crisis alpha is sensitive to the method for defining a crisis period. Both the volatility-based and returns-based approaches are backward-looking. Their performance is based on a few specific historical crisis events. As a result, crisis alpha is more appropriate for a stress test of the strategy over a longer historical period.[7] For strategic asset allocation decisions, a forward-looking performance measure is preferable. Forward-looking performance measures focus on structural relationships that may hold going forward as opposed to fitting to past events.[8] This measure should demonstrate the recent structural relationship

---

[7] For a shorter rolling window such as two years, frequently there are no crisis periods in a lookback window.

[8] Tail hedging is a field that is plagued with this particular problem. If a strategy hedges against a future Lehmann Brothers bankruptcy, it is highly unlikely that the next financial meltdown will manifest itself exactly like the ones in the past.

149

PROPERTIES OF TREND FOLLOWING RETURNS

between trend following and benchmark indices for traditional asset classes. Most asset classes can be examined using their corresponding betas to traditional betas. In this case, the traditional beta is roughly zero. As an alternative to this approach, **crisis beta** can be defined. Crisis beta is designed to estimate the conditional correlation with underlying indices. For example, trend following has positive correlation with equity bull markets and negative correlation with equity bear markets. In a traditional net correlation measure, these two good correlations cancel each other out as opposed to being additive. Given this property of trend following, the standard beta of trend following is close to zero. The standard beta is defined by the following expression:

$$\beta = \frac{cov(r, r_M)}{var(r_M)}$$

where r_M is the return of a corresponding benchmark. Taking both the positive and negative contribution of the covariance into account, a traditional beta can be decomposed into two expressions:

$$\beta = \frac{cov(r, r_M)}{var(r_M)} = \frac{cov(r, r_{\overline{M}})}{var(r_M)} + \frac{cov(r, r_M^+)}{var(r_M)}$$

Here, r_M^+ is a return series with only positive index returns and $r_{\overline{M}}$ is a return series with only the negative index returns. For both the positive and negative benchmark series, the remaining returns are replaced by zero. For a traditional beta, a negative beta indicates that the strategy generally moves in the opposite direction of the index. For traditional betas, negative beta is not usually desirable for an investor besides for possible diversification effects. As an example, a very negative beta can be achieved by shorting the benchmark index. Crisis beta can be defined by allowing the negative beta to remain negative and changing the sign of all positive contributions of the strategy in the traditional beta definition as in the following expression.

$$\beta_c = \frac{cov(r, r_M)}{var(r_M)} = \frac{cov(r, r_{\overline{M}})}{var(r_M)} - \frac{cov(r, r_M^+)}{var(r_M)}$$

With a simple manipulation to the traditional beta, the new measure crisis beta measures the level of conditional correlation for a trend following strategy. The lower the amount of crisis beta, the more beneficial the strategy can be for a long only investor in the underlying index. When compared with crisis alpha, crisis beta focuses on the recent relationship between trend following and a particular asset

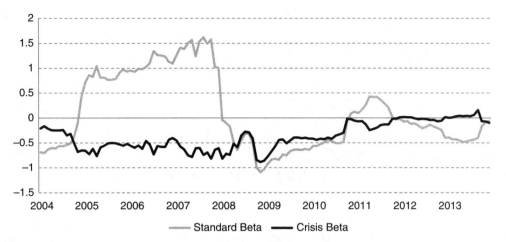

FIGURE 7.4 Two-year rolling crisis betas for trend following with the equity benchmark index: MSCI World Index.

Data source: Bloomberg.

class. This overcomes some of the specification problems of crisis alpha. A standardized definition of a crisis period is no longer necessary.

Using a representative pure trend following strategy from 2002 to 2013, Figure 7.4, Figure 7.5, and Figure 7.6 plot the rolling two-year rolling crisis betas with each of the equity, bond, and commodity indices. Figure 7.7 plots the overall average crisis beta, the simple average of the three-sector specific crisis betas. For

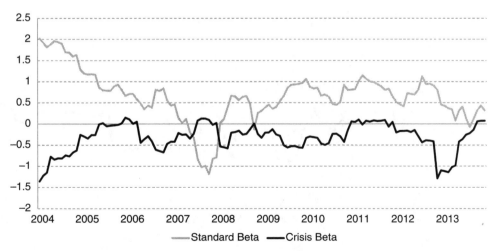

FIGURE 7.5 The two-year rolling crisis betas for trend following with the bond benchmark index: JPM Global Bond Index.

Data source: Bloomberg.

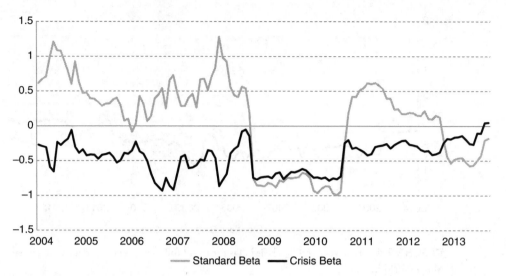

FIGURE 7.6 Two-year rolling crisis betas for trend following with the commodity benchmark index: CRB All Commodity Index.
Data source: Bloomberg.

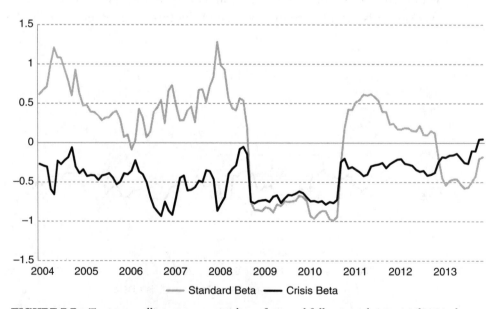

FIGURE 7.7 Two-year rolling average crisis betas for trend following where crisis beta is the average of the three-sector specific crisis betas for each of the three benchmark indices.
Data source: Bloomberg.

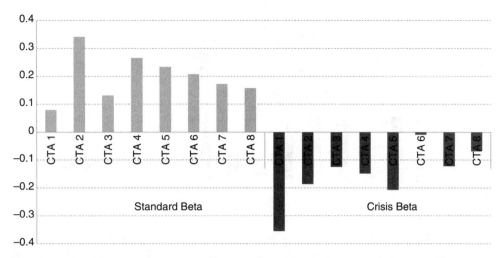

FIGURE 7.8 The average two-year rolling crisis beta of several CTAs with the CRB All Commodity Index.
Data source: Bloomberg.

comparison, each figure also plots the traditional beta for each corresponding index. From each of these figures, it is clear that the traditional beta is much more variable. Crisis beta is consistently rather negative.

The crisis betas of several major trend following CTAs can also be examined. Using performance data from 2002 to 2013, Figure 7.8 to Figure 7.11 plot both the

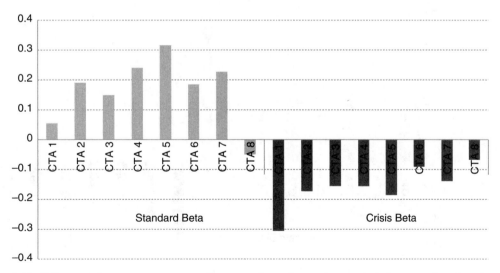

FIGURE 7.9 The average two-year rolling crisis beta of several CTAs with the equity benchmark index: MSCI World Index.
Data source: Bloomberg.

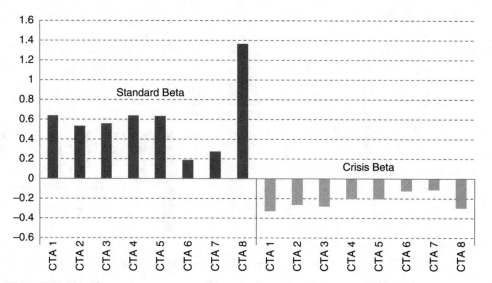

FIGURE 7.10 The average two-year rolling crisis beta of several CTAs with the bond benchmark index: JPM Global Bond Index.

Data source: Bloomberg.

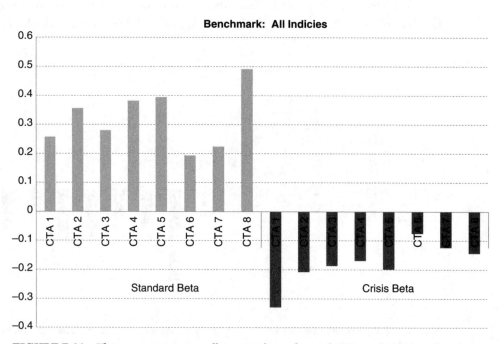

FIGURE 7.11 The average two-year rolling crisis beta of several CTAs with the three benchmark indices: MSCI World Index, JPM Global Bond Index, and the CRB All Commodity Index.

Data source: Bloomberg.

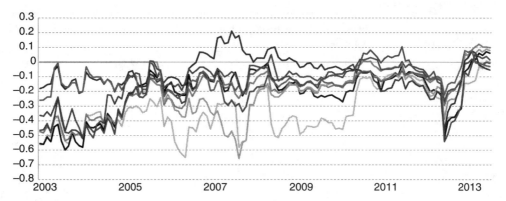

FIGURE 7.12 The time series of the two-year rolling crisis beta of several CTAs with the three benchmark indices.

Data source: Bloomberg.

average traditional asset class specific betas and the average of the two-year rolling crisis beta of the same eight CTA funds during the same period.[9] Some CTAs have negative crisis beta with all the benchmarks. Figure 7.12 depicts the time series for the two-year rolling crisis beta with all three benchmarks for all the CTA funds. This plot demonstrates how crisis beta is a stable property of trend following returns.

■ Key Statistical Properties

The previous sections outlined two unique measures for trend following. In this section, more general key statistical properties of trend following programs are outlined. To facilitate this discussion, the eight trend following systems are used to demonstrate how these statistics compare across different methods for trend following system construction. The partitioning of these trend following systems is listed in Table 7.2. The classification of these systems was introduced in Chapter 3.

Across the eight trend following systems, key statistical properties are summarized using box plots. Within each box, the central mark (the line in the charts) is the median, and the edges of the box represent the 25th and 75th percentiles, that is, the **interquartile range (IQR)**. The whiskers represent the most extreme points that are not outliers in the sample.[10] The individual plus signs outside of the whiskers are the outliers. Using a diversified set of 50 markets from equities, commodities, fixed income, and currencies, an analysis of these key characteristics can

---

[9] The return data is from June 2001 to December 2013 for all firms except for CTA5, which started in April 2004.

[10] The outlier boundaries for these charts are 1.5 times the box height away from the box edges.

	Equity Long Bias	Market Capacity Weighted	Long Horizon
1	No	No	No
2	Yes	No	No
3	No	Yes	No
4	No	No	Yes
5	Yes	Yes	No
6	No	Yes	Yes
7	Yes	No	Yes
8	Yes	Yes	Yes

be applied to the eight classifications of trend following.[11] Longer term returns, the Sharpe ratio, portfolio skewness, crisis alpha, crisis beta, and conditional correlation are examined to demonstrate how different approaches to trend following perform and differ from each other.

Long-Term Returns

Figure 7.13 depicts return dispersion over the past 20 years for each uniquely constructed trend following system. Systems 1, 2, 4, and 7 have provided the best performance during the past 20 years. All four of these profiles correspond to an equal dollar risk allocation approach. This suggests that risk allocation across more markets similar to an equal weighted approach is also more profitable in the long run.[12] This may also suggest that larger trend followers facing capacity constraints who focus mostly on the larger financials, similar to market capitalization weightings, may produce lower returns in the long run. Over the 20 year period, the addition of a long equity bias does not act as a performance differentiator for total return. This suggests that the positive effects of being long equity biased during bull markets may be outweighed by the consequences in bear markets.[13]

Skewness

Trend following strategies are often known for their **positive skewness**. Given their divergent risk taking approach, they take many smaller losses and earn fewer

---

[11] The dataset covers more than 20 years of daily data from 1993 to 2013.

[12] This observation foreshadows the style analysis in Chapter 12. A market size factor will be examined in further detail. The role of size, capacity, and less liquid markets is also discussed in Chapter 15.

[13] The role of equity bias will also be examined as a style factor in Chapter 12.

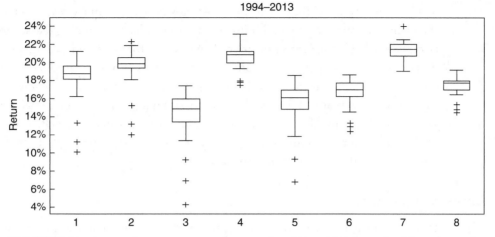

FIGURE 7.13 Return dispersion in annual returns for 1993 to 2013 for each of the eight trend following systems defined in Table 7.2.

larger gains. This approach should create positive skewness in the trend following return distribution. In statistical terms, this type of distribution is desirable since it exhibits lower drawdowns and has good diversification properties. Figure 7.14 plots the skewness for each unique trend following system. System 5 and System 8 exhibit substantially negative skewness (as opposed to positive skewness). System 5 and System 8 are trend following systems with both an equity long bias and

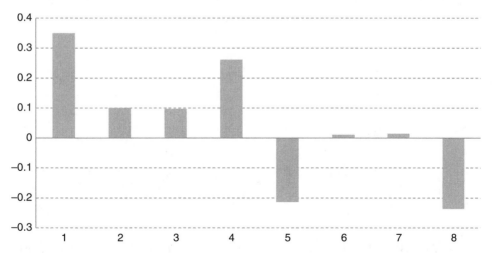

FIGURE 7.14 Average skewness of monthly returns for each of the eight trend following systems from 1993 to 2013.

market capacity weightings. This demonstrates how long equity bias and a focus on the financials can make a trend following more similar to a convergent strategy. The two systems with the largest positive skewness are the unbiased systems with equal dollar risk allocation (System 1 and System 4). This simple example demonstrates how a lack of view on the direction of equity markets and a lack of view on where to allocate risk creates the most divergent risk-taking approach in terms of positive skewness. Conceptually, adding equity bias and market capacity weights adds a view to the portfolio making the strategy more convergent. This property even shows up empirically in the skewness of returns.

Crisis Performance

Using a returns-based approach, crisis periods can be designated as months when the equity return is lower than one standard deviation below its long-term mean. Using the MSCI World Index for equity markets, Figure 7.15 plots the average monthly returns during crisis periods for each trend following system. Once again, System 1 and System 4 (no equity bias and equal risk allocation) produce the highest crisis alpha, while System 5 and System 8 (with an equity long bias and market capacity based allocation) deliver the least crisis alpha. This topic is examined in further detail in Chapters 14 and 15.

Correlation with Equity Markets

Investments with negative correlation can provide substantial diversification benefits. A negative correlation indicates that, when the benchmark is down, the return of the asset is likely positive. This relationship provides desirable diversification benefits.

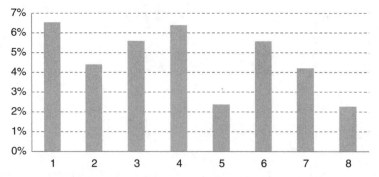

FIGURE 7.15 Average returns for each of the eight trend following systems during crisis periods when the MSCI Word Index had a return of one standard deviation or more below its mean from 1993 to 2013.

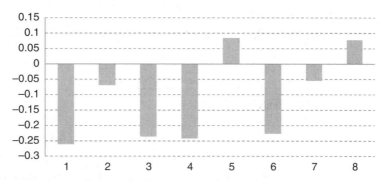

FIGURE 7.16 The average correlation between each trend following system's monthly returns and the MSCI World Index from 1993 to 2013.

The correlation of each trend following system with the MSCI World Index can be examined. From 1993 to 2013, Figure 7.16 plots the average correlation between the monthly returns for each trend following system and the MSCI World Index. System 1 and System 4 (no equity bias and equal risk allocation) are the most negatively correlated with the benchmark, while System 5 and System 8 (with an equity long bias and market capacity based allocation) are slightly positively correlated with the MSCI World Index. Because the correlation measure is a net measure, it may be less effective than crisis beta for evaluation.

In this section, key statistical properties of eight unique trend following systems are discussed. Across the different trend following systems, there is return dispersion as well as variation between the statistical properties from one system to another. The most divergent trend following systems, more notably the equal dollar risk weighted with no equity bias, exhibit return performance most consistent with a divergent risk-taking approach. They exhibit the highest crisis performance, most positive skewness, and lowest overall correlation with equity markets. Over the long run, similar to what has been found in risk-parity portfolios, equal risk-based approaches in trend following provide the highest return.

■ Summary

Trend following is an investment strategy that systematically allocates risk to a wide range of asset classes dynamically. Given the unique profile of this opportunistic strategy, two unique measures, crisis alpha and crisis beta, are discussed. Following this analysis, a range of statistical properties including total return, skewness, crisis performance, and conditional correlation is examined for a range of unique trend following systems. Consistent with their underlying market view, equal dollar risk allocation and no equity bias trend following systems provide higher crisis performance, lower overall correlation with equity markets, and the most positive skewness.

■ Appendix: A Summary of Common Performance Measures

Investment professionals use a wide range of performance metrics to evaluate performance. In this section, several commonly used performance metrics are summarized. Each of these measures has its own limitations and assumptions. Given this, the task of performance evaluation becomes even more complicated when trading strategies are dynamic.

Sharpe Ratio

The Sharpe ratio is one of the most widely used performance measures in investment management. The **Sharpe ratio** is a simple measure of risk-adjusted performance. Given its simplicity, the Sharpe ratio is intuitive, but it may fail to properly account for the complexities in dynamic trading strategies. In particular the Sharpe ratio may hide risks in many alternative investment strategies as it focuses on risk as defined by standard deviation of returns. In fact, Sharpe ratios require several assumptions about the distribution of returns. More explicitly, it requires both that returns are normally distributed and that standard deviation is an all-inclusive measure of risk. Standard deviations generally include price risk but other risks may be hidden. Trend following strategies take on mostly price risk resulting often in lower Sharpe ratios than many other alternative investment strategies that contain hidden risks. This concept is explained in more detail in Chapter 9.[14] The typical Sharpe ratio for long-only equities is 0.25 to 0.50. Sharpe ratios for trend following strategies generally range from 0.50 to 0.70 over the long run, while many hedge fund Sharpe ratios range from 0.50 to 1.50.

Omega Ratio

The **Omega ratio** provides an alternative to the Sharpe ratio. The Omega ratio is a ratio that compares the amount of weighted gains to weighted losses. This ratio does not make any assumptions about the distribution of returns. This fact allows the ratio

---

[14] It is also possible for hedge fund managers to manipulate Sharpe ratios. This can be done by selling options, by dynamic leveraging, smoothing returns, and other techniques. See Ferson and Siegel (2001), Goeztmann et al. (2002), and Lo (2002).

to take into account the information in higher moments of returns. In practice, a threshold can be used to define losses and gains relative to this threshold.

The Omega ratio takes the value of 1 when the threshold is the mean of the return series. In practice, the Omega ratio can be used to rank investments when the same time horizon is used. When returns are normally distributed or if there are no hidden risks, the Omega ratio and the Sharpe ratio tend to agree.

Information Ratio

Many investors use the information ratio to calculate relative performance when a benchmark is available. The **information ratio** is the ratio of the annualized excess return relative to a benchmark to the corresponding annualized tracking error. Tracking error is defined as the standard deviation of the excess return relative to the benchmark. One of the key challenges with the information ratio is that it requires an appropriate benchmark. In the trend following space, investors traditionally use common industry indices for benchmarking a trend following program. This benchmark represents a basket of managers, which is not investable.

Downside Risk

To understand the variability of performance during a drawdown many investors calculate downside risk. **Downside risk** measures the variability of underperformance below a minimum target rate. The minimum target rate can be zero, the risk-free rate, or any other fixed threshold. All returns above the threshold are included as zero in the calculation of downside risk.

Summary

This appendix provides a brief introduction to several commonly used measures for performance evaluation. Measures, such as the Sharpe ratio and Omega ratio, are used to help investors to rank and differentiate amongst trend following managers, thus they are important metrics for both managers and investors to understand.

■ Further Reading and References

Brunnermeier, M., and L. Pedersen. "Market Liquidity and Funding Liquidity." *Review of Financial Studies* 22, no. 6 (2009): 2201–2238.

Chan, N., M. Getmansky, and S. M. Haas. "Systemic Risk and Hedge Funds." In *The Risks of Financial Institutions and the Financial Sector*, edited by M. Carey and R. Stulz. Chicago: University of Chicago Press, 2006, 235–338.

Ferson, W., and A. Siegel. "The Efficient Use of Conditioning Information in Portfolios." *Journal of Finance* 3 (June 2001): 967–982.

Goetzmann, W., J. Ingersoll, M. Spiegel, and I. Welch. "Sharpening Sharpe Ratios." National Bureau of Economic Research Working Paper No. W9116, 2002.

Greyserman, A. "Crisis Alpha: ISAM Systematic." ISAM White paper, 2013.

Kaminski, K. "Managed Futures and Volatility: Decoupling a Convex Relationship with Volatility Cycles." CME Market Education Group, May 2012a.

Kaminski, K. "Unveiling the World of Uncertainty Specialists: A Short Guide to Investing in Volatility." Unpublished white paper, Stockholm School of Economics, 2012b.

Keating, C., and W. Shadwick. "An Introduction to Omega." London: The Finance Development Centre, 2002.

Khandani, A., A. Lo, and R. Merton. "Systemic Risk and the Refinancing Ratchet Effect." *Journal of Financial Economics* 108, no. 1 (2013): 29–45.

Lo, A. W. "The Statistics of Sharpe Ratios." *Financial Analysts Journal* 58 (2002): 36–52.

Lo, A., and A. Zhou. "A Comparison of Systemic Risk Indicators." Unpublished working paper, MIT Laboratory for Financial Engineering, 2012.

Pasquariello, P. "Financial Market Dislocations." *Review of Financial Studies*. Published electronically February 12, 2014.

Vayanos, D. "Flight to Quality, Flight to Liquidity, and the Pricing of Risk." NBER Working Paper, 2004.

CHAPTER 8

Characteristics of Drawdowns, Volatility, and Correlation

In Chapter 7, several key statistical properties for trend following strategies were discussed. These statistical properties take a first look at the performance of trend following across time. This chapter takes a closer look inside a trend following system at three core measures of risk and diversification: drawdowns, volatility, and correlation. These characteristics are examined at the portfolio level. This discussion provides greater insight into how trend following strategies experience drawdowns; into differences between market volatility, strategy volatility, and portfolio volatility; and into how diversification and correlation across markets impact trend following portfolios.

■ Understanding the Properties of Drawdowns

Drawdown measures the loss from an investor's peak past net asset value (NAV). Given the stochastic nature of return series, drawdowns are a natural part of any return series. In particular, the maximum drawdown over a given period is often used as an important risk measure. **Maximum drawdown** represents the worst loss an investor could have suffered by buying at the highest point and selling at the lowest. This measurement often gauges the worst case scenario. Other metrics

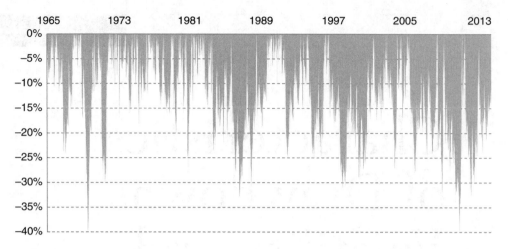

FIGURE 8.1 The drawdown profile based on daily returns of a simple trend following system in eight agricultural markets.

characterize the maximum drawdown itself. For example, many investors are interested in the **time to recovery** of a drawdown. There are also performance measures that adjust performance as a function of the maximum drawdown. For example, the **Calmar ratio** and **Sterling ratio** are common risk-adjusted return measures similar to the Sharpe ratio, which depends on the maximum drawdown.[1] Given that maximum drawdown depends on a specific time period, these measures are not easily scalable. More specifically, these ratios are not easily comparable across sampling frequencies, for example, daily ratios and annual ratios are not easily comparable.

Technically, the maximum drawdown is the extremum of the extremum of a return series (the maximum among the losses from a peak NAV to a trough in NAV). Given this definition, maximum drawdowns are highly path-dependent. The maximum drawdown will depend on several factors of a track record: data sampling frequency, length, volatility, mean return, and serial correlation of returns. Before discussing the statistics and properties of trend following drawdowns, Figure 8.1 presents an example of a drawdown profile for trend following applied across eight agricultural markets from 1965 to 2013. To examine a longer historical period, the system in Figure 8.1 is an agricultural-only trend following system.[2] Perhaps surprisingly, the system remains in a drawdown most of the time. In fact, in only less than 6 percent of the days in this example, the system is not in a drawdown, that

---

[1] The Calmar and Sterling ratios are the return in a given period normalized by the maximum drawdown in the same period. Typically, both ratios are calculated over a three-year period. For the Sterling ratio, the numerator is the maximum drawdown reduced by a fixed amount such as 10 percent.

[2] The system is based on a breakout signal. For this particular system, the Sharpe ratio is 0.9 and the monthly risk is 6 percent.

is, achieving a new high of NAV. During the roughly 50-year period, the system's maximum drawdown occurred in 1969 and the longest drawdown was from 1996 to 2001.

Several researchers have investigated the theoretical properties of the drawdown measure, and, in particular, expected maximum drawdown.[3] Most of the work in this area is based on returns that are generated using a Brownian motion via Monte Carlo simulation. Grossman and Zhou (1993) and Strub (2012) discuss portfolio optimization and trade size optimization with the objective to control drawdowns. In addition, Cukurova and Marin (2011) present interesting arguments for the use of both drawdown and survival status as a positive indicator of future fund performance. The following subsections review the theory for expected maximum drawdowns and the expected length and time to recovery for a drawdown. The **expected maximum drawdown** provides a baseline for investors to gauge the magnitude of observed drawdowns. The **expected drawdown length** provides an investor with a measure to gauge the severity of a drawdown. The **expected recovery time** gives an indication of the length of time needed to wait for recovery from a drawdown. Following the discussion of these two measures, trade statistics and other properties of returns during drawdown periods are discussed. Finally, the link between diversification and drawdowns is discussed as an introduction to how this relates to investor portfolios in Chapter 14.

Expected Maximum Drawdown

The expected maximum drawdown is the expected value of the maximum drawdown for a return series. Based on the assumption that the cumulative return series follows a random walk, Atiya, Abu-Mostafa, and Magdon-Ismail (2004) derive the expected maximum drawdown for a long-term horizon as a function of the mean, volatility, and track record length. The formula for the expected maximum drawdown $E[MDD]$ is valid when the drift is positive ($\mu > 0$) and can be written as follows:

$$E[MDD] = \frac{\sigma^2}{\mu}\left(0.63519 + 0.5\log T + \log\frac{\mu}{\sigma}\right)$$

where (μ) and (σ) are the drift and volatility of the return series per unit time. (T) represents the total time horizon. A simple manipulation of this function indicates that the expected maximum drawdown per unit of risk is a function of the Sharpe ratio and track record length. For a range of Sharpe ratios and track record lengths,

---

[3] Atiya, Abu-Mostafa, and Magdon-Ismail (2004), Casati (2010), and Belentepe (2003).

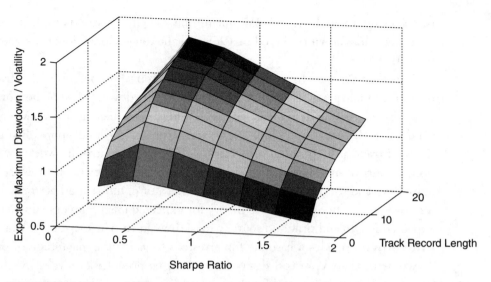

FIGURE 8.2 Expected maximum drawdown $E[MDD]$ per unit of risk as a function of the Sharpe ratio and track record length.

Figure 8.2 plots expected average maximum drawdown as a scalar multiple of volatility from $0x$ to $2x$ based on Monte Carlo simulation. Longer track records represent longer expected maximum drawdowns and higher Sharpe ratios result in lower expected maximum drawdowns. When the Sharpe ratio is between 0.75 and 1, the expected maximum drawdown over the period of a year is approximately $1x$ annualized volatility. To examine this using gross performance data from a trend following system, Table 8.1 lists the intrayear maximum drawdown from 2001 to 2013. For comparison, the S&P 500 Index is also listed in Table 8.1. Consistent with the simulation in Figure 8.2, on average the intrayear maximum drawdown is 17.35 percent, which is similar to $1x$ the volatility of the trend following system. The average intrayear maximum drawdown for the S&P 500 Index is 18.26 percent, which is also roughly $1x$ its volatility from 2001 to 2013.

For a given Sharpe ratio of 0.75 and 1.0, Table 8.2 displays the expected maximum drawdown for a track record of 10 to 30 years and an annualized volatility from 10 to 20 percent. Figure 8.3 plots a histogram for maximum drawdown over a 10-year period when the annual return and the annualized volatility are both 15 percent.

TABLE 8.1 Intrayear maximum drawdown for the gross returns of representative pure trend following system and the S&P 500 Index from 2001 to 2013. The trend following system has approximately 18 percent volatility during this period.

Year	2001	2002	2003	2004	2005	2006	2007	2008	2009	2010	2011	2012	2013	Average
Representative TF System	14.1%	14.5%	18.1%	24.5%	11.5%	25.0%	20.2%	19.7%	15.2%	10.2%	17.3%	17.2%	18.1%	17.35%
S&P 500 Index	29.7%	33.8%	14.1%	8.2%	7.2%	7.7%	10.1%	48.0%	27.6%	16.0%	19.4%	9.9%	5.80%	18.26%

TABLE 8.2	Expected maximum drawdown based on monthly returns for a track record of 10 to 30 years and an annualized volatility from 10 to 20 percent.						
	Sharpe = 0.75				Sharpe = 1.0		
	10	20	30		10	20	30
10%	16.40%	19.80%	21.60%	10%	14.10%	16.80%	18.20%
15%	23.50%	28.00%	30.60%	15%	20.20%	23.90%	26.10%
20%	29.60%	35.30%	38.50%	20%	25.90%	30.40%	33.10%

The theoretical formula purposed in Atiya, Abu-Mostafa, and Magdon-Ismail (2004) does not take into account serial correlation of returns. In practice, many return series exhibit some type of serial correlation. A simple Monte Carlo simulation can also confirm that positive (negative) serial correlation results in a higher (lower) maximum drawdown. Empirically, the serial correlation of daily returns for a trend following strategy can be as high as minus 10 percent. Trend following strategies tend to exhibit negative serial autocorrelation in returns over the longer run. This concept is revisited in Chapter 17 on dynamic allocation to trend following.

It is also important to discuss the path dependent nature of maximum drawdowns. Path dependence makes the maximum drawdown measure vary for different data sampling frequencies. The low (high) sampling frequencies result in lower (higher) expected maximum drawdowns. In Figure 8.4, the drawdown profile of the same system from Figure 8.1 is plotted for monthly returns as opposed to daily returns.

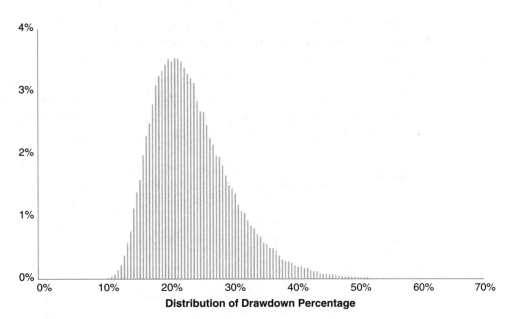

FIGURE 8.3 A histogram for maximum drawdown for a 10-year period with 15 percent annual return and 15 percent annual volatility.

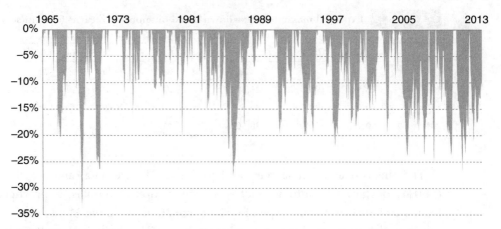

FIGURE 8.4 The drawdown profile based on monthly returns of a simple pure trend following system on eight agricultural markets.

When compared with Figure 8.1, both the maximum drawdown and the longest drawdown are reduced.

Expected Drawdown Length and Recovery

Investors are not only interested in the depth of drawdowns; they are also interested in **drawdown length** and recovery. Similar to the expected maximum drawdown, the expected longest drawdown length largely depends on the track record length and the Sharpe ratio. The drawdown length is defined as the length of time spent in a drawdown and the **expected longest drawdown length** is the expected value of the maximum length of time spent in a drawdown. Given this definition, it may not be the case that the maximum drawdown is the drawdown with the longest drawdown length. For example, given a representative trend following system,[4] the correlation between the drawdown length and depth is often lower than 70 percent among the drawdowns that are larger than 10 percent. For demonstrative purposes, Table 8.3

TABLE 8.3	Longest drawdown length (in months) for a given Sharpe of 0.75 and 1.0 over a period from 10 to 30 years.		
	10	20	30
Sharpe 0.75	30.4	43.1	52.2
Sharpe 1.0	22.8	30.8	36.2

[4] The representative trend following system is based on breakout signals with a set of lookback window sizes from 90 to 120 days over a diversified universe consisting of equity index, commodity, fixed income, and FX markets. The Sharpe ratio over the 30-year period is 1.07 with an annualized volatility of 14 percent.

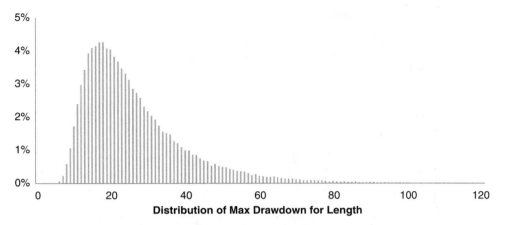

FIGURE 8.5 A histogram for longest drawdown length for a 10-year period with 15 percent annual return and 15 percent annual volatility.

summarizes results of a simple Monte Carlo simulation. In this simulation, for given Sharpe ratios of 0.75 and 1.0 over a period from 10 to 30 years, the longest drawdown length (in months) is listed in the table. Figure 8.5 presents the histogram of the longest drawdown length in a 10-year period with a Sharpe ratio of 1.0.

The total drawdown length can also be divided into two subperiods: the drawdown as measured from peak to trough and the recovery period. The drawdown measured from peak to trough is the total length of the loss of a drawdown and the **recovery period** is the amount of time it takes to recover from the specific drawdown. Figure 8.6 presents a scatter plot between the time from peak to trough (the

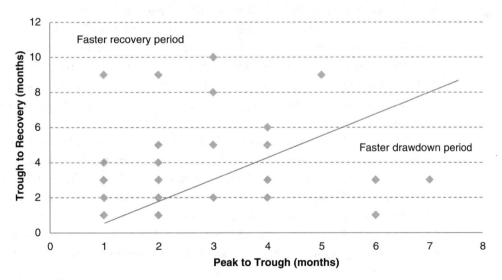

FIGURE 8.6 A scatter plot between the time from peak to trough (drawdown) and the recovery time for a representative trend following system.

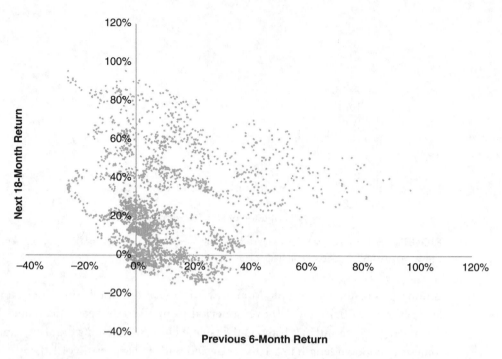

FIGURE 8.7 The relationship between the past return (rolling 6-month) and the following return (rolling 18-month) for a representative pure trend following system.

drawdown) and the recovery period for a representative trend following system. In practice, the median ratio between the recovery period and the entire draw-down period is roughly 0.5.[5] This implies that two-thirds of drawdowns are recovered in one-third of the time. The recovery is approximately twice as fast as the drawdown length. This shows the recovery (or recoverability) from drawdowns in trend following systems. This is consistent with the profile of a divergent risk-taking strategy outlined in Chapter 5. The strategy will take many small losses and then less often find larger gains. More explicitly, gains occur less often and are larger in magnitude than losses.

During periods following a drawdown (or the recovery period), the mean return tends to be conditionally higher than the long-term average. This also demonstrates the recoverability of the strategy from drawdowns. In Chapter 5, the market divergence index (MDI) was also cyclical over time. Connecting this to risk in markets, opportunities may potentially link to cycles in risk taking over time. From 2001 to 2013, Figure 8.7 plots the relationship between the past return (rolling 6-month) and the following return (rolling 18-month) for a representative pure trend following

---

[5] This estimate is a rough approximation but is representative across many independent calculations.

program.[6] When the past 6-month return was negative, the average 18-month return is 51.6 percent during this period. The long-term 18-month average is lower at 41.5 percent. Given a negative 6 month return, the conditional probability of an above-average 18-month return is 56 percent.

Winning/Losing Trade Ratios and Drawdowns

Using the gains and losses of a representative pure trend following system, trade and signal statistics during drawdown periods can provide further insight into risk allocation and into what drives drawdowns. Most trend followers are long to medium term with a typical holding period of several months. On a shorter horizon, round trip trade statistics (from entry to exit) are less meaningful for shorter windows as short as 22 days (approximately one month). Despite this, it is possible to take a closer look at all the trades that *exit* in a rolling window. As an example, using a representative pure trend following system 2001 to 2013, the **winning ratio** of trades and the **win/loss ratio (of trade PnL)** can be calculated. The winning ratio of trades is the ratio of trades that are winners to the number that are currently losers. This ratio gives some sense of if there are more winners or losers. It does not take into account the magnitude of a win or loss. The win/loss ratio of trade PnL is the ratio of trades, which have a winning PnL to the trades that have a losing PnL. In this example, drawdown has a minus 46 percent correlation with the winning ratio of the trades, but only a minus 14 percent correlation with the win/loss ratio of trade PnL. This may indicate that the lower winning trade ratio, rather than the lower win/loss PnL ratio, is the primary reason for the drawdowns. Put simply, the number of losers, not the magnitude, seems to drive drawdowns. Reverting back to the divergent risk-taking approach, many small losses are taken as opposed to large losses.

When using a short rolling window, instead of trade statistics, it can be more appropriate to examine signal statistics. At the signal level, both the **percentage of winning markets** with a positive PnL for a given rolling window and the win/loss ratio of PnL between winning markets and losing markets can be calculated. The percentage of winning markets with positive PnL provides some insight into the quantity of winners and losers. The win/loss ratio of PnL provides insight into magnitude from losers and winners. Using a 22-day rolling window, Figure 8.8 plots the percentage of winning markets with the drawdowns for a trend following program. The correlation between the percentage of winning markets and the drawdown magnitude is minus 64 percent. The correlation between the drawdown and the win/loss ratio of PnL between winning and losing markets is lower at minus 36 percent. Given these simple correlation statistics, a higher percentage of losing markets, rather than

---

[6] The analysis is based on gross daily returns.

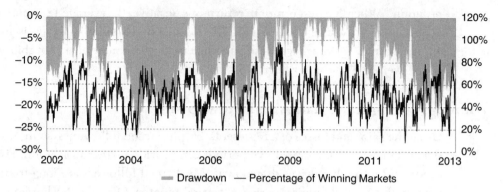

FIGURE 8.8 Percentage of winning markets in a 22-day rolling window and the drawdowns for a representative pure trend following program.

the larger losing PnL per market, cause the drawdowns in trend following portfolios. In other words, losses spread across markets cause drawdowns as opposed to large losses in individual markets. Daily signal statistics for PnL in a rolling window exhibit similar characteristics. A higher percentage of smaller losses, rather than larger daily losses, are more correlated with the size of a drawdown. This is intuitive as it also fits the divergent risk-taking approach discussed in Chapter 5. Trend followers spread risks across many markets; they avoid concentrating positions in one market and systematically cut losing positions. Both trade and signal statistics are consistent with this description.

> Drawdown periods represent times when many smaller losses occur together as opposed to a few large concentrated losses.

Given trade and signal statistics, the performance of trend following is clearly dependent on the number of winning markets. To demonstrate this relationship, Figure 8.9 presents a scatter plot between portfolio return and winning percentage in a 22-day rolling window. The correlation between return and winning percentage is close to 90 percent. Using a simple regression, when the percentage of winning markets is above 48 percent in a month, the expected monthly return is positive, and is negative otherwise. The relationship between drawdown and the percent of winning markets is robust for a 30-year sample period. In addition, the market divergence index (MDI), which is a measure for market divergence and potential profitability of trend following,[7] is highly negatively correlated with drawdown during the same 30-year period.

---

[7] A longer lookback window of 250 days is used to calculate the MDI in Chapter 5.

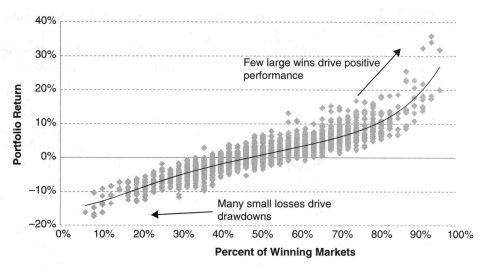

FIGURE 8.9 A scatter plot between the portfolio return and winning percentage in a 22-day rolling window for a representative pure trend following system.

■ Volatility of a Trend Following Portfolio

There are many misconceptions about the relationship between market volatility and the volatility of a trend following portfolio. From the outside, many investors intuitively think that the portfolio volatility is positively associated with market volatility, while others may believe that there should be no significant relationship between market volatility and portfolio volatility. The latter understands that the daily positions of a standard trend following system are adjusted by the rolling volatility of each market based on a pre-specified risk budget. This concept was explained in the discussion of systematic trend following in Chapter 3. When the volatility based on the rolling window of returns (σ_n) of a market rises, the nominal position is reduced accordingly.

$$v = s \times \left(\frac{\theta \times c}{\sigma_K(\Delta P) \times PV} \right) \times (PV \times P)$$

Despite this adjustment, rolling window estimates of volatility do not necessarily perfectly adjust for market volatility. This means that some undulations from market volatility still enter into a trend following portfolio. To clarify how volatility and correlation work at the aggregate and individual market level, Table 8.4 presents a list of key terms, notation, descriptions, and measurement proxies for reference during the discussion in the following sections.

TABLE 8.4 Key definitions of terms for volatility and correlation at the portfolio, strategy, and market level.

Aggregate Term	Individual Term	Description	Measured by/Proxy
Portfolio volatility (σ_p)		Total portfolio volatility	Standard deviation in portfolio returns (*average strategy volatility*, $\overline{\sigma}_s$)
Portfolio correlation (ρ_p)		Correlation across the portfolio	Weighted strategy correlation (average pair-wise strategy correlation $\overline{\rho}_{s,i,j}$)
	Strategy volatility $(\sigma_{s,i})$	Volatility for a strategy on individual market (i)	Standard deviation in strategy returns
	Strategy correlation $(\rho_{s,i,j})$	Correlation between two strategies (i) and (j)	Correlation between strategy returns (i) and (j)
Market volatility (σ_m)		Total market volatility	Weighted volatility for all future markets ($\overline{\sigma}_{m,i}$)
Market correlation (ρ_m)		Correlation across all markets	Weighted correlation between price returns ($\overline{\rho}_{m,i,j}$)
	Individual market volatility $(\sigma_{m,i})$	Price volatility for an individual market (i)	Standard deviation in price returns
	Individual market correlation $(\rho_{m,i,j})$	Correlation between two markets (i) and (j)	Correlation between price returns (i) and (j)

Standard portfolio theory states that total portfolio volatility is determined by the correlation structure between **strategy returns** of each market and the **strategy volatility** $(\sigma_{s,i})$ for each market. Here, a clear distinction needs to be made between *strategy volatility* $(\sigma_{s,i})$ and *market volatility* (either in aggregate or for an individual market). For each market (i), the strategy volatility $(\sigma_{s,i})$ is the volatility of the trend following strategy return on this particular market (i). The individual market volatility $(\sigma_{m,i})$ is volatility of a buy-and-hold return in the individual market (i). Market volatility (σ_m) is the total market volatility across all markets, often measured by a weighted average of individual market volatilities ($\overline{\sigma}_{m,i}$). Strategy volatility can be quite different from individual or aggregate market volatility. As explained in Chapter 3, this is due to the fact that trend following strategies determine position size based on each individual market's volatility and trend strength. It is also important to explain that the same distinction is also true for **strategy correlation** $(\rho_{s,i,j})$ and the standard individual and aggregate **market correlation**. Correlation effects are discussed more directly in the final section of this chapter. Figure 8.10 presents a schematic for the relationship between individual market and strategy volatility and portfolio volatility as a whole.

Trend following portfolio volatility (σ_p) is determined by an aggregation of strategy volatilities $(\sigma_{s,i})$ and correlations $(\rho_{s,i,j})$. Typically for an individual market, strategy volatility $(\sigma_{s,i})$ depends on market volatility $(\sigma_{m,i})$. In the case where position sizes are market volatility adjusted, this may no longer be the case. Later sections in

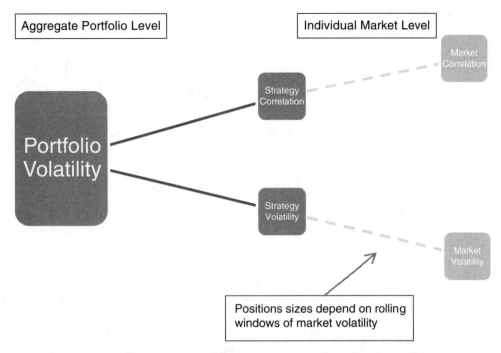

FIGURE 8.10 A schematic for strategy volatility for trend following and its relationship to market volatility and correlation.

this chapter discuss how the level of market volatility (σ_p) is not substantially correlated with individual strategy volatility empirically. Instead, changes in market volatility ($\Delta\sigma_{m,i}$ or $\Delta\sigma_m$) have the possibility of impacting strategy volatility.[8] Trend strength is also important for the total level of portfolio volatility. Empirically, the correlation between portfolio volatility (σ_p) and trend strength is statistically significant.

Returning to the basic tenets of standard portfolio theory, portfolio volatility is determined by both the correlation structure between the strategy returns and their corresponding volatilities. In addition to the schematic in Figure 8.10, portfolio variance (σ_p^2) can be written using the following formula:

$$\sigma_p^2 = \sum_i w_{s,i}^2 \sigma_{s,i}^2 + \sum_i \sum_{j \neq i} w_{s,i} w_{s,j} \sigma_{s,i} \sigma_{s,j} \rho_{s,i,j}$$

where ($\rho_{s,i,j}$) is the correlation coefficient between the strategy returns of markets (i) and (j), $\sigma_{s,i}$ is the strategy volatility for market (i), and ($w_{s,i}$) is the strategy weight

---

[8] This phenomenon is similar to classic delta hedging. A delta hedge portfolio may be delta neutral for small changes in the price but not remain gamma neutral. Position sizing in trend following is somewhat *vega neutral*, but for larger moves in volatility the strategy does not remain vega neutral. This concept relates to the importance of directional volatility discussed in Chapter 5.

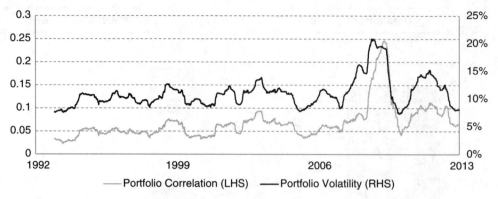

FIGURE 8.11 The relationship between the portfolio volatility (σ_p) and portfolio correlation (ρ_p).

for market (*i*). To discuss the core drivers and characteristics of portfolio volatility, a representative pure trend following system is used over a 20-year period.[9] As discussed earlier in this section, the total portfolio volatility (σ_p) is a function of strategy volatility and correlations. To simplify this analysis, two proxies are used to measure these quantities. First, the *average pairwise correlation* between strategy returns is used as a measure of **portfolio correlation** in aggregate ($\rho_p = \overline{\rho}_{s,i,j}$). Second, the *average strategy volatility* is used as a measure for portfolio volatility in aggregate ($\sigma_p = \sigma_s$). The following sections examine correlation and volatility at the portfolio level, the role of market volatility, the role of trend strength, and the concept of *good* volatility.

Correlation and Volatility at the Portfolio Level

Portfolio volatility (σ_p) measures how much a portfolio moves. Portfolio correlation gives insight into how interrelated strategies are. It is rather intuitive that portfolios moving and strategy interrelatedness would go hand in hand. Anecdotally, many practitioners suggest that correlation and volatility move together. As expected when examined empirically, the correlation between the rolling portfolio volatility (σ_p) and the rolling portfolio correlation ($\rho_p = \overline{\rho}_{s,i,j}$) is 0.87.[10] Figure 8.11 plots the relationship between the rolling portfolio correlation and portfolio volatility over time.

Lower portfolio correlation is associated with low portfolio volatility. While portfolio correlation is the result of numerous exogenous factors, empirically there also exists a strong relationship between portfolio correlation (ρ_p) and *market volatility*

---

[9] The representative pure trend following system consists of a diversified set of markets in equity indexes, commodities, fixed income, and FX sectors. Data is from 1993 to 2013.

[10] The rolling portfolio volatility and rolling portfolio correlation are both based on a 250-day rolling window.

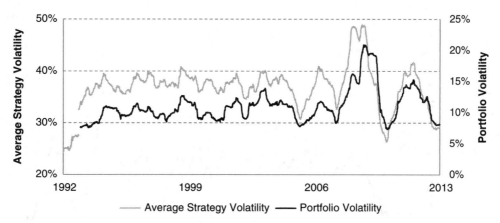

FIGURE 8.12 The relationship between the portfolio volatility (σ_p) and the average strategy volatility of all markets ($\overline{\sigma}_{s,i}$).

(σ_m). From 1993 to 2013, the correlation between rolling portfolio correlation (ρ_p) and rolling average of *aggregate market volatility* (σ_m) is 0.9. Despite this strong aggregate relationship, at the individual market level, market volatility ($\sigma_{m,i}$) is *not* highly correlated with the strategy volatility ($\sigma_{s,i}$).

Changes in Market Volatility

According to the general formula for portfolio volatility, the *strategy volatility* ($\sigma_{s,i}$) for each market is an important component of total portfolio volatility (σ_p). Figure 8.12 plots both portfolio volatility (σ_p) and *average strategy volatility* ($\overline{\sigma}_s$). The relationship is relatively strong. Empirically from 1993 to 2013, the correlation between the portfolio volatility and the *average strategy volatility* of all markets is 0.70.

As explained in the introduction to this section, at the individual market level, strategy volatility ($\sigma_{s,i}$) is different than market volatility ($\sigma_{m,i}$). Position sizing for each strategy is adjusted for past market volatility at the individual market level. As a result, at the individual market level, the correlation between the average strategy volatility ($\overline{\sigma}_{s,i}$) and average market volatility ($\overline{\sigma}_{m,i}$) is only 0.28. This number is still not close to zero. This indicates that there are still residual effects of individual market volatility that may be important.

At the individual market level, trend following systems uses past market volatility for position sizing. This is a *lagged* measure of volatility. When volatility is decreasing in a market, the lagged volatility measure under-allocates to the position and subsequently lowers the strategy volatility for that particular market. Likewise, when volatility is increasing in markets, the lagged volatility measure over-allocates to the position and subsequently inflates the strategy volatility for that particular market. Empirically from 1993 to 2013, the correlation between the average strategy

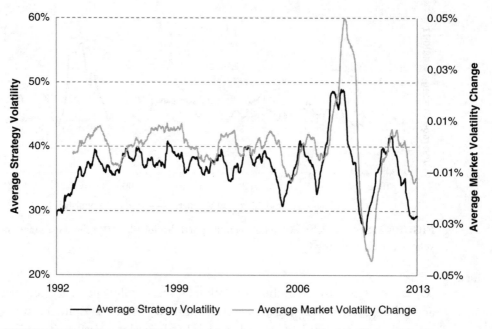

FIGURE 8.13 The relationship between the average strategy volatility ($\overline{\sigma}_{s,i}$) and the average market volatility change ($\overline{\Delta\sigma}_{m,i}$) from 1993 to 2013.

volatility ($\overline{\sigma}_{s,i}$) and the *average market volatility change* ($\overline{\Delta\sigma}_{m,i}$) is 0.68. Figure 8.13 plots the relationship between the average strategy volatility ($\overline{\sigma}_{s,i}$) and the *average market volatility change* ($\overline{\Delta\sigma}_{m,i}$) for this time period. This graph demonstrates how changes in market volatility relate to strategy volatility. Using lagged volatility measures to adjust positions roughly adjusts for market volatility but not perfectly.

If, for demonstrative purposes, the lookback window used for calculating position sizing is shortened, volatility updating would occur more frequently. This may reduce the mismatch from using a lagged measure of volatility for position sizing. Figure 8.14 displays the impact when the lookback window is shortened from 250 days to 20 days. Portfolio volatility appears to be more stable for the short lookback window. Empirically, the coefficients of variation for the rolling portfolio volatility are 0.24 for 250 days and 0.18 for 20 days.[11]

Trend Strength

Given the construction of trend following systems, trend strength is a significant factor for both strategy and portfolio volatility. As explained in Chapter 3, there are

---

[11] The coefficient of variation is the ratio of volatility to mean. This is the inverse of the signal-to-noise ratio. The lower the coefficient of variation the more similar two processes are.

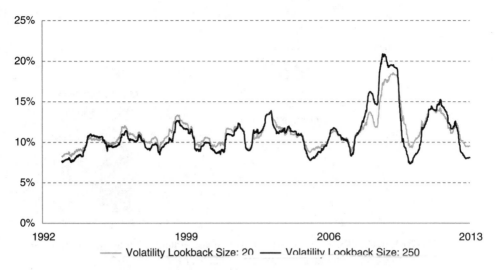

FIGURE 8.14 Portfolio volatility (σ_p) with both 20-day and 250-day lookback window sizes for adjusting position sizing based on past volatility.

many ways to measure trend strength as well as many ways to link trend strength to position sizing. Empirically and for simplicity, trend strength can be measured using the average absolute value of trend signals for all markets in a portfolio. As shown in Figure 8.15, the correlation between the strategy volatility (as measured by the rolling average strategy volatility) and trend strength (as measured by the rolling average

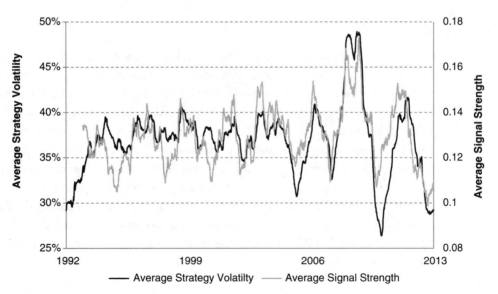

FIGURE 8.15 The relationship between strategy volatility (rolling average strategy volatility) and trend strength (rolling average signal strength).

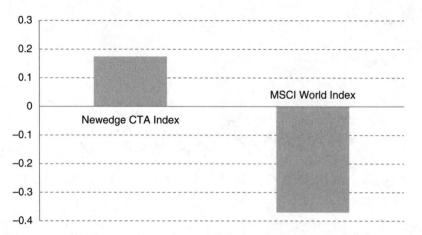

FIGURE 8.16 The correlation between two-year rolling portfolio volatility (σ_p) and skewness for the Newedge CTA Index and MSCI World Index from 2000 to 2013.
Data source: Bloomberg.

absolute value of trend signals for all markets) is rather high at 0.72. This result confirms the intuition that trend following strategies apply more risk when their conviction in the strength of trends is higher. The magnitude of signal strength also corresponds to a larger magnitude of PnL (either positive or negative). One might also expect that *serial* correlation of returns could result in higher volatility when trend strength is higher. Empirical data does not confirm this and signal strength and the serial correlation of returns are not significantly related.

Good Volatility

Positive skewness is one of the most desirable characteristics of a trend follow-ing return distribution. Returns with positive skewness have larger wins and rela-tively smaller losses avoiding some of the fat tail risks. As far as volatility goes, **good volatility** is the type of volatility where higher volatility is associated with a higher positive skewness. Empirically, the correlation between the rolling portfolio vola-tility (σ_p) and rolling skewness is rather positive. To put this into perspective, the correlation between rolling volatility and rolling skewness of equity index returns is quite negative. Given that most investors focus on equity markets, equity volatility is generally associated with negative skewness. Figure 8.16 demonstrates the different correlations between the two-year rolling volatility and skewness for the Newedge CTA Index and MSCI World Index. This figure demonstrates that there is some good volatility in CTA returns.[12]

---

[12] In contrast, equity volatility is *bad* volatility since it is associated with negative skewness.

■ Correlation and Diversification at the Portfolio Level

Correlation is a simple yet effective way for thinking about relationships between markets and diversification. Just as relationships change with time, correlation and diversification are also time varying. During certain time periods, intramarket correlation can increase substantially reducing the possibility to diversify across markets. It is also interesting to examine how newer markets and older, more established markets relate to each other across time. Figure 8.17 plots the correlations of 50 established markets (those that existed since 1992) and all markets (including an increasing set of markets over time). First, newer markets are less correlated than established markets. This effect can be seen by the fact that the overall market correlation is lower than that of only the established markets. Second, across time, correlations vary substantially. In particular, the financial crisis sticks out as a period of heightened correlation across all futures markets. Taking the analogy of correlation as a measure of relationships between asset classes, a period of financial crisis strengthened the relationships between all asset classes. Asset classes that typically behaved independently became highly related. Only several years post the credit crisis, these relationships, as measured by correlation, have weakened to precrisis levels. In general, high correlation often suggests low diversification. On the other hand, high correlation may also indicate large market divergence or trends. It is important to point out that the period with high correlation was one of the most profitable periods for trend following strategies. This point is important because correlation is a double-edged sword, it cuts both ways. If correlations are high,

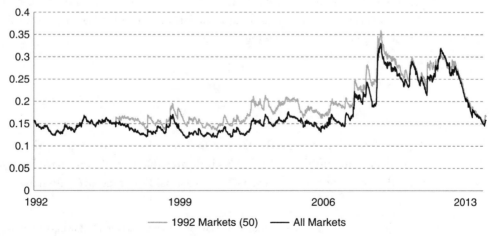

FIGURE 8.17 Average pair-wise market correlations for 50 established markets (those that exist from 1992 onward) compared with average pair-wise market correlations for all markets (including an increasing set of markets from 1992 onward). The sample period is 1992 to 2013.

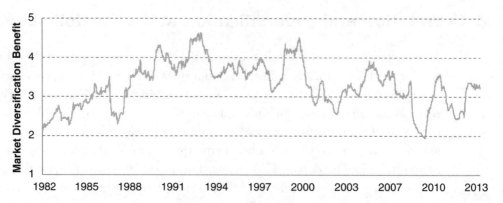

FIGURE 8.18 The market diversification benefit (MDB) up until the end of 2013 for a pure trend following system across a diversified universe of markets.

diversification may be lower across asset classes, but if this correlation comes from large trends across asset classes, this may be good for performance but possibly not for diversification.

Given the dynamic nature of trend following strategies and the complex relationship with correlation, simple market correlation is not the correct measure for diversification in trend following systems.[13] Put more simply, as opposed to a buy-and-hold strategy, periods of high correlation do not necessarily indicate low diversification in trend following portfolios. To evaluate the impact of correlation and diversification in a trend following portfolio, a straightforward metric, **market diversification benefit (MDB)**, can be defined. MDB is the ratio of average strategy volatility ($\overline{\sigma}_s$) for each individual market divided by total portfolio volatility (σ_p). When correlations between strategy returns for each market are higher, the MDB is lower and there is less diversification in a trend following portfolio. MDB can be written using the following simple ratio:

$$MDB = \frac{\overline{\sigma}_s}{\sigma_p}$$

Figure 8.18 plots the MDB starting in 1982. In recent periods, the MDB was steadily decreasing until late 2013. This indicates that correlations have been increasing for the strategy across markets.[14] A reasonable conjecture might be that both

---

[13] It can be confirmed that the correlation between the returns of a trend following system is generally the square of the correlation of the buy-and-hold returns.

[14] With an agricultural-only portfolio, a similar pattern can be observed for a much longer history since the 1960s.

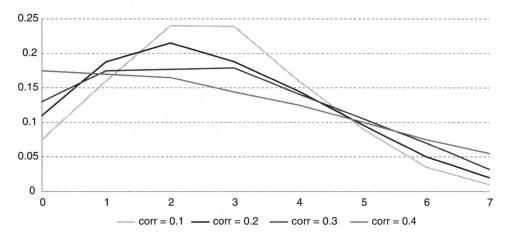

FIGURE 8.19 The theoretical probability of *n* sectors (*n* from 0 to 7) being negative simultaneously for various levels of correlation.

frequent government interventions and the commodity financialization contribute to this increase in correlation.[15]

The increased correlation might explain the recent performance of many CTA funds, which is negative across all seven sectors.[16] Theoretically, using a multidimensional normal distribution with various correlations between the sectors, a portfolio of seven sectors can be modeled. Figure 18.19 plots the theoretical probability of *n* sectors being negative simultaneously (for example, when *n* ranges from 0 to 7). The probability of all sectors being negative is noticeably higher when correlation is higher. On the other hand, the increase in the probability of all sectors being positive simultaneously is even larger. This phenomenon partially illustrates the fact that there is no conclusive, practical relationship between correlation and trend following performance. As shown in Figure 8.20, there is no apparent relationship between the rolling Sharpe ratio and rolling correlation between the sectors.

Correlation and Drawdown

Another characteristic of returns that may be linked to drawdown is portfolio correlation. To measure the portfolio correlation, market diversification benefit (MDB) can be used. As a reminder, MDB is the ratio between the average volatility of individual market returns in the portfolio and the volatility of the total portfolio

---

[15] The financialization of commodities documents increased correlation across commodities that are actively traded by commodity ETFs. The conjecture is that large capital flows increase correlation in previously less correlated commodity markets. Government intervention is discussed in more detail in Chapter 10.

[16] The seven sectors are equities, currencies, bonds, rates, agricultures, metals, and energies.

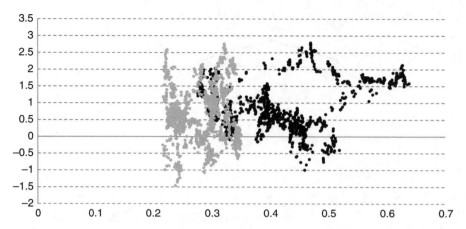

FIGURE 8.20 A scatter plot between the one-year rolling Sharpe ratio of a representative pure trend following portfolio (x-axis) and the one-year average rolling correlation between the sectors (y-axis). The light points are for the period from 2000 to 2007 and the dark points are for the period from 2008 to 2013.

return.[17] The higher the MDB is, the greater the diversification benefits are that the portfolio receives from the lower correlation between markets in the portfolio. During the past 10 years, the correlation between the MDB and drawdown was positive. However over a longer historical period, the correlation was quite negative. Figure 8.21 plots drawdown with the MDB of the representative pure trend following

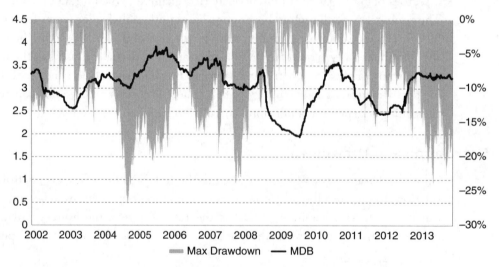

FIGURE 8.21 Market diversification benefit (MDB) and the drawdowns for a representative pure trend following program.

<hr/>

[17] Principal component analysis was also applied to ascertain the number of effective markets in the portfolio to analyze diversification benefits. The results were also similar and inconclusive.

system from 2001 to 2013. In late 2008 and early 2009, the MDB was at a historic low of 2.0, yet late 2008 was generally the strongest performance period for trend following. Conversely, 2005 was a period of relatively high market diversification, but the representative trend following system experienced a significant drawdown. Empirically, portfolio correlation as measured by the MDB seems to have an inconclusive relationship with drawdown.

■ Summary

This chapter reviews the concepts of drawdown, volatility, and correlation in trend following portfolios. There are several key methods for measuring and understanding drawdowns in trend following portfolios including expected maximum drawdown, drawdown length, and recovery periods. Trend following strategies are divergent risk-taking strategies that spread risk across many markets. Consistent with this approach, scenarios where many markets are losing represents periods when trend following strategies experience drawdowns. It is the number of successful markets and not the magnitude of successes that result in drawdowns. In addition to drawdowns, portfolio volatility and correlation were discussed in further detail. The following relationships are important for portfolio volatility.

- Portfolio volatility (σ_p) depends on the strategy volatility ($\sigma_{s,i}$) and strategy correlation ($\rho_{s,i}$) for each market.

- Strategy volatility ($\sigma_{s,i}$) is weakly related to market volatility ($\sigma_{m,i}$) (this is due to the position sizing approach, which adjusted using lagged volatility measures).

- Strategy volatility ($\sigma_{s,i}$) is related to *changes* in market volatility ($\Delta\sigma_m$).

- Portfolio volatility (σ_p) is also highly correlated with portfolio correlation (ρ_p).

- Portfolio volatility (σ_p) (as measured by average strategy volatility, $\overline{\sigma}_s$) and trend strength (as measured by average signal strength) are highly correlated.

- Portfolio volatility (σ_p) is positively related to skewness, which demonstrates how trend following strategies exhibit *good* volatility.

Lastly in this chapter, the discussion turns to the impact of correlation on trend following portfolios. Market diversification benefit (MDB) was defined as a measure for diversification in a portfolio. During recent times, the MDB measure has been decreasing. This suggests that recently the diversification in trend following portfolios has decreased. A closer examination of Sharpe ratios demonstrates that correlation has an inconclusive relationship with performance. This fact can be explained by the fact that correlation is both good and bad for trend following portfolios. This is further demonstrated by a closer look at drawdowns. The MDB measure does not directly link to drawdowns either.

■ Further Reading and References

Atiya, A., Y. Abu-Mostafa, and M. Magdon-Ismail. "On the Maximum Drawdown of a Brownian Motion." *Journal of Applied Probability* 41 (2004).

Belentepe, C. "Expected Drawdowns." Working paper, 2003.

Casati, A. "The Statistics of the Maximum Drawdown in Financial Time Series," Working paper, 2010.

Cukurova, S., and J. Marin. "On the Economics of Hedge Fund Drawdown Status: Performance, Insurance Selling and Darwinian Selection."Working paper, 2011.

Greyserman, A. "The Characteristics of Drawdown." ISAM white paper, 2012.

Greyserman, A. "Trend Following: Empirical Evidence of the Stationarity of Trendiness." ISAM white paper, February 2012.

Grossman, S., and Z. Zhou. "Optimal Investment Strategies for Controlling Drawdowns." *Mathematical Finance* 3, no. 3 (July 1993): 241–276.

Kaminski, K., and A. Mende. "Crisis Alpha and Risk in Alternative Investment Strategies." CME Group working paper, 2011.

Strub, I. "Trading Sizing Techniques for Drawdown and Tail Risk Control." Working paper, 2012.

Tang, K., and W. Xiong. "Index Investment and Financialization of Commodities." *Financial Analysts Journal* 68, no. 6 (2012).

CHAPTER 9

The Hidden and Unhidden Risks of Trend Following

Trend following strategies require dynamic allocation across many different asset classes. The dynamic nature of these strategies creates new challenges for traditional methods for dealing with risk. When it comes to risk in trend following, many traditional tools may mislead investors, sometimes providing a false sense of security, whereas other times overestimating the overall riskiness of a trend following strategy. In this chapter, four main sources of risk in alternative investments are discussed. These four include price risk, credit risk, liquidity risk, and leverage risk. Trend following is compared with other dynamic alternative investment strategies to demonstrate how price risk and leverage risk are the two key risks to evaluate in trend following. Following the discussion of core risk exposures, the Sharpe ratio and hidden risks in the Sharpe ratio are discussed. Following the discussion of the Sharpe ratio, the chapter turns to dynamic leverage and margin to equity. This discussion demonstrates how dynamic leverage can be used to inflate Sharpe ratios.

■ Directional and Nondirectional Strategies: A Review

Alternative investment strategies, of which futures-based trend following is one particular strategy, represent a wide range of dynamic investment approaches. These strategies differ from traditional investment strategies that focus on a passive, as opposed to an active, investment approach. The flexibility and dynamic nature of these strategies allows them to have drastically different return and risk profiles. It is this particular characteristic of alternative investments that has made them attractive to investors. In general, alternative investment strategies are divided into **directional** and **nondirectional strategies**. Directional strategies take long or short positions in financial securities in hopes to profit from directional moves. Common examples of these include managed futures (CTAs), equity long bias, equity short bias, and global macro, which are generally classified as directional strategies. Nondirectional strategies focus on taking relative value positions where the positions are both long and short (often) in the same asset class at the same time. Convertible arbitrage, fixed income arbitrage, merger arbitrage, equity long/short, and several others are often classified as nondirectional strategies. Due to investment restrictions, all traditional investment strategies including most mutual funds are long-only directional strategies.

Chapter 5 introduces the concept of convergent and divergent risk-taking strategies. Because nondirectional strategies rely on the assumption that values converge for either statistical or fundamental reasons, they are generally convergent risk-taking strategies. Directional strategies can be either divergent or convergent depending on how the direction is determined. If the direction is determined by fundamental analysis, such as many long-equity strategies, the strategy is a convergent risk-taking strategy. The positions do not converge but the risk-taking view of the strategy is founded on the belief that fundamental value is reflected in prices over the long run. On average, during normal market conditions this view works; during periods when there is a market crisis, this "convergent" approach is put to the test as fundamentals cease to drive prices temporarily. Convergent risk-taking strategies, as a class, tend to hold hidden risks, which come out during periods of stress.

■ Defining Hidden and Unhidden Risks

Dynamic investment strategies contain varying types of risks: both hidden and unhidden, measureable and difficult to measure. Risks in alternative investment strategies can be divided into four key groups: **price risk**, credit risk, liquidity risk, and **leverage risk**. As opposed to alternatives, traditional investments such as mutual funds often contain mostly price risk. For example, mutual fund performance depends mostly on the asset classes they invest in, where alternative strategies performance depends on their dynamic risk-taking profile. *Hidden risks are risks that cannot be detected by traditional performance measures such as the Sharpe ratio*. Risks that are difficult to measure are often also hidden because it may be difficult to perform appropriate risk adjustments.

Price risk and leverage risk should be unhidden as they should be measurable. Despite this fact, leverage risk can become hidden if improper risk measurement techniques are applied. This issue is investigated later in this chapter when dynamic

FIGURE 9.1 The four types of risk in alternative investments.

leveraging is discussed. Since both credit events and liquidity events often happen unexpectedly and in the form of shocks, credit risk and liquidity risk are often difficult risks to properly measure and forecast, creating the potential to embed hidden risks in performance measurement. In practice, fundamental models for pricing may be based on sound principles but credit and liquidity models have far less predictive and explanatory power. This highlights the point that credit and liquidity depend on the behavior of others, and human behavior is difficult to measure and predict. Figure 9.1 presents the four core risks in alternative investments from unhidden (price risk) to hidden. Trend following strategies tend to take on only price and leverage risk.[1] Convergent risk-taking strategies (especially those that are nondirectional) tend to hold hidden risks.

Due to the low counterparty risks and liquid nature of futures markets, trend following strategies maintain mostly price risk and leverage risk. To further explain this point, in the following sections, each of these four main types of investment risks is discussed. A simple comparison for each type of risk provides classification of the level of these types of risks in trend following in comparison with other dynamic investment strategies. For three of these risks (price risk, credit risk, and liquidity risk), crisis alpha and proxies for these risks are plotted for comparison. Before discussing the risks in alternative investment strategies, a crisis alpha decomposition can be applied to a set of dynamic risk-taking strategies. Figure 9.2 plots the crisis

---

[1] One caveat—dynamic investment strategies are typically a mix of convergent and divergent risk taking. Pure trend following is both a directional strategy and a divergent strategy. It avoids hidden risks common in convergent strategies. As a counterexample, a long volatility strategy that buys out-of-the-money OTC options applies divergent risk taking by limiting losses to the purchase of the option and riding the option payout in extreme events. Despite this, these long volatility strategies maintain and must manage some credit/via counterparty risk and liquidity risk.

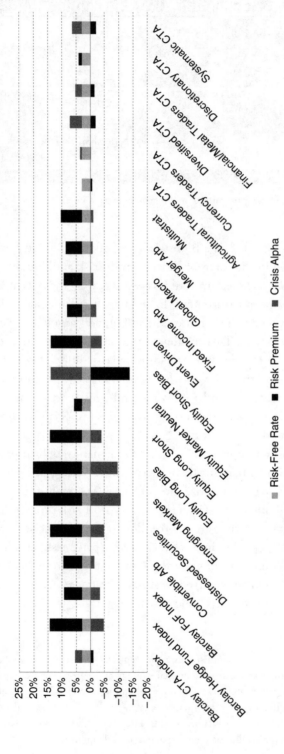

FIGURE 9.2 Crisis alpha decomposition for various alternative investment strategies from 1996 to 2013.

Source: BarclayHedge, RPM.

alpha decomposition for a set of alternative investment strategies similar to Chapter 4. Most strategies have hidden risks that often surface during crisis periods. As a result, for each type of risk in this section, crisis alpha can be used to classify if hidden risks are present in an alternative investment strategy.[2]

Price Risk

Price risk, often called *market risk*, is defined as the risk that the price of a security or portfolio will move in an unfavorable direction in the future. In practice, price risk is often proxied by volatility and it is a risk that is well understood in traditional investments. Price risk will be most relevant for directional strategies, which focus on long or short exposures. Strategies that are exposed primarily to price risk will behave similar to security markets over time and exhibit mean reversion in their return properties, similar to security markets over the long run. Price risk is a concept, which, although it can vary over time, is pervasive in all investments and is observable over time in performance (i.e., it is not a hidden risk). In Figure 9.3, the level of mean reversion in several alternative investment strategies is plotted (inverted) versus crisis alpha.

It is important to note that the S&P 500 Index is to the left in Figure 9.3. The level of mean reversion in this index represents mean reversion for a buy-and-hold strategy in equities. It is interesting to note that equity long bias is on the direct opposite side of this ranking. This is due the fact that equity long bias strategies do not buy-and-hold, they dynamically allocate risk over time. This simple graph can also demonstrate that equity long bias is possibly more convergent than a traditional buy-and-hold strategy in equities. Many CTA strategies are to the left, indicating price risk, and nondirectional strategies are in the middle or to the right.

Purely directional divergent risk-taking strategies, such as trend following, take on positions similar to the underlying prices. This connection should result in higher mean reversion in their returns over longer horizons if prices mean revert over time (for example, the S&P 500 in Figure 9.3). Directional and divergent risk-taking strategies seem to be more likely to obtain crisis alpha. Crisis alpha is much more negative for convergent risk-taking strategies and nondirectional strategies in aggregate.

Credit Risk

Credit risk is the risk associated with a counterparty not being able to repay their obligation or fulfill their side of a contract or position. Credit risk is often measured using the spread between low risk investments and their corresponding less credit

THE HIDDEN AND UNHIDDEN RISKS OF TREND FOLLOWING

---

[2] The discussion in this section is directly related to Kaminski and Mende (2011). Negative crisis alpha indicates losses during crisis as opposed to gains. *Source:* RPM and the CME Group.

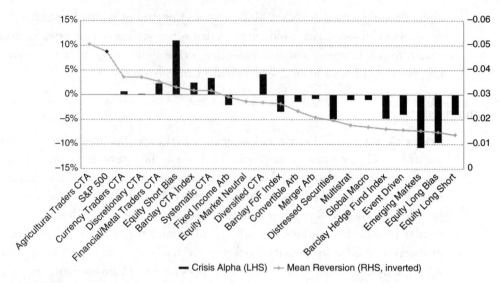

FIGURE 9.3 Crisis alpha and price risk (monthly mean reversion) for various alternative investment strategies from 1996 to 2013.
Source: BarclayHedge, RPM.

worthy counterparties, for example, the TED spread, which is the spread between LIBOR and three-month Treasury bill. Nondirectional strategies buy undervalued, cheaper investments and sell expensive, overvalued investments according to market prices. This mispricing, in addition to a lack of liquidity, can also be due to differences in credit and counterparty risk between these two relative assets. By buying the higher yielding investment and selling the lower yielding investment, a nondirectional strategy can also be described as providing credit to the market and earning a credit premium. A simple example of a *credit provider strategy* would be a long position in corporate bonds coupled with short positions in lower risk government debt. Strategies that provide credit in markets will earn credit premiums over time and they will suffer in situations when credit becomes an issue. Credit issues generally come in shocks and most of these shocks occur during moments of market stress. In Figure 9.4, as a proxy for credit risk, the level of correlation with the TED spread for several alternative investment strategies, is plotted (inverted) versus crisis alpha. Nondirectional strategies with high correlation to credit spreads perform worse during market crisis and directional strategies and those with lower correlation with credit spreads perform better during crisis periods.

Liquidity Risk

Liquidity risk stems from a lack of marketability or that an investment cannot be bought or sold quickly enough to prevent or minimize a loss. Nondirectional alternative investment strategies, often called *relative value strategies*, focus on buying

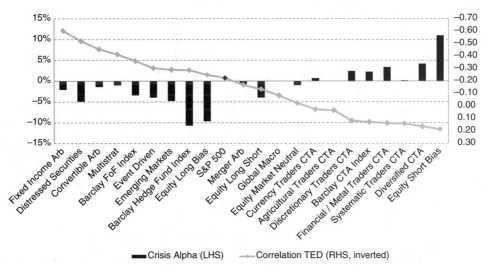

■ Crisis Alpha (LHS)   — Correlation TED (RHS, inverted)

FIGURE 9.4 Crisis alpha and credit risk (correlation with the TED spread) for various alternative investment strategies from 1996 to 2013.
Source: BarclayHedge, RPM.

cheaper assets that seem to be undervalued according to market prices and selling expensive assets that may be overvalued according to market prices. In this interpretation, these nondirectional market strategies are providing liquidity to the market by buying the assets investors do not value as highly and selling the assets investors seem to want to buy. Nondirectional strategies or relative value strategies become similar to a classic market maker who earns the bid-ask spread in a security. In the case of these alternative investment strategies, the relative spread between these two investments is its bid-ask spread. In this sense a hedge fund strategy is analogous to a *liquidity provider*.[3] If nondirectional strategies earn spreads similar to a market maker, their performance will also be similar. Market makers earn small seemingly "arbitrage-like" opportunities over time but the risk they carry comes when liquidity disappears as prices move drastically in one direction. Equity market crisis represents one of the few times when the majority of investors are forced and/or driven into action. This is one of the times when liquidity providers, or market makers, can get caught holding the wrong side of a highly levered trade resulting in large potential losses. A market making strategy will have high serial autocorrelation in returns over time since liquidity providers earn a rather positive arbitrage-like spread. Given this fact, serial autocorrelation in returns can be a good proxy for liquidity risk in an investment. In Figure 9.5, the level of serial autocorrelation in returns for several

THE HIDDEN AND UNHIDDEN RISKS OF TREND FOLLOWING

---

[3] Khandani and Lo (2010) discuss the existence of an illiquidity premium. The use of autocorrelation as a proxy for liquidity risk is also discussed in Getmansky, Lo, and Makarov (2004) in regard to systemic risk in hedge funds.

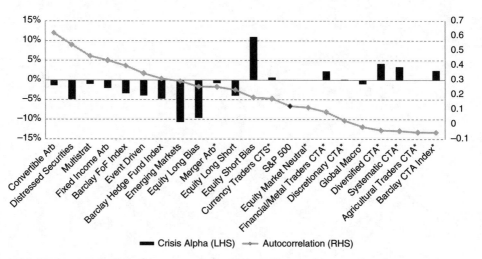

FIGURE 9.5 Crisis alpha and liquidity risk (serial autocorrelation) for various alternative investment strategies from 1996 to 2013. The (*) indicates that the estimate is statistically significant from zero. *Source:* BarclayHedge, RPM.

alternative investment strategies is plotted versus crisis alpha. Nondirectional strategies (or those strategies with higher serial autocorrelation) seem to carry more liquidity risk and the associated poor performance during crisis. Those strategies with insignificant serial autocorrelation seem to carry less liquidity risk. As a result, they are less impacted by a liquidity crisis.

Leverage Risk

Leverage risk is defined as taking exposure based on borrowed funds. One tricky thing with leverage is that it can be achieved by either borrowing funds directly or using derivatives that have implicit leverage. For example, in the world of trend following, leverage in futures contracts comes from the fact that the amount invested (as based on the margin to equity) is often many times less than the outstanding notional amount of the contract. For example, if there is $10 in margin and the contract has a notional value of $100 the contract is leveraged 10:1 because there is 9 times more borrowed money than money in equity. Leverage allows an investor to get more "bang for the buck." For a $100 notional value, a 10 percent increase to $110 for a position with only $10 in equity has a 100 percent return, which is 10 times the actual return. Leverage is a double-edged sword because if the price goes down by 10 percent the loss is also magnified resulting in a loss of 100 percent. Because options are essentially dynamically leveraged positions in underlying securities, another simple example of implicit leverage in derivatives is an option-selling strategy. In practice, the margin to equity ratio is a reasonable proxy for the level of leverage being used by a manager. Unfortunately, for less transparent strategies, this measure is not always available, especially for strategies with less liquid exposures. When returns are very positive, the key issue with leverage is in determining when results are due to high leverage (possibly excessive betting with very high margin to equity) or to a number of properly risk-controlled trades that went in the right direction.

■ The Myths and Mystique of the Sharpe Ratio

When it comes to performance measurement, there is no measure more commonly used than the Sharpe ratio (Sharpe 1994). The Sharpe ratio defines the risk-adjusted return in excess of the risk-free rate. The core assumption of the Sharpe ratio is risk adjustment based price volatility (as a proxy of price risk). *Sharpe ratios are measured with price risk in the denominator.* For dynamic strategies containing credit risk, liquidity risk, and leverage risk, the Sharpe ratio may underestimate hidden risks inflating performance in the short term.

Because price risk is mean reverting over the long run, Sharpe ratios should also decrease over the long run if price risk sufficiently accounts for the total risk in a strategy. This means that when price risk accounts for risk, consistent with mean reversion, short-term Sharpe ratios should be lower than long-term. In specific terms, annual Sharpe ratios should be higher than monthly Sharpe ratios. Figure 9.6 plots the monthly, quarterly, and yearly Sharpe ratios for trend following (a strategy with high levels of price risk), using the DJCS Managed Futures Index as a proxy, and hedge fund strategies, using the DJCS Hedge Fund Index. From this graph, it is clear that especially in the short term, Sharpe ratios for hedge fund strategies are

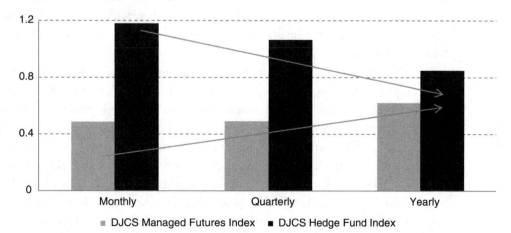

FIGURE 9.6 Sharpe ratios for Dow Jones Credit Suisse Managed Futures Index and Dow Jones Credit Suisse Hedge Fund Index across different sampling frequencies.
Data source: Bloomberg.

exposed to risks outside of price risk. Sharpe ratios are inflated in shorter horizons due to hidden risks. Sharpe ratios for trend following strategies are higher for longer horizons indicating that there are considerably less hidden risks in trend following.

Low Sharpe Ratios for Trend Following Are Prudent Performance Measures

Given the review of the four core risks in alternative investments, futures-based trend following strategies mostly contain price risk and even possibly leverage risk. This conclusion is consistent with intuition. As discussed in Chapter 2, futures strategies are highly liquid, efficient, low counterparty risk investments with minimal exposure to counterparty and liquidity risks. As a result, Sharpe ratios for trend following strategies prudently explain the amount of risk-adjusted return that is obtainable over time. In contrast, other alternative strategies that maintain other risks outside of price risk will have inflated Sharpe ratios that overstate performance in the short term. Because leverage risk depends on how a trend following system accelerates or decelerates positions, leverage risk is discussed in greater detail in the next few sections on dynamic leveraging.

■ Unraveling Hidden Risks of Dynamic Leveraging

Active derivatives-based trading strategies implicitly use leverage dynamically over time. Their use of leverage is often overlooked and misleading to investors. As a result, in this section, implicit leverage is explained. This helps to clarify how failing to properly evaluate for leverage may potentially glorify excessive risk taking. In simpler terms, it may be hard to distinguish the lucky big bettors from the calculated risk takers. This issue is important and unfortunately often overlooked by investors. A closer look at dynamic leveraging can help differentiate one trend following system from another.

For a futures manager, the simplest measure for the use of leverage is the margin to equity ratio. For example, many futures managers made exemplary returns in months like October 2008. A natural first question to ask: Is this due to luck or skill? If the return were due to luck, one would expect margin to equity ratios to be very high. This would mean that a manager took big bets (large notional positions) and they happened to pay off. For the month of October 2008, the opposite is actually true. Most trend followers were trading at margin to equity ratios well below their historical average. This means that their returns were skilled risk taking. In other words, if they had been taking more risks their returns would have been even larger than they already were. To put this into perspective, the October 2008 return for trend following was the highest from 2003 to 2013 while the margin-to-equity ratio was not even close to the highest. Given this example, it is clear that a closer look at how dynamic leveraging works and how it affects performance may help explain how to measure it, how to check for it, and how to evaluate when a manager is applying dynamic leveraging.

Defining Dynamic Leveraging

Dynamic leveraging is defined as a situation where the amount of leverage depends on the past profits and losses (PnL) of the portfolio. In simple terms, a dynamically leveraged portfolio, which increases (or decreases) its bet size when there are lots of past losers (or past winners), engages in a dynamic leverage strategy. Dynamic leveraging is similar to "doubling down" in poker. Dynamic leveraging is a convergent approach. Divergent strategies should cut their losses to manage risk. When divergent risk takers engage in dynamic leveraging, they are changing their approach to be convergent risk taking. Convergent strategies have a conviction regarding the structure of risks; when they are faced with a loss they *will not* cut the loss. In extreme cases, like dynamic leveraging, the approach will increase exposure to losing positions (a method of doubling down with position sizing).

Returning to the definition of dynamic leveraging, it is a situation where the amount of leverage depends on the past profits and losses (PnL) of the portfolio. For the example of options, the change in delta depends on the PnL of the option. Option selling is a simple type of dynamic leveraging. The delta (or the amount of shares of the underlying that are purchased using borrowed money) depends on the path of the underlying and the option's underlying PnL. Take the example of an investor who sold a call option and the price goes up. The PnL for the option seller is a loss but the delta of the call option has increased. The option seller's leverage also increases in tandem. For option sellers, leverage increases with losses and decreases with gains (or when the PnL is positive).[4]

The payoff characteristics and dynamic leverage use of option selling strategies can allow them to "get really lucky" in the short term, but the possibility that something can go devastatingly wrong in the longer term is nonnegligible. Put simply, dynamic leveraging, such as option selling, can be used to inflate performance in the short term. Dynamic leveraging is directly at odds with the divergent risk-taking approach.

Option Selling Strategies and Dynamic Leveraging

To compare the effects of dynamic leverage, a strategy such as option selling can be added to trend following. In this case, the performance for a representative pure

---

[4] Option selling is a convergent risk-taking strategy. The strategy takes small profits and has unbounded exposure on the downside similar to doubling down betting schemes. This type of convergent risk taking clearly adds hidden risks to Sharpe ratios.

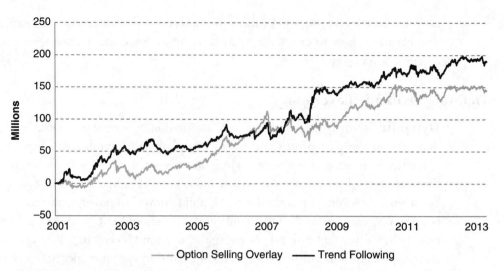

FIGURE 9.7 Cumulative performance for a representative crossover trend following system with and without an option selling overlay. Both time series are scaled to the same monthly risk of 5 percent. The sample period is from 2001 to 2013.

trend following system, both with and without an option selling overlay, can be compared both long and short term.[5] Position size is determined by the standard equal dollar risk approach from Chapter 3. The sample period for this analysis is from 2001 to 2013.

Option selling can be used as an overlay for trend following signals. When a trend following signal is positive (negative), the trend following system enters a short position in a put (call) option.[6] The overlay forces the trend following strategy to systematically sell call and put options instead of taking linear futures positions. In the option-selling case, position size is determined by the option's lambda and the volatility for each of the underlying markets. For simplicity in this example, option prices are calculated using the Black-Scholes formula. Figure 9.7 presents the performance of the crossover trend following system with and without the option selling overlay (both series are scaled to the same risk). During the 12-year sample

---

[5] A moving average crossover representative trend following system is used for this analysis. This system trades across a diversified universe of markets: commodity, fixed income, stock index, and FX sectors. In these experiments, shorter lookback window sizes range from 10 to 30 days and longer lookback window sizes range between 60 and 250 days.

[6] For simplicity, the trend following system enters an at-the-money option. Despite this assumption, the conclusions of this analysis are general and do not depend on the specific choices of parameters.

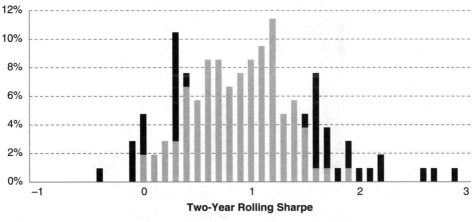

FIGURE 9.8 Histograms for two-year rolling Sharpe ratios for a trend following system with and without an option selling overlay. The sample period is from 2001 to 2013.

period, the Sharpe ratio for the trend following system is 0.92 while the Sharpe ratio for the trend following system with the option selling overlay is 0.82.

Due to the specific payoff characteristic of option selling and its use of implicit dynamic leveraging, there exists a significant probability for an option selling strategy to achieve seemingly superior performance for shorter periods such as less than two years. Figure 9.8 plots the histograms for the two-year rolling Sharpe ratio of the trend following system with and without the option selling overlay. In this histogram, the option selling overlay allows the trend following system the possibility of achieving a higher Sharpe ratio in excess of 1.5 over a two-year period. Over longer periods of time, the Sharpe ratio of the system with option selling overlay becomes lower than the trend following system. In Figure 9.9, the probability of achieving a rolling Sharpe ratio higher than 1.5 is plotted versus the number of years in the rolling window for calculating the Sharpe ratio. For the one-year rolling Sharpe ratio, the option selling overlay system has a 38 percent chance to be above 1.5 compared with a probability of only 18 percent without the overlay. When the Sharpe ratio is examined over four years, neither of the approaches are able to achieve a Sharpe ratio above 1.5.

Higher Sharpe ratios do not go unnoticed in higher order properties of returns. Higher short-term Sharpe ratios come at the cost of larger drawdowns and negative skewness. Without the overlay, the maximum drawdown is 26 percent; with the overlay, the maximum drawdown is 45 percent.[7] Without the option selling overlay,

---

[7] Both are scaled to the same monthly risk of 5 percent.

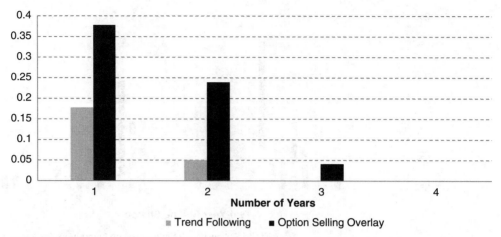

FIGURE 9.9 The probability of achieving a rolling Sharpe ratio higher than 1.5 versus the number of years for calculating the Sharpe ratio. The sample period is from 2001 to 2013.

the skewness is 0.51; with the overlay, the skewness becomes −0.34. Intuitively connecting to the convergent divergent discussion in Chapter 5, option selling is a convergent strategy; adding it to trend following adds hidden risks. Figure 9.10 presents histograms for another similar trend following system with and without an option selling overlay.

Another less obvious consequence of dynamic leveraging is the reduction of crisis alpha. Using a VIX-based criteria[8] to define crisis periods, Figure 9.11 plots the S&P

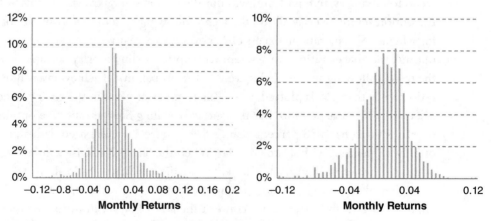

FIGURE 9.10 Histograms for monthly returns of the representative trend following system with (right panel) and without an option selling overlay (left panel) from 2001 to 2013.

---

[8] A month is defined to be a crisis period when the percentage change in the VIX is greater than 20 percent. This approach is consistent with several academic papers on this topic: see Vayanos (2004) and Brunnermeier and Pedersen (2009).

500 Index where the crisis periods are highlighted by the shaded bars. In this figure, 21 out of 129 months are defined as a crisis period. During the sample period from 2001 to 2013, Figure 9.12 presents the total return and crisis alpha for the trend following system with and without an option selling overlay. Based on the VIX definition of crisis, trend following returns 13 percent and delivers 5 percent crisis alpha. On the other hand, with the option-selling overlay the total return is 11.5 percent with a slightly negative crisis alpha at minus 0.5 percent. This simple comparison demonstrates how adding a convergent option-selling strategy overlay reduces crisis alpha for trend following. In summary, dynamic leveraging such as option selling gives access to higher short-term Sharpe ratios at the cost of deeper drawdowns, negative skewness, and loss of crisis alpha.

Martingale Betting and Dynamic Leveraging

Martingale betting is another type of explicit dynamic leveraging. Martingale betting works in the following way: when faced with a loss, the long position is increased until the first day of positive PnL. Bets are increased when they are losing (another form of doubling down). If Martingale betting is applied to a trend following system, the number of double-downs days must be limited to remain

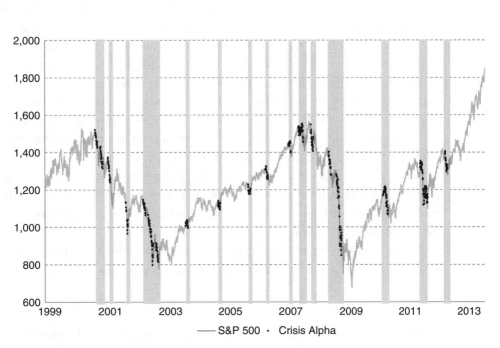

FIGURE 9.11 The S&P 500 Index with VIX-based crisis periods highlighted by the shaded bars.

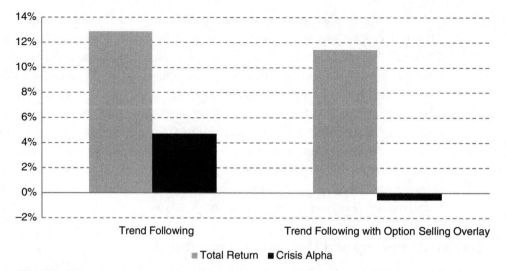

FIGURE 9.12 Total return and crisis alpha for trend following with and without an option selling overlay from 2001 to 2013.

tractable. In this case, the betting restarts when the number of consecutive days of loss reaches a predetermined number N or when the day's PnL is positive. The number N puts a limit on the amount of doubling down that can occur. In a simple example, N is set to be a maximum of five days. This means that the futures manager can double-down (increase the exposure of a losing position) for at most five days. Figure 9.13 plots the cumulative performance of a representative trend following system with and without Martingale betting. Both time series are scaled to the same risk. At first glance, a Martingale betting scheme appears to improve the performance of trend following in this sample period. During the sample period of just over 10 years, the Sharpe ratio for the trend following system is 0.92 and the Omega ratio is 0.65.[9] For the trend following system with a Martingale betting scheme, the Sharpe ratio is 1.09 and the Omega ratio is 1.20. This example creates a simple puzzle: How can a strategy with doubling down outperform a simple trend following system in terms of Sharpe ratio and Omega ratio? The answer is that these traditional measures ignore risks outside of price risk, not properly accounting for the use of dynamic leverage.

In this section, dynamic leveraging is introduced with two simple approaches. First, option selling overlay strategies is a simple approach to add dynamic leveraging

---

[9] A threshold of 2 percent is used for the Omega ratio. The Omega ratio is discussed in the appendix of Chapter 7.

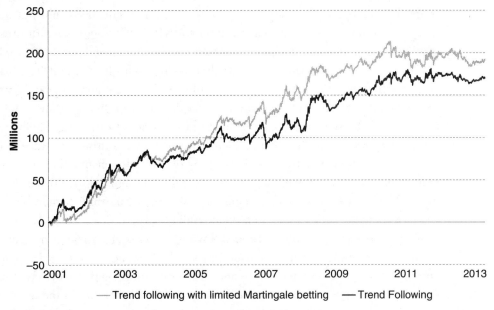

FIGURE 9.13 The historical performance for a representative trend following system and a trend following system with dynamic leveraging (via limited Martingale betting) from 2001 to 2013.

to trend following. This allows for access to higher Sharpe ratios in the short term at the expense of larger drawdowns, negative skewness, and the reduction of crisis alpha. Second, limited Martingale betting can be applied to trend following systems. In this case, doubling down increased the Sharpe ratio over the longer run, suggesting that aggressive dynamic leverage can be difficult to measure in high Sharpe ratios. Given that leverage risk may be hidden in traditional risk measures, the next logical step is to take a closer look at if or when dynamic leveraging occurs in trend following systems and how to measure it. Chapter 14 revisits dynamic leveraging and demonstrates how spectral analysis can help to filter out dynamic leveraging effects from Sharpe ratios. The next section discusses margin to equity and how it affects the portfolio volatility in trend following systems.

A Closer Look at Margin to Equity

The margin to equity ratio is a measure of the amount of traded capital that is being held as margin at any particular time. For example, if 25 percent of a fund's capital was held in margin accounts for trading, the margin to equity ratio is 25 percent. A conservative trader may have a margin to equity ratio around 15 percent and an aggressive trader may be at 40 percent margin to equity. Because most contracts require roughly 5 to 10 percent in margin, each dollar in a margin account represents a leveraged exposure in the underlying contract. If a conservative futures trader has \$100 and the margin requirement is 5 percent, he would put \$5 into a margin account and take on one contract for \$100. If an aggressive futures trader wanted to use more leverage, he could take on 5 contracts and put in \$25 giving him an exposure of \$500 notional, essentially levering up his investment. The margin to equity of the aggressive futures trader would be 25 percent and his gearing would be 4:1. All contracts vary in the amount of margin required. In aggregate, total margin to equity can be seen as a rough estimate of the amount of leverage being used. As futures traders change the size of their positions, add contracts, reduce contracts, and dynamically change their positions they dynamically change their leverage. The main question is: Do they use aggressive, so-called doubling down, dynamic leveraging such as in option selling strategies and Martingale betting? If there is excessive use of leverage, it may become a hidden risk in Sharpe ratios.

Margin to equity ratios in trend following systems are a rough measure of the amount of leverage that a system employs.[10] If dynamic leveraging is applied, the amount of leverage will accelerate and decelerate more aggressively creating more volatility in margin to equity. As a result, the level of variability in the use of margin to equity can be examined to determine if dynamic leveraging is being applied. In more practical terms, the coefficient of variation for the daily margin to equity can be examined. The **coefficient of variation** for daily margin to equity measures the normalized dispersion of margin to equity. For the same representative trend following system from earlier in this chapter, the coefficient of variation for the daily margin to equity ratio is 0.3. In the case of limited Martingale betting, the coefficient of variation for the daily margin to equity is 0.5. Although this type of dynamic leverage does not show up in the Sharpe ratio, the use of dynamic leveraging such as in Martingale betting does create higher variability in margin to equity ratios (or a higher coefficient of variation).

The correlation between past levels of leverage (margin to equity) and the magnitude of future returns (both positive and negative) can also demonstrate the use of dynamic leveraging.[11] If the correlation is high, past levels of high leverage resulted in the larger magnitude in returns (both positive and negative). This suggests that dynamic leveraging is being applied. Figure 9.14 presents scatter plots for daily positive and negative returns (absolute value) compared with lagged margin to equity for the representative trend following system. The correlation between lagged leverage and the magnitude of daily returns is relatively weak. More specifically,

---

[10] For the calculations in this section, in order to estimate margin a multiplier of 10 percent is applied to the gross exposure of markets in commodities, stock indices, and FX. A multiplier of 1 percent is applied to the gross exposure of fixed income to estimate margin.

[11] The margin to equity ratio is lagged by one day. This is because the return on day T depends on the positions at day T-1.

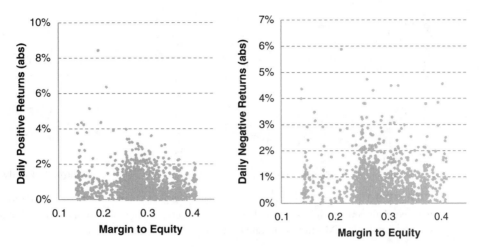

FIGURE 9.14 Scatter plots for lagged margin to equity and the absolute value of negative daily returns (left panel) and positive daily returns (right panel) for the representative trend following system from 2001 to 2013.

the correlation between the absolute value of daily negative returns and the lagged margin to equity is close to 0, and the correlation between the daily positive returns and the lagged margin to equity is even negative at −0.11. This suggests that trend following strategies do not engage in doubling down or the path dependent application of leverage such as option selling or Martingale betting. Higher returns for trend following most likely come from riding the price trend rather than the application of concentrated risks or dynamic leveraging.[12] This point can be illustrated further with a specific example. In October 2008, the return for the representative trend following system was its highest at 17.5 percent and the average margin to equity ratio for the same month was 16 percent, which is lower than the average for all months in the whole sample period. As a counterexample, in April 2009, the return of the trend following system was −5.5 percent and the average margin to equity ratio for the same month was also 16 percent.[13]

For comparison purposes, dynamic leveraging can be added to a trend following system. In this case, the correlation between the absolute value of daily negative returns and the lagged margin to equity ratio goes from close to zero to 0.37, and the correlation between positive returns and the lagged margin to equity ratio goes from −0.11 to 0.46. Figure 9.15 shows scatter plots for the negative daily returns (absolute value) and positive returns with lagged margin to equity ratios. For the

---

[12] In Chapter 8, this concept was discussed for the case of drawdowns. Trend following drawdowns are caused by lots of small losses as opposed to large concentrated bets.

[13] This effect can be called *asymmetric leverage*.

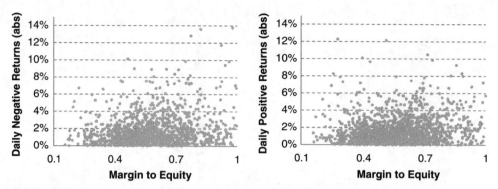

FIGURE 9.15 Scatter plots between the lagged margin to equity and the absolute value of negative daily returns (left panel) and positive daily returns (right panel) of the trend following system with limited Martingale betting from June 2001 to February 2012.

case of limited Martingale betting, the magnitude of returns is often derived from higher leverage.

In the case of dynamic leveraging, margin to equity ratios experience spikes in their volatility. This indicates that there may be hidden leverage risk. Figure 9.16 shows a comparison of the daily 22-day rolling volatility for the representative trend following system with and without a Martingale betting scheme. When both systems' monthly risks are scaled to 5 percent, their volatility behaves strikingly different across time. For the Martingale betting scheme, on a daily basis, volatility exhibits a cyclical pattern. The Sharpe ratio calculated by daily returns for Martingale betting

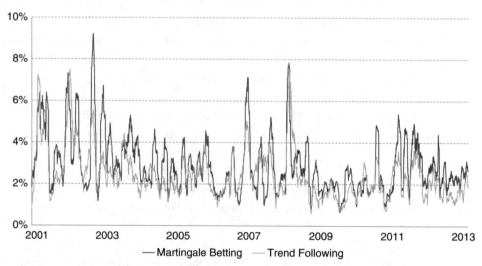

FIGURE 9.16 22-day rolling volatility for the representative trend following system and with Martingale betting.

should be expected to be quite different from the typical Sharpe ratio based on monthly returns. The aggregation of daily returns conceals the highly volatile daily path in PnL.[14] When daily data is used, the Sharpe ratio is reduced by roughly 20 percent. For the representative trend following system, the Sharpe ratios based on both daily and monthly returns are similar.

■ Summary

In this chapter, the core risks in alternative investment strategies were reviewed. These risks include price risk, credit risk, liquidity risk, and leverage risk. By comparing trend following with other alternative investment strategies, price risk and leverage risk were shown to be two main risks to discuss for trend following. By reviewing Sharpe ratios in contrast with key risks in alternatives, most risks in alternative investment strategies are hidden in Sharpe ratios. For the case of trend following that takes on only price risk, Sharpe ratios are prudent measures of risk taking with one caveat that needs to be examined further, leverage. If a strategy applies dynamic leverage, similar to doubling down in option selling or Martingale betting schemes, there may be leverage risk hidden in Sharpe ratios as well. A closer look at margin to equity ratios over time demonstrates that trend following strategies do not use dynamic leverage.

■ Further Reading and References

Brunnermeier, M., and L. Pedersen. "Market Liquidity and Funding Liquidity." *Review of Financial Studies* 22, no. 6 (2009): 2201–2238.

Foster, D., and H. Young. "The Hedge Fund Game: Incentives, Excess Returns, and Piggy-Backing." Working paper, 2007.

Getmansky, M., A. Lo, and I. Makarov. "An Econometric Model of Serial Correlation and Illiquidity in Hedge Fund Returns." *Journal of Financial Economics* 74 (2004): 529–609.

Goetzman, W., J. Ingersoll, M. Spiegel, and I. Welch. "Sharpening Sharpe Ratios." NBER Working Paper No. 9116, 2002.

Greyserman, A. "Dynamic Leveraging as a Factor of Performance Attribution." ISAM white paper, 2011.

Kaminski, K., and A. Mende. "Crisis Alpha and Risk in Alternative Investment Strategies." CME Group white paper, 2011.

---

[14]This is especially true if Martingale betting is applied earlier in the month.

Keating, C., and W. Shadwick. "A Universal Performance Measure." London: The Finance Development Centre, 2002.

Khandani, A., and A. Lo. "Illiquidity Premia in Asset Returns: An Empirical Analysis of Hedge Funds, Mutual Funds, and U.S. Equity Portfolios." Working paper, 2010.

Lo, A. W. "Risk Management for Hedge Funds: Introduction and Overview." *Financial Analysts Journal* 57, no. 6 (November/December 2001).

Lo, A. W. "The Statistics of Sharpe Ratios." *Financial Analysts Journal* 58, no. 4 (July/August 2002).

Sharpe, W. F. "The Sharpe Ratio." *Journal of Portfolio Management* 21, no. 1 (Fall 1994): 49–58.

Smith, S. W. "The Scientist and Engineer's Guide to Digital Signal Processing." California Technical Pub., 1997.

Vayanos, D. "Flight to Quality, Flight to Liquidity, and the Pricing of Risk." NBER Working Paper, 2004.

CHAPTER 10

Trend Following in Various Macroeconomic Environments

209

Trend following strategies perform well during periods of market divergence. Underlying macroenvironmental factors can drive market divergence creating tradable price momentum. In this chapter, several key macro aspects of markets are discussed: interest rate environments, postcrisis recovery in a period of quantitative easing, government interventions, and regulatory forces. The results across macro environments are mixed and often highly idiosyncratic. As a caveat, this chapter provides a summary of different perspectives on macro effects and market interventions. The analysis is qualitative, historical, and in some cases anecdotal. In addition to discussion of macro events, this chapter provides an analysis of the recent strong equity bull markets following the credit crisis, a period of quantitative easing. In general, the question of macro-wide effects and the link between these effects and trend following is complex. There are still many open questions that are left for future research.

■ Interest Rate Environments

Returning to the historical study of trend following in the introduction of this book, return data for a set of stock index, bond, and commodity markets going back as far as 1693 can be used to examine macro environments from a longer term perspective. Figure 10.1 illustrates the cumulative performance of a simple trend following system over the roughly 300-year period.[1] The Sharpe ratio for the entire 300-year sample period is 0.72. The average return is 0.9 percent monthly and monthly returns have a positive skew of 0.33. To quantify the relationship between trend following and traditional asset classes, an equity index and a bond index are constructed by averaging the monthly returns of several global equity indexes and bond markets with data starting in the 1870s.[2] Using monthly returns, the overall correlation between trend following and the equity index is 0.10, and 0.13 with the bond index. This correlation demonstrates that the overall correlation between trend following and traditional asset classes is low.

Figure 10.2 plots the average monthly return for a trend following system during periods of negative equity index or bond index performance. For equity markets,

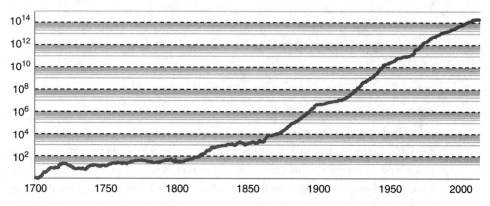

FIGURE 10.1 Cumulative performance (log scale) for a simple trend following system over a 300-year period from 1700 to 2012.

---

[1] The trend following system uses simple moving average based on monthly returns. Prior to 1900, the portfolio consists of 17 markets in the equity index, bond, and commodity sectors.

[2] The equity index is the average of monthly returns of FTSE 100 Index, S&P 500 Index, CAC 40 Index, and the Australian SPI 200 Index, and the bond index is constructed by the average monthly returns of U.S. 10-year Treasury note, Canadian 10-year Bond, and Japanese 10-year Bond. Before the existence of these several individual stock indexes or bond markets, the returns of equivalent markets were used to extend the data so that all components in these two indexes begin in the 1870s.

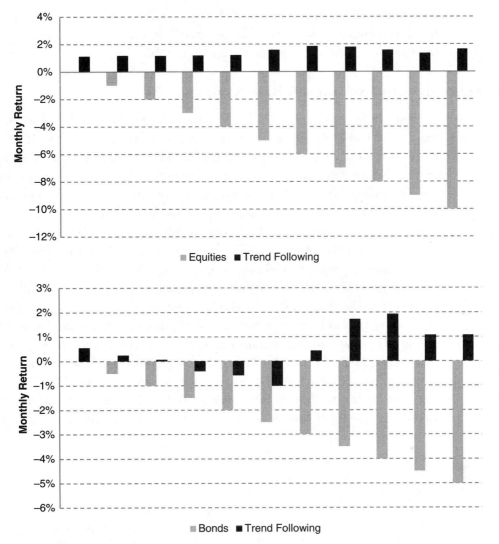

FIGURE 10.2 The conditional average monthly returns for trend following conditioned on negative returns for the equity index (top panel) and bond index (bottom panel).

the primarily top panel demonstrates that the average trend following return is positive during negative months for equity indices. More specifically, for the months where the equity index is down more than 10 percent, the average trend following return is almost 2 percent. For the case of the bond index, the bottom panel presents a less consistent pattern. It is important to point out that the average return for trend following is positive at times when the bond index is the most negative.

Much of this book is dedicated to crisis as defined by equity markets. It is also important to take a closer look at interest rates. Returning to the analysis in

Chapter 6, the potential impact of interest rates on trend following performance originates from two sources: additive interest income in funded investments and futures prices, inherent dependence on interest rates.

An Analysis of Two Interest Rate Regimes

Interest rate regimes have varied substantially during the past 800 years or even in the past 50 years. Figure 10.3 plots the Fed Funds rate from 1954 to 2013. During this almost 60-year period, there are two distinct interest rate regimes: rising interest rates before 1981, and falling interest rates after. The conditional performance of trend following during both of these regimes may provide some insight into how two very different interest rate regimes might impact performance.

Because futures prices for long-term bonds are not available until the 1980s, numerical methods can be applied to derive futures prices using yield data since 1962.[3] Using a portfolio made up of only the five-year and 10-year U.S. Treasury bonds, Figure 10.4 plots the portfolio Sharpe ratios for the rising and falling interest rate regimes. The Sharpe ratios are similar in magnitude with a slightly higher Sharpe ratio during the rising interest rate regime. Figures 10.5 and 10.6 plot the two-year rolling Sharpe ratio for trend following in the same two bond markets. From these two figures, the performance of trend following on both of these bond markets does not seem to be correlated with the corresponding change in yields.

In addition to the derived futures prices (where futures prices are derived from yields), the potential impact of rising interest rates can also be examined using

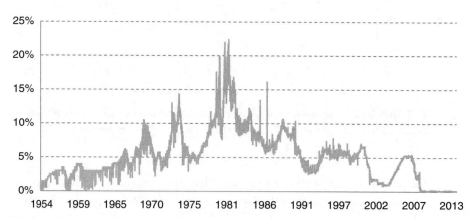

FIGURE 10.3   The federal funds rate from 1954 to 2013.
Data source: Global Financial Data.

---

[3] A linear relationship is derived using a regression between yields and futures prices. Empirically, the daily PnL of a trend following system based on the derived prices is highly correlated with actual futures prices.

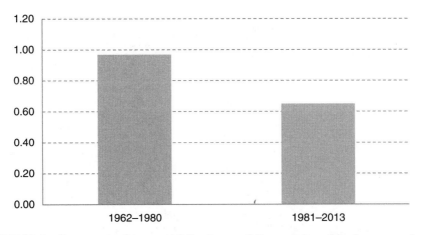

FIGURE 10.4 Sharpe ratios for a trend following portfolio consisting of the five-year and 10-year U.S. Treasury bond futures for two distinct interest rate regimes: rising from 1962 to 1981 and falling from 1981 to 2013.
Data source: Global Financial Data.

time-reversed prices series. The price formation process is time-irreversible, but this exercise is illustrative in the sense that increasing interest rates would create an environment where the fixed-income futures prices decrease. Table 10.1 displays the Sharpe ratios for nine long-term bond markets using real prices and time-reversed prices in the same period. On average, the Sharpe ratios using real prices (decreasing interest rate) are relatively close to those achieved using reversed prices (rising interest rate). These empirical tests demonstrate that trend following performance in long-term bond markets are unlikely to be significantly affected by different interest rate regimes. Trend following strategies take advantage of both upward and downward price trends in bond futures. Whether price trends are upward in decreasing interest rate environments or downward in rising interest rate environments seems to be *of little consequence* for trend following performance.

Short-Term Interest Rate Interventions

The analysis in the first part of this chapter has focused on longer-term interest rate regimes. Because most trend following systems are medium to long-term, these are the types of opportunities they are designed to capture. On the other hand, trend can occur in interest rate markets based on intervention or short-term shifts in interest rate markets. To examine the impact of short-term shocks in interest rates, interest rate hikes provide a simple example. Despite the evidence for long-term interest regimes, it can be argued that spikes in short-term interest rates can be detrimental for long-term strategies. This concept may be best explained with a simple interest rate intervention example. In early 2014, in comparison with other major currencies, the Turkish Lira exchange rate was at record lows. To boost the Turkish Lira, the

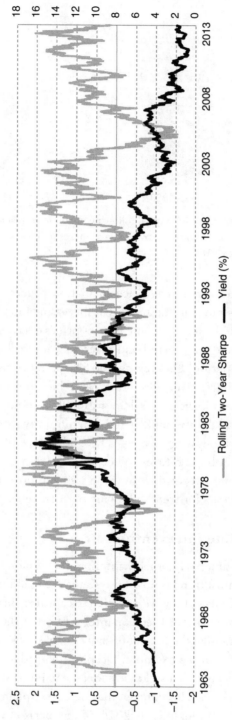

FIGURE 10.5 The two-year rolling Sharpe ratio for trend following five-year U.S. Treasury bond futures and the five-year yield from 1963 to 2013.

Data source: Global Financial Data.

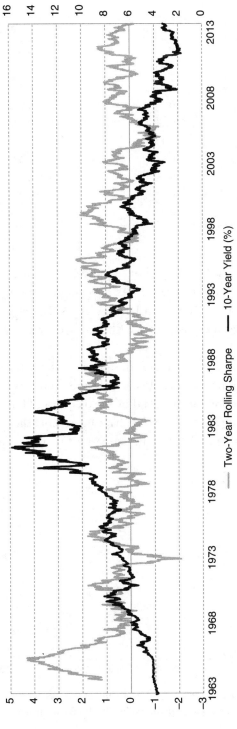

FIGURE 10.6   The two-year rolling Sharpe ratio for trend following the 10-year U.S. Treasury bond futures with the 10-year yield from 1963 to 2013.

Data source: Global Financial Data.

TABLE 10.1 Sharpe ratios for nine long-term bond futures based on real and time-reversed prices.

	Real Prices	Reversed Prices	Start Dates
Average	**0.42**	**0.33**	
U.S. 2-year	0.83	0.77	Dec. 1990
U.S. 5-year	0.37	0.29	Nov. 1988
U.S. 10-year	0.33	0.27	Oct. 1982
U.S. 30-year	0.24	0.14	Feb. 1978
Gilt Long	0.13	−0.16	May 1983
Euro Bund	0.61	0.50	June 1991
Euro Schatz	0.55	0.53	Nov. 1999
Euro Bobl	0.47	0.32	Nov. 1996
Japanese 10-year	0.22	0.34	Apr. 1986

Turkish Central Bank hiked up short-term interest rates. In Figure 10.7, the left graph plots short-term interest rates (overnight lending rates) for the Central Bank of the Republic of Turkey in January 2014. The right graph plots the Turkish Lira exchange rate in comparison with major currencies from October 2013 to January 2014.

From a one-month perspective, the jump in short-term interest rates presents itself as a spike in interest rates. Prior to the rate hike by the Turkish Central Bank, there was clearly a downward trend in Turkish Lira (TRY). This suggests that long-term trend following strategies would have been short the TRY up until the rate hike. The 4.25 percent rise in short-term interest rates and 5.5 percent rise in one-week

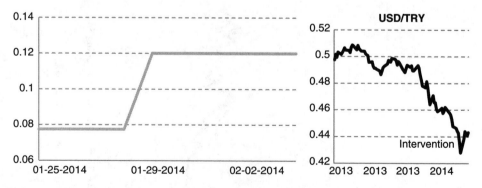

FIGURE 10.7 The left graph plots Central Bank of the Republic of Turkey Overnight Lending Rate in January 2014. The right graph plots the USD/TRY exchange rate from October 2013 through January 2014.

repo rates could have easily activated stops in trend following signals. This example demonstrates how government interventions can cause trends but they also have the ability to catch trend following systems off guard. Sustained trends are the most profitable for trend following, not short spikes. Not all trends are created equal.

■ Regulatory Forces and Government Intervention

Despite the concept of free markets, especially in recent times, markets have been overwhelmed by regulatory forces and incessant government intervention. The interaction of regulatory forces and government intervention is an interesting topic for trend following. It may be unclear if such effects can create or hinder price trends. Despite the fact that it is clear that both government intervention and regulatory changes will impact markets, how this occurs is somewhat unclear. To discuss this in further detail, some literature on government intervention is summarized followed by a few comments on regulatory forces.

Government Intervention

To discuss the impact of government intervention, first this section discusses several examples where government intervention was significant. The first example is the crude oil market. Since the 1950s, the crude oil market has been the focus of constant interventions by OPEC and other agencies. Stevens (2005) provides a comprehensive review of the factors that affect oil markets. More specifically, oil prices are influenced by factors related to supply and demand as well as the policies and agendas of government agencies. It is possible to argue that these factors may be cyclical or even structural. In either case, the price of oil exhibits evident price trends. Supporting this fact, trend following models on crude oil futures has demonstrated robust performance and a Sharpe ratio above 0.45 over the past few decades. This is higher than the average Sharpe ratio for trend following on individual markets, which is approximately 0.35.[4]

For a second example, the economic environment in Japan during the 1990s, often called the *lost decade*, is a period characterized by government intervention as well as frequent fiscal and monetary policy. To examine the effects of this period, the performance of trend following can be applied on the Japanese equity index (Nikkei), Japanese government bond index (JGB), and the yen (JPY). Table 10.2 displays the Sharpe ratios for trend following when applied to Japanese equity, bond, and currency

---

[4] Trend following individual markets has lower Sharpe ratios than an aggregate trend following system, which spreads risk across all asset classes.

TABLE 10.2 Sharpe ratios for a representative trend following strategy on the Nikkei, JGB, and JPY during the 1990s.

Index	Sharpe Ratio
Nikkei	0.37
JGB	0.97
JPY	0.67

markets during the 1990s. During this period of frequent intervention, all three markets exhibited price trends, which could have been captured by trend following. The Sharpe ratios for each of the asset classes, in particular the Japanese government bond index, are all above the overall average for a typical individual futures market.

The impact of government intervention on price volatility and trends has also been examined. For a specific example, Kneib and Wocken (2012) analyze prices in the dairy sector following EU interventions. They find that the impact of intervention on the price dynamics and volatility is mixed as well as determined by the intervention price. McCauley (2012) concludes that international flows of funds cast risk-on markets into a positive feedback loop. During risk-on periods, emerging market central banks tend to put downward pressure on global bond yields because of the capital inflows. This downward pressure further reinforces the risk-on mode. Kelly, Lustif, and Van Nieuwerburgh (2013) examine option markets and demonstrate a direct link between the financial sector and government bailout policy.

Following six specific significant interventions in currency markets, an InschQuantrend white paper (2011) examines the performance of trend following in FX markets during periods of intervention. The authors postulate that, when the purpose of intervention is to stabilize nervous markets, it has a favorable effect on the strength and smoothness of trends. Looking specifically in metal markets, Mingst and Stauffer (Winter 1979) estimate that the International Tin Council intervention caused a 10 percent rise in the price of tin from September 1968 to February 1969. In this particular case, the intervention resulted in a six-month trend in tin prices. For a range of metal markets (rubber, tin, and copper), Mingst and Stauffer (1979) show that it is difficult to recognize or measure how price interventions affect long-term price trends. For the case of stock markets, Bhanot and Kadapakkam (2006) analyze the Hong Kong Monetary Authority's massive stock market intervention in 1989. Their study concludes that the information effect of intervention contributed to a significant abnormal return on the Hang Seng. During the period following the intervention, the abnormal returns did not reverse indicating that the effect was not due to temporary price pressure.

Despite the fact that studies on government intervention are a relatively mixed bag, government intervention does not necessarily degrade trend following performance, and it may sometimes enhance it if longer term trends result. Despite this, Bond and Goldstein (2010, 2012) argue that government intervention can create trading risks for speculative trading. This is a particularly relevant point for commodity markets. For a concrete example, in the United States, the government performs a $20 billion subsidization for agricultural farmers. The question of whether this creates trends or increases risks is difficult to answer. Shorter term effects may be easier to examine. Although consistent with Bond and Goldstein, just as the Turkish Lira example earlier in this chapter, short-term intervention can be difficult for trend following. Using a specific example in commodity markets, in January 2014, the Egyptian agency GASC (General Authority for Supply Commodities) decreed that it will no longer accept wheat with a moisture content of higher than 13 percent. This simple declaration means that French wheat, which has a content of just over 13.5 percent, will be ineligible for trade in Egypt. Given that roughly 1 million tons of French wheat is exported to Egypt yearly, this new policy will have a substantial impact on French wheat prices. Not surprisingly, French wheat prices are down 22 percent in 2013. Short positions in French wheat would have benefited substantially from this policy change. U.S. wheat is a potential substitute with a moisture content of 12 percent, but the residual effect of this change coincided with only a 0.4 percent increase in price for U.S. wheat in 2013. Across a range of interventions, the evidence is highly idiosyncratic and difficult to predict from a case to case basis.

Returning to currency markets, several studies, including LeBaron (1999), Saacke (1999), and Sapp (1999) document strong correlations between periods of intervention (both German and U.S.) and positive performance for technical trading strategies in currency markets. This research might suggest that currency trends may be more tradable than interest rate trends. To support this claim, Neely (2002) finds evidence that interest rate interventions often come as a response to short-term trends and claims that intervention does not generate technical trading profits. The source of profits from the trends was the result of trends leading up to the intervention as opposed to after. To examine government intervention in currencies with an example, Figure 10.8 plots the dollar–yen exchange rate (USD/JPY) from 2000 to 2003. Consider the graph without the dots; do the interventions seem to substantially change price series in the graph? Neely (2002) may be correct in many cases as it is exorbitantly difficult to disentangle intervention from fundamental factors.

Regulatory Forces

In the wake of the previous financial crisis and infamous Bernard Madoff scandal, lawmakers and regulators are pushing for new regulations to help avoid future financial crises. There also has been a call for the harmonization of these regulations at the international level.

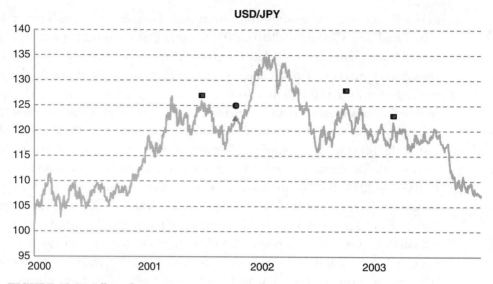

FIGURE 10.8 Effect of government intervention from 2000 to 2003. The "dots" represent the Bank of Japan's intervention.

The focus of these regulations has been on:

- Increasing transparency vis-à-vis the interconnectivity of market participants, counterparties, and contract-clearing methods.

- Regulations to limit and/or control risk taking.

- Potential bans and further control of short selling with the myopic goal is to avoid death spirals in prices.

Unintentional Impact of Regulation: A Comment Although well-intentioned, the push for further regulation may create even more structural reasons for why investors will be coordinated in their actions during losses in equity markets. First, the act of limiting or prohibiting short selling allows fewer investors to alleviate their long bias to equities possibly further exacerbating their need to sell during equity losses. Second, restrictions in the use of derivatives and commodity markets, such as those proposed for pension funds, can make them less diversified and less flexible in their portfolios in response to stress. Third, regulations that focus on risk taking, similar to Basel III, can further force investors into action when they take losses and volatility and correlation spike. Fourth, regulations for increased transparency in financial markets via the harmonization of regulation, reporting, and registration of positions and counterparties might help to reduce some of the problems seen in the banking sector during the last crisis. When it comes to future crises, many might criticize that harmonization of financial systems and the centralization of clearing and reporting could create new systemic risks financial monsters that also may be deemed "too big to fail." CCPs were discussed in Chapter 2. One of the key criticisms for CCP structures is based on systemic risks. The focus on the banking sector can unintentionally move problems to other market sectors, exchanges, insurance companies, shadow banking, and through other pathways.

As in all past financial crises, new regulation and rules are often well-intentioned. Despite these efforts, financial crises continue to manifest themselves in new areas, seemingly more often. The global market environment merely adapts to these rules and regulations. As a result, new rules and regulations may exacerbate the driving or forcing of market participants into action by limiting their adaptability and flexibility during times of market stress. If this is the case, in certain scenarios crisis alpha may be found across markets during these moments. Trend following is an opportunistic strategy that is poised to capture trends when they occur. Some trends are easier to catch than others. For example, the tulip mania bubble and the Wall Street crash of 1929 were discussed in the introduction to this book. In October 1929, a month when the Dow Jones index lost approximately half of the value, a representative trend following system had a slightly positive return. During the two years around the pre- and post–Black Monday, trend following realized a 90 percent return. On the other hand, during the Flash Crash of 2010 in the middle of the European debt crisis, capturing crisis alpha in this scenario proved more difficult.

■ Postcrisis Recovery

Post 2008, the financial world has been turned upside down. Reactions to the 2008 crisis have delivered an onslaught of regulation and nearly unprecedented fiscal and monetary policy. This includes, of course, quantitative easing. During this same period, for the five-year period from 2009 to 2013, the S&P 500 has slowly and steadily inched up to a whopping 175 percent! To put recent performance into perspective, this performance is in the 98th percentile of all five-year rolling periods since the S&P 500 index inception in 1928. Figure 10.9 plots the cumulative performance of the S&P 500 from 2009 to 2013.

It would seem that trend following systems should have profited strongly from this large "trend." Has this in fact been the case? In this section, a representative trend following system is used to examine performance on the S&P 500 Index. This analysis can provide insight into performance across trading speeds in general.

Fast, Medium, or Slow?

Although this "up-trend" is obvious to the naked eye, it is not obvious that any particular trend following strategy would be able to capture this trend. To discuss this in

FIGURE 10.9 The cumulative performance of the S&P 500 Index from 2009 to 2013.

further detail, the performance of different speeds of trend following systems over both the recent and entire histories can be examined. A trend following system will attempt to determine if the S&P 500 is climbing a hill or plummeting to new lows using sets of systematic rules. To classify different approaches to trend following, trend following systems are divided by trading speeds into buckets as a function of the average holding period. A fast system is defined as a holding period of less than four weeks. Medium systems are defined by 7- to 11-week holding periods and slow systems are defined by holding periods greater than 14 weeks. Although these cutoffs are relatively arbitrary, the results in this analysis remain relatively robust to this choice.[5]

For each holding period in Table 10.3, two arbitrarily selected generic trend following systems are used. For each particular trading speed, the correlation with the S&P 500 Index and Sharpe ratios are listed for 2009–2013 and since the inception of the S&P 500 Index in 1928. Since 1928, medium-term trend following systems have the highest Sharpe ratio with a low but positive correlation with the S&P 500 Index. The faster systems have the second-highest Sharpe ratio and they have a slightly negative to zero correlation with the S&P 500 Index since inception. The slowest systems have the lowest Sharpe ratio and the highest positive correlation with the S&P 500 Index since inception. During the postcrisis recovery, with a significant rise in the S&P 500 Index, the fast and medium systems have much lower Sharpe ratios than the slow systems.

---

[5] For each classification of speed, two trend following systems are selected arbitrarily that meet the holding period requirements.

Holding Period	Sharpe Ratio 2009–2013	Sharpe Ratio since 1928	Correlation to S&P 2009–2013	Correlation to S&P Returns since 1928
Fast	−0.026	0.466	0.037	−0.060
	0.156	0.492	0.125	−0.010
Medium	0.386	0.541	0.302	0.084
	0.120	0.522	0.420	0.056
Slow	0.503	0.415	0.804	0.214
	0.623	0.397	0.786	0.222
Combo[6]	0.379	0.581	0.514	0.102
Average[7]	0.294	0.472	0.412	0.084

In terms of correlation during the postcrisis recovery, all three speeds of trading systems have somewhat higher than average positive correlation, with the slow system having correlations as high as 80 percent. For the entire period, a typical slow system exhibits a correlation of roughly 20 percent with the S&P 500 Index, indicating that during the postcrisis recovery from 2009 to 2013, the uptrend was so strong that the correlation with a long equity strategy was four times the average correlation in history. This demonstrates how a slow system was the most similar to a buy-and-hold strategy in equity markets in this particular period. The high level of correlation between the slow systems and the buy-and-hold portfolio demonstrates the pure strength of the uptrend in equity markets post 2009.

Table 10.3 can also motivate a discussion of the impact of diversification. To examine diversification in a simple manner, the difference in performance of a combined system with several speeds and the average performance across all speeds can be compared. The difference between these two indicates the benefits of combining speeds in one trend following system. In both cases, the postcrisis recovery period and since inception, the combined Sharpe ratio is nearly 25 percent higher than the average Sharpe ratio of the individual trading speeds.

A Longer-Term Perspective 2009 to 2013 is a particular period where slow systems outperform. The natural next question to ask is whether this particular period is an anomaly. In order to put this into perspective, five-year rolling Sharpe ratios can be compared since inception of the S&P 500 Index in 1928. For the case of

---

[6] The Combo system is the combined strategy of all six systems.

[7] Equally weighted average of the six Sharpe ratios.

TABLE 10.4	The percentage of time each system (fast, medium, and slow) has the highest Sharpe ratio from 1928 to 2013.

	Percentage of Time with the Highest Sharpe Ratio (%)
Fast	37.42
Medium	35.80
Slow	26.78

overlapping five-year periods, there are a total of 81 data points. Table 10.4 lists the percentage of time that each system speed is the best performing in terms of Sharpe ratios. Throughout history (the postcrisis recovery period included), slow systems have performed the least often. During the entire period, either fast or medium-term speeds outperform slow systems roughly 73 percent of the time.

As seen in Table 10.4, the slow system was the best performer (over a rolling five-year period) only just over 25 percent of the time. It is also interesting to see which speeds have performed the best during periods across history. Figure 10.10 plots the best performer based on trading speed, where best performance is defined as the highest rolling five-year Sharpe ratio against the S&P 500 Index price chart (log-scale).

Figure 10.10 demonstrates how there are certain five-year periods where one strategy is the best performer. Because five years is a rather long period, shorter periods

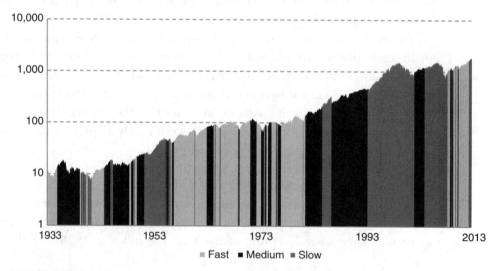

FIGURE 10.10 The best-performing five-year Sharpe ratios for fast, medium, and slow trend following systems from 1928 to 2013. These periods are plotted relative to the log-scale performance of the S&P 500 Index.

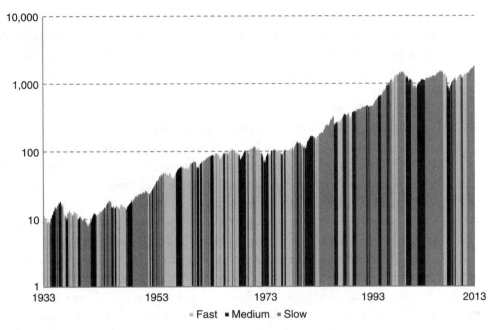

FIGURE 10.11 The best-performing one-year Sharpe ratios for fast, medium, and slow trend following systems on the S&P 500 Index from 1928 to 2013. These periods are plotted relative to the log-scale performance of the S&P 500 Index.

can also be examined for comparison. Figure 10.11 displays the best-performing trading speed in terms of one-year Sharpe ratios since the inception of the S&P 500 Index compared with the cumulative log-scale performance of the S&P 500 Index.

When slow systems outperform the medium and fast systems, it is also interesting to determine how extreme the outperformance is. Table 10.5 shows the frequency of time that the slow system's Sharpe ratio is greater than the respective

TABLE 10.5 The percentage of time the slow trend following system outperforms the medium-system Sharpe ratio by x and the fast-system Sharpe ratio by y from 1928 to 2013.

		Medium					
		$x = 0$	0.1	0.2	0.3	0.4	0.5
Fast	$y = 0$	26.78	13.87	9.23	6.90	5.75	5.16
	0.1	23.01	13.24	8.74	6.48	5.44	4.98
	0.2	18.84	12.45	8.01	6.01	5.00	4.55
	0.3	15.60	11.68	7.55	5.66	4.80	4.38
	0.4	14.02	10.73	7.30	5.52	4.66	4.30
	0.5	13.06	10.08	6.98	5.34	4.53	4.18

fast and medium systems (in combination). For example, the bold number 5.34 indicates that 5.34 percent of the time the slow-system Sharpe ratio is greater than the medium-system Sharpe ratio by 0.3 (*x*-axis) *and* the slow-system Sharpe ratio is greater than the fast-system Sharpe ratio by 0.5 (*y*-axis). The bold number is relevant because this represents the state of the S&P 500 Index during the postcrisis recovery period from 2009 to 2013.

The top left 26.78 number shows the percentage of time that slow is better than medium *and* slow is better than fast, which is the same result as in Table 10.4. In general from Table 10.5 it is clear that slow systems are fairly infrequently significantly better than both medium and fast. Put simply, it's relatively rare to see such substantial outperformance by the slow system.

The performance of fast, medium, and slow systems can also be examined in aggregate graphically. For the period of 1928 to 2013, Figure 10.12 plots a histogram of the five-year Sharpe ratios for fast, medium, and slow systems. For each histogram, the postcrisis recovery period is shown by the single highlighted bar for comparison. The distribution for fast systems is markedly different from the medium and slow systems. Faster systems do not seem to exhibit a normal distribution. Instead, fast systems are positively skewed with lower dispersion in performance. Table 10.6 lists the skewness for fast, medium, and slow systems applied on the S&P 500 Index in comparison with the S&P 500 Index itself.

It is interesting to note that the slow system has a very similar skew to the S&P 500 Index; intuitively this makes sense as the longer the holding period, the

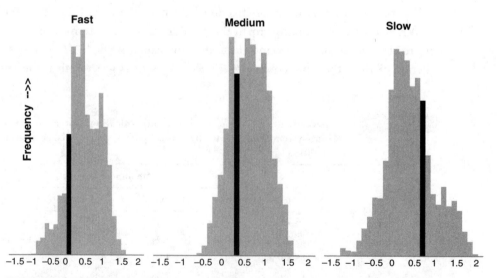

FIGURE 10.12 Histograms for five-year rolling Sharpe ratios for fast, medium, and slow trend following systems from 1928 to 2013. The postcrisis recovery period is shown by the single highlighted bar for comparison.

TABLE 10.6	Skewness for fast, medium, and slow systems on the S&P 500 and the S&P 500 from 1928 to 2013.			
	Fast	Medium	Slow	S&P 500
Skewness	0.21	0.03	−0.17	−0.22

more the system resembles a buy-and-hold strategy. For both the fast and medium speeds, the Sharpe ratios during the postcrisis recovery (2009–2013) are somewhat below their long-term averages. This demonstrates that although a buy-and-hold investor in the S&P 500 Index during this period is in the 98th percentile, this period does not appear to be a tail event for trend following systems.

The Need for Speed ... *Diversification*

Post 2008, equity markets have taken a slow and steady climb upward. The analysis in this section suggests (albeit not shockingly) that slow systems outperformed during this period. From a longer-term perspective, the occasional outperformance of a slow system is simply one data point and one period in time. This analysis and discussion does not imply that slow systems are better or worse than medium and fast. It only demonstrates the value of diversification across speeds and the importance of not overemphasizing individual time periods.

Since the inception of the S&P 500 Index, the average combined trend following portfolio has a Sharpe ratio of 0.58 with a low correlation of 0.1 with a buy-and-hold investment in the S&P 500 portfolio. This performance is greater than the Sharpe ratio of the S&P 500 Index itself. This, in and of itself, makes a compelling case for trend following as an alternative asset class.

To discuss diversification benefits more concretely, the addition of different speeds of trend following can be examined to determine how speed impacts total performance in combination with the S&P 500 Index. To do this, a long-only portfolio in the S&P 500 Index with a 50/50 allocation to trend following is considered. Since inception, the S&P 500 Index has had a Sharpe ratio of 0.37. Figure 10.13 compares the portfolio Sharpe ratio of a 50/50 mix of S&P 500 Index in combination with different types of trend following portfolios on the S&P 500 Index. The darker solid horizontal line indicates the original Sharpe ratio for a portfolio that is 100 percent long the S&P 500 Index with a Sharpe ratio of 0.37.

The benefit of diversification with trend following is quite apparent. One point that may be slightly counterintuitive in Figure 10.13 is the fact that the diversification benefits for the slow system are the lowest. This is due to the fact that the slow system is the most similar and also the most positively correlated with a long-only investment in the S&P 500 Index.

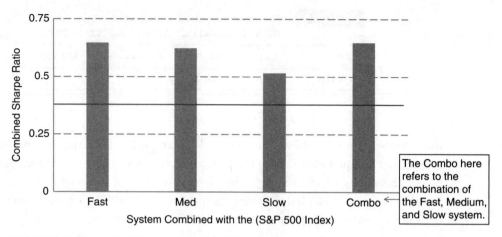

FIGURE 10.13 A 50/50 mix of the S&P 500 Index with fast, medium, and slow trend following systems on the S&P 500 Index. A combo system with all three speeds is listed for comparison. The period is 1928 to 2013.

Diversification over the Long Term It is undeniable that the postcrisis recovery period of 2009–2013 has been a joyous ride for the long-only equity investor. In this section, this slow and steady trend in equities is examined to determine which speed of trading systems would have performed during this period. During the postcrisis recovery, slower systems have performed rather well but not exceptional from a long-term perspective. Fast and medium systems would have found this trend difficult to follow. A historical perspective from 1928 to 2013 demonstrates how this five-year period is simply one sample period in history. The thought experiment uncovers a more important portfolio issue: the value of diversification across speeds. Slow systems tend to have a higher correlation to the market itself, providing marginal diversification benefits to an equities investor. Across time, diversifying across a wide spectrum of time frames provides a simple way to improve long-term performance of trend following from a portfolio perspective.

■ Summary

This chapter focuses on macro forces that may affect the performance of trend following over time. More specifically, interest rate regimes, government intervention, regulatory forces and the postcrisis recovery period were discussed. Interest rate regimes seem to have little impact on trend following performance. Government interventions are somewhat of a mixed bag but it seems that the act of forcing markets creates trends that may be exploitable. Shorter term interventions have the possibility of working against long-term trends following strategies. For a period of quantitative easing, a period of a large uptrend in equity markets, trend following performs in line with historical expectations. In aggregate, it is clear that it is very difficult to disentangle the impact of intervention and underlying fundamental factors. Lastly, regulatory forces are often well intentioned, yet they can create strange externalities in markets. Regulatory forces may from time to time create trends and thus opportunities for trend following strategies over time.

■ Further Reading and References

Bhanot, K., and P. Kadapakkam. "Anatomy of a Government Intervention in Index Stocks: Price Pressure or Information Effects?" *Journal of Business* (March 2006): 963–986.

Bond, P., I. Goldstein, and E. Simpson. "Market-Based Corrective Actions." *Review of Financial Studies* 23, no. 2 (2010): 781–820.

Bond, P., and I. Goldstein. "Government Intervention and Information Aggregation by Prices." Working paper, 2012.

"Central Bank Intervention: If the Trend Is Your Friend, Is Central Bank Intervention Your Enemy?," *InschQuantrend* 4 (April 2011).

Greyserman, A. "Trend-Following: Empirical Evidence of the Stationarity of Trendiness." ISAM white paper, February 2012.

Greyserman, A., and K. Kaminski. "S&P500: Is the Trend Your Friend?" ISAM white paper, 2014.

Kaminski, K. "Regulators' Unintentional Effects on Markets," *SFO*, 2011.

Kelly, B., H. Lustif, and S. Van Nieuwerburgh. "Too-Systematic-to-Fail: What Option Markets Imply About Sector-Wide Government Guartantees." Working paper, 2013.

Kneib, T., and M. Wocken. "Tobit Regression to Estimate Impact of EU Market Intervention in Dairy Sector." 123rd EAAE Seminar, Dublin, February 2012.

LeBaron, B. "Technical Trading Rule Profitability and Foreign Exchange Intervention." *Journal of International Economics* 49 (1999): 125–143.

McCauley, R. "Risk-On/Risk-Off, Capital Flows, Leverage and Safe Assets." BIS Working Paper, July 2012.

Mingst, K., and R. Stauffer. "Modeling Equilibrium Trends and Interventions in Commodity Markets." *Empirical Economics* 4, no. 2 (1979).

Mingst, K., and R. Stauffer. "Intervention Analysis of Political Disturbances, Market Shocks, and Policy Initiatives in International Commodity Markets." *International Organization* 33, no. 1 (Winter 1979).

Neely, C. "The Temporal Pattern of Trading Rule Returns and Central Bank Intervention: Intervention Does Not Generate Technical Trading Rule Profits." *Journal of International Economics* 58, no. 1 (October 2002): 211–232.

Saacke, P. "Technical Analysis and the Effectiveness of Central Bank Intervention." University of Hamburg, unpublished manuscript, 1999.

Sapp, S. "The Role of Central Bank Intervention in the Profitability of Technical Analysis in the Foreign Exchange Market." Unpublished manuscript, Ivey School of Business, University of Western Ontario, 1999.

Stevens, P. "Oil Markets." *Oxford Review of Economic Policy* 21, no. 1 (2005).

Tang, K., and W. Xiong. "Index Investment and Financialization of Commodities." NBER Working Paper 16385, 2010.

PART V

BENCHMARKING AND STYLE ANALYSIS

CHAPTER 11

Return Dispersion

For an allocator within the CTA space, high daily correlations among strategies often lead investors to believe that all trend followers are all roughly the same. In reality, the strategies vary substantially in their approach, style, positioning, and amount of nontrend strategies that are mixed in. Despite the misconception that there is a high degree of similarity, realized performance exhibits a significant amount of return dispersion. This chapter focuses on discussing return dispersion both empirically and conceptually. First, return dispersion is discussed across different strategy classifications in both the short term and long term. Second, two core drivers of return dispersion, lookback windows size and capital allocation approaches, are examined more specifically. Third, return dispersion is examined from the investor perspective. Finally, return dispersion is examined both theoretically and empirically using CTA returns. This chapter demonstrates how the idiosyncratic effects of parameter selection coupled with the importance of high correlation between programs results in return dispersion over time.

Before discussing return dispersion and its subsequent relationship with correlation, a simple thought-provoking example provides some perspective on the complexities of performance and correlation. Figure 11.1 plots realizations of three artificially generated assets (Asset 1, Asset 2, and Asset 3). At first glance, it appears that Asset 1 is much more correlated with Asset 2 than Asset 3. For this extreme example, the opposite is actually true. Asset 1 has a -1.0 correlation with Asset 2 and a $+1.0$ correlation with Asset 3! This example, albeit extreme, highlights the sometimes overdependence on correlation measure.[1]

---

[1] In Chapter 14, correlation is revisited again for the case of mark-to-market. The standardization of mark-to-market for futures trading provides one reason why cross-manager correlations in futures trading are prudent, and correlation may be understated in other strategies without standardized mark-to-market.

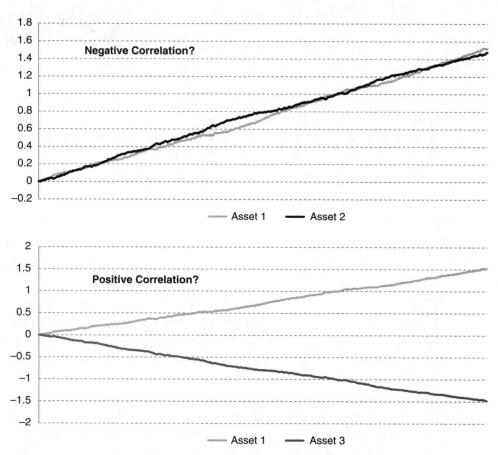

FIGURE 11.1 Realizations for three simulated assets (Asset 1, Asset 2, and Asset 3). This example illustrates seemingly deceptive correlation values between assets as Asset 1 has −1 correlation with Asset 2 and +1 correlation with Asset 3.

■ Strategy Classification and Return Dispersion

In Chapter 3, several key factors for classifying trend following programs were introduced. These include target risk levels, holding periods, capital allocation, and sector bias. Using holding period, capital allocation, and equity bias, trend following systems can be partitioned into eight systems. Table 11.1 summarizes the eight trend following systems. Chapter 7 returned to this partition of trend following systems and demonstrated that equal dollar risk portfolios provided higher long-term returns, equal dollar risk and no equity bias produced the highest crisis alpha, most positive skewness, and best conditional correlation properties. This analysis was relatively long term. In the short term, return dispersion can be even more substantial.

TABLE 11.1 The eight trend following systems based on three aspects of construction: equity bias, capital allocation, and holding horizon. Here, "No Long Horizon" indicates a median horizon.

	Equity Long Bias	Market Capacity Weighted	Long Horizon
1	No	No	No
2	Yes	No	No
3	No	Yes	No
4	No	No	Yes
5	Yes	Yes	No
6	No	Yes	Yes
7	Yes	No	Yes
8	Yes	Yes	Yes

To illustrate how these aspects of strategy construction link to return dispersion in both the long and short term, this section returns to the partitioning of trend following into eight systems.

Each trend following system is applied on a diversified set of 50 markets from equities, commodities, fixed income, and currencies.[2] Performance metrics and portfolio benefits, such as skewness, crisis alpha, and beta, help quantify how different approaches perform and differ across various market environments. In this section, performance measures across all eight trend following systems are summarized using box plots. Within each box, the central mark (the center line in the charts) is the median, and the edges of the box represent the 25th and 75th percentiles, that is, the interquartile range. The whiskers represent the most extreme points in the sample that are not outliers.[3] The individual plus signs in the charts outside of the whiskers are considered outliers.

Short-Term Performance Snapshots

To demonstrate return dispersion in the short run, performance snapshots for a specific calendar year can be examined. Figure 11.2 shows a box plot for return dispersion in 2012 for all eight trend following systems. In 2012, a symmetric system with equal dollar risk allocation and a medium holding horizon (System 1) had the worst performance. The median performance for System 1 was minus 15 percent. In contrast, System 8 with an equity long bias, market capitalization weightings, and

---

[2] The dataset includes daily data from 1993 to 2013. All returns are normalized to an annualized risk of 20 percent. Transaction costs are not deducted from the returns.

[3] The outlier boundaries in these charts are 1.5 times of the box height away from the box edges.

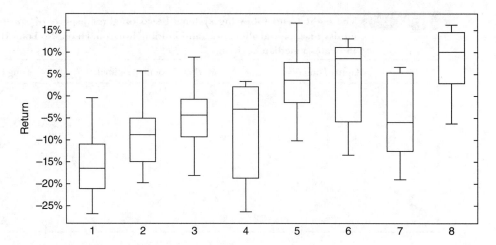

FIGURE 11.2 A box plot of return dispersion (with annualized returns) in 2012 for the eight trend following systems. The *y*-axis is annualized return.

long holding horizon had the best performance. The median performance for System 8 was 10 percent. For comparison, Figure 11.3 shows a box plot for the return dispersion in 2009 for all eight trend following systems. System 2 with equal dollar risk allocation, medium holding periods, and equity bias, had the best performance. In 2009, System 2 had a median performance of over 20 percent. In contrast, System 6

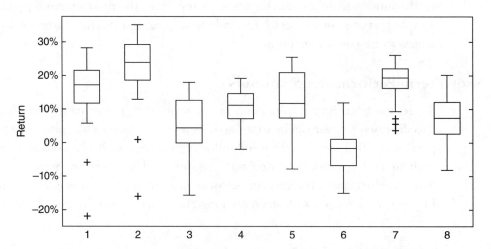

FIGURE 11.3 A box plot of the return dispersion (with annualized returns) in 2009 for the eight trend following systems. The *y*-axis is annualized return.

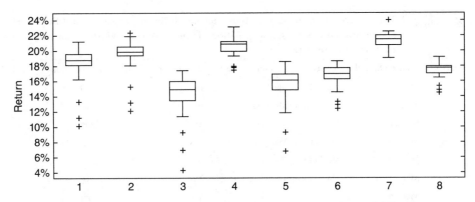

FIGURE 11.4 The return dispersion from 1994 to 2013 for the eight trend following systems. The *y*-axis is annualized return.

with no equity bias, market capacity weighting, and longer holding periods, had the weakest performance with a median return close to zero.

Partitioning the trend following space along aspects of strategy construction provides reasonable explanations for short-term performance dispersion. The level of return dispersion across trend following systems motivates the need for more sophisticated benchmarking in trend following. This issue is discussed in Chapter 12 and Chapter 13. Figure 11.4 shows a box plot for long-term return dispersion across the eight trend following systems. When compared with the snapshots from 2009 and 2012, it is clear that equal dollar risk allocation seems to outperform market capacity weightings over time. At least this seems to be the case from 1994 to 2013.

Position Sizing

Because the choice of system construction scheme seems to drive performance, it is possible to partition trend following systems even one step further. Returning to the discussion of systematic trend following system construction in Chapter 3, capital allocation explains how capital is distributed across markets. Position sizing depends on the past volatility for each individual market. To create further granularity as a function of system design, position sizing can be divided into long and short and equal dollar risk allocation (EDR) can be applied at either the individual market or sector level. For a shorter (longer) lookback window, position sizes will be adjusted by a shorter (longer) term estimate for volatility. Intuitively, a shorter lookback should perform better during risk on risk off environments where

TABLE 11.2 The 24 trend following systems across different types of holding periods, capital allocation, equity bias, and position sizing lookback windows and the corresponding performance in 2012.

Index No.	Trading Speed	Allocation Scheme	Equity Long Bias	Lookback (Pos Sizing)	2012 Return (%)
1	Median	Equal Risk (Markets)	No	Short	−17.5
2	Median	Equal Risk (Markets)	No	Long	−12.2
3	Median	Equal Risk (Markets)	Yes	Short	−9.3
4	Median	Equal Risk (Markets)	Yes	Long	−4.6
5	Median	Market Cap Based	No	Short	−5.0
6	Median	Market Cap Based	No	Long	−4.1
7	Median	Market Cap Based	Yes	Short	4.1
8	Median	Market Cap Based	Yes	Long	5.3
9	Median	Equal Risk (Sectors)	No	Short	−18.7
10	Median	Equal Risk (Sectors)	No	Long	−12.3
11	Median	Equal Risk (Sectors)	Yes	Short	−9.5
12	Median	Equal Risk (Sectors)	Yes	Long	−3.8
13	Slow	Equal Risk (Markets)	No	Short	−0.3
14	Slow	Equal Risk (Markets)	No	Long	−12.7
15	Slow	Equal Risk (Markets)	Yes	Short	5.2
16	Slow	Equal Risk (Markets)	Yes	Long	−5.4
17	Slow	Market Cap Based	No	Short	2.8
18	Slow	Market Cap Based	No	Long	−2.3
19	Slow	Market Cap Based	Yes	Short	9.0
20	Slow	Market Cap Based	Yes	Long	6.3
21	Slow	Equal Risk (Sectors)	No	Short	−3.6
22	Slow	Equal Risk (Sectors)	No	Long	−14.7
23	Slow	Equal Risk (Sectors)	Yes	Short	3.4
24	Slow	Equal Risk (Sectors)	Yes	Long	−6.3

volatility shifts rather quickly. Dividing equal dollar risk weighting by sector or individual market may explain how capital allocation impacts performance. Adding two options for equal dollar risk allocation and two approaches for position sizing, trend following systems can be divided into 24 systems. Table 11.2 demonstrates the partitioning of trend following into 24 systems with their corresponding performance in 2012.

Figure 11.5 shows a box plot for return dispersion with 24 subspaces in 2012. Systems 1, 9, and 22 experienced the worst performance in 2012. Across all types of trend following systems, market capacity weighting and equity long bias delivered the best performance. The further partitioning of trend following systems demonstrates even further how aspects of system construction affect return dispersion especially over shorter horizons.

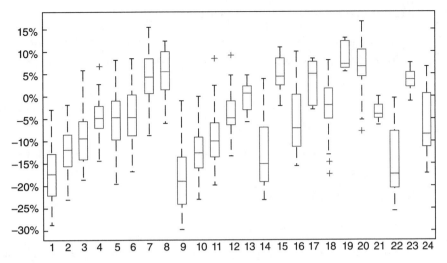

FIGURE 11.5   A box plot for return dispersion for 24 trend following systems in 2012.

■ A Closer Look at Capital Allocation and Position Sizing

In the previous section, several snapshots of trend following performance were compared across various aspects of system construction. Given that capital allocation was a core differentiator in performance over the longer term, a closer look into capital allocation can provide some insights into why capital allocation matters. Both capital allocation and position sizing contribute to the size of a position in a particular market. Both of these aspects are examined further in this section.

Instead of the eight trend following systems from Table 11.1, this section uses two generic trend following systems: a **channel breakout system** and a **moving average crossover system**. Using continuous price series, these systems use standard trend signals and a typical position sizing method using rolling volatility. They can be used to construct a representative of a trend following system.[4] To complement these two systems, a random entry system is used to increase the generality of the analysis.

Channel Breakout System

■ A long position is entered whenever the price is above the highest price in the lookback window.

■ A short position is entered whenever the price is below the lowest price in the lookback window.

■ The system also exits the position whenever a trailing stop is reached.

---

[4] It is important to note that a generic position sizing approach from Chapter 3 is applied.

Moving Average Crossover System

- A long position is entered when the moving average of the price in the shorter lookback window is higher than the moving average in the longer lookback window.

- A short position is entered when the shorter moving average is lower than the longer moving average.

- The system exits the position when the crossover signal changes sign or when a trailing stop is reached.[5]

Random Entry System

- There is no specific entry signal.

- The system consists of a large number of independent traders,[6] each of which enters a long or short position with equal probability initially.

- Each of the individual traders will exit positions when a trailing stop is reached.

The random entry system is an entry-independent trend following system. Despite the lack of entry decision, the system still follows trends when they develop. Short positions are stopped out when long upward trends occur and vice versa. The net position of the system of individual traders will become more aligned with the trend over time. The **tightness of the trailing stop** is defined by the number of rolling standard deviation of daily price change for setting a trailing stop. The tightness of trailing stops is similar to the lookback window size for a system with both entry and exit signals. The use of a random entry system is not for qualifying the importance of position management but to help demonstrate the robustness and generality of the results.

Roughly 50 markets are included in the portfolios across four sectors: equity indices, commodities, fixed income, and foreign currencies. Beginning in the 1990s, daily price data is available for most markets. Daily data for the agricultural markets is available since 1978.[7] To explain how positions are allocated, a closer look at the equation for number of contracts from Chapter 3 can help explain how these aspects

---

[5] For both the channel breakout and moving average crossover systems, the trailing stop is 12 times of the rolling standard deviation of daily price change in a 252-day lookback window.

[6] The system consists of 100 independent traders.

[7] Orders are assumed to be executed the same day at the Closing Price without considering slippage for all three trend following systems.

of system construction come into play. The nominal position (v) can be written as follows:

$$v = s \times \left(\frac{\theta \times c}{\sigma_K(\Delta P) \times PV} \right) \times \left(PV \times P \right)$$

In the numerator of this equation, the number of contracts for an individual market is a function of both the risk loading (θ) and invested capital (c). Capital allocation is set by adjusting (c) for each market. Risk adjustments can come from risk loadings (θ) and the risk adjustment based on past volatility ($\sigma_K(\Delta P)$) in the denominator. First, variations in position sizing based on the lookback windows (K) for past volatility ($\sigma_K(\Delta P)$) are analyzed to discuss return dispersion. Second, variations sector capital allocation (c) is examined to determine how sector allocation impacts return dispersion.[8]

Position Sizing and Lookback Window Size

Varying the size of the lookback window for position sizing based on volatility can provide some insights into how volatility adjustments in trend following systems impact performance. First, the channel breakout system can be examined as a function of position sizing. Using lookback windows varying in size from 20 days to 200 days, Table 11.3 displays the annual returns from 2001 to 2013 for a channel breakout system.[9] The impact of lookback window size appears to be random across the sample period. Certain years seem to be more sensitive to lookback size. For example, in 2009, a lookback of 50 days would have a positive return of 3.91 percent. During the same year, when the lookback window is reduced to only 20 days, the performance plunged downwards by 14.52 percent. On the other hand, in 2003, every lookback in this example would have resulted in a positive return. To gauge the level of return dispersion across different construction styles, the interquartile range (IQR) can be used as a measure for return dispersion. The IQR is defined as the difference between the 25 percent quartile and the 75 percent quartile of all returns within each year. In 2003, the IQR was only 3.77 percent while in 2008 the IQR was 13.74 percent. The dispersion of returns in Table 11.3 demonstrates how for some years shorter lookback windows outperform longer lookback windows and vice versa.

---

[8] Among the three typical factors of return dispersion, portfolio leverage and risk loadings (θ) are the most straightforward and thus not discussed here. The results in this section are all scaled to an annual net-of-fee annualized volatility of 15 percent over the entire testing period.

[9] In this subsection, for this system as well as the other two systems, capital allocation among markets in the portfolio is based on equal dollar risk. In this case, the position size is inversely proportional to the rolling volatility of the market.

TABLE 11.3 Annual returns for channel breakout systems with lookback window size ranging from 20 days to 200 days. The second row is return dispersion as measured by the interquartile range (IQR) for each year due to the varying lookback window size.

	2001	2002	2003	2004	2005	2006	2007	2008	2009	2010	2011	2012	2013
IQR	4.96	4.03	3.77	6.92	4.78	3.49	3.99	13.74	6.20	4.40	2.49	6.77	9.56
20	15.15	16.46	17.34	1.39	2.09	−9.00	14.03	51.47	−10.23	−0.89	−13.97	−2.31	−7.12
30	14.10	16.89	14.93	8.00	−1.06	1.70	0.97	64.20	−14.52	6.08	−9.99	−0.26	−6.17
40	13.47	25.46	9.63	6.25	−6.23	2.53	−5.72	65.17	−3.91	7.65	−2.51	−2.91	−6.61
50	8.84	25.31	6.78	9.24	−0.11	7.23	−8.54	63.58	3.91	5.90	3.96	−7.31	−8.69
60	6.34	27.72	7.40	6.30	0.22	13.27	−2.03	62.44	12.72	7.89	4.81	−5.81	−8.72
70	12.54	25.34	8.38	2.15	1.24	12.54	3.43	59.59	12.24	12.72	5.35	−10.28	−7.42
80	11.46	24.92	11.07	−2.09	2.49	13.14	0.09	58.32	9.75	12.13	10.78	−9.91	−9.17
90	9.34	26.45	13.41	−4.88	2.26	15.73	−0.61	60.95	8.82	16.50	11.28	−12.98	−7.61
100	11.42	23.97	17.21	−6.11	4.81	13.42	0.56	60.92	7.06	15.44	10.92	−8.63	−1.22
110	10.09	25.71	18.25	−5.43	4.76	9.61	2.45	57.32	8.15	17.15	8.89	−5.39	0.17
120	10.07	25.01	17.51	−0.61	6.13	7.33	3.54	57.26	8.24	16.91	6.03	−1.25	2.81
130	10.19	24.11	17.80	0.01	5.66	9.55	5.02	55.08	6.11	14.46	5.39	−1.98	1.61
140	15.98	26.66	16.85	−0.27	3.51	9.84	3.16	54.08	7.11	14.29	8.55	−1.11	1.14
150	16.75	25.08	15.82	0.71	4.36	10.31	3.41	52.01	5.76	14.14	7.18	−1.73	2.53
160	15.59	23.43	16.53	0.10	6.80	9.83	4.80	51.34	5.93	15.20	6.13	1.18	3.07
170	16.79	22.04	18.06	2.84	8.46	8.91	4.59	50.39	6.08	15.26	5.52	0.99	2.03
180	16.94	20.09	17.03	1.34	7.79	9.05	3.53	47.61	5.08	15.25	5.41	1.51	0.69
190	16.43	19.81	18.23	4.24	7.71	10.65	3.57	46.56	4.20	15.44	5.32	1.39	1.20
200	16.26	21.21	18.58	6.93	6.70	11.19	4.49	45.06	3.85	16.20	6.15	0.35	2.15

Moving average systems depend on both the shorter and longer lookback windows for determining when positions are long or short. In this example, for the moving average crossover system, longer lookback ranges from 100 days to 240 days and the shorter lookback ranges from 10 days to 60 days. Figure 11.6 plots the returns for each combination of the longer and shorter lookback window sizes within each year from 2001 to 2013. As seen with the channel breakout system, return dispersion varies significantly from year to year. For example, 2008 returns were highly sensitive to the choice of both lookback sizes. In contrast, in 2005, the choice of lookback size was less important.

Both the channel breakout system and the moving average crossover system depend on the decision to use a specific signal to enter and exit positions. To demonstrate if these results are robust or simply a function of the entry signal, a random entry system can also be examined for return dispersion. The annual returns and IQR for the random entry system from 2001 to 2013 are listed in Table 11.4. For the

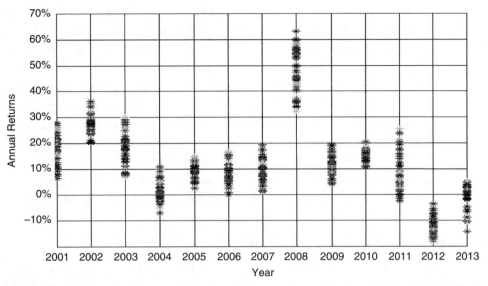

FIGURE 11.6 Annual return dispersion for moving average crossover systems. The longer lookback window ranges from 100 to 240 days and the shorter lookback window ranges from 10 to 60 days.

TABLE 11.4			Annual returns for the random entry system with varying tightness of trailing stops, or the number of rolling standard deviations of daily price changes, ranging from 2 to 20. The first row is return dispersion as measured by the interquartile range (IQR) for each year due to the varying tightness of trailing stop.										

	2001	2002	2003	2004	2005	2006	2007	2008	2009	2010	2011	2012	2013
IQR	**4.43**	**12.52**	**7.31**	**8.33**	**10.39**	**4.18**	**11.94**	**21.65**	**7.32**	**14.59**	**13.82**	**10.38**	**4.41**
2	2.44	−0.36	13.56	−7.66	4.97	1.83	4.44	75.43	−23.74	10.79	−6.26	−1.84	−7.90
3	11.49	12.13	8.42	−13.34	−4.21	−1.78	11.09	64.37	−42.00	3.18	−11.32	4.78	−4.44
4	5.57	24.84	15.22	−9.03	−6.77	−3.93	2.93	94.03	−14.60	3.16	−17.42	−4.16	3.07
5	18.25	26.08	9.10	3.90	−3.09	1.09	3.45	86.60	−9.55	11.23	5.26	−5.41	−2.81
6	19.27	26.21	7.64	2.13	−6.99	−0.03	−5.81	89.54	1.26	12.96	5.93	−11.93	−1.18
7	13.91	29.01	3.95	3.29	−5.51	2.35	−7.09	89.62	2.47	17.85	12.80	−17.70	−3.74
8	15.73	32.16	4.71	4.08	−8.88	5.11	−10.40	75.36	4.28	18.61	14.40	−18.73	−2.84
9	12.07	35.88	5.40	2.26	−7.95	4.29	−5.57	69.82	2.90	17.85	14.62	−27.27	0.09
10	11.36	33.01	6.24	−2.41	−6.75	6.02	−1.28	75.69	8.17	18.80	17.13	−21.41	1.41
11	12.19	36.03	9.80	−2.04	−8.23	5.08	−4.85	75.62	8.06	17.55	9.81	−19.47	−0.63
12	10.38	38.50	11.88	−3.15	−7.97	1.24	−4.19	69.09	5.66	17.22	10.41	−19.32	−0.64
13	10.86	40.73	14.96	−3.44	−5.72	−1.52	−2.40	70.76	3.04	12.86	10.21	−17.35	−0.95
14	14.61	39.55	15.45	−6.82	−3.55	2.85	0.41	60.61	1.80	23.77	4.03	−13.35	−3.33
15	17.11	40.62	15.97	−9.68	−2.35	3.21	3.03	58.06	−0.44	24.79	2.75	−9.90	2.11
16	15.90	39.65	12.44	−2.80	2.71	2.65	7.33	49.95	1.39	33.15	−1.65	−9.52	0.53
17	16.28	43.04	15.15	−2.49	4.32	8.52	7.51	40.16	3.96	37.97	−0.16	−8.77	7.23
18	13.50	38.83	17.47	5.16	7.66	6.12	7.94	24.28	3.29	34.24	−1.77	−8.90	8.65
19	15.81	42.26	19.03	3.10	10.04	6.17	7.76	18.18	−4.37	30.21	−5.26	−6.91	1.75
20	15.69	43.04	16.44	11.05	9.08	5.58	10.14	17.86	−3.02	31.44	−7.90	−8.76	1.09

random entry system, position sizing and speed of trading will depend directly on the tightness of the trailing stops. The tightness of the trailing stop, or the number of rolling standard deviations of daily price changes, is ranged from 2 to 20. A tightness of 2 would stop out frequently creating a faster system. A tightness of 20 would rarely stop out with longer term holding horizons. Even with a random entry system, return dispersion varies substantially from year to year. For example, changing the tightness of the trailing stop parameter from 3 to 4 in 2009 would improve the annual return from minus 42 percent to minus 14.6 percent. In 2010, the same shift in from 3 to 4 would have little to no impact on the performance difference. The results for return dispersion are robust across three different types of trend following system constructions. Position sizing seems to matter in some years and not matter in others.

Sector Specifics and Capital Allocation

In order to illustrate the impact of capital allocation by sector, as demonstrated in the previous subsection, a channel breakout system is examined for a range of lookback window sizes from 90 to 120 days. In Table 11.5, capital allocation to each sector is varied from 10 percent to 50 percent averaged over 90- to 120-day lookback windows from 2001 to 2013. The remaining capital is divided equally between the other three sectors. Within each sector, capital allocation for each of the markets in the sector is based on the equal dollar risk allocation. The sector position size is then roughly defined by the following expression:

$$\text{Sector Position Size} = \frac{\text{Sector Capital} \times \theta}{N \times \overline{\sigma}_{sector}}$$

where (θ) is the risk loading, (N) is the total number of markets in the sector, and $(\overline{\sigma}_{sector})$ is the average dollar risk for markets in a particular sector. As with position sizing, the sector allocation overweighting and underweighting creates substantial variation over the 13-year period. For example, in 2013, an overweighting to the fixed income sector would result in very negative performance. On the other hand, an overweighting to equity in 2013 would result in a substantially higher return. Sector performance varies substantially from year to year. In 2005 and 2008, return dispersion is relatively low regardless of sector capital allocation. In contrast, during 2011, the difference in returns is quite large from overweighting one sector or another.

Return Dispersion and Market Volatility

The previous two sections discussed the potential impact of different approaches for position sizing and sector capital allocation. Given wide ranges of values of parameters for both position sizing and sector capital allocation, return dispersion in

TABLE 11.5 Annual returns for a channel breakout system with different capital allocation among the four sectors. The first row is return dispersion as measured by the interquartile range of different returns in each year due to the varying capital allocation.

Eqty	Cmdt	FI	FX	2001	2002	2003	2004	2005	2006	2007	2008	2009	2010	2011	2012	2013
			IQR	5.55	3.46	3.99	2.72	1.92	2.96	4.07	1.32	2.83	3.59	5.99	3.27	4.27
25	25	25	25	5.84	27.61	17.52	−7.03	4.90	11.90	−3.44	62.25	8.87	13.61	11.40	−16.03	−3.87
10	30	30	30	0.49	27.54	15.32	−8.15	3.81	11.74	3.96	64.01	4.75	21.41	19.17	−14.40	−11.96
15	28	28	28	2.27	27.56	16.05	−7.78	4.18	11.79	1.49	63.42	6.12	18.81	16.58	−14.94	−9.27
20	26	26	26	4.06	27.59	16.79	−7.40	4.54	11.85	−0.97	62.83	7.50	16.21	13.99	−15.49	−6.57
30	23	23	23	7.62	27.63	18.25	−6.65	5.27	11.96	−5.90	61.66	10.25	11.01	8.80	−16.58	−1.18
35	21	21	21	9.40	27.66	18.98	−6.28	5.63	12.02	−8.36	61.07	11.62	8.41	6.21	−17.12	1.52
40	20	20	20	11.19	27.68	19.71	−5.90	6.00	12.07	−10.83	60.48	13.00	5.80	3.62	−17.67	4.21
45	18	18	18	12.97	27.70	20.44	−5.53	6.36	12.13	−13.29	59.89	14.38	3.20	1.03	−18.21	6.91
50	16	16	16	14.75	27.73	21.17	−5.16	6.73	12.19	−15.75	59.30	15.75	0.60	−1.56	−18.76	9.60
30	10	30	30	6.15	32.49	18.80	−11.11	7.38	10.13	−5.41	62.59	8.45	12.07	14.45	−17.98	−3.56
28	15	28	28	6.05	30.86	18.37	−9.75	6.56	10.72	−4.75	62.47	8.59	12.58	13.43	−17.33	−3.66
26	20	26	26	5.94	29.24	17.94	−8.39	5.73	11.31	−4.09	62.36	8.73	13.10	12.41	−16.68	−3.77
23	30	23	23	5.73	25.98	17.09	−5.67	4.08	12.50	−2.78	62.13	9.01	14.12	10.38	−15.38	−3.98
21	35	21	21	5.63	24.35	16.66	−4.31	3.25	13.09	−2.12	62.02	9.15	14.64	9.36	−14.73	−4.08
20	40	20	20	5.53	22.73	16.23	−2.95	2.43	13.68	−1.46	61.90	9.30	15.15	8.34	−14.08	−4.19
18	45	18	18	5.42	21.10	15.81	−1.59	1.60	14.27	−0.80	61.79	9.44	15.66	7.32	−13.43	−4.29
16	50	16	16	5.32	19.47	15.38	−0.23	0.78	14.86	−0.14	61.67	9.58	16.18	6.30	−12.78	−4.40
30	30	10	30	2.51	21.32	22.92	−3.03	5.46	8.96	−8.25	62.81	11.72	7.75	2.60	−18.39	5.50
28	28	15	28	3.62	23.41	21.12	−4.36	5.28	9.94	−6.65	62.62	10.77	9.70	5.53	−17.60	2.37
26	26	20	26	4.73	25.51	19.32	−5.69	5.09	10.92	−5.04	62.43	9.82	11.66	8.46	−16.82	−0.75
23	23	30	23	6.95	29.71	15.72	−8.36	4.72	12.89	−1.83	62.06	7.92	15.56	14.33	−15.25	−7.00
21	21	35	21	8.06	31.80	13.92	−9.70	4.53	13.87	−0.22	61.87	6.97	17.51	17.26	−14.46	−10.12
20	20	40	20	9.17	33.90	12.12	−11.03	4.35	14.85	1.38	61.68	6.02	19.47	20.19	−13.68	−13.25
18	18	45	18	10.28	36.00	10.32	−12.37	4.16	15.83	2.99	61.49	5.07	21.42	23.12	−12.89	−16.37
16	16	50	16	11.39	38.10	8.52	−13.70	3.97	16.81	4.60	61.30	4.12	23.37	26.06	−12.11	−19.50
30	30	30	10	14.20	29.09	13.03	−5.83	2.96	16.79	−4.03	59.57	10.57	13.20	9.36	−13.37	−5.48
28	28	28	15	11.41	28.60	14.52	−6.23	3.61	15.16	−3.83	60.46	10.01	13.34	10.04	−14.25	−4.94
26	26	26	20	8.63	28.10	16.02	−6.63	4.26	13.53	−3.63	61.35	9.44	13.47	10.72	−15.14	−4.41
23	23	23	30	3.05	27.11	19.01	−7.43	5.55	10.28	−3.24	63.14	8.31	13.74	12.07	−16.92	−3.34
21	21	21	35	0.26	26.62	20.51	−7.83	6.20	8.65	−3.04	64.03	7.74	13.88	12.75	−17.81	−2.81
20	20	20	40	−2.52	26.13	22.01	−8.23	6.85	7.02	−2.84	64.92	7.17	14.02	13.43	−18.70	−2.27
18	18	18	45	−5.31	25.63	23.50	−8.63	7.49	5.39	−2.65	65.82	6.61	14.15	14.11	−19.59	−1.74
16	16	16	50	−8.10	25.14	25.00	−9.03	8.14	3.76	−2.45	66.71	6.04	14.29	14.79	−20.48	−1.20

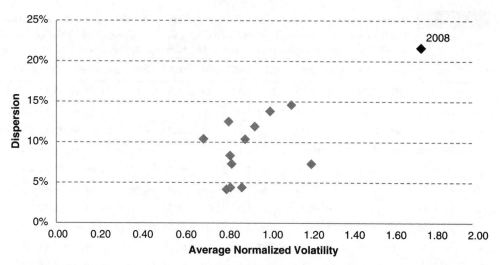

FIGURE 11.7 A scatter plot between return dispersion (IQR) due to different lookback size and market volatility (average normalized market volatility). The sample period is 2001 to 2013.

trend following seems to be relatively random with periods where return dispersion is relatively high. For all trend following systems in the last subsections, 2008 represents a year where return dispersion was at the highest levels for all parameterizations of position sizing. Given the wide range of return dispersion from year to year, the next natural question to ask is how overall market volatility may relate to return dispersion. For the simplicity of this analysis, market volatility can be defined as the average normalized volatility across all markets that are included in trend following portfolios. In this section, each individual market is normalized by the average 252-day rolling standard deviation of daily price change for the relevant sample period.

First, return dispersion, as measured by the interquartile range (IQR) based on a range of lookback windows, can be compared with the corresponding market volatility for each year in the sample period. Figure 11.7 displays a scatter plot between the return dispersion (IQR for a range of lookback size as in Table 11.3) and the overall market volatility (average normalized 252 day volatility across all included markets). When the outlier of 2008 is removed from the scatter plot, there remains no obvious correlation between the return dispersion, as a function of lookback size, and overall market volatility.[10] The same analysis can be applied to variations in sector capital allocation. Figure 11.8 presents a scatter plot between return dispersion (IQR due

---

[10] Given that this result is for only a 10-year period, longer horizons were also examined with a smaller set of included markets. The results are similar when applied to a portfolio of 12 markets over 32 years of historical prices.

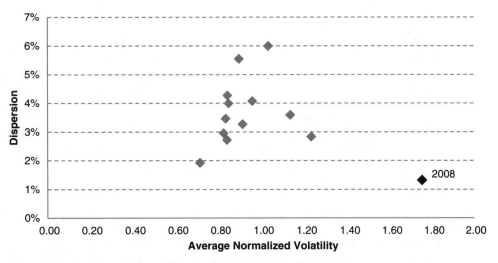

FIGURE 11.8 A scatter plot between return dispersion (IQR), due to different sector capital allocations, and market volatility (average normalized market volatility). The sample period is 2001 to 2013.

to the range of sector capital allocations from Table 11.5) and the market volatility (average normalized market volatility). When the outlier of 2008 is removed, again there remains no obvious correlation between return dispersion, as a function of sector capital allocation, and market volatility.

Chapter 8 discussed the relationship between market volatility and portfolio volatility. In this chapter, it was explained that the volatility adjustment approach to position sizing in trend following systems should make them somewhat "vega neutral." During periods when the volatility moves much more drastically, the volatility adjustment of positions will not be able to remain as "vega neutral." Given this explanation, the lack of correlation between return dispersion and market volatility is to be expected. A year like 2008 represents a year when volatility spikes and return dispersion is substantial. As a robustness check, when the volatility of the Newedge index is used, instead of average normalized volatility, return dispersion still remains uncorrelated with market volatility.

■ Return Dispersion from an Investor's Perspective

From the investor's perspective, return dispersion due to varying parameters is still an important issue. Return dispersion may provide additional information for evaluating and understanding manager performance in the cross section. For example, if return dispersion is large, it is normal that trend following programs experience a

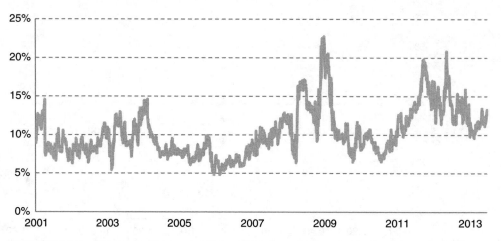

FIGURE 11.9 The Return Dispersion Index (RDI) from 2001 to 2013. The index value is the interquartile range (IQR) of the rolling annual returns due to different lookback window sizes and sector capital allocations for breakout and moving average crossover systems.

wide range of performance. On the other hand, when the return dispersion is low, an investor may be rightfully skeptical of performances that deviate substantially from their peers (when normalized by volatility). A simple example could be trend following managers who decided to begin allocating a substantial portion of their capital to carry trades or even credit spreads. Since carry trades are not a traditional trend following strategy, a trend following with lots of additional carry may deviate substantially from other trend followers even when return dispersion is low for trend following systems as a group.

To gauge the level of return dispersion in trend following systems over time, a Return Dispersion Index (RDI) can be measured using both the breakout and moving average crossover systems. Lookback window sizes for the breakout system range from 20 to 250 days as in Table 11.3 and sector capital allocation percentages range according to Table 11.5. The RDI is measured as the IQR for rolling annual returns across variations in lookback window size and sector capital allocation. The RDI provides an aggregate view into the level of return dispersion to be expected across trend following programs. Figure 11.9 plots the RDI, as measured by the IQR for 12-month rolling trend following returns based on both a breakout system and a moving average crossover system, from 2001 to 2013. For a specific example, at the beginning of 2012, the RDI peaked close to 20 percent. This value is among the top 5 percent of past values for return dispersion in the given sample period.[11]

---

[11] According to the Barclay Flash Report for CTA trading programs managing at least $50 million, the maximum of 2011 YTD (up to July 31, 2011) return was 27 percent and the minimum YTD return was −30 percent. In 2010, the highest return was 66 percent while the lowest was −15 percent.

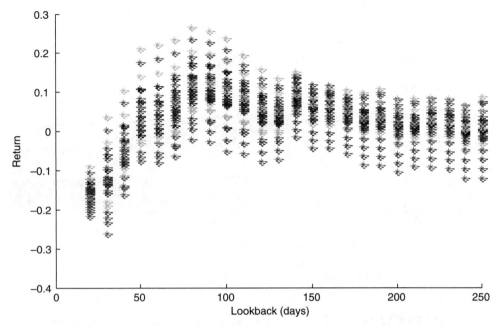

FIGURE 11.10 Portfolio return as a function of lookback window size and sector capital allocation in 2011. Each point represents a specific combination of lookback window size and sector capital allocation.

To examine return dispersion in further detail, a specific year can be examined more closely. For example, 2011 will be examined in closer detail for demonstrative purposes. Figure 11.10 plots the portfolio return distribution for a breakout system across a range of lookback window sizes and sector capital allocations in 2011. Figure 11.10 demonstrates that specifically in 2011, a shorter lookback window size would have resulted in the best performance. To take this example to an even more granular sector level, Figure 11.11, Figure 11.12, Figure 11.13, and Figure 11.14 plot return as a function of both lookback window size and sector capital allocation.[12] For the specific example of 2011, a lower equity allocation would produce higher returns. Large commodity allocations would have performed worse for shorter lookback windows and irrelevant if the lookback window was longer. For fixed income in 2011, larger allocations to fixed income would increase return regardless of lookback window size. Finally for currencies, an overweighting would improve performance but the improvement was relatively variable as a function of lookback window size.

---

[12] As in other examples in this section, when the allocation changes in a specific sector, capital is divided equally among the remaining three sectors.

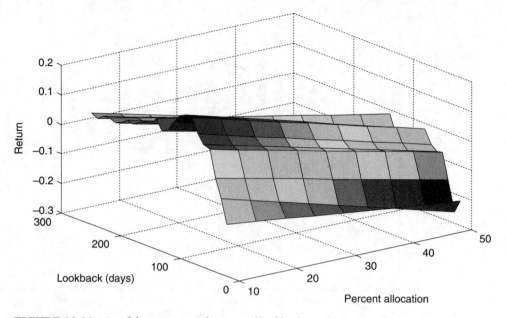

FIGURE 11.11 Portfolio return as a function of lookback window size and equity sector allocation in 2011.

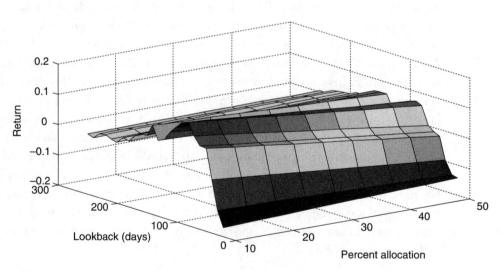

FIGURE 11.12 Portfolio return as a function of lookback window size and commodity sector allocation in 2011.

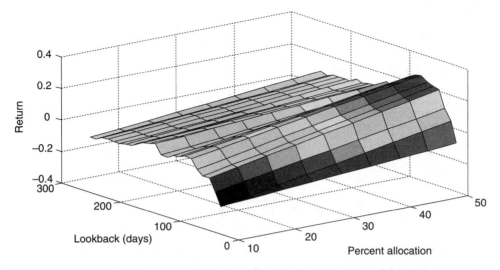

FIGURE 11.13 Portfolio return as a function of lookback window size and fixed income sector allocation in 2011.

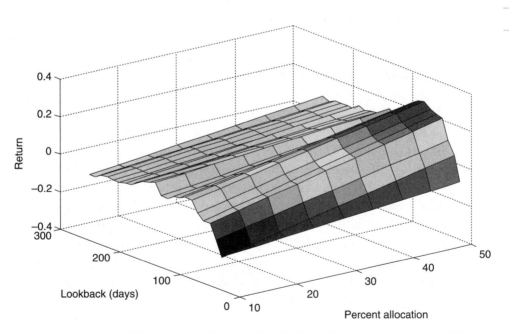

FIGURE 11.14 Portfolio return as a function of lookback window size and currencies (FX) sector allocation in 2011.

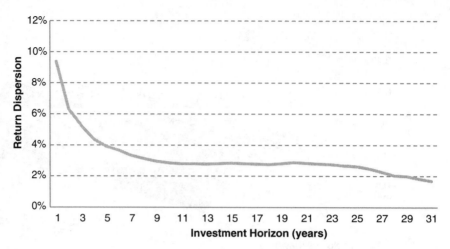

FIGURE 11.15 Return dispersion of average annual returns due to different lookback window sizes as a function of investment horizon. The vertical axis is return dispersion as measured by the mean of the interquartile range for different average annual returns in each given investment horizon.

Diminishing Return Dispersion with Time

Despite causing high levels of return dispersion in the short term, the impact of the specific choice of lookback window size and sector capital allocation has a decreasing impact on return dispersion as the investment horizon increases. In the long run, return dispersion decreases due to the randomness of the parameters. This effect can be demonstrated with a simple empirical experiment using 12 markets with prices dating back to 1978. Figure 11.15 plots average return dispersion, measured by the IQR of the different average annual returns in the investment period for lookback window size ranging from 20 to 200 days, as a function of investment horizon. Return dispersion gradually decreases with the increasing investment horizons. For investment horizons greater than four years, return dispersion, or the mean interquartile range of the different average annual returns in the investment period, has decreased to levels as low as 5 percent. Figure 11.16 demonstrates a similar pattern for sector capital allocations. The sector capital allocation approaches are the same as in Table 11.5. As in Figure 11.15, return dispersion is measured by the IQR for the average annual returns over a range of sector capital allocations. As with lookback window size, return dispersion as a function of sector capital allocation gradually decreases as the investment horizon increases.

The Perils of Dynamic Parameter Selection

Several sections of this chapter have demonstrated that it seems to be relatively random which set of parameters is the best performing in any given year. This

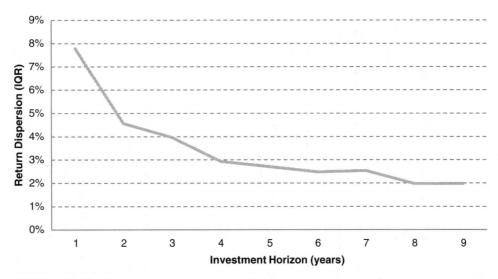

FIGURE 11.16 Return dispersion as measured by the interquartile range for the average annual returns over a range of sector capital allocations. The vertical axis is the mean interquartile range of different average annual returns in the investment horizon.

observation alone suggests that dynamic parameter selection may be an overly myopic or possibly a naive goal. Needless to say, it is natural that someone might wonder if parameters can be selected to outperform.

This section performs a simple empirical experiment. For each year, a system searches across a wide range of lookback window sizes and sector capital allocations. This set of parameters is roughly 10,000 combinations of lookback window sizes from 20 to 250 days and sector capital allocations from 0 to 100 percent. The parameter set that has the highest return for the following year is selected. Unlike future returns, because the experiment is performed on historical data, the future best performer is known. Given the set of 10,000 different combinations of parameters, a simple optimization of parameters based on the previous year's return results in an average annual return of 8.8 percent much lower than the average return over the sample period. Among the 10,000 combinations of lookback window size and sector capital allocations over the same period, only 13 percent of the parameter sets have an average return worse than what is achieved by dynamic adjustment of parameters annually.

There are other methods to dynamically select parameters based on past performance.[13] For another example, parameters can also be selected based on past

---

[13] It is also possible to apply advanced optimization methods and experiment with other technical variations. These approaches are likely to suffer from data-snooping biases.

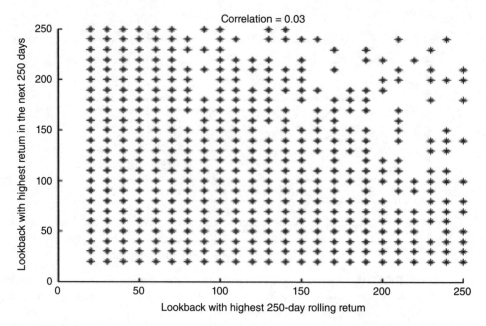

FIGURE 11.17 A scatter plot of the relationship between the lookback window size for the highest *current* 250-day rolling return and the lookback window size for the highest *subsequent* return over the following 250-day period.

Sharpe ratios. Instead of choosing the parameters with the best past performance (either return or Sharpe ratio), the parameters with the worst performance can also be tested. Interestingly enough, but not surprisingly, the overall performance of choosing the parameters of the worst performance in the past is similar to what was achieved by parameters of the best past performance.

Due to the apparent randomness of return dispersion, dynamic parameter adjustment based on past performance does not provide better results. To demonstrate this graphically, Figure 11.17 plots the relationship between the lookback window size with the highest *current* 250-day rolling return and the lookback window size with the highest *subsequent* return over the following 250-day period. The correlation between current and subsequent highest performing lookback windows is 0.03 or approximately zero. This scatter plot demonstrates that dynamic parameter selection is most likely doomed to be an ill-fated task.

Despite a concerted effort to find a filter to select the best parameters over time, in the short run the idiosyncratic nature of parameter selection seems to make this task somewhat insurmountable. The perils of dynamic parameter selection provide a convincing argument for diversifying across trend following programs.

Diversification Across Trend Following Programs

A closer analysis of return dispersion over time demonstrated that return dispersion seems to diminish with an increasing investment horizon. Another simple way to diversify a trend following strategy is to include a basket of trend following strategies. This combination helps to diffuse some of the idiosyncratic effects of parameter selection discussed earlier in this chapter. The impact of adding trend following strategies to a portfolio can be demonstrated with a simple empirical example. Let n be the number of included trend following programs. For each year, n trend following strategies are randomly selected from the pool of trend following strategies based on both breakout and moving average crossover systems with the same lookback window size and sector capital allocation ranges in this chapter. For each year from 2001 to 2013, 200 combinations of n randomly selected programs are used to calculate the level of return dispersion. In this case, return dispersion as a function of the number of trend following programs is measured by the IQR for the average annual returns of the n trend following programs. More simply, the return dispersion is the mid-range of values for the average annual portfolio return for a portfolio of n trend followers where there are 200 randomly selected examples of this portfolio. Average annual returns are calculated from 2001 to 2013 in this example.

Figure 11.18 plots annual return dispersion as a function of n, the number of included trend following programs for the sample period of 2001 to 2013. This figure demonstrates how return dispersion decreases as the number of trend following

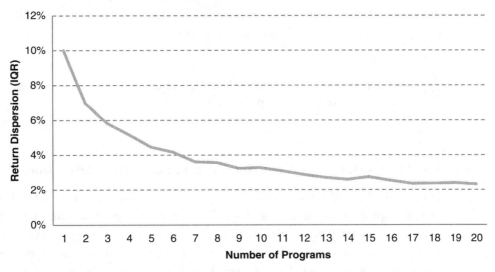

FIGURE 11.18 One-year return dispersion for average annual returns as a function of the number of included trend following programs. The vertical axis is return dispersion as measured by the mean interquartile range across each individual year from 2001 to 2013.

programs increases. This figure also demonstrates the approximate number of trend following programs that are needed to reduce the impact of return dispersion even at a one-year horizon. Based on Figure 11.18, the expected return dispersion for one-year returns is reduced from 10 percent for one program to below 5 percent for only five programs. As the portfolio increases to 20 trend following programs, return dispersion converges to a very low level of 2 percent. This example demonstrates how the *idiosyncratic effects of parameter selection* reduce with a pool of trend following strategies with different parameters. At a certain point there remains a level of return dispersion that cannot be diversified away. This "systematic" effect is due to the fact that portfolios of correlated, but not perfectly correlated, return series maintain some level of return dispersion. This concept is discussed in further detail in the following section.

■ Empirical and Theoretical Considerations for Correlated Return Series

The previous sections in this chapter focused on documenting and explaining return dispersion for trend following systems. Two trend following strategies with different parameterizations represent two correlated return series. From both an empirical and theoretical perspective, this section takes a step back and looks at the properties of correlated return series and its connection with return dispersion. First, return dispersion is examined theoretically for the case of two correlated return series. Second, CTA return dispersion is compared with the theoretical values for return dispersion. This section clarifies how diversification is still necessary across a large group of correlated trend following programs.

> Despite high correlations, diversification across trend following programs reduces the idiosyncratic effects of parameter selection.

Theoretical Considerations for Correlation and Return Dispersion

Given two stochastic-correlated return series, it is only natural that there will be return dispersion in the time series of these returns. The next question is how to determine the level of return dispersion to be expected over a particular observation period for both series. To simplify this analysis, the two return series (r_t^X, r_t^Y) are assumed to be normally distributed random variables. In this section for simplicity, return distribution is defined as the absolute difference between the two return series. For two normal random variables the absolute value of the difference between the two return series follows a folded normal distribution. In the special case where the two normal random variables have both the same mean (μ) and standard deviation (σ), with a correlation of (ρ), the expected value for return dispersion, the absolute difference between these two variables, is equal to the following expression:

$$E[|r^X - r^Y|] = \frac{S\sqrt{2}}{\sqrt{\pi}}$$

where $S = \sigma\sqrt{2(1-\rho)}$. The variance for return dispersion (the absolute difference) is equal to the following expression:

$$Var\ (|r^X - r^Y|) = S^2\left(1 - \frac{2}{\pi}\right)$$

Based on these two formulas, the following observations can be made:

- On average, return dispersion is linearly related to the volatility for the original two returns. Higher (lower) volatility, higher (lower) return dispersion.

- In the special case where the two correlated series have the same mean, return dispersion does not depend on the means of the two return series.

- The variance of return dispersion decreases linearly as a function of correlation. The expected value for return dispersion decreases as a square root of the correlation.

- Both the expected value and variance of return dispersion decrease when the correlation (ρ) increases.

- When the correlation (ρ) is close to 1, the expected value for return dispersion can still be quite substantial.

Simulation and Theoretical Return Dispersion

Using the theoretical framework for relating return dispersion to correlation, return dispersion can be examined in simulation to compare theoretical values with simulated return series. First, two correlated return series are simulated via Monte Carlo Simulation. Over a group of simulations, correlations are varied from 0 to 1. In this example, both return series have the same mean and same volatility. The volatility is set at 18 percent annualized. In Figure 11.19, the top graph plots the mean for return dispersion of rolling annual returns, and the lower graph plots the probability of the return dispersion being larger than 10 percent. The bars represent the estimates from simulation and the dark line represents the theoretical values derived earlier in this section. For a specific example, in the top graph, when the correlation

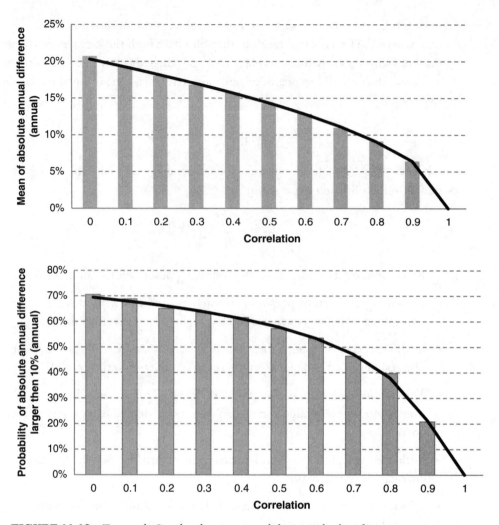

FIGURE 11.19   Top graph: Simulated estimates and theoretical values for average return dispersion for rolling annual returns as a function of correlation. Lower graph: Simulated estimates and theoretical values for the probability that return dispersion for rolling annual returns is greater than 10 percent. For both graphs, bar plots are simulation estimates and the dark line is the theoretical value.

is 0.7 between the two series, the average return dispersion should be around 11 percent. For the same correlation of 0.7 in the lower graph, there is almost a 50/50 chance that return dispersion will be greater than 10 percent.

From both of these figures, even in the case when the two return series are highly correlated, there is still a substantial chance for return dispersion. Figure 11.20 plots the same comparison of simulated and theoretical values for return dispersion using rolling monthly returns (as opposed to annual in Figure 11.19). The top graph plots

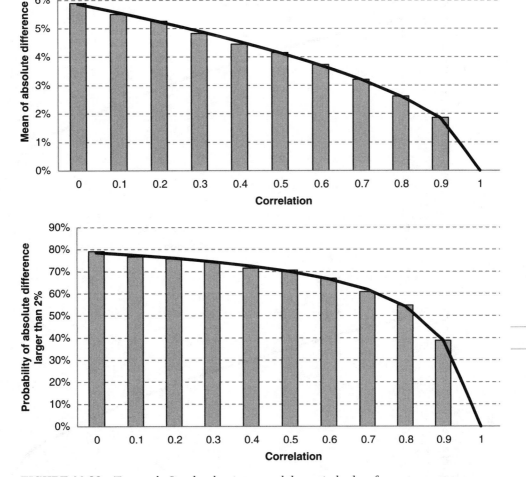

FIGURE 11.20 Top graph: Simulated estimates and theoretical values for average return dispersion for rolling monthly returns as a function of correlation. Lower graph: Simulated estimates and theoretical values for the probability that return dispersion for rolling monthly returns is greater than 2 percent. For both graphs, bar plots are simulation estimates and the dark line is the theoretical value.

the average return dispersion as a function of correlation and the lower graph plots the probability of the rolling monthly return dispersion being larger than 2 *percent*. For instance, using a specific example, when the two return series are correlated with 0.7, the average monthly return dispersion is greater than 3 percent, and the probability of observing a monthly return dispersion, which is larger than 2 percent, is as high as 61 percent.

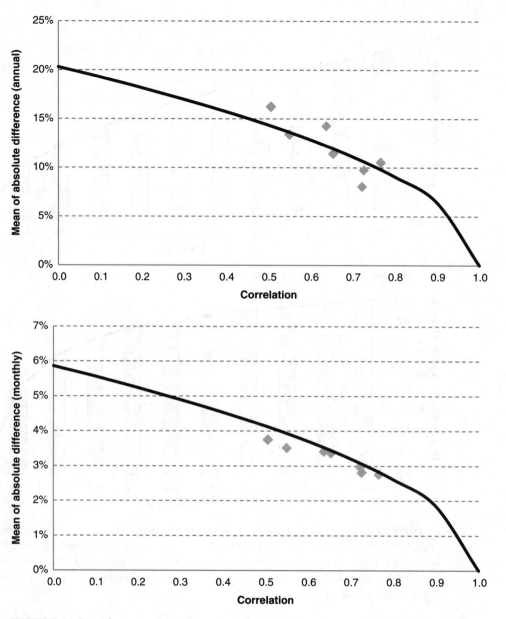

FIGURE 11.21 The mean return dispersion of annual rolling (top graph) and monthly (lower graph) returns between pure trend following and seven other CTAs from 2001 to 2012. The line shows the theoretical value for return dispersion as measured by mean of the absolute return difference.

Empirical Analysis of Correlation in Trend Following

The previous two sections discussed theoretical aspects of return dispersion for correlated return series. The relationship was examined both theoretically and via simulation. This section turns to an empirical analysis of return dispersion in trend following, using actual track records for CTA returns. For the typical trend following CTA, 0.7 is a good estimate for the correlation between various trend following CTA programs. For illustrative purposes, a pure trend following system can be compared with seven large trend following CTAs' actual track records. In this example, both monthly and annual rolling returns can be examined.[14] Figure 11.21 plots both the theoretical values for return dispersion and point values for the mean return dispersion between pure trend following and the seven actual trend following CTA track record returns. For both monthly and annual returns, mean return dispersion from actual CTA performance is in line with theoretical expectations for correlated return series.

When two return series are perfectly correlated, return dispersion is zero. In contrast, when correlations decrease from one, return dispersion becomes nonnegligible. Based on both the theoretical and empirical results in this section, for the simple case where correlations range between 0.6 and 0.8, for the same Sharpe ratios and an annual volatility of 18 percent, estimates for the average return dispersion are listed in Table 11.6. Even in the case where correlations range between 0.6 and 0.8, typical trend following correlations, this table demonstrates that return dispersion is relatively substantial from month to month and even annually.

Combining Correlated Return Series

Given the theoretical, simulated, and empirical evidence in this chapter, highly correlated return series still exhibit nonnegligible return dispersion. The results for this section have focused on comparing two return series. This section turns to the addition of several highly correlated return series empirically using actual track records

TABLE 11.6 Given a typical correlation of 0.6–0.8, the same Sharpe ratio, and annual volatility of 18 percent, approximate estimates of average return dispersion between two correlated series.

Frequency	Approximate Average Return Dispersion
Annual	10%
Biannual	7.5%
Monthly	3%

[14] All CTA track records start in June 2001 and end in December 2012. Each track record is first scaled to the same 18 percent risk for the given sample period. The Sharpe ratios for the CTAs vary from 0.42 to 0.90 in the sample period for this example.

for CTAs. Individual CTAs often have correlation between 0.6 and 0.8 depending on the observation period. As a group, for an individual year, return dispersion can be quite substantial. For example, in 2012, CTA returns, for managers with at least $1 billion in assets under management, ranged from more than 30 percent to minus 35 percent.[15]

One common mistake among investors is the assumption that the high correlation among CTAs suggests that all CTAs are created equal. At the extreme, this conclusion may even convince an investor to think that one CTA manager is only needed to represent the space. Returning to Figure 11.17, individual trend following strategies have substantial idiosyncratic effects due to their individual choice of parameters. These idiosyncratic effects create substantial return dispersion from year to year between individual trend following programs. As more trend following strategies are added into a portfolio the idiosyncratic effects of each individual trend following strategies parameters are averaged out. When this is done in aggregate, the systematic effects of combining correlated return series results in a low but nonnegligible level of return dispersion.[16]

Instead of using trend following systems, as was done earlier in this chapter, actual track records for CTA managers can be combined to see how return dispersion is affected by adding additional managers to a portfolio. Figure 11.22 plots return dispersion, as measured by the average interquartile range for investing in n unique trend following programs, as a function of n. As in Figure 11.18, the number of trend following programs ranges from 1 to 20. Despite the high level of correlation between the actual CTA track records, return dispersion decreases substantially with the addition of more trend following programs. This demonstrates that there are risks to selecting a single manager to represent an exposure to trend following. Selecting one manager will cause high levels of return dispersion due to the idiosyncratic effects of the parameters for an individual manager. This point was discussed at the beginning of this chapter when ranges of parameterizations for both position sizing and sector capital allocation were discussed. Just as with the simple breakout and moving average crossover trend following systems, adding several managers to a trend following portfolio reduces the idiosyncratic effects of parameter selection even for a one-year period.

[15] *Source:* Newedge Nelson Report 2012. The average return for 2012 was minus 1.1 percent. It is important to note that some of these managers are not necessarily trend following managers, and their use of leverage or target risk levels can vary substantially.
[16] The analogy of idiosyncratic and systematic risks in stock returns provides a good way to consider the importance of parameter dependence. For a large enough portfolio, only the systematic effect of correlated return series remains. This effect is systematic as it affects all strategies and it cannot be diversified away since the correlation between strategies is less than 1.

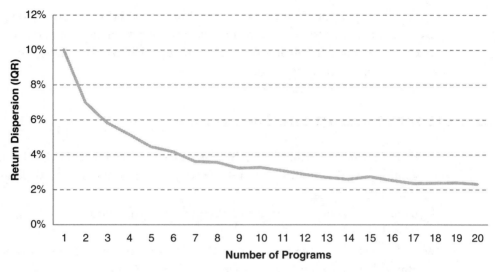

FIGURE 11.22 Return dispersion, as measured by the interquartile range for average annual returns, as a function of the number of trend following programs in a portfolio. Actual CTA track records are used for these calculations.

■ Summary

This chapter discusses the role of return dispersion in trend following. First, the chapter turns to strategy classification in trend following and examines two key aspects of strategy construction: position sizing and sector capital allocation. Over large ranges of parameter values, empirically return dispersion was shown to be both pervasive and highly random across time. These results were true for both position sizing and sector capital allocation. When market volatility was taken into account, volatility did not seem to drive the level of return dispersion for either position sizing or sector capital allocation. Given the random nature of return dispersion, the chapter turned to return dispersion from an investor perspective. Since optimal selection of parameters was shown to be a rather impossible task, an investor should consider the effects of adding several trend following programs into a portfolio. Adding several trend following programs, either actual track records or trend following systems, reduces the idiosyncratic effects of parameter selection. Finally, the chapter turned to a theoretical analysis of correlated return series and return dispersion. This analysis, when compared with actual CTA returns, demonstrated that return dispersion in the CTA industry is in line with expectations for highly correlated return series theoretically. As a summary, return dispersion is a natural effect for highly correlated return series. Each individual trend follower exhibits idiosyncratic effects due to parameter selection. These idiosyncratic effects can be reduced by combining unique trend following programs into a portfolio. When the portfolio is large enough, some level of return dispersion will remain. This level of return dispersion represents the systematic effects that remain from combining a portfolio of correlated return series that are not perfectly correlated.

■ Further Reading and References

Agarwal, V., and N. Naik. 2000, "Performance Evaluation of Hedge Funds with Option-Based and Buy-and-Hold Strategies." EFA 0373; FA Working Paper No. 300.

"Dynamic Leveraging as a Factor of Performance Attribution." ISAM white paper, May 2011.

Fama, E., and K. French. "Common Risk Factors in the Returns on Stocks and Bonds." *Journal of Financial Economics* 33 (1993): 3–56.

Fung, W., and D. Hsieh. "Empirical Characteristics of Dynamic Trading Strategies: The Case of Hedge Funds." *Review of Financial Studies* 2 (1997): 275–302.

Fung, W., and D. A. Hsieh. "Asset-Based Style Factors for Hedge Funds." *Financial Analyst Journal*, 58, no. 1 (2002).

Sharpe, W. E. "Asset Allocation: Management Style and Performance Measurement." *Journal of Portfolio Management* 18, no. 2 (Winter 1992): 7–19.

TREND FOLLOWING WITH MANAGED FUTURES

CHAPTER 12

Index and Style Factor Construction

Each individual trend following system includes a complex integration of risk allocation, signal generation, filtering, and trade execution. Each of these aspects combines to create a somewhat unique yet similar system. As discussed in the previous chapter, daily correlations between programs are often high, yet return dispersion in the cross section can be quite substantial. This provides a unique challenge for an investor as programs often deviate substantially from common industry benchmarks and from other trend following funds. Investors are concerned about performance evaluation, strategy classification, appropriate benchmarking, and monitoring style drift. Without a proper benchmark to compare with, results can be misleading and manager skill is difficult to characterize. A simple comparison to an industry benchmark is often too naive, and peer-based analysis can be relatively subjective. To alleviate this problem, Greyserman et al. (2014) present an analytic framework for performing return based style analysis in managed futures. By focusing on the divergent risk-taking aspect of trend following, their paper provides a direct link between strategy construction and performance in the cross section of CTA returns. In Figure 12.1, the rolling 12-month normalized returns for eight large CTAs is plotted. This plot demonstrates how difficult it can be to compare one trend follower with another.

This chapter reviews the construction of a new benchmark for divergent risk taking and three corresponding style factors from Greyserman et al. (2014). First, divergent risk taking is revisited and used to design a basic divergent trend following strategy. The construction of this simple strategy allows for the construction of

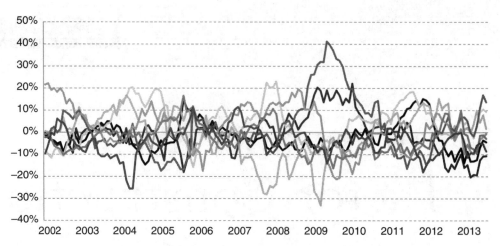

FIGURE 12.1 Twelve-month rolling returns for eight large trend following CTAs. All programs are normalized to the same risk for comparison.

Data source: Bloomberg.

"the market" for trend following, which is dubbed the divergent trend following index (DI). Second, three style factors based on market size, equity bias, and trading speed are constructed. Third, the DI and three factors are compared with common manager based indices, academic indices, and traditional asset classes. The analysis in this chapter provides the background for the returns based style analysis and its corresponding applications in Chapter 13.

■ Divergent Risk Taking Revisited

Divergent and convergent risk taking was discussed at length in Chapter 5. As opposed to convergent, divergent risk takers often assume relative ignorance to the distribution of asset returns. They systematically cut their losses on the downside and they "follow" or even double-up on winners. In distribution, divergent risk takers take many smaller losses but few larger wins. This means that these strategies have positive skewness, positive convexity, and lower **success rates** per trade. In practice, trend followers may have less than a 50 percent success rate in their positions. Trend following strategies are also some of the few hedge fund strategies to exhibit positive skewness in returns. Put simply, trend following strategies apply a divergent risk-taking approach across futures markets.

Contrary to popular belief, predictability on entry is often less important than the exit decision over time. As a description, this often leaves substantial room for interpretation and strategy construction. Each trend following strategy involves several key decisions: position entry mechanisms, risk allocation across markets, loss thresholds, and position selectivity. Position entry is often determined by noisy

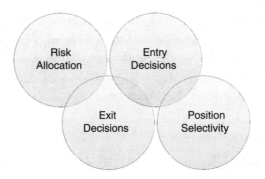

FIGURE 12.2 The core components of a trend following strategy.

price-based signals that deem when a trend is upward or downward. Risk allocation rules determine how much risk is allocated from one market to another. Loss thresholds determine when an upward trend or downward trend is deemed not to exist. Position selectivity explains how a strategy may prefer one market over another or uptrends in one market to downtrends in the same market.

A trend following strategy can be divided into four core components: risk allocation, entry decisions, exit decisions, and position selectivity. (See Figure 12.2.) Each of these components are reviewed from the perspective of a divergent risk taker.

The Entry Decision

The **entry decision** determines when a position is taken on. A pure divergent risk taker may have no view on the entry of a position.[1] As discussed in Chapter 3, a simple trend following system may use a moving average to enter a position. For example, Pedersen, Ooi, and Moskowitz (2012) use a 12-month period for both entry and exit in their time series momentum strategy.[2] The entry decision is perhaps the most controversial as the use of a sophisticated entry mechanism may suggest that returns are predictable over time.[3] Greyserman et al. (2014) use a naive

---

[1] The concept of momentum has been widely discussed by academics. The main problem with momentum is that both an entry and an exit decision are required to implement a momentum strategy. In fact, the term momentum has often caused investors and academics to assume that momentum strategies imply predictability in asset prices. One difference in a divergent risk-taking approach is that it is asymmetric; the exit decision is more important and more complex than the entry decision.

[2] As another example, the Newedge Trend Indicator is a simple 20/120 moving average crossover strategy on roughly 50 different futures markets.

[3] Pedersen, Ooi, and Moskowitz (2012) use one characterization of time series momentum, which includes a 12-month lookback window. They vary this characterization but their results also show that return dispersion varies with the construction of a strategy. Their entry window and exit window are based on past returns and they document a time series momentum asset pricing anomaly.

entry decision to avoid making any assumptions about predictability in asset prices across time. On the other end of the spectrum, Fung and Hsieh (1997b) demonstrate mathematically how trend following strategies are similar to lookback straddle options. In this case, entry and exit decisions are simply replication (or delta hedging) of a portfolio of exotic options.[4]

The Exit Decision

The decision to exit a position for a trend following system is the most critical one. The simple tulip crisis example from the first chapter of this book demonstrated this asymmetry. The decision to enter could be quite naive, but the decision to get out and when to get out will have a much larger impact on overall performance. Taking a detour into the behavioral finance literature, there is a plethora of evidence that confirms an implicit asymmetry between losses and gains.[5] The exit decision will depend explicitly on the **loss tolerance** of the strategy. The loss tolerance is simply the amount of loss a position can maintain before a divergent risk taker cuts the position. In the simple tulip example, as seen in Figure 12.3, a divergent risk taker with low loss tolerance would sell as soon as there was a small loss, for example 10 percent, getting out of the position in February. In contrast, a second divergent risk taker with higher loss tolerance than the first might have sold tulips in March. Finally, a third divergent risk taker with extreme levels of loss tolerance (perhaps exhibiting the disposition effect when faced with losers) becomes a buy-and-hold investor riding the tulip bubble up and crashing down with it.

Position Selectivity and Risk Allocation

Outside of entry and exit mechanisms, there are also two other key aspects to the construction of a trend following strategy. For a purely divergent risk taker, they should not engage in **position selectivity** as they may have no explicit view on any type of position. In practice, a system can be constructed to select certain positions

---

[4] Theoretically Fung and Hsieh (1997b) explain how trend following works mathematically in the absence of assumptions for predictability in asset returns. The problem for most investors is that lookback straddles are not traded. This provides some challenges for benchmarking returns.

[5] There is a wide range of behavioral finance topics that suggest an asymmetry. First and foremost, prospect theory, a positive theory in behavioral economics, demonstrates loss aversion in utility functions where losses are weighted more than gains. Investors also exhibit the disposition effect. They tend to hold onto their losers and sell their winners too fast. The snake bite effect also causes investors to avoid investing again once they have lost money. The issue of asymmetry in losses is also discussed in the context of stop loss rules in Kaminski and Lo (2014).

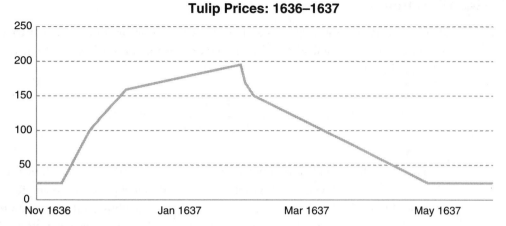

Tulip Prices: 1636–1637

FIGURE 12.3   A standard price index for tulip bulb contracts.
Source: Thompson (2007).

over others (a process often called *filtering*). A divergent risk taker should have "no conviction" or view on the value of one asset class versus another. For example, a purely divergent approach would not prefer equities to bonds; only the signal strength of these asset classes would dictate the position decision.

The second aspect to examine is risk allocation and correspondingly capital allocation. Risk allocation defines the allocation of risk across different markets. In theory, the simplest approach for allocating risk is equal dollar risk allocation based on past volatility. This approach is similar to risk parity without taking correlation into account. A strategy that deviates from the equal dollar risk allocation approach may be focusing on the size of the market, liquidity, or taking an implicit view on which risk premia they expect to outperform.

■ Defining a Divergent Trend Following Strategy

To characterize the divergent risk-taking approach, a simple divergent trend following strategy can be defined. A **divergent trend following strategy** (D) with returns (r_t^D) includes a basic entry decision, uses a trailing stop for exit decisions, and employs equal dollar risk allocation across markets. The entry decision is intentionally basic to avoid making assumptions about the predictability of future asset returns. A trailing stop is a simple stopping rule that updates stop levels and "trails" prices as they move. Equal dollar risk allocation is a simple, "agnostic," and robust method to allocate risk across markets. It relies only on the assumption that volatility is relatively persistent over time.

Risk Allocation

The nominal position (v) in a particular market, long or short, is equal to a sizing function times the total adjusted dollar risk times the nominal value of one contract. This can be written as follows:

$$v = s \times \left(\frac{\theta \times c}{\sigma_K(\Delta P) \times PV} \right) \times (PV \times P)$$

The sizing function is a number between -1 and 1 ($s \in [-1,1]$). It determines the size and direction of a contract based on entry and exit signals. The sizing function is discussed in more detail later in this section. The total adjusted dollar risk allocated is equal to the allocated dollar risk divided by the futures contract dollar risk. The allocated dollar risk is simply the risk loading (θ) times the allocated capital (c) per market. The futures contract dollar risk is the realized dollar risk ($\sigma_K(\Delta P)$ of each contract price over a lookback window of time (K) times the point value (PV)).[6] The nominal value of one contract is equal to the point value (multiplier) times the contract price.

Taking a closer look at this equation, there are several generalizations and extensions. First, in the simple case, the risk loading (θ) is set to be equal for all markets and it is often quoted in basis points, for example, 0.02 for each market. The risk loading is set up in this way to allow for gearing of a trend following system. Capital allocated to the strategy can also vary from market to market, but in the simple case, capital can be equal dollar weighted. This means that the capital for an individual market is equal to the total capital (c_T) divided by the number of traded markets (N).

$$c = \frac{c_T}{N}$$

An example, such as a long position in corn, can further clarify this equation. Suppose that future contracts for corn have a realized dollar risk $\sigma_K^{Corn}(\Delta P) \times PV = \$7,000$, the risk loading is 0.02, the capital allocated is \$1,000,000, the contract size (point value) is 50, and a typical price of \$430. If the sizing of the position was simply 1 ($s = 1$), the nominal position is \$61,427.57 long in corn. For comparison, corn contracts can be compared with a typical oil contract. For example, suppose that crude oil futures have a realized dollar risk of $\sigma_K^{oil}(\Delta P) \times PV = \$24,000$, the risk loading is 0.02, the capital allocated is \$1,000,000, the point value is 1,000, and the typical price is \$95.

---

[6] The point value is a multiplier that is used for the size of futures contracts.

For $s = 1$, this would constitute a long position of \$79,166.67 to oil.[7] The relative sizing is the most important. Total risk of the trend following system can be geared upward or downward by changing the risk loading. For example, if the risk loading for each contract is doubled to 0.04, the positions would also double for each market with \$122,857.14 in corn and \$158,333.33 in oil for the same allocated capital.

Entry and Exit Decisions

In the expression for the nominal position in each market, there is one key variable that needs to be characterized. The sizing function determines the implementation of a trend following strategy. At any particular time t, the sizing function (s_t) determines the position sizing and direction, long or short.[8]

The entry and exit decisions should be constructed to be consistent with a basic divergent risk-taking approach. A trailing stop is a simple, consistent method for cutting losses in positions. It is a stopping rule that is activated when a certain threshold of losses are acquired. The key feature of a trailing stop is the fact that the threshold for losses varies as a function of the past price history effectively "trailing" the price. In a simple characterization, the key parameter is the **trailing stop loss tolerance (γ)**. This quantity can simply be referred to as loss tolerance as it defines the tightness of the stops for a particular trend following strategy. If (γ) is large, the strategy has high loss tolerance and the trailing stops are only hit with larger losses. This is similar to a slow trend following system. On the other hand, if (γ) is small, the strategy has low loss tolerance and the strategy exits positions rather quickly. Using the same analogy, this is similar to a faster trend following system. The trailing stop updates the stop level as a function of (γ) and the past price history. Both a long and short **trailing stop indicator** ($I_t^{TS,long}$, $I_t^{TS,short}$) can be defined. These indicators are activated when either long or short trailing stop levels are hit. ($I_t^{TS,long}$) can be defined as follows

$$I_t^{TS,long}(\gamma) = \begin{cases} 1 & \text{if } P_t \leq TS_{t-1}^{long} & \text{Stop long position} \\ 0 & \text{if } P_t > TS_{t-1}^{long} & \text{maintain long position} \end{cases}$$

where (P_t) is the price at time t and (TS_{t-1}^{long}) is the trailing stop level at time $t - 1$ where (TS_t^{long}) is updated for each time t by the following expression:

$$TS_t^{long} = \max (P_t - \gamma\sigma_m, TS_{t-1}^{long})$$

---

[7] It is important to point out here that the total notional exposure is not the same as the capital allocated. The total capital allocated will also depend on the margin requirements for the contracts, as set by the futures exchange.

[8] Without loss of generality, as the approach is the same for all included markets, a particular market (i) is assumed and the subscript is dropped from this characterization.

with (σ_m) as the volatility of the price over a time window (m).[9] The trailing stop level follows the movement of prices over time. As prices rise, the trailing stop level follows them and vice versa. The trailing stop level is always the maximum of the previous trailing stop level and the new stop level based on the current price. If the current price is $100, the loss tolerance is 5, and the past volatility is 10 percent, the current stop level would be $50. The trailing stop level will depend on whether the price has risen or fallen in the recent past. For example, if prices had fallen to a current price of $100, the current trailing stop level could be $99. In this case, the new trailing stop level will be 99 (much higher than 50). On the other hand, if prices rose to the current price of $100, the previous trailing stop level could be $48. In this case, the next trailing stop level will be the same as the current stop level at $50.

Entry Mechanisms

Although intentionally very simple, the entry for a divergent trend following strategy is more subtle. First, to motivate the choice of entry heuristic, a little detour into behavioral finance can help explain a common behavioral heuristic, **probability matching**. As individuals, when we are faced with a decision between two choices, H or T, we will randomly select H at the same frequency as the underlying distribution. This process is deemed as probability matching by the field of heuristics. For example, if a coin is biased at 75 percent heads (or H), we will select heads or tails (H or T) at a similar frequency. For example, we will select HHTHHHTHTHHHHTHT as opposed to selecting HHHHHHHHHHHHHHHHH. In the case where the frequency to expect H is not known, the best estimate for this frequency is applied and H will be selected at that frequency. This behavioral heuristic can also be shown to be an optimal behavior when faced with a sequence of binary decisions over time.[10]

Trend following is a sequence of binary decisions. Similar to heads or tails, at each point of entry the decision is whether the trend is up or down (H versus T). In this

---

[9] The short trailing stop indicator is defined in a similar manner with:

$$I_t^{TS,short}(\gamma) = \begin{cases} 1 & if \ P_t \geq TS_{t-1}^{short} \quad Stop \ short \ position \\ 0 & if \ P_t < TS_{t-1}^{short} \quad maintain \ short \ position \end{cases}$$

where (P_t) is the price at time t and (TS_{t-1}^{short}) is the short trailing stop value at time $t-1$:

$$TS_t^{short} = \min(P_t + \gamma\sigma_m, TS_{t-1}^{short})$$

[10] In their paper, "The Origin of Behavior," Brennan and Lo (2011) explain that probability matching is an optimal strategy for success over time in a population. They examine a simple sequential decision model that can explain many behavioral heuristics in the behavioral finance literature including prospect theory, probability matching, risk foraging, and several others.

case, any individual trend follower will simply decide whether to go long or short at the same frequency as their best net estimate of an uptrend (H) or downtrend (T) denoted by $(\hat{p}_t^{up}, \hat{p}_t^{down})$. This means the average would be the best net estimate for an aggregated system of such decisions. Put more simply, the sizing function should be set to the net estimate of up or down trends.

$$s_t = \hat{p}_t^{up} - \hat{p}_t^{down}$$

When a trailing stop is hit, this is the same as realizing an H or T depending if the trailing stop was for the long or short position. For example, if two short trailing stops are hit, this is the same as realizing two tails (TT). The frequency for uptrends and downtrends should be updated accordingly as new information is available. The expression for updating the estimate for the probability of an up and down trend can be written as follows:

$$\hat{p}_t^{up} = \hat{p}_{t-1}^{up} + 0.5 \times (\hat{p}_{t-1}^{down} I_t^{TS,short} - \hat{p}_{t-1}^{up} I_t^{TS,long})$$

$$\hat{p}_t^{down} = \hat{p}_{t-1}^{down} + 0.5 \times (\hat{p}_{t-1}^{up} I_t^{TS,long} - \hat{p}_{t-1}^{down} I_t^{TS,short})$$

At each point in time when a trailing stop is reached for either the long or short position, the sizing function is adjusted to reflect the best net estimate for the trend upward or downward. Note that the probability of an uptrend plus a downtrend adds to one but the sizing function ranges between −1 and 1.

This system is perhaps best explained with an example. It can be assumed that initially there is no prior view on the probability of an uptrend or downtrend at time 0. In this case, $p_0^{up} = p_0^{down} = 0.5$ and the sizing function is 0 ($s_0 = 0$). Suppose that the first trailing stop occurs at time (τ_1) and a second at time (τ_2) with ($\tau_1 < \tau_2$). Suppose also that both trailing stops are for the short position. In this case, the indicator for the short trailing stop is one and the indicator for the long trailing stop is 0: $I_{\tau_1}^{TS,short} = 1$ and $I_{\tau_1}^{TS,long} = 0$. At the time of the first trailing stop (τ_1) the estimate for the probability that this market is in an uptrend is

$$\hat{p}_{\tau_1}^{up} = \hat{p}_{\tau_1-1}^{up} + 0.5 \times (\hat{p}_{\tau_1-1}^{down} I_{\tau_1}^{TS,short} - \hat{p}_{\tau_1-1}^{up} I_{\tau_1}^{TS,long})$$

$$= 0.5 + 0.5 \times (0.5(1) - 0.5(0)) = 0.75$$

This estimate is used to determine the sizing function, which is long with a loading of 0.5

$$s_{\tau_1} = \hat{p}_{\tau_1}^{up} - \hat{p}_{\tau_1}^{down} = 0.75 - 0.25 = 0.5$$

At time (τ_2) the time of the next (short) trailing stop, the probability estimates are updated again:

$$\hat{p}^{up}_{\tau_2} = \hat{p}^{up}_{\tau_2-1} + 0.5 \times (\hat{p}^{down}_{\tau_2-1} I^{TS,short}_{\tau_2} - \hat{p}^{up}_{\tau_2-1} I^{TS,long}_{\tau_2})$$

$$= 0.75 + 0.5 \times (0.25(1) - 0.75(0)) = 0.875$$

This estimate is used to adjust the sizing function to a long position with a loading of 0.75.

$$s_{\tau_2} = \hat{p}^{up}_{\tau_2} - \hat{p}^{down}_{\tau_2} = 0.875 - 0.125 = 0.75$$

The intuition is that when a trailing stop is hit, the estimated probability is adjusted based on the frequency that trailing stops are reached. The trading strategy is relatively naive and it depends directly on the frequency of trailing stops, which is characterized by the corresponding level of loss tolerance.[11]

Defining "The Market" for Trend Following

In the previous section, a simple divergent risk-taking approach for trend following was characterized. This strategy involves a few simple assumptions. First, the strategy uses estimates of an up or down trend to enter positions as a function of trailing stop frequencies. The decision to exit is a simple trailing stop heuristic with some level of loss tolerance (γ).

The next step is to determine, similar to what is the market for equity risk, the market for divergent risk taking. "The market" for equities is an equity index or a market capitalization weighted basket of long positions in company stock. In this case, the market for divergent risk is a basket of trading strategies, which represent a range of loss tolerances (γ). A **divergent trend following index (DI)** can be defined as an equal weighted basket[12] of trading strategies over a wide range of loss tolerances. Practically, the index can be constructed with a finite number of strategies over a reasonable range of loss tolerances ($\gamma = 4, 6, \ldots 20$). For this case, as opposed to in equities, an equal weighted approach is more suitable for the market as it is the simplest to implement. The DI represents the average market return for

---

[11] The trading system is essentially a Bayesian system with no prior. A simple 50/50 initial estimate is updated as stopping rules are hit over time.

[12] The simple baseline divergent trend following index has equal weighting to different loss tolerances. Perturbations of this index and how the strategies are put together will allow for the construction of style factors later in this chapter.

divergent risk taking. Given this characterization, a straightforward construction for the DI with returns (r_t^{DI}) can be defined as:

$$r_t^{DI} = \frac{1}{N} \sum_{i=1}^{N} r_t^D (\gamma_i), \quad \gamma_i = 4, 6, 8, \ldots 20$$

where $r_t^D (\gamma_i)$ is the return of a divergent trend following strategy with loss tolerance (γ_i) over a set of (N) different loss tolerances.

Intuitively, the DI is made up of an equal weighted basket of deterministic strategies over a range of loss tolerances. Unlike a manager-based industry index or even one specific trend index, the DI is not built by aggregating a large group of highly subjective and specifically parameterized strategies. The simplicity of this approach allows for modifications in the methodology to design style factors. The construction of style factors can help explain how the baseline divergent risk-taking approach can be modified to achieve different risk and return profiles. Before moving forward to construct style factors, the five key assumptions and characterizations that create the DI are summarized below:

1. Risk allocation: Equal dollar risk allocation across all markets (positions are based on past dollar risk levels. Market size or liquidity is not taken into account).
2. Loss tolerance: Assumed to be equal across all markets (i.e., there is no preference over losses in one market versus another).
3. Exit strategy: Completely characterized by a trailing stop, which depends on the loss tolerance of the strategy.
4. Entry strategy: Entry decisions happen immediately following an exit. The sizing of positions is based on the simple best net estimates for the probability of an uptrend minus a downtrend.
5. Position selectivity or bias: No implicit bias to any sector, asset class, or market.

It is also important to point out that the DI is an equal weighted combination of tradable investment strategies, which are completely defined by a small number of parameters. The index represents a wide range of tradable strategies in futures markets, which are differentiated by their approach to spreading risk and taking losses over time. Any individual trend following strategy may deviate from this approach, but at the core, trend following strategies are about diligent risk allocation and cutting losses.

Despite the simplicity of the DI, the index is relatively representative of the trend following industry. In Figure 12.4 and Figure 12.5, the historical performance of the DI is plotted with several common manager-based indices and trend indices. The manager-based indices represent a basket of trend following strategies constructed by individual managers whereas the trend indices are defined by a set of parameters.

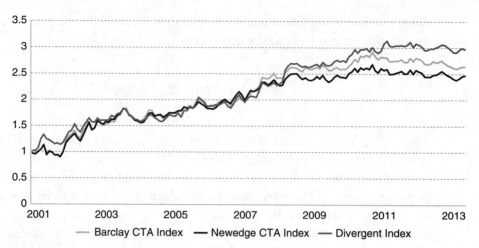

FIGURE 12.4 Historical performance of the Barclay CTA, Newedge CTA, and divergent trend following indices from June 2001 to December 2013. All series are normalized to a risk of 6 percent.

Data source: Bloomberg.

For example, the Newedge Trend Indicator is a simple 20/120 moving average crossover system in roughly 50 futures markets and TSMOM is defined by rolling 12-month windows from Pedersen, Ooi, and Moskowitz (2012).

For example, Figure 12.6 plots the correlation of the divergent trend following index with several manager-based indices and trend indices. The correlation with most manager-based indices is roughly 80 percent, which demonstrates that divergent risk taking is at the core of trend following. This is also evident in the trend indices from both industry and academia. The Newedge Trend Indicator is the

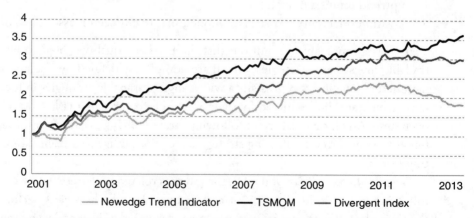

FIGURE 12.5 Historical performance of the Newedge Trend Indicator, TSMOM, and divergent trend following index from June 2001 to December 2013. All series are normalized to a risk of 6 percent.
Source: Bloomberg, Moskowitz, Ooi, and Pedersen (2012).

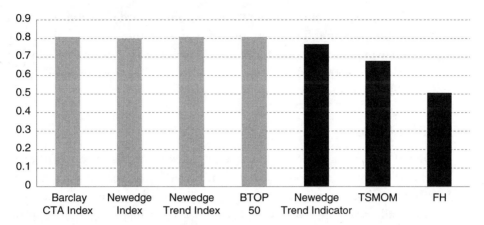

FIGURE 12.6 Correlation between the divergent trend following index (DI) with both common industry manager indices (Barclay CTA, Newedge, Newedge Trend, and BTOP50) and trend indices (Newedge Trend Indicator, TSMOM, and Fung and Hsieh). The sample period is June 2001 to December 2013.

Source: Bloomberg; Moskowitz, Ooi, and Pedersen (2012); and Fung and Hsieh (2001).

most correlated with a simple divergent trend following system that focuses most explicitly on loss tolerance. The Fung and Hsieh (1997b) lookback straddle option strategy[13] seems to have the lowest correlation with the DI.

At a first glance, although simply constructed, the DI seems to capture a key aspect in trend following. It is also interesting that a system that has most of the focus on the exit decision and the process of cutting losses seems to represent the trend following space rather well. The next step is to modify the strategy construction to better explain a wider range of approaches in trend following.

■ Constructing Style Factors

The previous section outlined the divergent trend following index (DI) or the market for divergent risk taking in futures markets. Similar to the construction of an equity index, the construction of the index provides a baseline for understanding "market beta" and the general valuation of equity risk. In this case, the divergent trend following index provides a baseline for understanding **trend beta** and the general valuation of divergent risk-taking activity. In the equity market, the method of constructing the market index cannot explain certain anomalies in the CAPM such as the small firm effect, value effect, and so on. Similar to the Fama and French

---

[13] The data for the Fung and Hsieh index can be obtained at http://faculty.fuqua.duke.edu/~dah7/DataLibrary/TF-FAC.xls.

(1993) factors, one can construct three straightforward CTA style factors. These factors can help account for deviations in the construction of a trend following strategy. Greyserman et al. (2014) construct style factors based on market size, equity bias, and trading speed. In this section, the construction of these three style factors is detailed to explain the intuition for each style factor.

Market Size Factor

One of the main assumptions for the DI index is the use of equal risk weightings to all markets based only on realized volatility. At the other extreme, risk can be allocated based on the market capacity of each individual futures market. For a review of risk allocation approaches see Chapter 3. For a market capacity approach to risk weighting, risk allocations are still adjusted by past volatility, but the capital allocation (c^i) can be set as a function of market capacity. In practical terms, market capacity can be measured by the volume multiplied by price volatility.[14] Capital will then be allocated as a function of the total market capacity. The nominal position for a market capacity weighted strategy for each individual market (i) is:

$$v^{MCW,i} = s^i \times \left(\frac{\theta \times c^i}{\sigma_K(\Delta P^i) \times PV^i} \right) \times (PV^i \times P^i)$$

where

$$c^i = \frac{MCAP_i}{\sum_{j=1}^{N} MCAP_j}$$

Using this logic, the **market size factor** (small minus big) with returns (r_t^{SMB}) is the difference between a divergent trend following strategy with equal risk weightings and one with market capacity weightings. In net, the market size factor represents the impact of allocating more capital to smaller and often less liquid markets which are typically capacity constrained. This is similar to the SMB factor for equities described by Fama and French (1993). In this case, the market size factor is defined as:

$$r_t^{SMB} = r_t^{DI} - r_t^{MCW}$$

Similar to equity markets, a market capacity approach will place more risk in large, liquid futures markets. Larger trend following systems, those with larger assets

---

[14] Market capacity (MCAP) is equal to 250-day rolling average daily volume and rolling average daily volatility (lagged by one day).

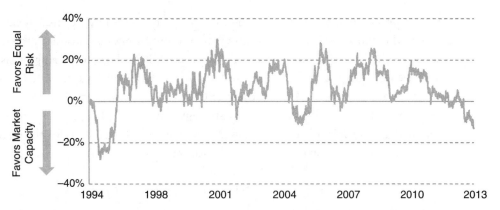

FIGURE 12.7 Twelve-month rolling returns for the market size factor (small minus big) (SMB) from December 1994 to December 2013.

under management and capacity constraints, may be restricted to this approach based purely on their size in assets under management. This may be a function of trading costs, slippage, and market impact in smaller markets. Practically, a size factor will indicate when divergent risk-taking opportunities or trends are coming from smaller markets or larger cash rich futures markets. Figure 12.7 plots the annual rolling returns of the market size factor (SMB) from December 1994 to December 2013. From September 1993 to December 2013, the SMB seems to be positive with an average of 6.3 percent. This indicates that there seems to be a small-market effect over time. The allocation of risk to smaller markets has added return over this 20-year sample period. It is important to note that similar to the small cap effect in equities, this premium is not stable. In certain periods, smaller markets greatly underperform larger markets. For example, since 2009 the SMB has been steadily decreasing. It is possible to speculate as to why this may be the case. The first candidate would be quantitative easing and its ability to create bigger trends in large, highly liquid bond and equity markets. If there are profound trends in these larger markets, the smaller markets may underperform in comparison. The size factor is directly linked to liquidity and issues with capacity in smaller markets. These issues are discussed in further detail in Chapter 15.

Equity Bias Factor

The divergent trend following index (DI) avoids having any specific preference to one particular market or another. Taking a small detour again into behavioral finance, investors tend to anchor to certain values or assets to make relative valuations. In financial markets, the main anchor for comparison is always equity markets. Most of investors' attention is focused on equity markets in aggregate. Given this fact, it is not surprising that a trend following manager may be tempted to include an equity bias in the construction of the strategy. If an equity-long bias is added, this changes some of the statistical properties of the strategy, including decreasing crisis alpha. This aspect of equity bias is discussed in further detail in Chapter 14. To examine equity bias, an **equity bias factor** (EQB) can be constructed as the difference between a divergent trend following strategy with an explicit equity-long bias and one with an explicit short-equity bias. Mathematically, the returns for the equity bias factor (r_t^{EQB}) can be characterized by the following expression:

$$r_t^{EQB} = r_t^{DI}(v_t^i > 0) - r_t^{DI}(v_t^i < 0), \; i \in Equities$$

The equity bias factor isolates the impact of adding rules or filters to slant a system more than usual. More specifically, under the assumption that there is an equity risk premium, over time there are more uptrends in equities than downtrends. In practice this is the case, but it is important to clarify that an equal dollar risk allocation approach does not mean equal capital allocation to long and short. The long and short ratio will depend only on the existence of long or short trends in a particular market. In equities, there are many more long than short signals. This means that an equal risk weighted approach already has a net long bias over time. If managers were interested in anchoring returns to an equity index even further, they might consider filtering out negative signals or restricting short positions in equities. The equity bias factor explains in relative terms how much a trend following strategy overallocates risk to long positions in equities.

Figure 12.8 plots the average annual rolling 12-month returns for the equity bias factor from December 1994 to December 2013. In this figure, it is clear that the

FIGURE 12.8 Twelve-month rolling returns for the equity bias factor (EQB) from December 1994 to December 2013.

equity bias factor tracks the performance of equity indices. This is evident from the drawdowns in equity markets from both the credit crisis and the tech bubble. Adding an extra bias toward equities is similar to adding equities to the portfolio or adding equity beta to the strategy. Intuitively, a system with equity bias will have a higher Sharpe ratio but will lose some of the positive characteristics of trend following during equity crisis periods. For example, the annualized mean return of equity bias factor is 6.7 percent from 1993 to 2013. The equity bias factor changes some of the statistical properties of trend following and reduces crisis alpha. This is discussed in further detail in Chapter 14.

Trading Speed Factor

In practice, most CTA investors ask managers for their average holding horizon. This is a simple number that investors often ask to get some idea of the speed of a trading program. The problem with this number is that it is an average and it is a complex combination of an enormous range of parameters in a trend following system. Using the divergent trend following approach, the performance of faster strategies with low loss tolerance and slower strategies with higher loss tolerance can be compared. A **trading speed factor** (*slow minus fast*) (SMF) is defined as the difference between a portfolio of slower, high loss tolerance strategies and a portfolio of faster, low loss tolerance strategies. Greyserman et al. (2014) define the trading speed factor return (r_t^{SMF}) as:

$$r_t^{SMF} = r_t^{DI}(\overline{\gamma}_{slow}) - r_t^{DI}(\overline{\gamma}_{fast})$$

where

$$\overline{\gamma}_{fast} = 4, \ldots 10; \overline{\gamma}_{slow} = 14, \ldots 20$$

The trading speed factor links trading speed to loss tolerance. When the trading speed factor is higher, slower trading systems (with higher loss tolerance) are more effective than faster trading strategies (with lower loss tolerance). Figure 12.9 plots the rolling annual returns for the trading speed factor from December 1994 to December 2013. The annualized average net return is roughly 8.8 percent, which suggests that slower systems have outperformed faster systems during the past 20 years. One interpretation of this result could be that higher loss tolerance is compensated over time by the market. It is also important to point out that similar to the market size factor, the trading speed factor is highly period dependent. There are certain periods where slow trading speeds with high loss tolerance are not compensated. For example, it is interesting to point out that faster systems perform better during crisis periods.

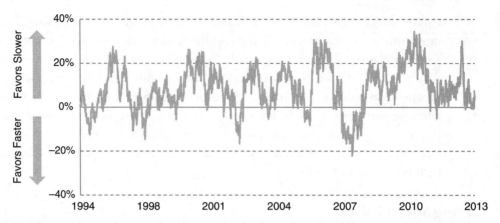

FIGURE 12.9 Twelve-month rolling returns for the trading speed factor (slow minus fast) (SMF) from December 1994 to December 2013.

■ Characteristics of the Style Factors

Given the construction of the three style factors, one issue of concern is correlation and collinearity of the style factors. If these factors explain the same effects, they may provide little help in explaining the cross section of CTA returns. Figure 12.10 plots the 12-month rolling returns for the divergent trend following index (DI) and the three style factors. There is considerable variation in their performance over time. In Table 12.1, the correlations between the factors and divergent trend following index are listed. The correlations are not zero and the factors seem to be reasonably different from each other. This suggests that they may be able to provide some explanatory power for different aspects in trend following systems.

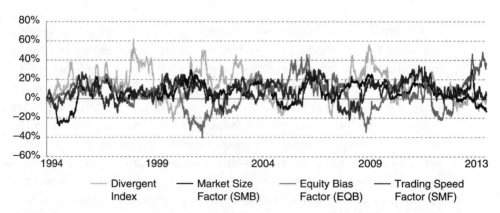

FIGURE 12.10 A comparison of the 12-month rolling returns for the divergent index (DI) and three style factors from December 1994 to December 2013.

TABLE 12.1		Correlations between the divergent trend following index (DI) and the three style factors: market size (SMB), equity bias (EQB), and trading speed (SMF).		
	DI (Trend Index)	Market Size Factor (SMB)	Equity Bias Factor (EQB)	Trading Speed Factor (SMF)
DI (Trend Index)	1	0.365	0.009	0.250
Market Size Factor (SMB)	0.365	1	−0.046	0.178
Equity Bias Factor (EQB)	0.009	−0.046	1	0.106
Trading Speed Factor (SMF)	0.250	0.178	0.106	1

As demonstrated in Figure 12.10, the divergent trend following index and three style factors exhibit significant variation. To examine this further, Table 12.2 presents summary statistics for the divergent trend following index (DI) and the size, equity, and speed factors.

Figure 12.11 plots the statistics for each of the style factors. The size factor has a smaller positive mean, positive skewness, and the highest kurtosis over the 20-year period. Neither the divergent trend following index nor any of the style factors have substantial serial correlation. Both the equity and trading speed factor have higher means than the size factor but negative skewness. Of all three style factors, the equity factor has the largest drawdown at 51.4 percent. To make the comparison more straightforward, it is important to volatility adjust the style factors. In Figure 12.12, the Sharpe ratios for the divergent trend following index (DI) and the three style factors are plotted for comparison. The DI has a Sharpe ratio of 0.81, which is in line with the CTA industry. More interesting among the style factors, the trading speed factor (SMF) has the highest Sharpe ratio of 0.60. The Sharpe ratios for the equity bias factor (EQB) and the market size factor (SMB) are lower at 0.48 and 0.57 respectively.

TABLE 12.2		Annualized statistics from 1993 to 2013 for the divergent trend following index (DI) and the three style factors: market size (SMB), equity bias (EQB), and trading speed (SMF). Statistics include mean, median, standard deviation, Sharpe ratio, skewness, kurtosis, serial autocorrelation, and maximum drawdown.						
Index and Factors	Mean (%)	Med (%)	St.Dev (%)	Sharpe	Skew	Kurt	ρ (%)	MDD (%)
DI (Trend Index)	14.80	11.20	18.20	0.81	0.56	4.24	7.50	20.50
Market Size Factor (SMB)	6.30	1.50	11.00	0.57	0.10	8.05	−6.60	25.50
Equity Bias Factor (EQB)	6.70	7.10	14.00	0.48	−0.38	3.94	−4.50	51.40
Trading Speed Factor (SMF)	8.80	14.90	14.60	0.60	−0.55	3.15	−1.30	21.20

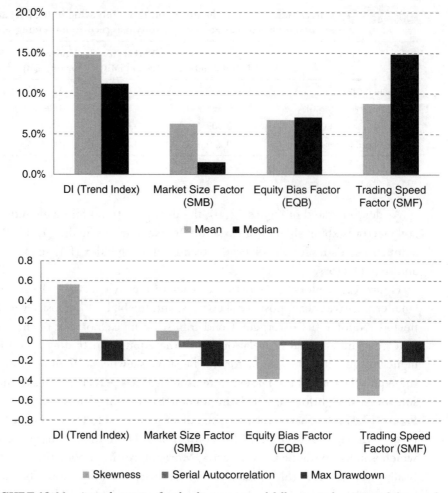

FIGURE 12.11 Annual statistics for the divergent trend following index (DI) and three style factors from 1993 to 2013.

FIGURE 12.12 Sharpe ratios for the divergent trend following index (DI) and three style factors from 1993 to 2013.

Comparing with Common Industry Indices

To better understand how the style factors relate to common manager-based industry indices and trend indices, in Figure 12.13 the correlation between these indices with the divergent trend following index and the three style factors is plotted. The style factors are generally positively correlated with the indices although they have much lower correlation than the predominant "trend" factor, the DI. This motivates the use of DI as a measure of trend beta. Of all three factors, the equity bias factor has the lowest correlation with all indices. The equity bias factor also has the most variation especially compared with the trend indices.

Comparing with Traditional Asset Classes

Most alternative investment strategies boast low correlation with traditional asset classes. Many investors choose to invest in trend following based on its complementary properties and conditional correlation with their investment portfolios. As a result, it is interesting to take a closer look at how style factors relate to traditional asset classes. Figure 12.14 plots the correlation of the DI and the three style factors (size, equity, speed) with traditional assets. Traditional assets include equities (MSCI World Index), emerging equities (MSCI EM Index), fixed income (JPM Global Bond Index), commodities (S&P GSCI), and volatility (VIX Index). As expected during the 20-year period, the DI has a low negative correlation with equities and low

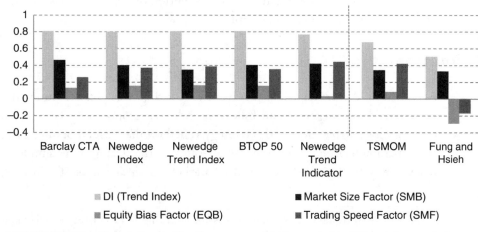

FIGURE 12.13 Correlation for the divergent trend following index (DI) and three style factors with several common industry manager-based indices and several trend indices from June 2001 to December 2013.

Data source: Bloomberg; Moskowitz, Ooi, and Pedersen (2012); and Fung and Hsieh (2001).

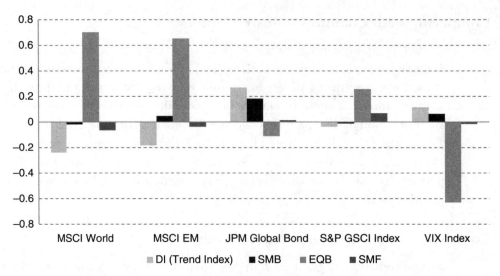

FIGURE 12.14 The divergent trend following index (DI) and size, equity, and speed factors correlation with other asset classes: Equity (MSCI World Index), Emerging Equity (MSCI EM Index), Fixed Income (JPM Global Bond Index), Commodities (S&P GSCI Index), and Volatility (VIX Index). The sample period is 1993 to 2013.
Data source: Bloomberg.

positive correlation with fixed income and volatility.[15] The size factor (SMB) has low positive correlation with bonds. The equity factor has the highest correlations in absolute terms with a high positive correlation with equity markets and large negative correlation with volatility. The trading speed factor has the lowest correlations in absolute terms with all of the traditional asset classes. In absolute terms, very few of the correlations are substantial with the exception of the equity bias factor. This will be discussed in more detail in Chapter 14.

■ Summary

By revisiting the principles of divergent risk taking, this chapter outlined the construction of a divergent trend following index as proposed by Greyserman et al. (2014). The construction of this strategy relied on the least amount of assumptions and is parameterized by only the loss tolerance of the strategy. This simple definition led the way to the construction of a "market" or *trend beta* as it will be called in

---

[15]The positive correlation with fixed income is not surprising. In Chapter 6, the roll of interest rates was discussed. The contribution of interest income for futures trading strategies is nonnegligible. Volatility was also discussed in for defining crisis periods in Chapter 7 and in the context of portfolio volatility in Chapter 8. Trend following is related to changes in volatility on the upside, which in net makes the strategy slightly positively correlated with volatility over the long run.

Chapter 13, the DI and three corresponding style factors based on market size, equity bias, and trading speed. The Sharpe ratio for the DI and three style factors are all positive with moderately low correlations between them. The divergent trend following index and three style factors were then compared with manager-based indices, price-based trend following indices, and traditional asset classes. The analysis in this chapter provides the background for the returns-based style analysis in the following chapter.

■ Further Reading and References

Agarwal, V., and N. Y. Naik. "Performance Evaluation of Hedge Funds with Option-Based and Buy-and-Hold Strategies." EFA 0373; FA Working Paper No. 300, 2000.

Brennan, T., and A. Lo. "The Origin of Behavior." *Quarterly Journal of Finance* 1, no. 55 (2011).

Fama, E., and K. French. "Common Risk Factors in the Returns on Stocks and Bonds." *Journal of Financial Economics* 33 (1993): 3–56.

Fung, W., and D. Hsieh. "Empirical Characteristics of Dynamic Trading Strategies: The Case of Hedge Funds." *Review of Financial Studies* 2 (1997a): 275–302.

Fung, W., and D. Hsieh. "Survivorship Bias and Investment Style in the Returns of CTAs." *Journal of Portfolio Management* 23 (1997b): 30–41.

Fung, W., and D. Hsieh. "A Primer on Hedge Funds." *Journal of Empirical Finance* 6 (1999): 309–331.

Fung, W., and D. Hsieh. "The Risk in Hedge Fund Strategies: Theory and Evidence from Trend Followers." *The Review of Financial Studies* 2 (2001): 313–341.

Fung, W., and D. Hsieh. "Performance Characteristics of Hedge Funds and Commodity Funds: Natural vs. Spurious Biases." *Journal of Financial and Quantitative Analysis* 35 (2000): 291–307.

Fung, W., and D. Hsieh. "Asset-Based Style Factors for Hedge Funds." *Financial Analysts Journal*, 58, no. 1 (2002).

Fung, W., and D. Hsieh. "Hedge Fund Benchmarks: A Risk-Based Approach." *Financial Analysts Journal* 60 (2004): 65–80.

Greyserman, A., K. Kaminski, A. Lo, and L. Yan. "Style Analysis in Systematic Trend Following." Working paper, 2014.

Kaminski, K., and A. Lo. "When Do Stop-Loss Rules Stop Losses?" *Journal of Financial Markets* 18, issue C (2014): 234–254.

Moskowitz, T., Y. Ooi, and L. Pedersen. "Times Series Momentum." *Journal of Financial Economics* 104 (2012): 228–250.

Thompson, E. "The Tulipmania: Fact or Artifact?" Public Choice 130, nos. 1–2 (2007): 99–114.

CHAPTER 13

Benchmarking and Style Analysis

Return-based style analysis is a commonly used technique to identify a fund's exposures to a mixture of indices or factors. It can be used to evaluate a fund's performance, to reveal asset allocation tilts, and to detect style drift. Originally proposed by Sharpe (1992) for mutual fund return analysis, Fama and French (1993) would go on to develop a similar methodology, based on three factors, to explain the cross-section of stock returns. This chapter develops the same methodology for trend following. It is worthwhile to note that, while focused on the strategy of trend following, this type of analysis can also be generalized to other strategies. Using the divergent trend following index (DI) as the baseline strategy or "market" portfolio and three construction style factors similar to Greyserman, Kaminski, Lo, and Yan (2014), this chapter develops a framework and discusses applications for return-based style analysis in managed futures.

The trend following style factors are not based on index returns; they are constructed similar to those of the Fama and French (1993) three-factor model. A framework of this kind is necessary as work on hedge fund–style analysis focuses only on higher interstrategy (as opposed to intrastrategy) variations. More specifically, in the literature, hedge fund returns are often characterized by the returns of buy-and-hold strategies of assets manager portfolios, returns attributed to their dynamic trading strategies, and other style factors.[1] For example, Fung and Hsieh (1997a) identify five general strategy categories to explain the return differential among a wide range

---

[1] See also Hasanhodzic and Lo (2007).

of hedge funds: systems/trend following, systems/opportunistic, global/macro, value, and distressed. Studies of this type are useful for determining the general **strategy category** of a hedge fund. They cannot provide a more detailed, intra-strategy differentiation among the funds within the same category. The framework, as proposed by Greyserman et al. (2014), is designed to fill the void in style analysis at the intrastrategy level for trend following within managed futures.

■ A Framework for Return-Based Style Analysis

Return-based style analysis is based on explicitly defining a relationship between a strategy's returns and the corresponding baseline strategy and style factors. Following the discussion in Greyserman et al. (2014), any trend following return series (either a fund or an index) can be decomposed into the contribution from the baseline strategy (the divergent trend following index, DI), and the contribution from the corresponding construction style factors. The trend following style factors include the market size factor (SMB), the equity bias factor (EQB), and the trading speed factor (SMF).[2] Given this framework, the following linear relationship between a trend following return series and the baseline strategy and each corresponding style factor can be written as:

$$r_t^{CTA} - r_f = \alpha + \beta^{Trend} r_t^{DI} + \beta^{SMB} r_t^{SMB} + \beta^{EQB} r_t^{EQB} + \beta^{SMF} r_t^{SMF} + \varepsilon_t$$

This relationship is defined by the gross return at time t of the baseline strategy net the risk-free rate (r_f) compared with the return of the divergent trend following index (r_t^{DI}), the return of the market size factor (r_t^{SMB}), the return of the equity bias factor (r_t^{EQB}), and the return of the trading speed factor (r_t^{SMF}). The corresponding betas (coefficients) can be interpreted as the "*trend beta*" and "*style betas*" for market size, equity bias, and trading speed. To analyze the validity of this relationship, a simple linear regression between a trend follower's gross return series and the corresponding return series for the divergent trend following index (DI) and three style factors can provide estimates for the beta coefficients and alpha (the intercept). The estimates for betas will provide a quantitative measure for determining the style of an individual manager or index. The R-squared for this regression will provide a measure for the goodness of fit of the model. Given the variability in manager returns, high R-squared values suggest that the linear relationship explains a substantial portion of the variability of returns for a given return series. The intercept of the

TREND FOLLOWING WITH MANAGED FUTURES

---

[2] Chapter 12 included a thorough discussion and analysis of both the divergent trend following index (DI) and three corresponding style factors.

linear relationship represents the alpha, or the amount of performance that remains once all of the effects of each style and baseline strategy are taken into account.

Analyzing Common Industry Benchmarks

A natural first step is to return to commonly used manager-based indices and price-based trend indices discussed in the previous chapter. A review of manager-based indices provides an aggregate view of the average style of CTA managers. A review of price-based trend indices, both industry oriented (the Newedge Trend Indicator) or academically motivated (TSMOM;[3] Fung and Hsieh[4]), provide perspective into their construction style. The differences between the manager-based indices, which include actual track record returns, and price-based indices allow for perspective on how styles may be adjusted when the rubber meets the road (when theory meets practice).

A return-based style analysis can be applied to each of these indices by regressing their excess return series on trend (DI), market size (SMB), equity bias (EQB), and trading speed (SMF). Table 13.1 describes the results of this analysis for the relevant time periods.[5] The R-squared values for each of these indices range from 0.48 for the Fung and Hsieh model (2001) to 0.69 for Newedge Trend Index. This suggests that the return-based style analysis explains a substantial portion of the variation in CTA index returns. Figure 13.1 compares the trend beta for each of the indices. The Newedge Trend Index has the highest trend beta and both trend indices have

TABLE 13.1 Return-based style analysis on common manager-based CTA indices (Newedge CTA Index, Newedge Trend Index, BTOP 50 Index) and price-based trend indices (Newedge Trend Indicator, TSMOM, Fung and Hsieh). Significant coefficients are labeled in bold for p values less than 5 percent and italics for p values less than 10 percent.

Manager-Based Indices and Price-Based Trend Indices	Trend	Size	Equity	Speed	R-Squared	Intercept (%)
Newedge CTA	**0.37**	0.00	**0.08**	0.04	0.67	*−0.23*
Newedge Trend	**0.65**	−0.13	**0.16**	*0.08*	0.69	**−0.41**
BTOP 50	**0.35**	0.00	**0.08**	0.02	0.68	*−0.21*
Newedge Trend Indicator	**0.54**	0.13	−0.03	**0.16**	0.62	**−0.40**
TSMOM	**0.46**	−0.03	0.06	**0.16**	0.50	*0.43*
Fung and Hsieh	**1.44**	**0.74**	**−0.72**	**−1.08**	0.48	**−2.39**

Data source: Bloomberg; Moskowitz, Ooi, and Pedersen (2012); and Fung and Hsieh (2001).

---

[3] Data source for TSMOM is Moskowitz, Ooi, and Pedersen (2012).

[4] The data for the Fung and Hsieh index can be obtained at http://faculty.fuqua.duke.edu/~dah7/DataLibrary/TF-FAC.xls.

[5] The return series begin in 2000 with the start of the Newedge CTA index. Some indices, for example the BTOP50 index, have longer data histories. For consistency, this analysis begins in 2000.

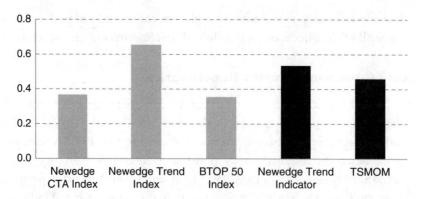

FIGURE 13.1 Estimates of "Trend Beta" for select industry manager-based CTA indices (Newedge CTA Index, Newedge Trend Index, BTOP 50 Index) and price-based trend indices (Newedge Trend Indicator, TSMOM).
Data source: Bloomberg; Moskowitz, Ooi, and Pedersen (2012).

relatively high betas as well. Given that the DI runs at a volatility of 18.2 percent, it is not surprising that the trend beta is less than one for most indices. It is also consistent that the Newedge Trend Index, which contains exclusively trend followers, has the highest trend beta. Both the Newedge Trend CTA and BTOP 50 indices contain funds with a wider range of nontrend following strategies.

Figure 13.2 compares the *style betas* for each of the indices. The market size beta (SMB) is not statistically significant for any of the indices except the Fung & Hsieh (2001). Although not significant, the market-size beta (SMB) is close to zero for the Newedge CTA and BTOP 50 indices. The Newedge Trend Index is slightly negative indicating that the trend followers in this index might have a slight preference for larger markets. For the Fung and Hsieh trend index, which does not represent an actual track record, the market size factor is large and positive, suggesting a small market bias in this theoretical price-based index. The comparison between the trend indices and the indices based on actual track records suggests the practicalities of smaller markets, due possibly to liquidity and volume constraints, might cause a slight style shift when practice is compared with theory.

Returning again to Figure 13.2, the equity bias beta is positive and significant for all manager-based indices. On the other end, the Fung and Hsieh (2001) lookback straddle portfolio has a large negative statistically significant loading to the equity bias factor. When theory is compared with practice, the manager-based indices exhibit somewhat larger equity bias than the price-based indices. From a style perspective, this suggests that in aggregate, fund managers may choose to slightly overweight long positions in equity markets. For the price-based trend indices, the TSMOM also has a slight but not statistically significant style slant toward equity markets. This style slant may be due to the parameter selection of 12 months in the paper by Moskowitz,

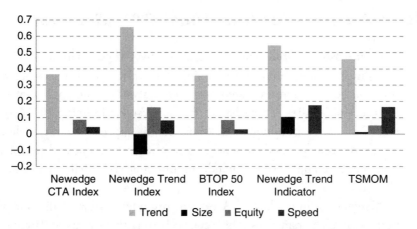

FIGURE 13.2 Trend beta and three factors betas (size, equity, and speed) for select manager-based CTA indices and price-based trend indices.
Data source: Bloomberg, Moskowitz, Ooi, and Pedersen (2012).

Ooi, and Pedersen (2012). It is possible that the choice of 12 months happens to be a very good lookback window size for long equity markets in particular. Relative to a general divergent trend following approach, this may cause a slight equity bias based on specific parameter selection.

The trading speed betas are almost all positive except Fung and Hsieh (2001) although they vary in significance. The TSMOM series uses a window of 12 months. Since the speed factor loading is positive, this indicates that TSMOM trades slower than the typical trend following system.[6] Both the Newedge Trend Indicator and TSMOM have higher trading speed betas than the manager-based indices. Among the manager-based indices, the Newedge Trend Index, which contains only managers labeled as trend followers, has the highest trading speed beta, which is significant. This suggests that trend followers in this index tend to trade slower than the average CTA. This qualitative point is well known in the CTA industry. Many nontrend managers may use short-term, relative value, or mean reversion strategies. These strategies typically trade more often than trend followers. Even at the aggregate level, this style difference between a pure trend following index and an aggregate CTA index can be demonstrated quantitatively using style analysis. For both manager-based and price-based trend indices, trend beta is much larger than the other style factors. Intuitively, the aggregate index level style analysis in this section suggests that trend followers are primarily divergent risk takers. In aggregate, they may also make certain style adjustments due to market constraints and frictions, an implicit desire for equity bias, and possibly trading costs.

_____

[6]A 12-month window will mean that the observation period is 12 months, not that the holding period is 12 months.

■ Style Analysis for Individual CTA Managers

The return-based style analysis proposed by Greyserman et al. (2014) provides a straightforward method for discussing intrastrategy differences between CTAs. The previous section demonstrated how this analysis can be applied at the index level. This section applies return-based style analysis on individual CTA returns and discusses the corresponding applications of this approach. First, style analysis allows for more strategy specific benchmarking, classification, and performance attribution. Further applications include monitoring style drift, manager selection, and allocation.

A review of individual CTA returns provides a view of the underlying styles of individual CTA managers. This section begins this discussion by considering eight large trend following CTA managers. Table 13.2 shows the results of a return-based style analysis using the monthly returns of eight large CTAs against the returns of the baseline system (DI) and the return series of the three factors.[7] For simplicity these CTAs are labeled CTA1 to CTA8. The R-squared for the regressions are between 0.52 and 0.74, indicating the explanatory power of the return-based style analysis. Alpha is the intercept of each regression and the betas are the coefficients with (DI) and the three style factors.[8]

In Figure 13.3, the trend beta for each CTA is plotted for comparison. When compared with the manager composite indices, individual CTA trend beta exhibits variation from one CTA to another. Figure 13.4 plots the market size, equity bias, and trading speed factors for each individual CTA. The exposure to different style factors seems to vary substantially for each of the factors. This demonstrates how not all CTAs are created equal. Unlike the aggregate indices, each of the individual CTAs seem to have their own loadings to the various style factors. For example, CTA1 is the only CTA with a negative beta with the equity bias factor (EQB) and a positive yet insignificant beta with market size factor (SMB). This suggests that CTA1 may allocate more risk to small markets and clearly avoids long equity bias more than its peer group. For the case of CTA4, the market size beta is very large and negative, the equity bias beta is large and positive, and the trading speed beta is large and positive. This suggests that CTA4 has more risk allocated to larger markets (most likely financials), a select excess long bias toward equity, and a somewhat slower system than its peer group. Even in the peer group of large CTAs, there is significant variation in trading styles.

---

[7] All returns are monthly between June 2001 and December 2013.

[8] Unlike the standard return-based style analysis, the coefficients are not constrained to be larger than 0 and to sum to 1.

	Trend	Size	Equity	Speed	R-Squared	Intercept (%)
CTA1	**0.78**	0.12	*–0.11*	**0.16**	0.70	–0.11
CTA2	**0.82**	**–0.21**	**0.12**	–0.02	0.71	–0.25
CTA3	**0.69**	**–0.26**	**0.20**	–0.05	0.52	0.27
CTA4	**0.50**	*–0.20*	**0.17**	**0.13**	0.49	–0.12
CTA5	**0.51**	**–0.16**	**0.14**	*0.09*	0.62	–0.12
CTA6	**0.47**	–0.03	**0.20**	–0.01	0.56	0.11
CTA7	**0.81**	–0.14	**0.14**	*–0.09*	0.74	–0.30
CTA8	**0.59**	–0.14	**0.24**	*0.11*	0.60	*–0.43*

TABLE 13.2 Return-based style analysis of eight large trend following CTAs. Significant coefficients are labeled in bold for *p* values less than 5 percent and italics for *p* values less than 10 percent.

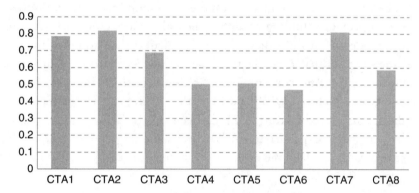

FIGURE 13.3 "Trend Beta" with the divergent trend following index (DI) for eight individual large trend following CTAs.

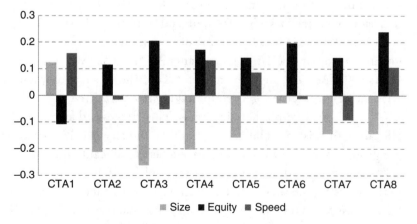

FIGURE 13.4 Size, equity, and speed betas for eight large trend following CTAs.

It is important to remember that this analysis is based only on the return series of these managers. This classification is not based on anecdotal comments or qualitative classifications. Although an investor might be able to ask a CTA manager for information regarding the style of their program, most of this information may be difficult to quantify or classify systematically. This quantitative CTA style analysis was able to classify a CTA's trend following construction style and link this directly to their return series. The only input is the monthly return series, and the fit is rather impressive given the level of volatility in manager return series.

Appropriate Benchmarking and Performance Attribution

After the factor loadings are known for each CTA, it is possible to establish a specific benchmark based on the CTA's own exposures to the three factors and the base system (DI). A positive alpha can be interpreted as skills of the specific CTA in relation to the benchmark with the corresponding style exposures. For example, CTA3 provides the largest alpha when all style factors are taken into account in the model. CTA3 also has a lower R-squared than some of the other managers. This suggests that other factors may be necessary to explain the positive excess performance. Another simple application is performance attribution: in 2013 the equity bias factor (EQB) is positive, the market size factor (SMB) is negative, and the trading speed factor (SMF) has been relatively low and insignificant. Given the large negative exposure to small markets and large positive equity bias, one might expect CTA3 to lead the pack. This is indeed the case; CTA3 well outperformed its peers in 2013.

Smaller and Nontrend Managers

The analysis can now be turned to other types of trend followers outside of large CTAs. First, a group of small CTAs (small in AUM, labeled SCTAs) and a group of managers who are classified as "nontrend" (strategy classifier is nontrend, labeled NCTAs). Table 13.3 lists the results of a return-based style analysis on the original group of eight large CTAs, eight smaller AUM CTAs (SCTAs), and three nontrend CTAs (NCTAs). Among the smaller CTAs, the R-squared values are consistent with the original large CTA group ranging from 0.25 to 0.62. A few of the smaller CTAs have positive market size betas. This suggests that some of them seem to allocate more risk to smaller markets than the larger CTA managers. In this sample group, most small CTAs also have a less significant equity bias than the larger CTAs and their trading speed betas vary substantially. Consistent with discussion in the industry, the smaller CTAs seem to have a wider range of styles and possibly have access to certain opportunities in small markets that larger CTAs may not. In the nontrend group, both NCTA1 and NCTA3 have R-squared estimates close to

TABLE 13.3 Return-based style analysis on a group of large CTAs, smaller CTAs, and nontrend CTAs. Significant coefficients are labeled in bold for p values less than 5 percent and italics for p values less than 10 percent.

	Trend	Size	Equity	Speed	R-Squared	Intercept (%)
CTA1	**0.78**	0.12	*−0.11*	**0.16**	0.70	−0.11
CTA2	**0.82**	**−0.21**	**0.12**	−0.02	0.71	−0.25
CTA3	**0.69**	**−0.26**	**0.20**	−0.05	0.52	0.27
CTA4	**0.50**	**−0.20**	**0.17**	**0.13**	0.49	−0.12
CTA5	**0.51**	*−0.16*	**0.14**	*0.09*	0.62	−0.12
CTA6	**0.47**	−0.03	**0.20**	−0.01	0.56	0.11
CTA7	**0.81**	−0.14	**0.14**	**−0.09**	0.74	−0.30
CTA8	**0.59**	−0.14	**0.24**	*0.11*	0.60	*−0.43*
S CTA1	**0.52**	**0.45**	−0.01	**0.26**	0.44	−0.22
S CTA2	**0.53**	0.19	**0.34**	**0.28**	0.52	**−0.83**
S CTA3	**1.13**	0.20	−0.07	−0.20	0.35	−0.03
S CTA4	**1.45**	**−0.52**	0.03	**0.34**	0.62	*−0.95*
S CTA5	**0.38**	0.00	0.11	−0.11	0.25	0.12
S CTA6	**0.63**	−0.07	0.04	0.02	0.49	−0.29
S CTA7	**0.87**	0.14	**0.20**	**−0.21**	0.51	0.07
S CTA8	**0.57**	**0.32**	**0.14**	**−0.25**	0.60	−0.12
N CTA1	−0.04	0.01	−0.05	0.02	0.01	**0.53**
N CTA2	**0.73**	**−0.53**	−0.11	**0.18**	0.46	**0.74**
N CTA3	0.06	*0.16*	0.03	0.01	0.08	0.05

zero. This suggests that their returns are not characterized by any style of trend following. On the other hand, NCTA2 sticks out with an R-squared value of 0.46. NCTA2 may label themselves as nontrend but a trend following style analysis paints a very different picture. In the peer group of all CTAs in this set, NCTA2 does differ from other managers by having a very negative and significant market size beta, a less significant negative equity bias beta, and a large and significant trading speed beta. This suggests that this manager favors the larger markets, may have a relative short equity bias, and slower trading systems.[9] From the perspective of an investor, this type of analysis will help to nonsubjectively classify and compare CTA managers.

---

[9] Personal discussions with this manager, NCTA2, confirm that this analysis is indeed the case. This particular manager does not employ as frequent stops creating a slower trading system and has a rather unique approach for trend signals. Despite the uniqueness in the peer group, the manager is still very much a trend following manager.

Carry Trading

Given that carry is a common futures strategy, it is not uncommon for investors to consider carry as an additional factor for CTA style analysis. Despite this, most trend following managers include less exposure to carry. To demonstrate this, a carry factor is added to the return-based style analysis for the eight large trend following CTA managers. R-squared values improve slightly for some managers and not others. Overall, the impact of adding a carry factor is relatively minimal. For the set of eight large CTAs, only CTA4 has a significant and positive loading to the carry factor. The results are similar for smaller CTA managers. For a manager who explicitly states that they trade carry strategies, it is easy to simply add a fourth carry factor to characterize the effect of carry on that portfolio.

Monitoring Style Drift

Another difficult issue in the CTA space is monitoring and determining style drift. Since trend following systems are rather complex, performance is noisy, and strategy construction is not as transparent as some might like, it is hard to understand if performance is due to the market or to changes in the trend following strategy

TABLE 13.4 CTA style analysis with and without the carry factor. Significant coefficients are labeled in bold for p values less than 5 percent and italics for p values less than 10 percent.

No Carry	Trend	Size	Equity	Speed	Carry	R-Squared	Intercept (%)
CTA1	**0.78**	0.12	*−0.11*	**0.16**	—	0.70	−0.11
CTA2	**0.82**	**−0.21**	0.12	−0.02	—	0.71	−0.25
CTA3	**0.69**	**−0.26**	0.20	−0.05	—	0.52	0.27
CTA4	**0.50**	**−0.20**	0.17	0.13	—	0.49	−0.12
CTA5	**0.51**	*−0.16*	0.14	*0.09*	—	0.62	−0.12
CTA6	**0.47**	−0.03	0.20	−0.01	—	0.56	0.11
CTA7	**0.81**	−0.14	0.14	−0.09	—	0.74	−0.30
CTA8	**0.59**	−0.14	0.24	*0.11*	—	0.60	*−0.43*
With Carry	**Trend**	**Size**	**Equity**	**Speed**		**R-squared**	**Intercept**
CTA1	**0.78**	0.11	−0.09	**0.16**	−0.12	0.70	−0.02
CTA2	**0.81**	**−0.23**	0.14	−0.01	−0.15	0.71	−0.13
CTA3	**0.69**	**−0.27**	0.22	−0.05	−0.10	0.52	0.35
CTA4	**0.51**	−0.18	0.13	0.13	**0.23**	0.50	−0.29
CTA5	**0.51**	*−0.16*	0.15	*0.09*	−0.05	0.62	−0.08
CTA6	**0.47**	−0.01	0.17	−0.01	0.12	0.57	0.02
CTA7	**0.81**	−0.16	0.16	−0.09	−0.11	0.74	−0.21
CTA8	**0.59**	−0.14	0.23	*0.11*	0.02	0.60	*−0.45*

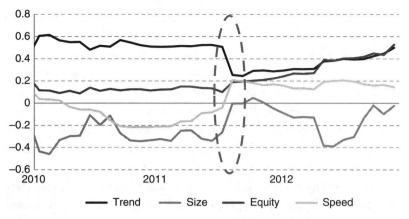

FIGURE 13.5 Rolling 24-month betas for the size, equity, and speed factors for CTA5 from 2005 to 2012.

itself. Using the style factors as a measure of exposure to certain styles, an investor can examine rolling windows of the style factors to determine if these seem to be changing substantially over time. For example, for the period of 2010 to 2013, Figure 13.5 plots the 24-month rolling factor betas for each of the style factors: size, equity, and speed for CTA5. In this graph, the trend following system seems to have been adjusted slightly in 2011, the trend beta reduced substantially, the equity bias is increasing, and the trading speed was slowed down. This analysis could be used to ask CTA managers to explain how their system may have changed and if and what they are doing differently during 2011. Typically, it is very difficult to measure style drift for trend following systems. Over the past few years, several individual trend following managers have created both good and bad press for adding carry strategies, moving more into cash equity markets, and/or adding credit spreads.[10] CTA style analysis provides a method for monitoring the style of a strategy to determine when or if there are structural changes in the trading approach.

■ Sector Level Analysis of the Market Size Factor

The previous section discussed style analysis for individual manager returns. This analysis demonstrated how style analysis can be used for performance attribution, appropriate benchmarking, and monitoring style drift. This section takes a closer look at the market size factor and demonstrates how style analysis can be extended to the sector level.

---

[10]The move from pure trend following to a multistrategy approach is discussed in Chapter 16.

Among the three factors, size, equity, and speed, which are proposed for style analysis of CTA returns, the market size factor (SMB) has recently exhibited a large downward trend. This suggests that trend following systems with a market capacity–based allocation scheme would have outperformed equal dollar risk-based systems. Peer analysis confirms this conclusion. Despite the recent negative market size factor, over a 20-year period, the mean return of the SMB is 6.3 percent. This positive premium may indicate that over the longer-term, smaller markets outperformed, analogous to a "small cap" effect in equities. An intrasector analysis may help provide some insights into what is driving the recent negative market size factor.

For a portfolio that includes equity, fixed income, FX, and commodity sectors, Figure 13.6 depicts the aggregate SMB. Despite the long-term average, allocating more risk to smaller markets has not been beneficial recently. To understand the recent deterioration of this factor, the performance of the size factor in each sector can be analyzed for comparison.

Figure 13.7 plots the sector specific market size factors. From each of these graphs, unlike the market size factor (SMB) at the portfolio level, the sector specific market size factors are not all consistently downward trending with the exception of possibly equity markets. It is important to clarify that the portfolio level market size factor is not exactly the weighted average of the sector specific market size factors. Each sector specific market size factor is computed for a portfolio only in this particular sector. Equal risk in that sector is compared with market capacity weighting performance. When the sector specific market size factor is positive, this means that there are more trends in smaller markets in that sector.

The equity sector is the only sector where the size factor shows an increasingly degrading performance since 2006. This indicates that the smaller equity index markets have underperformed in comparison with large equity index markets. More specifically, larger equity markets are trending and smaller equity markets

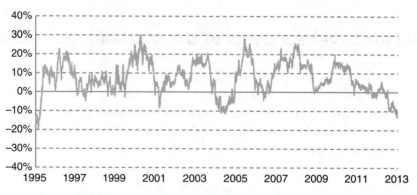

FIGURE 13.6 The market size factor (SMB) from 1995 to 2013.

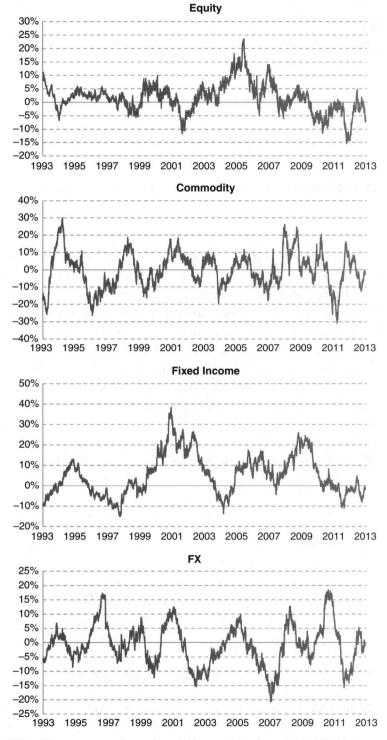

FIGURE 13.7 The sector specific market size factor (SMB) from 1993 to 2013.

FIGURE 13.8 The S&P 500 Index and Hang Seng Index from January 2010 to January 2014. *Source:* Bloomberg.

are range bound. As an example, Figure 13.8 plots the S&P 500 Index and Hang Seng Index from January 2010 to January 2014. It appears that the S&P 500 Index is much trendier than the Hang Seng Index. These effects can be quantified by calculating the difference in level of divergence for between large and small markets via the Market Divergence Index (MDI large − MDI small). Figure 13.9 plots the difference in market divergence based on the MDI (large − small). This plot confirms that the larger equity markets have trended strongly while smaller markets seem to be range bound (not exhibiting divergence). This seems to demonstrate that at the equity sector level, there is an implicit emerging market focus in the equal dollar risk approach.

Turning next to the fixed income markets, the fixed income market size factor has been in a recent downward trend. Combining all of these graphs together, since

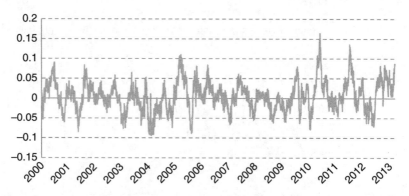

FIGURE 13.9 Differences in market divergence for larger equity markets and small equity markets as measured by the market divergence index, MDI (large − small) from September 2000 to December 2013.

2006, larger equity markets have trended more than emerging markets. Large fixed income markets have trended more than smaller ones. Coupling this with a rough period for smaller commodities in 2010 to 2011, and a rough period for smaller currencies in 2011 to 2012, an equal dollar risk allocation has provided poor performance.

Commodity and currency markets seem to exhibit less consistent behavior recently. This suggests that the equity sector may be the main driver for the decrease in the market size factor (SMB) during recent times. To empirically examine each individual sector's impact on the portfolio level size factor, an alternative intrasector market size factor can be calculated. In this example, individual sector allocations are set to be the same for each sector for both equal dollar risk and market capacity weighting allocation approaches. Within each sector, equal dollar risk allocation is compared with the market capacity based allocation. Figure 13.10 shows the intrasector size factor. In contrast to the market size factor in Figure 13.6, the intrasector size factor performance has actually improved during the past two years. The intrasector market size factor demonstrates that the sector allocation also plays an important role in the recent downtrend of the size factor performance. More specifically, a purely equal dollar risk allocation approach would have allocated less capital to equity markets in general at the sector level in addition to allocating less risk to the larger equity markets (within the equity sector as a whole).

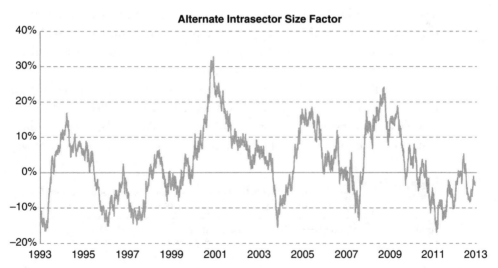

FIGURE 13.10 The intrasector market size factor: The difference between the average annual rolling returns of systems with an equal risk allocation scheme and a market capitalization–based allocation scheme within each sector (equal risk-market capitalization). Sector allocations are held constant for both approaches.

Style Analysis Clarifications

Despite the ease of use and intuitive nature of linear returns–based style analysis, this technique is not a panacea for performance analysis. The ease and applicability of the Fama-French model may cause a somewhat premature confidence in the use of factor analysis. In addition to this issue, the choice of the baseline system and factor construction is instrumental for interpreting results. Because the results of style analysis are relatively easy to achieve, it is important to examine core aspects of their use: the interpretation of style coefficients, the choice of baseline system and style factor construction.

Style Coefficients: Handle with Care

Before discussing CTA-style factor analysis, it is important to take a step back and review the well-known Fama-French model in equities. This discussion provides a few important rules and words of caution for factor analysis as a general methodology. Using the Fama-French three-factor model with the market, the size factor (SMB), and the value factor (HML), consider a set of four funds consisting of either mutual funds or ETFs: F1 to F4. The Fama-French three-factor model is estimated for each of these funds. The funds are then ranked on their loading to value (their corresponding value beta). These values are listed in Table 13.5.

Using simple point estimates from the Fama-French three-factor model, Fund 1 has the highest loading on value. Does this mean that Fund 1 is really the most representative value fund? It turns out that Fund 1 is the United States Short Oil Fund. This is a randomly selected fund, clearly not a value-focused mutual fund. What produces these apparently counterintuitive results?

The devil is in the mathematical details of factor model estimation. Instead of showing the table as in 13.5, the point estimates in Table 13.6 are listed with their t-statistics and those point estimates that are statistically significant from zero with 95 percent confidence are marked in bold. The estimates and their corresponding statistics are

TABLE 13.5 Coefficient estimates for the Fama-French three-factor model for mutual funds and ETFs 1 to 4. The funds are ranked by their weighting to value.

Fund	Market Beta	Size Loading	Value Loading	Alpha (%)
1	−1.20	−0.05	0.66	1.25
2	0.90	0.03	0.31	−0.24
3	0.97	−0.26	0.31	−0.24
4	0.97	0.06	0.25	−0.33

Data source: Bloomberg; French.

TABLE 13.6 Coefficient estimates and *t*-statistics for the Fama-French three-factor model for mutual funds and ETFs 1 to 4 from Table 13.5. Highlighted coefficients indicate *p* values less than or equal to 5 percent.

Fund	Market Beta	T-stat	Size Loading	T-stat	Value Loading	T-stat	Alpha (%)	T-stat	R-Squared
United States Short Oil Fund	−1.2	−5.48	−0.05	−0.13	0.66	1.48	1.25	1.52	0.44
iShares Russell 1000 Value ETF	0.9	42.05	0.03	0.87	**0.31**	10	−0.24	−2.48	0.93
Vanguard Value ETF	0.97	57.31	−0.26	−7.93	**0.31**	10.89	−0.24	−3.79	0.98
iShares S&P 500 Value Index Fund ETF	0.97	43.00	0.06	1.60	**0.25**	7.61	−0.33	−3.23	0.93

Data source: Bloomberg; French.

listed in Table 13.6. In this case, Fund 1, the short-strategy oil fund, clearly has a reasonable negative loading on the market and a considerably lower fit to the model with an R-squared of only 0.44. Despite being higher in absolute terms, Fund 1's value loading is statistically insignificant with a *t*-statistic of only −0.31. A coefficient is only statistically significant from zero with 95 percent confidence if it is larger in magnitude than 1.96. The other three funds are large-cap, value ETFs with a very close fit in terms of R-squared using the Fama-French three-factor model.

Suppose instead that the goal is to select a growth fund. Table 13.7 lists a summary of estimates from the Fama-French model for funds 1 to 7: F1 to F7. The seven funds are sorted by their loading on value, with the most negative loading representing the highest loading to growth.

TABLE 13.7 Coefficient estimates for the Fama-French three-factor model for mutual funds and ETFs 1 to 7. The funds are ranked from the lowest value weighting to the highest value weighting. Negative weightings indicate growth as opposed to value.

Fund	Market Beta	Size Loading	Value Loading	Alpha (%)
1	0.75	−0.41	−0.72	−0.41
2	1.04	−0.69	−0.45	−1.00
3	0.23	−0.19	−0.41	0.86
4	1.07	−0.10	−0.38	−0.10
5	0.87	−0.49	−0.33	−0.25
6	1.04	−0.01	−0.30	−0.09
7	0.97	−0.19	−0.23	−0.09

Data source: Bloomberg; French.

When the funds are replaced with their names and their corresponding t-statistics, Fund 1 is a gold ETF. Why would a gold fund be the largest growth fund, even larger than the growth ETF? Although there may exist some correlation between gold and equities, it is not completely clear that this ETF could be expected to have the highest growth loading. The fit of the Fama-French three-factor model can be very good for traditional ETFs and funds, but it provides misleading results in many other cases. The estimates for poorly fit models cannot be compared with those that have a good fit. It is important to note that the iShares S&P 500 Growth Index Fund has the lowest absolute loading for growth out of the seven funds. Despite this low absolute loading, the coefficient is highly statistically significant, consistent with what would be expected given the name of the fund. (See Table 13.8.)

Similar to the lousy fit for the gold ETF, the Fama-French three-factor model does a relatively poor job of explaining CTA performance. For most CTA funds, the R-squared ranges from 0.00 to 0.15. Estimates for the size and value factors are also useless. As with any model, the coefficients can be estimated but they are meaningless without proper statistical significance.

Following the discussion of classic-style analysis models, CTA-style factor analysis can also be discussed with the same level of scrutiny. For each of the eight large CTAs from Table 13.2, the coefficient estimates are displayed with the corresponding p-values in Table 13.9.

TABLE 13.8 Coefficient estimates for the Fama-French three-factor model for mutual funds and ETFs 1 to 7. The funds are ranked from the lowest value weighting to the highest value weighting. Negative weightings indicate growth as opposed to value. Significant coefficients are labeled in bold for p values less than 5 percent and italics for p values less than 10 percent.

Fund	Market Beta	T-stat	Size Loading	T-stat	Value Loading	T-stat	Alpha (%)	T-stat	R-Squared
Market Vectors TR Gold Miners ETF	0.75	2.77	−0.41	−0.71	−0.72	−1.49	−0.41	−0.37	0.08
Goldman Sachs Commodity Strategy Fund Class A	1.04	6.92	**−0.69**	−2.08	−0.45	−1.62	−1.00	−1.54	0.38
SPDR Gold Shares ETF	0.23	1.66	−0.19	−0.69	−0.41	−1.76	0.86	1.63	0.04
iShares Russell 1000 Growth ETF	1.07	71.66	**−0.10**	−4.13	**−0.38**	−17.58	−0.10	−1.60	0.97
PowerShares DB Commodity Index Trac ETF	0.87	7.13	−0.49	−1.94	−0.33	−1.54	−0.25	−0.51	0.36
Vanguard Growth ETF	1.04	61.89	−0.01	−0.17	**−0.3**	−10.77	−0.09	−1.37	0.98
iShares S&P 500 Growth Index Fund ETF	0.97	63.46	**−0.19**	−7.47	**−0.23**	−10.50	−0.09	−1.32	0.96

Data source: Bloomberg; French.

TABLE 13.9 Coefficient estimates for the CTA Style Factor Analysis for CTAs 1 to 8. The R-squared value for the Fama-French three-factor model is listed for comparison. Significant coefficients are labeled in bold for p values less than 5 percent and italics for p values less than 10 percent.

	Trend	Size	Equity	Speed	R-Squared	Fama-French R-Squared
CTA1	**0.78**	0.12	*−0.11*	**0.16**	0.70	0.13
CTA2	**0.82**	**−0.21**	**0.12**	−0.02	0.71	0.04
CTA3	**0.69**	**−0.26**	**0.20**	−0.05	0.52	0.01
CTA4	**0.50**	**−0.20**	**0.17**	**0.13**	0.49	0.00
CTA5	**0.51**	*−0.16*	**0.14**	*0.09*	0.62	0.02
CTA6	**0.47**	−0.03	**0.20**	−0.01	0.56	0.00
CTA7	**0.81**	−0.14	**0.14**	*−0.09*	0.74	0.04
CTA8	**0.59**	−0.14	**0.24**	*0.11*	0.60	0.04

Data source: Bloomberg; French.

In this example set, all eight CTAs have significant trend beta. For the market size factor and trading speed factor, several of the CTAs do not have significant coefficients. For example, CTA8 has an insignificant coefficient for the market size factor (SMB); this means that the coefficient of CTA8 to size cannot be compared directly with, for example, CTA3, which has a significant negative size loading. There are two interpretations of the market size coefficient for CTA8. First, it may be the case that the fund has a very small size exposure. This exposure could be so small that the model could not perceive it with the small set of monthly returns. On the other hand, CTA8 may simply not have a particular loading to market size.

Since many CTAs blend trend following with other nontrend strategies, it is not surprising that they have varying R-squared values. For portfolios with more non-trend strategies, it is intuitive that a trend following model proposed for CTA-style analysis would not be as good a fit. This will create some challenges when comparing factor loading coefficients between strategies. For example, CTA3 has an R-squared of 0.52. When compared to its Fama-French R-squared of 0.01, this shows that while the goodness of fit of the model is increased greatly by including the proposed factors, additional factors would need to be included to improve the explanatory power of the model for this manager.

Baseline Strategy and Model Design

For any style analysis framework, there are several key assumptions:

1. Choice of baseline system
2. Selection of style factors
3. Factor construction

The results in this chapter follow the discussion in Greyserman et al. (2014). In this framework, any trend following return series (either a fund or an index) can be decomposed into the contribution from the baseline strategy (the divergent trend following index, DI), and the contribution from the corresponding construction-style factors. The trend following style factors include the market size factor (SMB), the equity bias factor (EQB), and the trading speed factor (SMF).

In this section, the first aspect of style analysis design is discussed in greater detail. For the choice of a baseline strategy, the divergent trend following index provides a baseline that maintains the least bias or particular market view. This strategy is the most ideologically aligned with a pure trend following approach. Style factors explain certain deviations from this approach. Depending on the objective of style analysis, this choice of baseline strategy has both its pros and its cons. Returning to the Fama-French analogy, the choice of an equal weighted or value weighted index for the equity market will change the results and their interpretation. For the case of trend following, one can consider the same substitution of using market capacity weighted as opposed to an equal weighted approach. To examine the difference between these two indices, Figure 13.11 plots the cumulative performance for the divergent trend following index (DI) and the market capacity weighted index (MCAPI). The two indices are relatively similar with a correlation of 0.88.

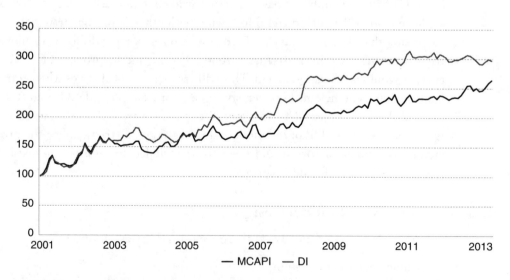

FIGURE 13.11 Cumulative performance of the divergent trend following index (DI) and the market capacity weighted trend following index (MCAPI) from 2001 to 2013.

Depending on the type of CTA under analysis, one baseline strategy or another may be more appropriate. The choice of baseline strategy will also affect the interpretation and determination of the other style coefficients. The pros and cons of the choice of baseline strategy are best explained by doing a simple experiment. Suppose the divergent trend following index is substituted with a market capacity weighted index (MCAPI). Using the same time series from Table 13.2 earlier in this chapter, style analysis can be reapplied to the eight large CTAs using the market capacity weighted index instead of the DI. The results of style analysis with the original model and the new model with the market capacity weighted as the baseline strategy are listed in Table 13.10.

The most straightforward way to interpret these results is to look at a few key trends first. Since the set of CTAs in this sample is large (in terms of AUM), it is logical to expect them to be the most similar to the market capacity weighted index. Contrary to this fact, the R-squared stays the same or goes down for all eight managers. The coefficients to the size factor increase across the board and all coefficients become significant. For equity bias, the use of the market capacity weighted baseline strategy includes a bias toward equity markets, which reduces the explanatory power of the

TABLE 13.10 Coefficient estimates for the CTA-style factor analysis for CTAs 1 to 8. Significant coefficients are labeled in bold for p values less than 5 percent and italics for p values less than 10 percent.

Original (DI)	Trend	Size	Equity	Speed	R-Squared	Intercept (%)
CTA1	**0.78**	0.12	*−0.11*	**0.16**	0.70	−0.11
CTA2	**0.82**	**−0.21**	**0.12**	−0.02	0.71	−0.25
CTA3	**0.69**	**−0.26**	**0.20**	−0.05	0.52	0.27
CTA4	**0.50**	**−0.20**	**0.17**	**0.13**	0.49	−0.12
CTA5	**0.51**	**−0.16**	**0.14**	*0.09*	0.62	−0.12
CTA6	**0.47**	−0.03	**0.20**	−0.01	0.56	0.11
CTA7	**0.81**	**−0.14**	**0.14**	*−0.09*	0.74	−0.30
CTA8	**0.59**	**−0.14**	**0.24**	*0.11*	0.60	*−0.43*
(MCAPI)	Trend	Size	Equity	Speed	R-Squared	Intercept (%)
CTA1	**0.69**	**0.79**	**−0.12**	**−0.16**	0.67	−0.10
CTA2	**0.64**	**0.49**	0.07	*−0.14*	0.64	−0.27
CTA3	**0.52**	**0.34**	**0.18**	−0.13	0.47	0.25
CTA4	**0.46**	*0.30*	**0.15**	−0.10	0.49	−0.10
CTA5	**0.45**	**0.28**	**0.12**	*−0.10*	0.62	−0.09
CTA6	**0.37**	**0.31**	**0.13**	*−0.11*	0.49	0.17
CTA7	**0.60**	**0.54**	*0.09*	*−0.12*	0.64	−0.35
CTA8	**0.51**	**0.45**	**0.16**	−0.09	0.58	*−0.42*

equity bias factor. The role of the speed factor also changes when the baseline strategy is changed. When the market capacity weighted baseline strategy is used, many of the strategies look faster.

For the size factor, the broad increase in the coefficients demonstrates that when the benchmark is equal weighted, many of the managers are biased toward larger markets. On the other hand, when the market is market capacity weighted, many of these CTAs bias more to smaller markets than would be dictated by their market capacity. For a concrete example, CTA1 and CTA2 can be compared and examined. Both of these CTAs have high R-squared, with the original model at 0.70 and 0.71. When a market capacity weighted baseline strategy is used, both have a worse fit at 0.67 and 0.64. CTA1's size coefficient goes from 0.12 to a significant 0.79. For CTA2, the size coefficient goes from a significant −0.21 to a significant positive 0.49. Comparing these two, both CTAs are closer to a pure trend following approach and in a relative sense CTA1 seems to allocate more risk than CTA2 to smaller markets.

The speed factor is somewhat more complicated. For example, under the original model CTA1 looks slow relative to the DI. But when the market capacity weighted baseline strategy is used, CTA1 looks faster. This may be confusing to interpret but it means that this fund is faster than a market capacity weighted index but slower than the divergent trend following index.

■ Manager Selection and Allocation

A return-based approach for CTA style analysis allows for strategy classification, performance evaluation, peer analysis, and monitoring style drift. Manager selection and allocation is another challenge for any investor. As with any portfolio choice problem, the optimization problem is a function of both preferences and assumptions regarding the distribution of asset returns. To explain how style factors can be used for manager selection and allocation, a simple experiment is performed using data from the eight large CTA managers from June 2001 to December 2012. Table 13.11 presents the Sharpe ratios for the divergent trend following index and three style factors. Table 13.12 lists the Sharpe ratios, trend betas, and three corresponding style betas for each of the eight large CTA managers.

TABLE 13.11 Sharpe ratios for the divergent trend following index (DI) and three style factors from June 2001 to December 2012.

	Trend (DI)	Size (SMB)	Equity (EQB)	Speed (SMF)
Sharpe Ratio	0.80	0.96	0.36	0.65

TABLE 13.12 Sharpe ratios and betas for the divergent trend following index (DI) and three style factors for eight large CTA managers from June 2001 to December 2012.

	CTA1	CTA2	CTA3	CTA4	CTA5	CTA6	CTA7	CTA8
Sharpe ratio	0.73	0.56	0.83	0.59	0.67	0.9	0.53	0.42
Trend beta (DI)	0.78	0.82	0.69	0.50	0.51	0.47	0.81	0.59
Size beta (SMB)	0.12	−0.21	−0.26	−0.20	−0.16	−0.03	−0.14	−0.14
Equity beta (EQB)	−0.11	0.12	0.20	0.17	0.14	0.20	0.14	0.24
Speed beta (SMF)	0.16	−0.02	−0.05	0.13	0.09	−0.01	−0.09	0.11

Imagine a scenario where an investor is considering allocating capital to some or even all of these eight CTA managers. First, instead of making assumptions regarding the existing portfolio or preferences of each individual investor, it is much more straightforward to assume that the investor has access to the divergent trend following and style factor return series and can select desired exposures to these. For example, in the case of the Fama-French three-factor model (1993), any investor can examine these factors in comparison with their own individual portfolio and decide which exposure to these factors they deem appropriate.[11] In the case of the eight trend following managers (CTA1 to CTA8), the same assumption is made. Given this assumption, there are many different exposures that could be desirable depending on the individual investor. Table 13.13 presents a list of several possible investor choices for exposures to each of the three style factors. Choices A, B, and C represent an investor who would like a certain style exposure and not the other two. Choice D may represent an investor who wants an equal exposure to all three style

TABLE 13.13 A list of example investor choices for exposures to each of the three style factors using data from June 2001 to December 2012.

Investor Choice	Size Beta (SMB)	Equity Beta (EQB)	Speed Beta (SMF)	Sharpe Ratio
A	1.00	0.00	0.00	0.96
B	0.00	1.00	0.00	0.36
C	0.00	0.00	1.00	0.65
D	0.33	0.33	0.33	0.91
E	0.70	0.09	0.21	1.09

[11] Paralleling the example of Fama and French (1993), in the case of equities, an investor may choose a small cap portfolio or a value or growth portfolio. In the case of trend following, an investor may prefer small markets or "search for crisis alpha."

TABLE 13.14	A list of portfolio weights for investor choices (A to E). Allocations are determined by maximizing the Sharpe ratio with given desired exposure for each corresponding investor choice (A to E). The CTA1 to CTA8 are possible candidates for each portfolio.

Investor Choice	Portfolio Weights								Sharpe
	CTA1	CTA2	CTA3	CTA4	CTA5	CTA6	CTA7	CTA8	
A	0.38	0.00	0.00	0.00	0.00	0.62	0.00	0.00	0.90
B	0.00	0.00	0.00	0.06	0.15	0.59	0.00	0.20	0.80
C	0.21	0.00	0.00	0.34	0.28	0.00	0.00	0.17	0.72
D	0.00	0.00	0.00	0.16	0.28	0.20	0.00	0.36	0.67
E	0.37	0.00	0.00	0.14	0.03	0.33	0.00	0.13	0.82

factors. Choice E is the choice for an investor who wants the maximum Sharpe ratio possible from all possible combinations of exposures of the divergent trend following index and three corresponding style factors.[12]

For a given investor choice, for example A, B, or D, a portfolio of CTA managers can be selected to arrive at the same desired factor weights with the highest Sharpe ratio. For this optimization problem, the objective is to maximize the Sharpe ratio with the constraints that the weights for each factor loading are set to the investor's choice. As an example, Table 13.14 lists the corresponding weights to each CTA and the Sharpe ratio for this portfolio choice.

Choice A is a size portfolio. CTA1 is the only large CTA manager that has a positive exposure to the size factor (SMB). It is not surprising that the optimization problem suggests a 38 percent exposure to CTA1 and 62 percent exposure to CTA6. This portfolio mimics the size (SMB) factor with the highest Sharpe ratio. The Sharpe ratio is comparable with the size factor (SMB). It is also important to remember that the size factor is not an investable strategy but CTA1 and CTA6 represent two large CTA managers. Choice B is a portfolio with a loading on the equity bias factor (EQB) with the highest Sharpe ratio. This portfolio includes an allocation of 6 percent to CTA4, 15 percent to CTA5, 59 percent to CTA6, and 20 percent to CTA8. Since CTA1 is the only large CTA that has a negative exposure to the EQB, it is not surprising that this manager is not included in this portfolio. Interestingly enough, CTA2, CTA3, and CTA7 are not included in any of the portfolios. These three managers have lower Sharpe ratios, so it is not surprising that they are not included. This demonstrates the drawbacks of a Sharpe ratio–based approach. Using Sharpe ratios is just one example of an objective function. It is also possible to use many

---

[12] These portfolio weights are selected by solving a simple optimization problem with four return series (DI, SMB, EQB, and SMF). The objective function is the Sharpe ratio and the constraint is that the weights sum to 1.

other approaches to select managers. For example, if a particular investor wanted to find the exposure to the style factors that provides the largest crisis alpha. The weights for this portfolio would create a maximum crisis alpha portfolio. The results from this section are also confined to the small set of eight large CTAs. Returning to Table 13.3, there is a much larger range of exposures to the factors when smaller CTAs are also included in manager selection. For example, a crisis alpha portfolio may include a large positive exposure to the size factor and negative exposure to the equity bias factor. Qualitatively, CTA1, SCTA1, SCTA3, and possibly even NCTA2 are three managers that might be candidates for consideration.

This section discusses a simple approach for using style factors to perform manager selection and allocation. There are several drawbacks to using Sharpe ratios in sample, but the approach does provide a simple way to select and allocate to CTA managers based on their construction styles.

■ Summary

This chapter discusses a return-based approach to style analysis for trend following managers and its corresponding applications. Using the benchmark and style construction as proposed by Greyserman et al. (2014), common industry benchmarks, trend indices, and individual manager returns can be analyzed based on their construction style. The R-squared for trend following managers, manager-based benchmarks, and trend indices are high, suggesting that the style analysis framework explains a considerable portion of variation in CTA returns in the cross section. Applications of CTA style analysis include performance attribution, appropriate benchmarking, and new tools for monitoring style drift. Given a specific set of investor preferences for different CTA styles, manager selection and allocation can also be determined using CTA style factors.

■ Further Reading and References

Agarwal, V., and N. Naik. "Performance Evaluation of Hedge Funds with Option-Based and Buy-and-Hold Strategies." EFA 0373; FA Working Paper No. 300, 2000.

Brennan, T., and A. Lo. "The Origins of Behavior." *Quarterly Journal of Finance* 1, no. 55 (2011).

Fama, E., and K. French. "Common Risk Factors in the Returns on Stocks and Bonds." *Journal of Financial Economics* 33 (1993): 3–56.

French, K. http://mba.tuck.dartmouth.edu/pages/faculty/ken.french/data_library.html.

Fung, W., and D. Hsieh. "Empirical Characteristics of Dynamic Trading Strategies: The Case of Hedge Funds." *Review of Financial Studies* 2 (1997a): 275–302.

Fung, W., and D. Hsieh. "Survivorship Bias and Investment Style in the Returns of CTAs." *Journal of Portfolio Management* 23 (1997b): 30–41.

Fung, W., and D. Hsieh. "A Primer on Hedge Funds." Journal of Empirical Finance, 6 (1999), 309–331.

Fung, W., and D. Hsieh. "Asset-Based Style Factors for Hedge Funds." *Financial Analysts Journal* 58, no. 1 (2002).

Fung, W., and D. Hsieh. "Performance Characteristics of Hedge Funds and Commodity Funds: Natural vs. Spurious Biases." *Journal of Financial and Quantitative Analysis* 35 (2000): 291–307.

Fung, W., and D. Hsieh. "The Risk in Hedge Fund Strategies: Theory and Evidence from Trend Followers." *Review of Financial Studies* 2 (2001): 313–341.

Fung, W., and D. Hsieh. "Hedge Fund Benchmarks: A Risk-Based Approach." *Financial Analysts Journal* 60 (2004): 65–80.

Greyserman, A., K. Kaminski, A. Lo, and L. Yan. "Style Analysis in Systematic Trend Following." Working paper, 2014.

Kaminski, K., and A. Lo. "When Do Stop Loss Rules Stop Losses?" *Journal of Financial Markets* 18, issue C (2014): 234–254.

Hasanhodzic, J., and A. Lo. "Can Hedge-Fund Returns Be Replicated?" *Journal of Investment Management* 5 (2007): 5–45.

Moskowitz, T., Y. Ooi, and L. Pedersen. "Time Series Momentum." *Journal of Financial Economics* 104, no. 2 (2012): 228–250.

Sharpe, W. E. "Asset Allocation: Management Style and Performance Measurement." *Journal of Portfolio Management* 18, no. 2 (Winter 1992).

Trend Following in an Investment Portfolio

CHAPTER 14

Portfolio Perspectives on Trend Following

Up until this point, trend following has been examined somewhat in isolation. The remainder of this book turns to trend following from a more global perspective. This chapter reviews three core issues that represent advanced topics: the role of equity markets and crisis alpha, understanding cyclicality in trend following volatility, and the role of mark-to-market for manager-to-manager correlations. This chapter opens the discussion of trend following from an investor perspective. Chapter 15 discusses the role of size, liquidity, and capacity. Chapter 16 examines the act of diversifying away from pure trend following. Chapter 17 discusses dynamic allocation to trend following across time.

■ A Closer Look at Crisis Alpha

Chapter 4 introduced the concept of crisis alpha in the context of adaptive markets. Throughout the following chapters the importance of crisis alpha is discussed using an array of measures and across construction styles for trend following. For an institutional investor, crisis alpha is a key characteristic for understanding how trend following strategies can perform during difficult periods for traditional portfolios. Chapter 7 discussed how crisis alpha can be applied for different asset classes. This section focuses on diving deeper into how equity markets relate to crisis alpha.

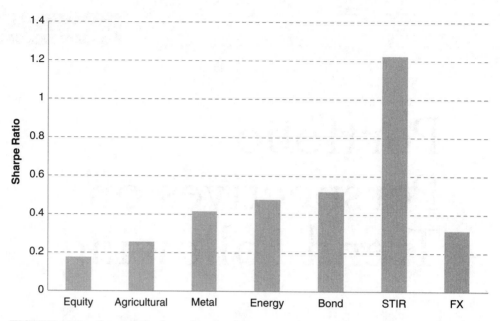

FIGURE 14.1 Sharpe ratios for each sector for a representative trend following system. The sample period is from 1999 to 2012.

Equity Dependence

A typical trend following portfolio consists of seven sectors: equity indices, bonds, short-term interest rates (STIR), foreign currencies (FX), agriculturals, energies, and metals. Figure 14.1 plots the respective sector Sharpe ratios for a representative trend following system from 1999 to 2012.[1] This sample period is chosen intentionally as the total buy-and-hold return for equity markets during this time period is approximately zero. Concurrently, trend following performance has been the weakest in the equity sector.[2] To further examine the level of market divergence for each sector, the market divergence index (MDI) can be calculated at the portfolio level for each sector. When the MDI is greater than a threshold of 0.1, this indicates a period of higher divergence. For the specific case of equities, the probability that the sector MDI is greater than 0.1 can be used to measure the prevalence of trend following opportunities. As seen in Chapter 3, 0.1 is used as a threshold for a trend following portfolio as this is the MDI level where the system tends to have nonnegative performance on average. If the MDI is high, the signal-to-noise

---

[1] The representative trend following system is a diversified system with equal dollar risk allocation.

[2] For the analysis in this section, the equity sector includes two North American markets, four European markets, and three Asian markets.

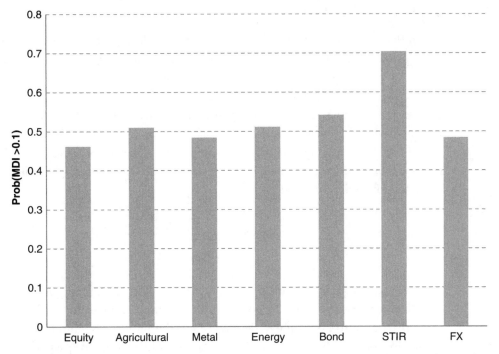

FIGURE 14.2 The estimated probability for each sector MDI being larger than 0.1. The sample period is from 1999 to 2012.

ratio for prices in that sector was high often indicating profitability for trend following strategies. Figure 14.2 plots the estimated probability that each sector MDI is greater than 0.1 for the sample period of 1999 to 2012. Across all sectors, equity markets have the lowest probability of being above the threshold of 0.1. Some might hypothesize that equity markets are more "efficient" in relative terms due to increased competition. There is also ample academic literature, for example, Monoyios and Sarno (2002) asserting that equity indices exhibit mean reversion in the long term. It is not clear if underperformance in trend following equities is due to increased competition or the underlying lack of market divergence in equity markets as an asset class.

Crisis alpha is a simple measure of how a strategy performs during periods of market stress. Chapter 7 demonstrated how crisis alpha was related to performance across many sectors where equity market crisis is the stimulus. The sample period of 1999 to 2012 includes two extreme negative equity bear markets, yet equity markets exhibit the least divergence (or signal-to-noise ratios). This demonstrates how equity markets may be the *instigator* but clearly not the main source of crisis alpha.

Long- or Short-Equity Trends

Given that equity markets exhibit the least market divergence on a sector basis, this section examines the role of positive and negative equity trends. To examine directional effects in market divergence, it is possible to revisit the construction of the market divergence index (MDI) from Chapter 5. The signal-to-noise ratio is a ratio between the trend and individual price changes over a specific period. In order to measure the level of price divergence for a particular price series, the signal-to-noise ratio is used. For any specific day, at time (t), the signal-to-noise ratio (SNR_t) for a particular price series with lookback period (n) can be calculated mathematically using the following formula:

$$SNR_t(n) = \frac{\left|P_t - P_{t-n}\right|}{\sum_{k=0}^{n-1}\left|P_{t-k} - P_{t-k-1}\right|}$$

where (P_t) is the price at time (t) and (n) is the lookback window for the signal, or the signal observation period. For medium- to long-term trend followers, this is typically chosen to be roughly 100 days. The MDI on day t is simply the average of (SNR_i^t) for all markets in the portfolio. Based on historical data, when the MDI is above 0.1, markets are trend-friendly and on average positive returns are expected in the corresponding period.

When the absolute value is removed from the numerator for the signal-to-noise ratio, the result is a new market divergence index with signs (sMDI). When the sMDI is large and positive, this indicates a market environment with stronger uptrends. Figure 14.3 plots the estimated probability for each sector sMDI

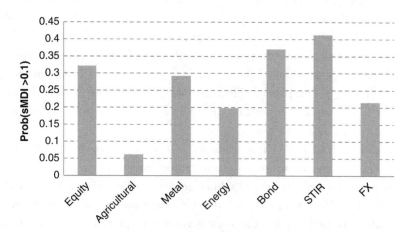

FIGURE 14.3 The estimated probability for each sector sMDI being larger than 0.1. The sample period is from 1999 to 2012.

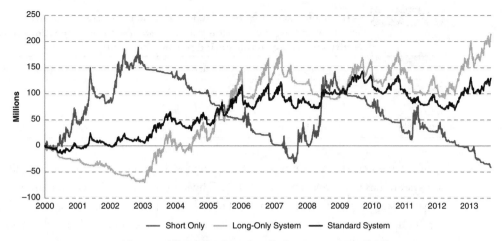

FIGURE 14.4 Cumulative performance for a standard symmetric trend following system, a system with long positions only, and a system with short positions only in the equity sector. The sample period is from 1999 to 2013.

being larger than 0.1. Second only to fixed-income markets, equity markets have a high probability of having an sMDI greater than 0.1. Comparing Figure 14.2 and Figure 14.3, uptrends make up more than two-thirds of the periods when the MDI is higher than 0.1.[3]

To examine directional equity positions only (long or short), the performances of a standard, a long-only, and a short-only trend following system can be compared. In this case, a long-only trend following system takes signals only in the long direction (flat or long), while a short-only trend following system takes signals only in the short direction (flat or short). Figure 14.4 plots the performance of these three systems from 1999 to 2013. By comparing these three systems, it can be observed that short positions in a standard symmetric trend following system contribute to substantially negative PnL. During this sample period, restricting short positions would have improved performance in the equity sector. Table 14.1 presents performance statistics for the equity sector across all three trend following systems: the standard symmetric trend following system, one with only long positions, and one with only short positions.

For the sample period from 1999 to 2012, the long-only system has the highest Sharpe ratio. The long-only system has positive performance beginning in 2009. In contrast, the standard trend following system has remained down from 2009 to 2012. Despite the increase in Sharpe ratio, the trend following system, which is long only in

---

[3] The other scenario for the MDI being larger than 0.1 is when sMDI is lower than –0.1, which counts approximately one-third of the cases.

TABLE 14.1	Performance statistics for a standard symmetric trend following system, a system with long positions only, and a system with short positions only in the equity sector. The sample period is from 1999 to 2013.		
	Sharpe	Return (monthly) (%)	Risk (monthly) (%)
Standard	0.36	0.80	7.52
Long Only	0.41	1.32	10.95
Short Only	−0.07	−0.25	11.36

equities, has negative skewness of −0.25 whereas the standard symmetric trend following system has positive skewness of 0.23. The shift in return skewness from positive to negative suggests that there are larger tail risks and possibly a less desirable risk profile for the long-only system in equities. This motivates a closer look at what happens in equity markets during extreme market events such as crisis.

Crisis Alpha

Crisis alpha is a measure of performance during periods of market stress. Using the VIX-based approach from Chapter 7, any month with a move in the VIX greater than 20 percent over the previous level of the VIX is labeled as a crisis month. Figure 14.5 displays the S&P 500 Index where the VIX based crisis periods are highlighted by the shaded bars.

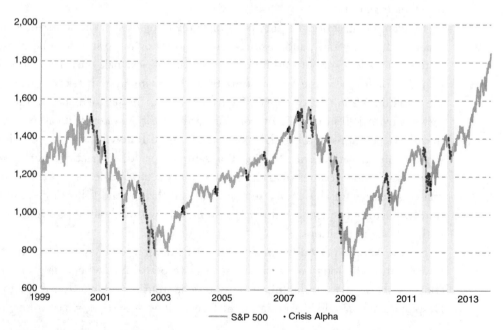

FIGURE 14.5 The S&P 500 index from 1999 to 2013 with VIX-based crisis periods highlighted by the shaded bars.

Data source: Bloomberg.

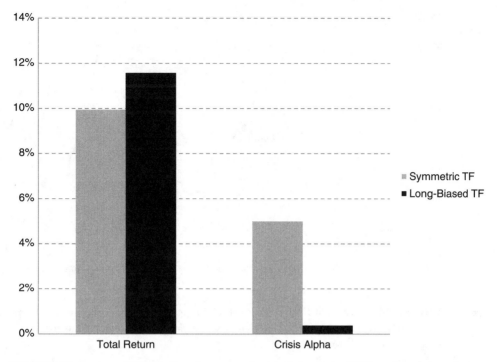

FIGURE 14.6 A comparison of total return and crisis alpha, with a VIX-based crisis period definition, for both a standard symmetric trend following system and a trend following system with equity-long positions only. The sample period is from 1999 to 2012.

Realistically, trend followers do not completely remove short-equity signals. Instead of examining long-only positions in the equity sector, a bias of 5:1 for long positions versus short positions is applied. Figure 14.6 compares the crisis alpha contribution for both the standard symmetric and long-biased (in the equity sector) trend following systems. It is important to note that equity is only one of the seven sectors of the whole portfolio. From Figure 14.6, the impact of removing short-equity signals from a trend following system increases total return by more than 1 percent. This restriction increases total return, but it comes at the cost of crisis alpha. Crisis alpha performance is reduced from roughly 5 percent to close to zero. More specifically, an improvement in the Sharpe ratio (from 0.77 to 0.86 for the whole portfolio) is at the cost of 4.6 percent crisis alpha.

To demonstrate the robustness of this effect, a second definition for a crisis period can be used based on past returns. A crisis month can be defined as any month with a lower than minus 5 percent return for the S&P 500 Index. Figure 14.7 displays the S&P 500 Index with the returns-based crisis periods highlighted by the shaded bars. Figure 14.8 compares the crisis alpha contribution for both the standard symmetric

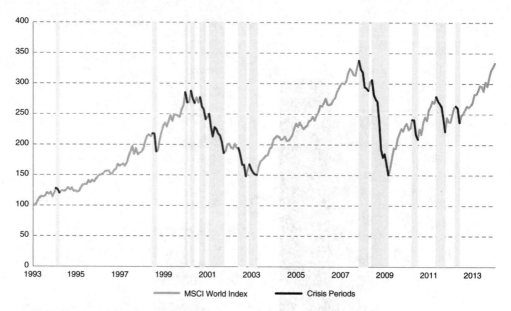

FIGURE 14.7 The MSCI World Index with crisis periods, where crisis is defined by monthly returns less than minus 5 percent, highlighted by the shaded bars from 1993 to 2013. *Data source:* Bloomberg.

and long-only (in the equity sector) trend following systems. Despite the different definition for crisis periods and change in index, the results are roughly the same. Removing short equity signals from a trend following system increases the total return at a corresponding cost in crisis alpha. From Figure 14.8, the net reduction in crisis alpha is approximately the same at 4.6 percent (from 8.7 to 4.1 percent).

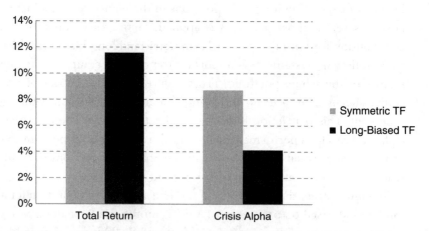

FIGURE 14.8 A comparison of total return and crisis alpha, with an SPX return-based crisis period definition, for both a standard symmetric trend following system and a trend following system with equity-long positions only. The sample period is from 1999 to 2012.

Portfolio Effects of Long Equity Bias

The first part of this section demonstrated how equity-long bias comes at the cost of crisis alpha. To examine this effect from an investor's perspective, the impact should also be examined at the total portfolio level. For simplicity, two institutional portfolios are considered in this analysis: the traditional 60/40 equity bond portfolio and a fund of funds (FoF) portfolio. The 60/40 portfolio can be examined using a 60 percent allocation to the MSCI World Index and 40 percent allocation to the JPMorgan Global Bond Index (GBI). The fund of funds portfolio will be represented by an allocation to the HFRI Fund of Fund Index (HFRIFOF). The hedge fund indices are not necessarily investable but their return series can represent how a fund of funds investor might have performed over time. Each of the institutional portfolios will be combined with a 20 percent allocation to trend following. The first combined portfolio consists of an 80 percent allocation to the 60/40 portfolio (48 percent stocks, 32 percent bonds) and 20 percent allocation to trend following. The second combined portfolio is an 80 percent allocation to the fund of funds index (HFRIFOF) and 20 percent in trend following.[4]

Table 14.2 displays the performance statistics for a traditional 60/40 portfolio when compared with adding trend following both with or without a long bias in equity positions.[5] The standard symmetric trend following program has a larger increase in Sharpe ratio and larger reduction in maximum drawdown. Adding a long equity bias increases the average return more than the symmetric system. Table 14.3

TABLE 14.2	Performance statistics for both a 60/40 portfolio and a 60/40 portfolio combined with trend following. The total combined portfolio consists of 48 percent stocks, 32 percent bonds, and 20 percent trend following over a sample period from 1999 to 2012. The combined portfolio includes either a symmetric trend following program or a trend following program with long equity bias.

	Sharpe Ratio	Monthly Return (%)	Monthly Volatility (%)	Maximum DD (%)
Traditional Institutional (60/40)	0.68	0.72	3.55	44.47
With 20% Trend Following (Symmetric)	0.94	0.80	2.86	24.97
With 20% Trend Following (Long-Biased Equity Sector)	0.91	0.82	3.02	27.57

Data source: Bloomberg.

---

[4] For each investment prior to combining them into a single portfolio, monthly volatility is normalized to 5 percent.

[5] Instead of examining long-only positions in the equity sector, again for realistic purposes, a bias of 5:1 for long positions versus short positions is applied.

Performance statistics for both a fund of funds portfolio and a fund of funds portfolio combined with trend following. The total combined portfolio consists of 80 percent in the HFRIFOF and 20 percent trend following over a sample period from 1999 to 2012. The combined portfolio includes either a symmetric trend following program or a trend following program with long equity bias.

	Sharpe Ratio	Monthly Return (%)	Monthly Risk (%)	Max DD (%)
Fund of Funds Index (HFRIFOF)	0.73	1.08	4.96	71.23
With 20% Trend Following (Symmetric)	1.23	1.54	4.25	22.97
With 20% Trend Following (Long-Biased Equity Sector)	1.12	1.18	3.56	19.84

Data source: Bloomberg.

displays the performance statistics for an institutional investor with a fund of funds allocation compared with adding trend following with or without long bias in equity positions. For the fund of funds investor, adding a long bias to a trend following program reduces both the average return and the Sharpe ratio.

In the first part of this section, long equity bias in a trend following portfolio was shown to increase total return and Sharpe ratios at the cost of crisis alpha. From the perspective of a trend following manager, this may be desirable. From the perspective of an institutional investor, when trend following programs are combined with common institutional portfolios, long equity bias decreases the Sharpe ratio for a total portfolio. For the 60/40 portfolio, removing the long bias is more effective for drawdown reduction. Although the results are somewhat mixed, there seems to be compelling evidence that long bias may be in the interest of the manager more than the interest of the investor.

■ The Impact of Mark-to-Market on Correlation

Correlation is undoubtedly one of the most commonly used quantitative measures to classify relationships between managers. Lower correlations between managers generally imply a diversification of styles and approaches. This typically leads investors to conclude that it is more beneficial to invest in a larger number of managers in a particular space. Given the reliance on correlation as a measure, it is highly important that correlation estimates are accurate. Turning to the futures industry, there is one particular technical aspect of futures trading that is often ignored, standardized mark-to-market for net asset value (NAV) calculation. This section demonstrates empirically how, for strategies without standardized mark-to-market on settlement prices, correlation may be understated. In simple terms, correlations in managed futures are high and appropriate. For managers outside of managed futures, correlations may be lower simply due to the lack of a standardized mark-to-market mechanism.

Mark-to-Market and Illiquid Markets

Several academic papers have illustrated the impact of illiquidity on hedge fund returns. For example, Getmansky, Lo, and Makarov (2004) provide strong evidence that mark-to-market or mark-to-model practice has caused high serial autocorrelation of hedge fund returns in most categories as a result of market illiquidity. One of the often overlooked impacts of illiquid markets is the impact on the correlation *between managers* (or funds). Mark-to-market or mark-to-model practice is a potential source of significant variation in settlement pricing in illiquid markets. This variation artificially decreases the correlations between managers trading these assets as they may adopt different settlement and pricing methods for the purposes of calculating returns and net asset value (NAV).

An important source of variation for mark-to-market pricing in less liquid markets is the simple bid-ask spread. Arakelyan and Serrano (2012) examine the bid-ask spread for various credit default swap (CDS) markets. To put bid-ask spreads outside of futures contracts into perspective, the average bid-ask spread for a one-year maturity CDS market, with a rating of BBB, is 13 bps with a standard deviation of 22 bps. A bid-ask spread of this magnitude is often of the same order of magnitude as the daily volatility of CDS markets. For futures markets, the bid-ask spreads are considerably lower. Across the industry, standardized settlement prices are used to mark-to-market positions daily regardless of bid-ask spreads.

Liquidity and Correlation

For illustrative purposes, a simple scenario can be used to explain the potential impact of the bid-ask spread on correlation. First, consider a situation with two identical managers. In this case, both managers have the same return series and their correlation is 1. Next, variations between these identical managers can be imposed by adding a bid-ask spread to the original returns. This can be achieved by modeling a certain spread distribution. Instances of this distribution are chosen randomly for a mark-to-market price within the bid-ask distribution. Figure 14.9 shows the histogram of correlations between the identical manager returns after the assumed bid-ask spread has been added. In this example, the average bid-ask spread is set as 20 percent of the daily volatility for the original return series and the standard deviation of the bid-ask spread is set at 40 percent of the daily return volatility. In this example on average the correlation drops from 1 to 0.8. This example shows how the addition of variation in the bid-ask spread can reduce correlation (even if return series are perfectly correlated). In many less liquid security markets (i.e., the credit space), the bid-ask spread can be even larger than the one used in the example.

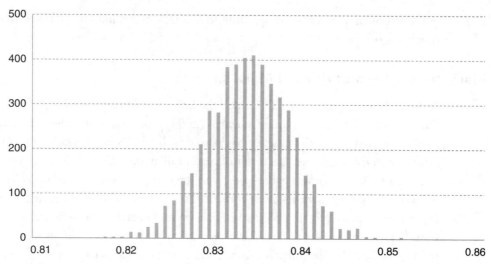

FIGURE 14.9 The distribution of the correlation between two return series (perfectly correlated) after the assumed bid-ask spread is added.

In the CTA industry, managers may have correlations as high as 80 percent. For two CTA managers with an 80 percent correlation, without mark-to-market and standardized settlement prices, the observed correlation can be as low as 50 percent. These examples show how simple variations in bid-ask spread and mark-to-market may potentially decrease correlations. Put in another way, the lack of standardization and consistent mark-to-market mechanism reduces correlations between managers. To examine how this relates to managed futures, variation in mark-to-market and its relation to intermanager correlations is examined in greater detail in the following section.

Mark-to-Market and Trend Following

The previous section demonstrated how illiquidity and variations in the bid-ask spread may understate correlation between managers. This section examines two highly correlated representative trend following systems trading a diversified universe of liquid futures markets. Over the past 20 years, the correlation between the daily returns of these two trend following systems is 0.96.

As explained earlier in this section, managed futures funds trade mostly liquid futures markets, which provide the daily settlement price at the exchange. As a result, there is no need for a discretionary decision in the mark-to-market methodology. However, to demonstrate the possible impact of mark-to-market variability, the variation of mark-to-market pricing is simulated by imposing a statistical price distribution around the daily settlement price. Instances for the price series are sampled to set the mark-to-market calculation of daily PnL. It is important to note that this noise is added for the PnL calculation only. The signals and positions for the

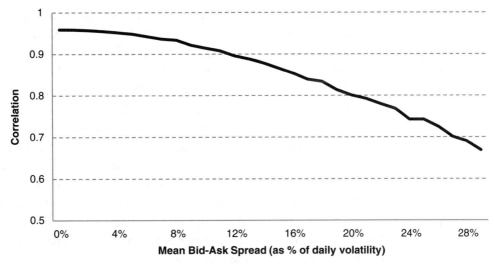

FIGURE 14.10 The correlation between the daily returns of two trend following systems at various assumed mean bid-ask spread as a percentage of the volatility of daily price changes.

underlying systems are not impacted in any way. Daily returns for various assumed bid-ask spreads are expressed as a percentage of the daily price volatility for each market. Figure 14.10 shows the correlation between the two highly correlated trend following funds as a function of the average bid-ask spread for mark-to-market. For a specific example, when the mean bid-ask spread is assumed to be 20 percent of the daily price volatility, the impact of this variation on the daily settlement price reduces correlation from 0.96 to 0.8, a reduction of 17 percent in correlation. From an investor perspective, without standardized mark-to-market for daily settlement prices, these highly similar managers look seemingly more dissimilar.

The important takeaway from this example is that if trend following strategies did not mark-to-market by daily settlement prices set by the exchange, they would have substantially lower correlations between managers. This means that many other strategies, which they are often grouped with, in the alternative space may have understated intermanager correlation. The lack of a standardized mark-to-market mechanism can augment their potential value for diversification.

■ Understanding Volatility Cyclicality

Volatility is an important part of risk taking and understanding risk over time. In practice, volatility is not constant but time varying. This concept especially holds true for dynamic trading strategies. One way to examine how volatility changes over time is to look at volatility cyclicality. **Volatility cyclicality** is defined as the relative speed of cycles in volatility for a particular trading strategy. If a strategy is relatively slow over time, volatility cycles should be low frequency. This means that a period of a volatility cycle is perhaps as long as a year. Volatility in trend following is time varying and it tends to exhibit lower cyclicality. On the other hand, for aggressive position taking approaches where volatility quickly accelerates and decelerates, this exhibits high cyclicality in volatility. As discussed in Chapter 9, dynamic leveraging is a perfect example of an approach that should cause high-frequency volatility cycles. A closer look at option selling strategies and Martingale betting in Chapter 9 demonstrated spikes in volatility and high cyclicality in volatility patterns. As a review, dynamic leveraging is defined as a situation where the amount of leverage depends on the past profits and losses (PnL) of the portfolio. In simple terms, a dynamically leveraged portfolio, which increases (or decreases) its bet size when there are many past losers (or past winners), engages in dynamic leveraging. Dynamic leveraging is similar to "doubling down" in poker. Chapter 9 discussed how dynamic leveraging can include hidden leverage risk in Sharpe ratios.

Volatility cyclicality can be examined more directly using spectral analysis. Practically, Fourier transforms can be used to extract and identify volatility cycles. A Fourier transform converts a signal from the time domain to the frequency domain allowing for both the identification and filtering of volatility cycles.[6] The Fourier transform can be applied to 22-day (approximately one month) rolling volatilities to reveal the corresponding high and low frequency components.[7] Periods are plotted as a function of their power (strength), which can be plotted as a periodogram.[8] More specifically, a periodogram is the spectral density of a signal; it power weights the frequencies by their importance in a signal. To begin the discussion of volatility cyclicality of trend following, Figure 14.11 plots the periodograms for trend following (Newedge Trend Index) and equity markets (MSCI World Index). The periodogram of the trend following index shows no obvious dominant frequency corresponding to a period shorter than 252 days. In contrast, the periodogram for the 22-day rolling volatility of the equity index shows several dominant higher frequencies. Figure 14.11 demonstrates that volatility cycles in trend following are longer and perhaps smoother then volatility cycles in equity markets. A simple spectral analysis of trend following and equity markets demonstrates how, in contrast with equity markets, the volatility adjustment for positions in trend following is able to smooth out the cyclical effects in volatility over time. The volatility adjustment for trend following was introduced in Chapter 3 and explained in further detail in Chapter 8.

---

[6] The Fourier transform is a commonly used signal processing tool, converting a signal from the time domain to the frequency domain. For technical details see Smith (1997).

[7] In this analysis, all time series are normalized to the same volatility.

[8] This concept was introduced and discussed in Chapter 5.

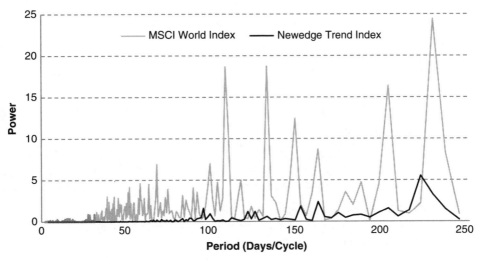

FIGURE 14.11 The periodograms of higher frequency components for the 22-day rolling volatility of the Newedge Trend Index and the MSCI World Index.

Extracting Dynamic Leveraging from Manager Performance

The previous section introduced the concept of cyclicality in volatility. A view over both low and high frequencies demonstrated that trend following exhibits lower cyclicality in volatility than equity markets. In contrast to looking at volatility cyclicality over lower frequencies, this section returns to the discussion of dynamic leveraging and the impact of high-frequency volatility cycles. In practice, spikes and high cyclicality in volatility patterns is a signature of dynamic leveraging. Trend following systems are not designed to accelerate positions as a function of PnL. Returning to the example in Chapter 9, Martingale betting is an example of a dynamic leveraging scheme that can boost Sharpe ratios. As a review, Martingale betting works in the following way: when faced with a loss, the long position is increased until the first day of positive PnL. Bets are increased when they are losing (another form of doubling down). If Martingale betting is applied to a trend following system, the number of double-down days must be limited to remain tractable.

Dynamic leveraging is similar to "doubling down" in poker. Aggressive patterns in the application of leverage can be isolated in a manager return series. This allows an investor to determine at which level dynamic leveraging may potentially be inflating Sharpe ratios. Again for the case of high-frequency effects, Fourier transforms can be used to extract and identify volatility cycles. To demonstrate the power of a Fourier transform in extracting dynamic leveraging effects, Figure 14.12 displays the periodograms for only the high-frequency components for the 22-day rolling volatility of the representative trend following system (left panel)

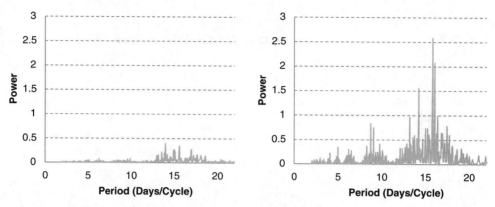

FIGURE 14.12 Periodograms including the higher frequency components for the 22-day rolling volatility of the representative trend following system (left panel) and the system with limited Martingale betting (right panel).

and the system with limited Martingale betting (right panel). The periodogram of the representative trend following system shows no dominant frequency corresponding to a period less than 22 days. In contrast, the periodogram for the 22-day rolling volatility with limited Martingale betting shows several dominant frequencies. The strength of these high-frequency effects represents the accelerating doubling down behavior in position taking. Returning to the discussion in Chapter 9, the leverage effects from Martingale betting was not measurable in Sharpe ratios. Spectral analysis tells a very different story. Martingale betting is clearly adding high-frequency effects in volatility.

One of the main benefits of converting signals into the frequency domain is that it is relatively easy to filter out different frequencies from a signal. Once the frequency domain signal is filtered it can then be converted back into a time series via the Inverse Fourier Transform. The result is a time signal with high-frequency effects removed from the series. To demonstrate this approach, Figure 14.13 presents a flow chart for the filtering process to remove high-frequency effects. In practical terms, once the high-frequency doubling down effects are removed, it is possible to see how much of the performance in terms of Sharpe ratios was attributed to these accelerating betting schemes.

To make this example even more concrete, the returns of six trend following managers (CTA1 to CTA6) and one trend following program (with and without Martingale betting) can be examined.[9] For CTA managers, their performance is

_____

[9] The Fourier transform and inverse Fourier transform are performed for the absolute value of returns. After filtering and applying the inverse Fourier transform, the recovered returns are assumed to have the same sign as the original returns. For tractability, extreme outliers in the power spectral density are removed before applying the inverse Fourier transform.

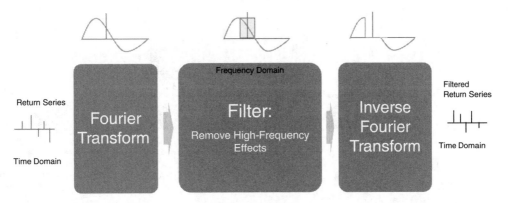

FIGURE 14.13 A schematic for the process of filtering out high-frequency effects in return series. The inputs are return series in the time domain. Outputs are filtered return series in the time domain. Filtering occurs in the frequency domain.

converted into the frequency domain and subsequently filtered to remove high-frequency effects. An inverse Fourier transform is then applied to the remaining frequency series to convert it back into a time series. Table 14.4 lists the performance measures for the original Sharpe ratio and postfiltering Sharpe ratios. Graphically, Figure 14.14 plots the original Sharpe ratio and the postfiltering Sharpe ratio without high-frequency effects. Filtering out high-frequency effects reduces the performance for all CTA managers except CTA4. It is important to note that certain managers exhibit more high-frequency effects in their returns than others. For a specific example, CTA2's performance is cut by more than half

TABLE 14.4 The original two-year Sharpe ratio and the two-year Sharpe ratio after removing the dominant high-frequency components for six managers (CTA1 to CTA2) and two trend following systems (TF and TF with limited Martingale betting).

	Original Series	Removing High Frequencies
CTA1	1.05	0.84
CTA2	2.01	0.94
CTA3	2.31	1.49
CTA4	0.64	0.69
CTA5	2.51	2.32
CTA6	0.17	−0.65
TF	0.56	0.53
TF with Martingale Betting	1.34	0.88

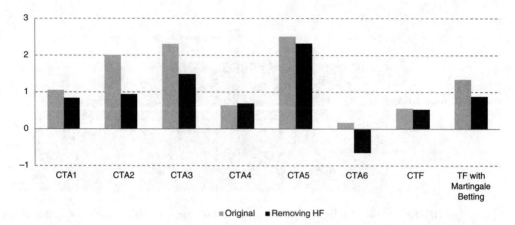

FIGURE 14.14 Two-year Sharpe ratios for six trend following CTAs and a representative trend following program with and without limited Martingale betting. Sharpe ratios are calculated with and without filtering out high-frequency effects via Fourier Transform.

when high-frequency effects are removed. This indicates that CTA2 is more likely to use dynamic leveraging in their position taking. More specifically, the Sharpe ratio reduces from 2.01 to 0.94 when high-frequency effects are removed. On the other hand, CTA1 and CTA5 are only mildly affected by removing high-frequency effects. This suggests that these two managers do not accelerate or decelerate positions similar to dynamic leveraging. This point is also true for a trend following system when compared with a trend following system with limited Martingale betting. High-frequency effects explain 0.46 of the performance of trend following with limited Martingale betting and only 0.03 of the performance for a standard trend following program. The difference in Sharpe ratios demonstrates how Fourier transform can be used to analyze the performance impact of dynamic leveraging. This approach is a tool that reveals potential hidden leverage risk due to dynamic leveraging. The Sharpe ratio provides a risk-adjusted performance measure. Despite this risk adjustment, the impact of dynamic leveraging is not always measurable in Sharpe ratios. The use of Fourier transforms allows for the removal of dynamic leveraging effects from return series providing insights into position taking for CTA managers.

■ Summary

This chapter presents three advanced topics from an investor perspective. First, the impact of equity markets on crisis alpha is discussed. A closer analysis of crisis alpha and equity bias demonstrates that equity markets are often the instigator for crisis but not the main driver of performance. Despite this fact, when equity positions are long biased this may improve performance from the manager perspective. From the investor perspective, a long equity bias may increase performance for a manager on a stand-alone basis but in a global perspective this shift comes at the cost of crisis alpha, reducing some of the diversifying properties of the strategy.

Second, the chapter turned to mark-to-market in managed futures. Due to the standardization of mark-to-market in managed futures, high correlations are representative of actual correlations between strategies. In contrast, for strategies outside of managed futures, the lack of standardized mark-to-market mechanisms has the ability to understate correlations between managers overstating the diversification properties of many dynamic hedge fund strategies.

Finally, this chapter turned to cyclicality in volatility for trend following. Even in comparison with equity markets, standard trend following systems exhibit low-frequency cyclicality in volatility. The use of the Fourier transform as a tool to examine the spectral components in trading series is discussed. The discussion of dynamic leveraging as a hidden risk in Sharpe ratios was also reexamined. Using filtering techniques, return series for managers can be filtered for the impact of dynamic leveraging and its corresponding impact on Sharpe ratios. An analysis of several managers demonstrated the heterogeneity across individual managers. In addition, the comparison of trend following systems with and without limited Martingale betting demonstrated the ability of spectral analysis and filtering to capture hidden risks in dynamic leveraging.

■ Further Reading and References

Arakelyan, A., and P. Serrano. "Liquidity in Credit Default Swap Markets." Mimeo, University CEU Cardenal Herrera, Spain, 2012.

Brunnermeier, M. K., and L. H. Pedersen. "Market Liquidity and Funding Liquidity." *Review of Financial Studies* 22, no. 6 (2009): 2201–2238.

Getmansky, M., A. Lo, and I. Makarov. "An Econometric Model of Serial Correlation and Illiquidity in Hedge Fund Returns." *Journal of Financial Economics* 74, no. 3 (2004): 529–609.

Greyserman, A. "The Impact of Mark-to-Market on Return Correlations," ISAM white paper, 2013.

Greyserman, A. "Trend Following in Equity Markets: The Cost of Crisis Alpha." ISAM white paper, 2012.

Monoyios, M., and L. Sarno. "Mean Reversion in Stock Index Futures Markets: A Nonlinear Analysis." *Journal of Futures Markets* 22, no. 4 (2002).

Smith, S. "The Scientist and Engineer's Guide to Digital Signal Processing." California Technical Pub., 1997.

Vayanos, D. "Flight to Quality, Flight to Liquidity, and the Pricing of Risk." NBER Working Paper, 2004.

CHAPTER 15

Practicalities of Size, Liquidity, and Capacity

Many argue that diversification may be the only free lunch in finance. Diversification can come in various forms, including varying investment styles, exposures to risk factors, choice of sectors/markets and asset classes, speed of trading, and many other parameters. Chapter 3 introduced four key differentiators in trend following systems: risk targets (leverage), market allocation, trading speed (holding period), and directional bias. Chapter 11 discussed return dispersion by examining both position sizing and sector capital allocations. Chapters 12 and 13 presented a framework for analyzing the importance of construction style. In each of these discussions, the practicalities of size, capacity, and liquidity was mentioned but not examined in detail. This chapter examines the diversification benefits of trend following as a function of size, capacity, and liquidity. First, size is examined as a function of capital allocation and trading speeds. Second, the diversification benefits of adding less liquid markets are discussed.

■ Does Size Matter?

As funds grow in assets under management, there are several important considerations. First, capital allocation may be constrained by market liquidity and volumes imposing capacity constraints on managers. This will effectively require larger funds to slant their allocations based on market size similar to market capacity weighting.

Second, trading speeds will be limited to slower systems as large positions will need to be phased into the market similar to block trades. Based on the analysis in Chapter 13, a larger manager will most likely have a negative beta with the market size factor, a positive beta with the equity bias factor, and a positive beta with the trading speed factor. For the eight CTAs in Chapter 13, this was relatively true in aggregate. Because the market size factor has a positive premium over the long run, a negative market size beta would indicate possible missed opportunities in smaller markets. On the other hand, as discussed in Chapter 14, a positive equity bias may increase expected return at the cost of skewness and crisis alpha. A positive trading speed beta has performed better over the long run with the most negative skewness. This section first examines two aspects that may impact diversification inside trend following portfolios: correlation properties in the underlying included assets and trading speeds. Following this discussion, trend following programs are analyzed for both intraportfolio diversification and the corresponding diversification benefits as part of a larger portfolio.

Correlation, Diversification, and the Inclusion of Smaller Markets

Before discussing diversification in a trend following portfolio, for motivation and frame of reference, this section begins with a detour into standard portfolio theory to review the main drivers of diversification. Standard portfolio theory demonstrates rather simply how correlation can create diversification benefits in a portfolio. A trend following portfolio benefits from correlation in the same manner. Each individual position can be seen as components in one trend following portfolio. The correlation properties between these positions dictate the amount of diversification across the entire portfolio. To examine diversification benefits more explicitly, the value-at-risk measure can be used. In the case where there is no diversification, the sum of the value-at-risk for every component is the same as the total portfolio value-at-risk. When there is diversification, the sum of value-at-risk for each component will be higher than the total portfolio value-at-risk. A **diversification ratio** can be measured as the ratio of the total sum of the individual value-at-risk divided by the total portfolio value-at-risk. If the diversification ratio is 1, there is no diversification between the portfolio components. As this ratio increases from 1, there is increasingly more diversification in a portfolio.

Mathematically, if there are N components, which are all assumed to have the same risk (σ) and correlation (ρ), the diversification ratio can be characterized by the expression:

$$Diversification\ ratio = \frac{\sqrt{N}}{\sqrt{1+(N-1)\rho}}$$

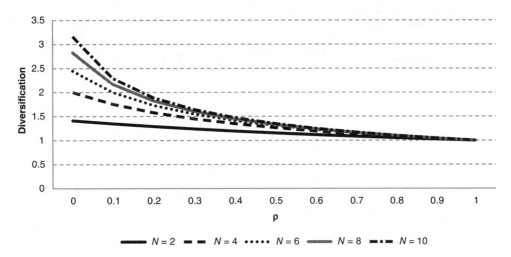

FIGURE 15.1 The diversification ratio as a function of increasing correlation (ρ).

Using this simplified expression for the diversification ratio, when correlation is 1, all components are the same and there is no diversification. To demonstrate how the diversification ratio varies with correlation and the number of components, Figure 15.1 plots the diversification ratio for correlations from 0.1 to 1 and for (N) components from 2 to 10. Consistent with intuition, as correlation increases, diversification across a portfolio decreases. As in modern portfolio theory, when correlation is zero, there are still diversification benefits. Mathematically when ρ is zero, the diversification ratio is $\sqrt{N}$, which is much higher than 1. The number of components in a portfolio also impacts the diversification ratio. As more unique components are included, there are more diversification benefits. This can also be seen in Figure 15.1. Despite the simplicity of the example in this section, the intuition can be applied easily to trend following portfolios. The more unique the positions with low correlation that can be included in a trend following portfolio, the greater the diversification in the portfolio. From the perspective of a constrained trend following program, restrictions in both the number and types of assets that can be included may impact diversification at the portfolio level.

Smaller and Newer Markets Given the discussion of the futurization of the derivatives industry in Chapter 2, it is clear that modern day futures markets present a wide and expanding array of investment opportunities. Across the spectrum of futures markets that are traded, there is a vast range of liquidity, volume, and turnover. Some markets, especially the high turnover financial contracts, are highly liquid. Outside of these, there are smaller, less liquid agricultural and newer markets. Examples of newer markets are deliverable swap futures or emissions markets. Across the industry, there has been concern over growing correlations across the historically

TABLE 15.1 Correlations between sector returns for a representative trend following system in 2012.

	Agriculturals	Bonds	Currencies	Energies	Equities	Rates	Metals
Agriculturals		0.05	0.19	−0.12	0.01	0.08	0.01
Bonds	0.05		0.19	0.06	−0.14	0.21	0.22
Currencies	0.19	0.19		0.32	0.48	0.14	0.55
Energies	−0.12	0.06	0.32		0.39	0.08	0.28
Equities	0.01	−0.14	0.48	0.39		0.04	0.3
Rates	0.08	0.21	0.14	0.08	0.04		0.01
Metals	0.01	0.22	0.55	0.28	0.3	0.01	
Average	3.70%	9.80%	31.20%	16.80%	18.00%	9.30%	22.80%
Average ABS CORR	7.70%	14.50%	31.20%	20.80%	22.70%	9.30%	22.80%

less correlated commodity markets. This phenomenon is termed commodity financialization. As correlations across markets increase, diversification in the portfolio decreases. Smaller, less liquid, and newer markets may be less subject to the effects of financialization.[1] To examine the correlation effects inside a portfolio, a correlation analysis across asset classes for a representative trend following program can demonstrate this more explicitly. Table 15.1 shows a correlation snapshot for 2012 between sector returns for a representative trend following system. The agricultural sector's average correlation with other sectors was only 3.7 percent in 2012. Despite the low correlation, the majority of markets that are less correlated remain the smaller and less liquid ones. When liquidity and volumes are a constraint, as it will be for larger trend following programs, allocation to these markets would shrink to the point of insignificance.[2]

Trading Speed

Trading speed is another aspect of trading affected by total asset size. As programs grow and trade size increases, there are more issues with implementation and potential for market impact. To examine this issue, this section returns to the lookback window size for trading signal generation as a proxy for trading speed. For example, one way to diversify within a trend following program is to use different lookback windows to pick up trading signals at different speeds. A program that has both medium- and long-term lookback windows will pick up medium- and long-term

---

[1] Financialization is a widely documented phenomenon. In fact, even in real estate, real estate investment trusts (or REITs) have documented high correlations with equity markets as they are exchange traded.

[2] The Newedge research note on capacity (Burghardt, Kirk, and Liu 2013) demonstrates this empirically and is consistent with this point.

	20	30	45	60	90	120	170	250	350	500
20	100	74	50	36	19	16	12	7	4	3
30	74	100	71	50	28	22	17	11	6	4
45	50	71	100	74	45	34	27	17	13	6
60	36	50	74	100	65	51	37	26	19	14
90	19	28	45	65	100	81	61	43	32	22
120	16	22	34	51	81	100	78	56	43	29
170	12	17	27	37	61	78	100	74	55	35
250	7	11	17	26	43	56	74	100	78	53
350	4	6	13	19	32	43	55	78	100	72
500	3	4	6	14	22	29	35	53	72	100

FIGURE 15.2   A correlation matrix for simulated returns series for a representative trend following system with lookback window sizes varying from 20 to 500 days. The correlation is listed in percentage value.

trends. A combination of trading speeds will pick up very different trend signals across time. Theoretically, the correlation between systems with different lookback window sizes can be approximately ranked as the square root of the shared time of the two lookback windows as a fraction of the longer lookback window. Figure 15.2 displays the correlations between simulated return series for a representative trend following system with the lookback window sizes varying from 20 to 500 days.[3]

From Figure 15.2, the correlation between 20-day lookback windows and 500-day lookback windows is close to zero. Given the low correlations across lookback window sizes, there are clear diversification benefits for employing a wide range of trading speeds. For systems limited to only slower systems due to transactions costs or market impact, their ability to diversify across trading speeds will be more limited. Larger trend following systems will be constrained to slower trading systems.

Empirical Analysis of Size on Diversification

The previous two sections discussed two aspects that may affect diversification in trend following programs with larger assets under management. Both an inability

---

[3] For simplicity, the simulation is applied using geometric Brownian motion.

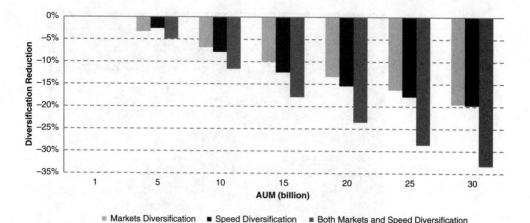

FIGURE 15.3 An empirical analysis for representative trend following systems of the reduction in diversification as a function of asset size allowing either or both limitations on market size and trading speeds.

to significantly allocate to smaller and newer markets and limiting to slower speeds may affect the ability of a larger trend following program to achieve intraportfolio diversification. This section performs an empirical analysis of the size issue by limiting markets and trading speeds. Assuming representative allocations for each level of assets under management, the analysis is conducted across markets and over various trading speeds based explicitly on market liquidity and transaction costs. The market universe consists of the following sectors: equity, fixed income, FX, agricultural, energy, and metals. For a range of trading speeds, holding horizons range from several days to several months. For each corresponding trend following program with a respective size, the diversification reduction is measured relative to the diversification level of a portfolio with a size of $1 billion. For each individual trend following system, based on the level of assets under management, appropriate limitations on market allocations and trading speeds are applied.[4] Using a representative trend following system, Figure 15.3 displays the impact of size on diversification. As asset size increases, allocations to relatively less liquid markets must decrease accordingly. Faster systems must also cede ground to slower systems. Intraportfolio diversification benefits decrease with size. The reduction in intraportfolio diversification occurs across both trading speeds and market allocations. Accounting for the impact of size across trading speeds and market depth, the level of diversification within

---

[4] In this simple illustration, for a typical sector allocation for a trend follower with $1 billion in assets under management and a trend follower with $30 billion in assets under management, the sector allocation is linearly decreased as a function of assets under management. The sample period is 1993 to 2013.

the portfolio decreases by more than 15 percent as assets under management reach $15 billion and 30 percent when assets reach $25 billion. The empirical analysis in this section demonstrates that limiting trading speeds and limiting markets decreases intraportfolio diversification in larger trend following programs.

Portfolio Diversification Benefits and Size

The first part of this section discussed how intraportfolio diversification benefits decrease as a function of asset size. This section discusses the issue from the perspective of an outside investor. The impact of size on the diversification benefits of adding trend following is examined from a total portfolio perspective. A traditional 60/40 portfolio is used as a representative investor portfolio. In this particular case, the 60/40 portfolio is 60 percent in equities using the MSCI World Index and 40 percent in bonds using the JPMorgan Global Bond index (GBI). By limiting markets and trading speeds linearly as a function of asset size, the impact on correlation and crisis alpha can be measured directly.

A combined portfolio of 60/40 and trend following can be seen as a portfolio with two assets. If both assets have similar levels of volatility, the correlation between the two remains the best measure for diversification between the two assets. Using the same market and trading speed limitations from the previous section, Figure 15.4 displays the correlations between the 60/40 portfolio and the

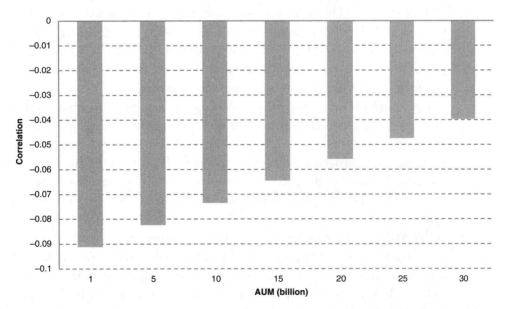

FIGURE 15.4 Correlation between trend following programs and a traditional 60/40 portfolio as a function of asset size (AUM) in the trend following program.

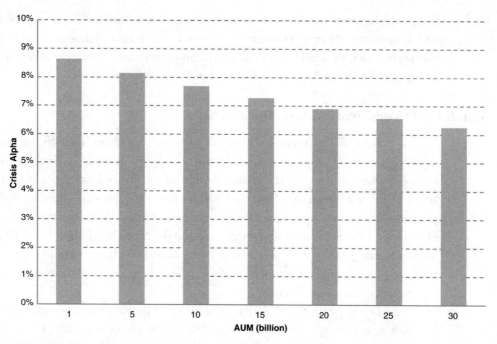

FIGURE 15.5 Crisis alpha as a function of asset size. Crisis alpha is defined by months when the 60/40 portfolio has a return one standard deviation or below its mean.

trend following program as a function of asset size (AUM). As asset size increases, the correlation between the traditional portfolio and the trend following program steadily increases. This indicates reduced diversification benefits as a function of size. Consistent with the style analysis discussion in Chapter 13, the increased correlation can be explained by a tilt toward the financials futures markets. Clearly, the financial positions are more correlated with the bonds and equities in a traditional 60/40 portfolio. The empirical results confirm this assertion.

Crisis alpha is an important diversifying characteristic of trend following programs. Crisis alpha measures the strategy's performance during periods of market stress. In this particular case, crisis alpha is measured as the performance of the trend following program during the crisis periods for the traditional 60/40 portfolio. Crisis periods are defined as months when the 60/40 portfolio has a return that is one standard deviation from its mean. Using the 60/40 portfolio to define crisis periods, Figure 15.5 plots crisis alpha as a function of asset size (AUM). Compared with a $1 billion fund, at an asset size of $25 billion, crisis alpha is almost a quarter lower (roughly 24 percent less). In addition to higher allocation to financial futures markets in larger funds, an inability to use faster trading speeds may also contribute to the reduction in crisis alpha. This effect is also seen for the trading speed factor in Chapter 13. Slower systems seem to underperform relative to faster ones during crisis periods.

■ The Impact of Less Liquid Markets

Given both the discussion and empirical analysis in the first half of this chapter, market size and liquidity present key capacity issues for larger trend following programs. The inclusion or exclusion of less liquid markets is examined in further detail in this section. This section examines the impact of including less liquid markets on several key statistical properties of trend following returns. These include Sharpe ratio, drawdowns, and crisis alpha. Over more than a 20-year period, the impact of including less liquid markets resulted in slightly lower total returns. Despite this, the diversification benefits for including less liquid markets improved Sharpe ratios, reduced maximum drawdowns, and increased crisis alpha.

Instead of measuring individual markets by sector, each market can be evaluated based on liquidity. To measure the level of liquidity across markets, it is necessary to rank markets by their corresponding level of liquidity. For the empirical analysis in this section, the universe of markets includes 50 markets in the equity index, commodity, fixed-income, and FX sectors.

For simplicity, the average daily dollar volume for each market over the past 10 years can be used as a simple measure of liquidity.[5] Given this measure, each market can be ranked accordingly. Figure 15.6 plots the liquidity rankings for all 50 markets. Market symbols are available in the appendix of this chapter. The most liquid markets are dominated by fixed income. Among the fixed-income markets, only the Euroswiss bond futures are not included in the top 50 percent of the most liquid markets. The bottom 50 percent of the least liquid markets significantly consists of those in the commodity sector. Among the commodities in this sample, only crude oil, gold, natural gas, and RBOB gasoline are included in the top 50 percent most liquid markets. Within commodities, the agricultural markets are at the bottom of the liquidity ranking. In this sample, currency markets include seven currency futures markets traded on the CME. Out of these seven currencies, the Mexican Peso is the least liquid. Among the equity indices, the Asian equity markets are the least liquid.[6]

Measuring Diversification Benefits

Using the liquidity ranking system, the marginal impact of including less liquid markets can be examined in more detail. For the empirical analysis in this section, a

---

[5] The daily dollar volume of all traded contracts for each market is aggregated based on price and volume data (*Source:* Reuters). Volume is only one measure of liquidity; there are many more complex liquidity measures that are not considered in this analysis.

[6] It is important to note that liquidity is a relative term. In this context, less liquid implies less liquid than the highly liquid, most heavily traded contracts in futures markets. For all practical purposes, the appropriate term should be less liquid, liquid, which is confusing.

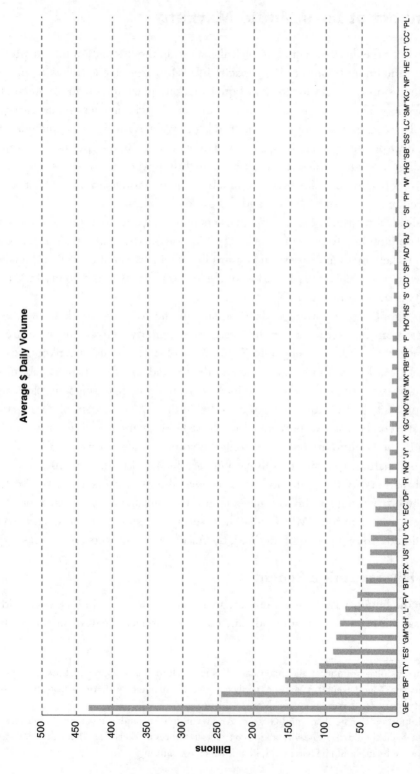

FIGURE 15.6 A liquidity ranking measured by the average dollar daily volume of all contracts traded for each market from 2003 to 2013.

Data source: Bloomberg.

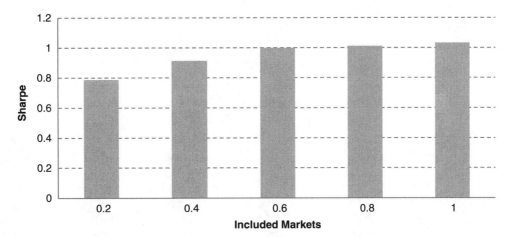

FIGURE 15.7 Sharpe ratios as a function of included markets as a function of their liquidity ranking from 1993 to 2013.

representative trend following system is used.[7] Several key characteristics of trend following portfolios can be measured as a function of including less liquid markets. These measures include total return, Sharpe ratio, maximum drawdown, and crisis alpha.

Sharpe Ratio Total return is important, but risk-adjusted performance is often a more prudent measure of performance. Sharpe ratios are the simplest way to measure risk adjusted performance. For a more than 20-year period, Figure 15.7 plots Sharpe ratios when less liquid markets are included. The Sharpe ratio steadily increases as more *less* liquid markets are included in a trend following program. This increase suggests that the diversification benefits or correlation properties of these markets outweigh the lower aggregate return they provide.

Maximum Drawdowns Drawdowns are also an important characteristic of a portfolio. Using a representative trend following system, Figure 15.8 plots the maximum drawdown as more less liquid markets are included into the program. Maximum drawdown is reduced from almost 50 percent to roughly 32 percent when a trading program includes more of the less liquid markets.[8]

Crisis Alpha Crisis alpha measures a strategy's performance during market crisis. For this example, crisis alpha is defined using a VIX-based measure. Figure 15.9 plots crisis alpha as more *less* liquid markets are included into a portfolio. A portfolio,

---

[7] A breakout system with lookback window sizes ranging from 60 to 250 days is used. Allocation between markets is based on equal dollar risk allocation.

[8] The maximum drawdown is scaled to the same portfolio risk of 5 percent monthly.

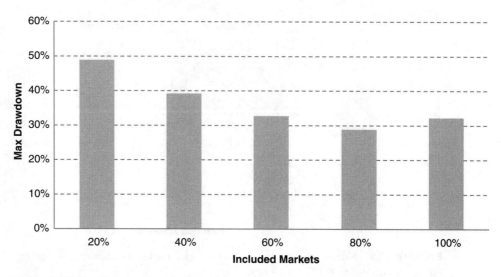

FIGURE 15.8 The maximum drawdown for a representative trend following system as more *less* liquid markets are included in the portfolio. The analysis is done using liquidity rankings.

which includes only the top 20 percent most liquid markets (primarily fixed-income markets), delivers much lower crisis alpha than a more diversified portfolio including the less liquid markets, such as the commodity markets.

Diversification across Time

The previous section suggests that adding more *less* liquid markets increases diversification benefits. These benefits were measured by increased Sharpe ratio,

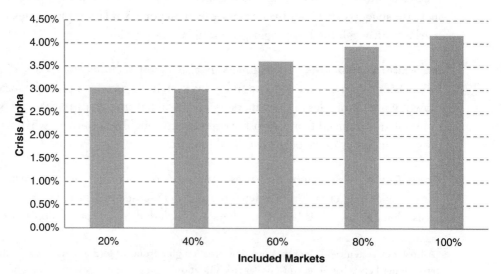

FIGURE 15.9 Crisis alpha as more less liquid markets are included into a trend following portfolio. Markets are ranked by liquidity.

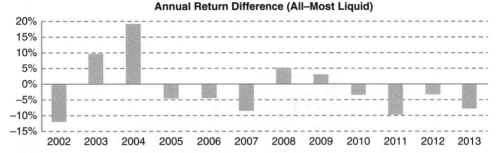

FIGURE 15.10 The average annual return difference between the portfolio consisting of all markets and the portfolio of the top 50 percent most liquid markets only from 2002 to 2013.

decreased maximum drawdowns, and increased crisis alpha. Despite this, there may be some nontrivial timing issues for the inclusion of less liquid markets. To examine this closer, Figure 15.10 plots the difference in average annual returns between a portfolio with only the top 50 percent most liquid markets and a complete portfolio with all markets included from 2002 to 2013. From Figure 15.10, 2003 and 2004 as well as 2008 and 2009 are years when including all markets outperformed the top 50 percent most liquid markets. Figure 15.11 plots the Sharpe ratio as more markets are included for the past 10 years. The results from 2002 to 2013 are consistent with the 20-year period examined earlier in this chapter. On average, Sharpe ratios increase as more *less* liquid markets are included in a trend following portfolio.

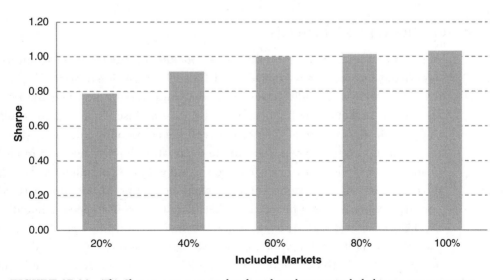

FIGURE 15.11 The Sharpe ratio as more less liquid markets are included into a representative trend following portfolio. The sample period is 2002–2013. Markets are added based on their liquidity rankings.

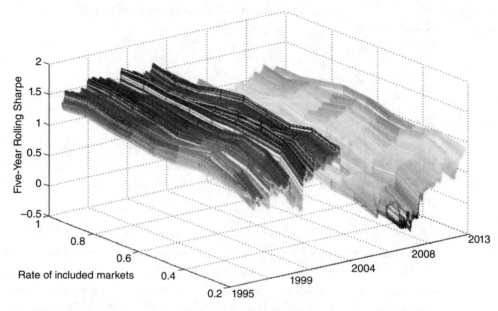

FIGURE 15.12   Five-year rolling Sharpe ratios as a function of included markets and time periods.

To examine the robustness in diversification benefits in terms of Sharpe ratios, five-year average rolling Sharpe ratios can be examined with varying allocations to less liquid markets. Figure 15.12 plots five-year rolling Sharpe ratios as a function of both the allocation to less liquid markets and over time. Although rolling Sharpe ratios vary across time, the relative improvement in Sharpe ratios is robust for including less liquid markets.

Commodities versus Financials

Across all sectors, the most liquid markets include mostly the financial futures markets (fixed income, equity indices, and FX). The least liquid markets include primarily physical commodity markets. Given the diversification benefits for adding less liquid markets, it is important to also take a closer look at how significantly these results depend on differences between the commodity futures markets versus the financial futures markets. To examine the relationship between commodities and financials, a stratified portfolio can be compared with the portfolio based on liquidity ranking. A stratified portfolio is the portfolio consisting of the same percentage of commodity markets and financial markets based on their respective liquidity ranking. Figure 15.13 demonstrates that the stratified portfolio consistently outperforms the other liquidity ranking portfolio as less liquid markets are included (except for at 100 percent, both portfolios are the same). Significant diversification benefits are earned by including commodity markets into a trend following portfolio. Even for the stratified portfolio, when the number of included less liquid markets increases,

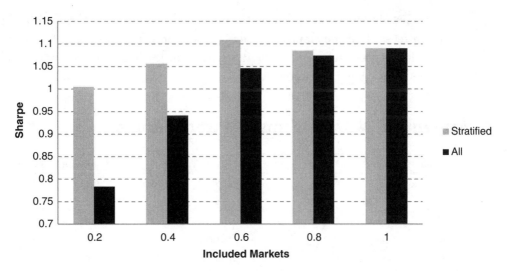

FIGURE 15.13 Sharpe ratios of the stratified portfolio based on the liquidity ranking of financial and commodity markets and the portfolio based on the liquidity ranking. The sample period is 1993 to 2013.

the Sharpe ratio of the portfolio improves. This confirms that the diversification benefits are not solely the outcome of including the commodity sector, but also of including more less liquid markets. With the same allocation between commodities and financials in the stratified portfolios, adding less liquid markets consistently improves the Sharpe ratio. The analysis in this section demonstrates that both the unique properties of commodities and the inclusion of less liquid markets improve diversification benefits.

■ Summary

Explosive growth in the CTA industry and growing assets under management has raised questions regarding diversification and capacity issues. This chapter first discussed key issues related to size and its impact on diversification. Increasing size in assets under management was shown to restrict intraportfolio diversification by limiting access to smaller and newer futures markets as well as limiting some of the faster trading speeds. These limitations result in a higher correlation to traditional portfolios with a larger slant toward the financials and decreased crisis alpha. Following the discussion of size, the role of liquidity in diversification benefits was also discussed. The inclusion of less liquid markets increased diversification benefits from a total portfolio perspective. The inclusion of less liquid markets increased Sharpe ratios, decreased maximum drawdowns, and increased crisis alpha. Finally, the role of commodity markets in driving the diversification benefits of trend following was also discussed. In the empirical analysis, both commodity markets, for their unique correlation properties, and less liquid markets improve the diversification benefits of a trend following program.

■ Appendix: Market Symbols and Names

Symbol	Name	Symbol	Name	Symbol	Name
C-	Corn	US	U.S. 30-year T-Note	CD	CME CAD/USD
CC	Cocoa, NY	CL	Crude Oil	JY	CME JPY/USD
CT	Cotton	HO	Heating Oil	NP	CME MXN/USD
KC	Coffee	NG	Natural Gas	SF	CME CHF/USD
LC	Live Cattle	RB	RBOB Gasoline	EC	CME EUR/USD
HE	Lean Hogs	ES	E-Mini S&P 500 Index	PL	Platinum
S-	Soyabeans	MX	CAC 40	GC	Gold
SB	Sugar, #11	DF	DAX Index	HG	Copper
SM	Soyameal	X-	FTSE 100 Index	SI	Silver
W-	Wheat	HS	Hang Seng	GE	Eurodollar
BF	Euro-BUND	NO	Nikkei	B-	Euribor
GM	Euro-BOBL	NQ	E-Mini Nasdaq 100 Index	F-	Euroswiss Franc
GH	Euro-SCHATZ	SS	Taiwan MSCI Index	L-	Short Sterling
R-	Gilts	FX	Euro-STOXX		
FV	U.S. 5-year T-Note	RJ	E-Mini Russell 2000 Index		
BT	Japanese Bond	PI	Australian SPI200 Index		
TU	U.S. 2-year T-Note	AD	CME AUD/USD		
TY	U.S. 10-year T-Note	BP	CME GBP/USD		

■ Further Reading and References

Burghardt, G., E. Kirk, and L. Liu. "Capacity of the Managed Futures Industry." Newedge Alternative Edge Note, July 2013.

Greyserman, A. "Diversification: Size Matters." ISAM white paper, 2012.

Greyserman, A. "Trend Following: Empirical Findings of Diversification by Less Liquid Markets," ISAM white paper, 2012.

CHAPTER 16

Diversifying the Diversifier

Diversification is the act of introducing variety into an investment portfolio. Diversification is often touted as the only method to achieve some protection during periods of distress. For an investment manager, diversification can be either **intrastrategy** or **interstrategy**. For example, Chapter 15 discussed how fund size can impact intrastrategy diversification by limiting access to smaller, less liquid markets as well as examining statistics that affect interstrategy diversification benefits at the total portfolio level. This chapter focuses on diversification at an interstrategy or total portfolio level and discusses the prospect of moving from pure trend following into a more multistrategy approach. The empirical analysis in this chapter demonstrates that, on a stand-alone basis, a multistrategy approach may be beneficial to a trend following manager. Despite this, from an outside perspective, diversifying away from trend following may decrease some of the desirable properties in a larger portfolio context. More explicitly, the move from pure trend following to multistrategy results in reducing both the positive skewness and the potential for delivering crisis alpha. To demonstrate this more explicitly, portfolio benefits of a pure trend following program versus a multistrategy approach are compared empirically from the perspective of an institutional investor. From the perspective of the manager, a multistrategy approach may be desirable, but from the perspective of an external investor it may be less desirable. Given that relative value strategies and many other hedge fund strategies tend to be convergent strategies, this chapter also returns to issues related to hidden risk in the use of nondirectional convergent strategies.

■ From Pure Trend Following to Multistrategy

The move from pure trend to multistrategy has been increasingly popular in the CTA space. It is conceivable that adding nontrend strategies may be a simple way to increase Sharpe ratios over time. As discussed in Chapter 9, there are often hidden risks in high Sharpe ratios. In addition to the quantitative benefits, there are other concerns for an investor regarding the move to multistrategy. Most importantly, the shift from pure divergent strategies like trend following into convergent strategies makes a trend following strategy more similar to the underlying portfolios of investors. Other issues also include the constant concern of style drift, clarity of investment process, and transparency.

By taking a closer look at the statistical properties of a multistrategy approach in contrast with pure trend following, the pros and cons of this approach can be examined more explicitly. This section takes a first look at the impact of a multistrategy approach on Sharpe ratios, portfolio skewness, and crisis alpha. This analysis provides the background for an empirical analysis of portfolio performance from the perspective of an institutional investor in the next section.

Sharpe Ratios

Chapter 9 discussed the myths and mystique of the Sharpe ratio as a performance measure. Nondirectional strategies may introduce hidden risks in investment strategies. More specifically, this means that adding nondirectional strategies may increase Sharpe ratios without exposing the potential for hidden risks. To demonstrate this, a simple multistrategy CTA can be modeled by combining the return series of a representative trend following system with the HFRI Fund of Funds (FoF) index. The return of the HFRI Fund of Funds index is used as a simple proxy for a pool of diversified nontrend following strategies. The empirical results are based on a diversified universe of markets inclusive of equity indices, bonds, rates, FXs, and commodities.

In this simulation at the end of each month, 80 percent risk is allocated to trend following and 20 percent risk is allocated to the HFRI FoF index. As shown in Figure 16.1, the multistrategy portfolio is able to improve the standalone performance for all trend following strategies. At first glance, this may seem appealing as the move from pure trend following to multistrategy increases Sharpe ratio for a CTA manager *on a standalone basis*. To understand the implications for diversification, other desirable statistical properties such as negative skewness and crisis alpha should also be examined.

Negative Skewness

One of the desirable return characteristics of a divergent trading strategy like trend following is positive skewness. Most hedge fund strategies are convergent trading strategies and they exhibit negative skewness. Figure 16.2 plots a comparison of

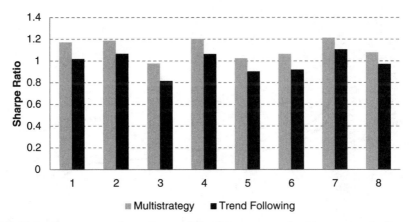

FIGURE 16.1 Sharpe ratios for each trend following system with a 20 percent risk allocation to the HFRI FoF index (multistrategy).
Data source: Bloomberg.

skewness in monthly returns between a pure trend follower (pure TF System) and a variety of other strategies. From this figure, it is evident that pure trend following is one of the few strategies with very positive skewness in returns. Other hedge fund strategies tend to be negatively skewed.

Skewness measures the degree of asymmetry in a distribution. A negatively skewed distribution has a long tail on the left side of the mean, while positive skewness indicates a long tail on the right side. To put the skewness values into perspective, Figure 16.3 illustrates the probabilities of a monthly return series

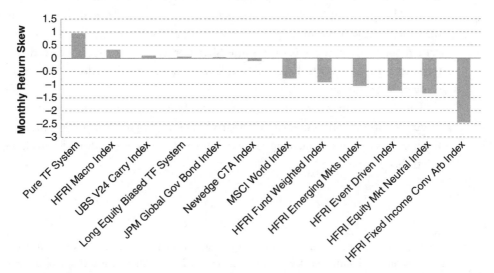

FIGURE 16.2 Monthly return skewness for pure trend following (Pure TF System) and a variety of other strategies.
Data source: Bloomberg.

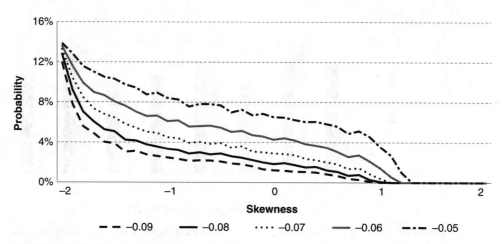

FIGURE 16.3 The probability that a monthly return series achieving a return below *x* percent for various levels of skewness: *x* ranges from –5 to –9 percent.

generating a return below *x* percent, where *x* ranges from –5 to –9 percent, at various skewness levels.[1] Note that, though all the return series have the same Sharpe ratio, the probability of achieving an outsized negative return diverges significantly across different skewness levels, for example, the probability of achieving a return below –5 percent at skewness –1.0 is more than twice that of a distribution with skewness of 1.0.

Skewness in returns also has a direct impact on the expected value of maximum drawdown. Negatively skewed returns have higher maximum drawdowns and vice versa. Using a simple Monte Carlo simulation, Figure 16.4 displays the expected maximum drawdown in *n* years, $2 \leq n \leq 10$, at each skewness level for the various return series depicted with the same Sharpe ratio. A positively skewed return distribution is expected to have a much lower maximum drawdown than a negatively skewed distribution.

The act of adding convergent, negatively skewed, trading strategies to a trend following strategy will decrease the positive skewness. This can potentially undermine the benefits of trend following such as decreasing maximum drawdowns from a total portfolio perspective.

---

[1] Several simulated monthly returns are generated with the same mean, standard deviation, and kurtosis, but with different skewness varying from –2 to 2. All return series have the same Sharpe ratio of 1.0. Each return series has an average monthly return of 1.25 percent and standard deviation of 4.3 percent.

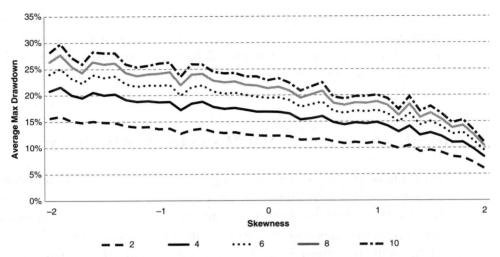

FIGURE 16.4 Average maximum drawdown in a period of n years, for $2 \leq n \leq 10$, for a range of return skewness levels. Each simulated return series has the same Sharpe ratio.

Crisis Alpha

Crisis alpha measures a strategy's performance during market stress. It is one of the most important portfolio benefits of trend following. Figure 16.5 shows the crisis alpha of pure trend following and several other hedge fund strategies and indices during equity market crises.[2] Although most other hedge fund strategies and indices

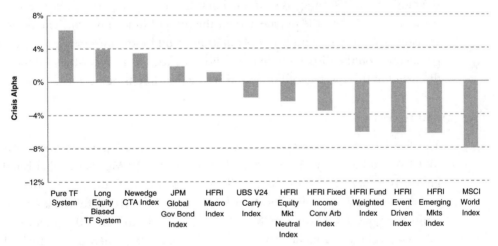

FIGURE 16.5 Crisis alpha for pure trend following (Pure TF System) and several other strategies and indices.

Data source: Bloomberg.

---

[2] In this example, crisis alpha is defined as the average monthly return of each strategy/index during the months when the MSCI World Index's return was one standard deviation or below its mean.

provide negative crisis alpha, the pure trend following system provides a monthly crisis alpha of 6 percent. Given the performance of most traditional portfolios during market crisis, crisis alpha provides substantial diversification benefits for an institutional investor. The impact of trend following strategies is examined from a total portfolio perspective in the following sections.

■ Portfolio Analysis of the Move to Multistrategy

From the perspective of a CTA manager, the move from pure trend following to multistrategy may increase Sharpe ratios, especially in the short run. On the other hand, with the traditional 60/40 or fund-of-funds, institutional investors already hold a significant allocation to nontrend following strategies. From the perspective of the institutional investor, the move from pure to multistrategy may degrade some of the portfolio benefits of investing in CTAs in general. To demonstrate this, a simple multistrategy CTA can be modeled by combining the return series of a representative trend following system with the HFRI Fund of Funds (FoF) index. The return of the HFRI Fund of Funds index is used as a simple proxy for a pool of diversified nontrend following strategies. This proxy is only one proxy and results for other nontrend strategies may vary. The empirical results are based on the 20-year period between 1993 and 2013, using a diversified universe of markets inclusive of equity indexes, bonds, interest rates, FXs, and commodities. In the following two sections, the move to multistrategy is examined first from the perspective of the 60/40 investor and second from the perspective of the fund of funds investor. The performance statistics are compared both across different trend following substrategies to provide perspective on the dispersion in portfolio benefits. Lastly, robustness of the results is discussed in the absence of bonds and across multiple time periods.

The 60/40 Investor

The 60/40 investor is represented by combining a 60 percent allocation to the MSCI World Index and 40 percent allocation to the JP Morgan Global Bond Index. Figure 16.6 depicts the five-year rolling Sharpe ratio of the 60/40 portfolio combined with a 20 percent allocation to either a pure trend following system or a multistrategy CTA.[3] From 1998 to 2013, the portfolio with 20 percent pure trend following achieved a higher Sharpe ratio. In particular, when the traditional 60/40 portfolio is in a significant drawdown, the pure trend following strategy benefits the investor more significantly than the multistrategy CTA. To put this into further

---

[3] The multistrategy CTA is represented by the 50/50 combination of the trend following system and the HFRI Index.

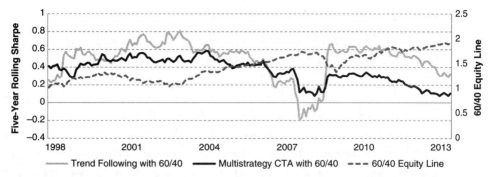

FIGURE 16.6 Five-year rolling Sharpe ratio for a representative trend following system and a multistrategy CTA plotted together with the cumulative performance of a traditional 60/40 strategy. The sample period is from 1998 to 2013.
Data source: Bloomberg.

perspective, Figure 16.7 plots the deteriorating drawdown profile as a CTA allocates more risk to nontrend following strategies. For example, when a multistrategy CTA is compared with a 50/50 allocation to nontrend following strategies and a pure trend following program, pure trend following has a 2.5 times larger impact on drawdown reduction. Both improved long-term Sharpe ratios and better drawdown reduction demonstrate how from a global portfolio perspective a multistrategy approach may be less desirable.

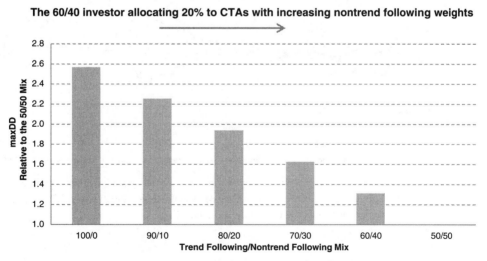

FIGURE 16.7 Maximum drawdown relative to a 50/50 allocation to trend following mix of trend and nontrend strategies as a function of the percentage invested in pure trend following to nontrend strategies. The vertical axis is the ratio between the maximum drawdown reduction of the various allocations to nontrend following strategies and that of the 50/50 allocation. The sample period is from 1998 to 2013.

The Fund-of-Funds Investor

As with the traditional 60/40 investor, a fund-of-funds investor observes the same disparity of portfolio benefits between a pure trend following strategy and a multistrategy CTA. Using the HFRI FoF index as a proxy for the portfolio of a fund-of-funds investor, Figure 16.8 displays the five-year rolling Sharpe ratio of a portfolio combining a traditional fund-of-funds investment with an allocation to a CTA in an 80/20 ratio. CTAs in the analysis are a pure trend follower and a multistrategy CTA with 50 percent of risk taken in nontrend following methodologies.[4] Similar to the 60/40 investor, over a 20-year period, the fund-of-funds portfolio combined with a 20 percent allocation to pure trend following, achieved a higher Sharpe ratio. In cases where the HFRI FoF index is in a significant drawdown, pure trend following strategies benefit the investor more significantly than the multistrategy CTA. Consistent with the drawdown profiles for the 60/40 portfolio, Figure 16.9 presents a similar pattern for the fund of fund portfolio for maximum drawdowns as a CTA allocates more risk to nontrend following strategies. For example, when a multistrategy CTA is compared with a 50/50 allocation to nontrend following strategies with pure trend following, the impact on drawdown reduction is 3.1 times larger for the pure trend following approach.

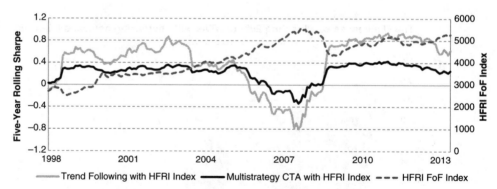

FIGURE 16.8 Five-year rolling Sharpe ratios for the fund of funds portfolio combined with 20 percent of the representative trend following system and a multistrategy CTA, respectively, plotted with the cumulative performance of the HFRI FoF Index.
Data source: Bloomberg.

[4] In this case, the nontrend strategy is perfectly correlated with the fund of funds portfolio. This is simply a proxy; in practice the correlation is clearly not one but the concept is the same. In practice, if the approach is not trend following, an investor can select their own nontrend strategies. In this case, a multistrategy CTA adds nontrend strategies to their portfolio.

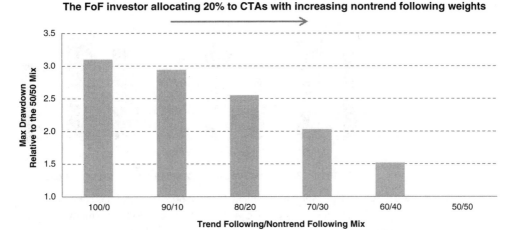

The FoF investor allocating 20% to CTAs with increasing nontrend following weights

FIGURE 16.9 Maximum drawdown for a fund of funds (FoF) investor with an increasing allocation to nontrend strategies. The vertical axis is the ratio between the maximum drawdown reduction of the various allocations to nontrend following strategies and that of the 50/50 allocation. The sample period is from 1993 to 2013.

The Disparity of Portfolio Benefits and System Design

The previous section demonstrates and documents how the move from pure trend following to multistrategy may improve Sharpe ratios on a standalone basis while potentially deteriorating the portfolio benefits of pure trend following. To document the robustness of these effects, portfolio benefits are compared across eight trend following systems, described in Table 16.1. Portfolio benefits are examined in terms of Sharpe ratio improvement, maximum drawdown reduction, and change in

TABLE 16.1 Eight trend following systems along three dimensions: equity bias, capital allocation, and holding horizon. Here, "No Long Horizon" indicates a median horizon.

	Equity Long Bias	Market Capacity Weighted	Long Horizon
1	No	No	No
2	Yes	No	No
3	No	Yes	No
4	No	No	Yes
5	Yes	Yes	No
6	No	Yes	Yes
7	Yes	No	Yes
8	Yes	Yes	Yes

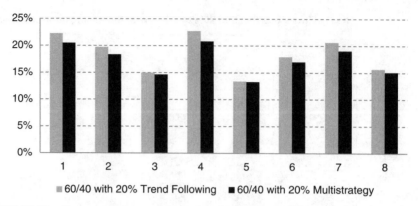

FIGURE 16.10 Sharpe ratio improvement after the 60/40 portfolio is combined with 20 percent overlay of either a trend following portfolio (Systems 1 to 8) or a multistrategy CTA (with Systems 1 to 8).

beta.[5] Figure 16.10 plots the Sharpe ratio improvement after the 60/40 portfolio is combined with 20 percent overlay of either a trend following portfolio or a multi-strategy CTA portfolio. Both approaches can improve the Sharpe ratio consistently, but the benefit of a multistrategy CTA is consistently lower than the corresponding trend following systems. From Figure 16.11 depicting the reduction of maximum drawdown, the same conclusion can be made. Based on maximum drawdowns, a pure trend following portfolio delivers more significant benefits to a 60/40 portfolio. In Figure 16.12, the pattern for the change in beta is somewhat mixed, but it is

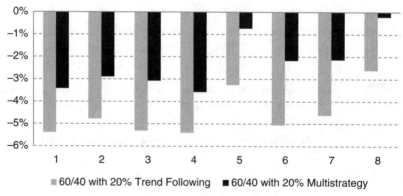

FIGURE 16.11 Maximum drawdown reduction after the 60/40 portfolio is combined with 20 percent overlay of either a trend following portfolio (Systems 1 to 8) or a multistrategy CTA (with Systems 1 to 8).

---

[5] Beta is defined using the MSCI World Index for equity exposure. The S&P 500 Index and the Nikkei Index produces similar results.

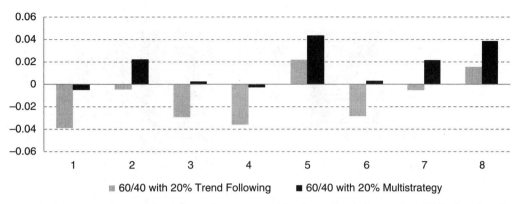

FIGURE 16.12 Change in beta (using the MSCI World Index) after the 60/40 portfolio is combined with 20 percent overlay of either a trend following portfolio (Systems 1 to 8) or a multistrategy CTA (with Systems 1 to 8).

still relatively consistent that a multistrategy CTA fund is less effective at reducing the beta of the portfolio.

After comparing trend following with a multistrategy CTA and an examination of the traditional 60/40 investor, now the portfolio benefits of each trend following system can be examined in more detail for the fund of funds (FoF) investor. Figure 16.13, Figure 16.14, and Figure 16.15 show Sharpe ratio improvement, reduction of maximum drawdown, and beta change after the 60/40 portfolio and the HFRI FoF index are combined with the 20 percent overlay of the average returns of each subspace. Pure trend following (System 1 and System 4, with the latter being a slower system) consistently provides the largest portfolio benefits in terms of Sharpe ratio improvement, maximum drawdown reduction, and beta reduction. This conclusion stands for both the traditional 60/40 investors and the fund of funds (FoF) investors.

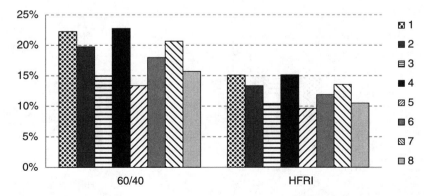

FIGURE 16.13 Sharpe ratio improvement for the 60/40 portfolio and HFRI FoF Index when combined with a 20 percent overlay from each of the eight trend following systems.

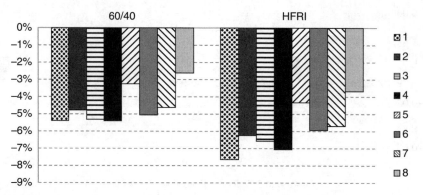

FIGURE 16.14 Reduction in maximum drawdown for the 60/40 portfolio and HFRI FoF Index when combined with a 20 percent overlay of each of the eight trend following systems.

The Robustness of Portfolio Benefits

The empirical results in the previous sections are derived from a diversified universe of markets consisting of equity indexes, bonds, interest rates, FXs, and commodities. The past 20 years represent a period of prolonged falling interest rates. This long-term trend has played a major role in trend following performance (as all trends should). Despite this, removing bonds from the portfolio may provide some indication how much of the results may depend on bonds or on even the most recent extreme low interest rate environment. To gauge the robustness of portfolio benefits, this section provides two alternative views: the absence of bonds for the entire period and a closer look at the recent 10 years where interest rates have decreased to extremely low levels. For the sake of brevity, the discussion is focused on the Sharpe ratio improvement.

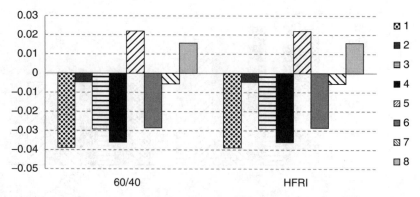

FIGURE 16.15 Change in beta (using the MSCI World Index) for the 60/40 portfolio and HFRI FoF Index when combined with a 20 percent overlay from each of the eight trend following systems.

The Absence of Bonds Trend following has clearly benefited by capturing the strong trends created by an extended falling interest rate environment over the past several decades. Currently, interest rates are near historically low levels; investors are naturally concerned about the potential impact of a rising rate environment on trend following. In both the multicentennial analysis in Chapter 1 and the discussion of interest rate environments in Chapter 6 and Chapter 10, rising interest rate environments are not necessarily detrimental to trend following performance. Despite this, there have been substantial trends in fixed income during the past 20 years. To isolate the impact of portfolio benefits in absence of this rather large trend, it is interesting to examine the portfolio benefits of trend following in the absence of bonds. Figure 16.16 shows the comparison between the Sharpe ratio improvement

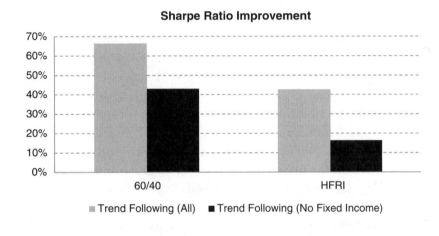

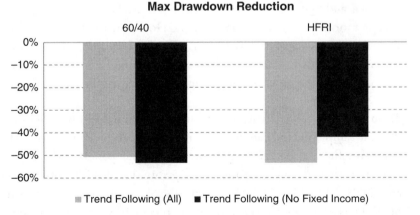

FIGURE 16.16 The impact on the Sharpe ratio improvement and maximum drawdown reduction both with and in the absence of fixed income using a 20 percent allocation to trend following for both the 60/40 portfolio and the HFRI FoF Index.

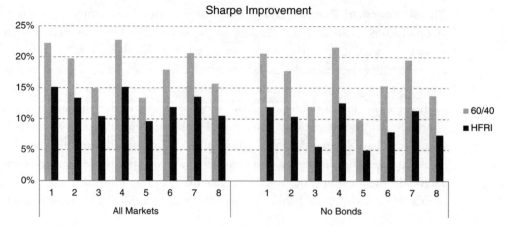

FIGURE 16.17 The impact of removing fixed income from trend following portfolios in terms of Sharpe ratio improvement for both the 60/40 portfolio and the HFRI FoF Index. Each index has a 20 percent allocation to trend following with or without fixed income.

(upper panel) and maximum drawdown reduction (lower panel) for both the 60/40 portfolio and HFRI FoF index when the trend following portfolio acts inclusive and exclusive of bond markets. Although the exclusion of bond markets does reduce the magnitude of Sharpe ratio improvement, with comparatively more impact on the fund-of-funds investor, the Sharpe ratio still remains positive. Moreover, it appears that the maximum drawdown reduction for both investor types is largely indifferent to the removal of bond markets in a trend following program.

To examine the impact of bonds at a more granular level, different types of trend following systems can be examined. Figure 16.17 shows the comparison between the Sharpe ratio improvement for both the 60/40 portfolio and HFRI FoF Index when the trend following portfolio includes or excludes bond markets. For trend following System 4 and System 7, the absence of bond markets does not appear to reduce the Sharpe ratio improvement substantially. However, for the trend following systems with the market capacity based allocation, for example, trend following Systems 3 and 5, the negative impact for the absence of bonds is more significant. As discussed in Chapter 15, the fixed-income futures markets are the largest and most liquid.

Time Periods To evaluate the robustness of portfolio benefits through time, the 20-year sample period can be split into two separate 10-year periods. Figure 16.18 compares the Sharpe ratio improvement (upper panel) and maximum drawdown reduction (lower panel) for the two separate decades for both the 60/40 portfolio and the HFRI FoF Index. Interestingly, the Sharpe ratio improvement for the 60/40 portfolio is noticeably lower in the more recent 10 years, but the benefit to the HFRI FoF Index has been relatively robust throughout. The impact on maximum drawdown has been more stable in both time periods.

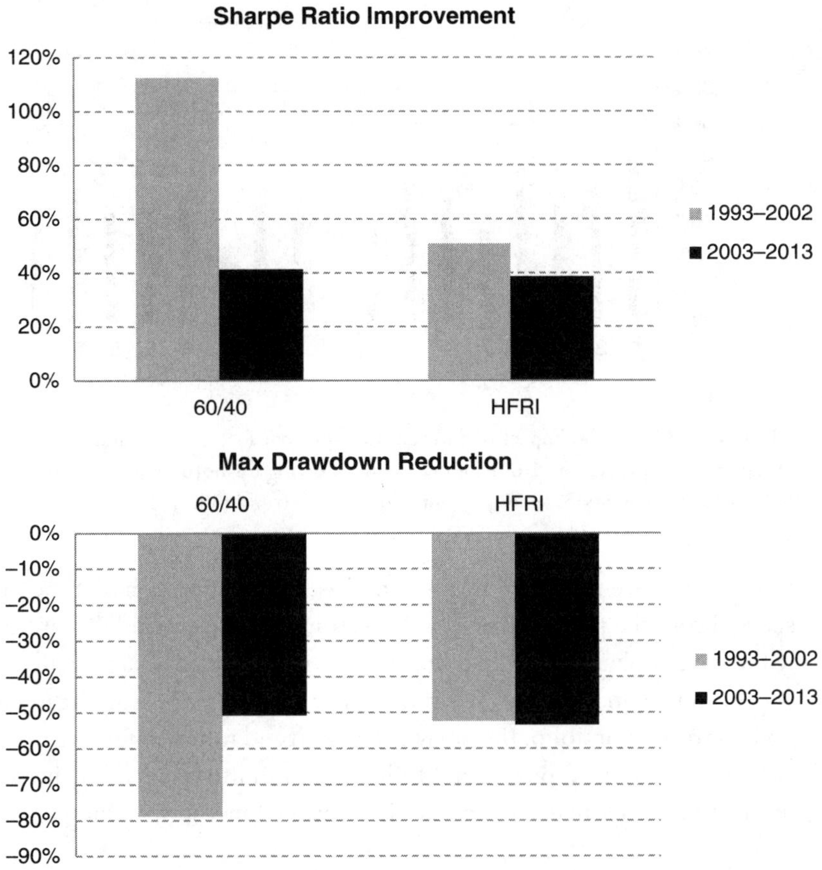

Sharpe Ratio Improvement

Max Drawdown Reduction

FIGURE 16.18 A comparison of Sharpe ratio improvement and maximum drawdown reduction using a 20 percent of allocation to trend following over time periods (1993–2002 and 2003–2013) for both the 60/40 portfolio and the HFRI FoF Index.

It appears that portfolio benefits for the 60/40 portfolio are noticeably lower in the more recent 10 years, but the benefit for the HFRI FoF Index is relatively robust. Overall, significant portfolio benefits can be observed in the more recent past for both types of institutional portfolios. Moreover, in both decades, pure trend following strategies (System 1 and System 4) consistently provide larger benefits to an institutional investor.

In this section, it was observed that despite increasing Sharpe ratios on a standalone basis, a multistrategy CTA with an allocation to nontrend following strategies may provide reduced portfolio benefits for institutional portfolios. To demonstrate the robustness of this conclusion, the disparity of portfolio benefits between distinctive trend following programs was also discussed. Empirical results show that pure trend following, characterized by system symmetry and equal dollar risk allocation, achieves the largest portfolio benefits for both traditional 60/40 traditional investors and fund of funds investors. This analysis provides some important insights into the

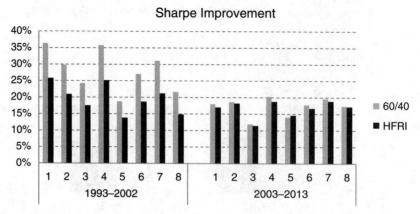

FIGURE 16.19 The impact of different time periods (1993–2002 and 2003–2013) in terms of Sharpe ratio improvement from adding trend following for both the 60/40 portfolio and the HFRI FoF Index. Each index has a 20 percent allocation to trend following.

move from pure trend following to multistrategy approaches in the managed futures space. From the perspective of an investor, they must decide what their objective is. If they are looking for a one-stop shop with a higher Sharpe ratio, a multistrategy approach may make sense. If, on the other hand, an investor already holds a diversified nontrend portfolio, they may invest in trend following for diversification. In this case, the move from pure trend following to multistrategy may be more in the best interest of a CTA manager than an institutional investor seeking diversification.

■ Hidden Risk of Leveraging Low-Volatility Strategies

Although there are many ways to diversify a trend following program interstrategy, a common method is to add purely convergent risk-taking strategies such as relative value.[6] These strategies often have high Sharpe ratios especially over shorter periods of time. To achieve adequate returns, they often also require substantial use of leverage. The use of leverage magnifies the impact of tail risks in convergent risk-taking strategies. This section discusses the hidden risks (or tail risks) in leveraging low-volatility relative value strategies.[7] For this discussion, a generic long/short relative value strategy is considered. This long/short strategy involves two highly correlated

---

[6] Relative value strategies are convergent risk-taking strategies because they take the view that a certain relative relationship holds. Over time they tend to exhibit low price risk but higher hidden risks such as leverage risk. Risks in alternative investment strategies were discussed in Chapter 9 on hidden and unhidden risks.

[7] A relative value strategy is used as an example in this illustration. A similar analysis was also applied in Chapter 9 when the use of dynamic leverage inside a trading strategy was discussed.

portfolios, one long and one short, both with the same dollar risk (σ). If the long and short legs of the relative value strategy have correlation (ρ), the volatility of the relative value strategy (σ_{RV}) can be expressed by the following expression:

$$\sigma_{RV} = \sigma\sqrt{2(1-\rho)}$$

when $\rho > 0.5$, the volatility of the relative value strategy (σ_{RV}) is lower than (σ). Due to the typically strong correlation between the long and short portfolios, standard portfolio theory suggests that the long/short relative value strategy's volatility becomes quite low as correlations increase. For example, if correlation is 0.9 and volatility is 20 percent, the relative value strategy has a net volatility of 8.94 percent (much lower than 20 percent). In a portfolio consisting of strategies with heterogeneous risk profiles, significant leverage is often necessary to maintain equal risk for low-volatility strategies of this type. Using even simple risk budgeting techniques, required leverage can be substantial.

Consider first a hypothetical portfolio consisting of a long/short relative value strategy and two other managed futures strategies. In a simple case, both the long and short leg of the relative value strategy have risk of (σ) and both managed futures startegies have risk of (σ). To achieve equal dollar risk allocation between the three portfolios, a leverage factor of n (where $n > 1$) would need to be applied to the relative value strategy. In this specific case, the required leverage would be as follows:

$$n = \frac{1}{\sqrt{2(1-\rho)}}$$

For the case when the correlation is 0.9, the required leverage factor is 2.24. When the correlation is 0.98, the required leverage factor is 5.[8] In the case with three strategies, the relative value strategy has a risk exposure of ⅓ or 33 percent. Instead of net risk exposure, gross risk exposure can also be considered. The *gross* leveraged risk level of the relative value strategy is $2n\sigma$. In the case when both of the two other strategies have the same risk (σ), the net and gross risk exposures for the relative value strategy can be characterized by the following:

$$\text{net exposure}_{RV} = \frac{n\sigma\sqrt{2(1-\rho)}}{n\sigma\sqrt{2(1-\rho)} + \sigma + \sigma} = \frac{1}{3}$$

$$\text{gross exposure}_{RV} = \frac{2n\sigma}{2n\sigma + \sigma + \sigma} = \frac{n}{n+1}$$

---

[8] The required leverage is set by setting the relative value strategy equal to the other strategies' risk. Solving for (n) in this case gives the formula above.

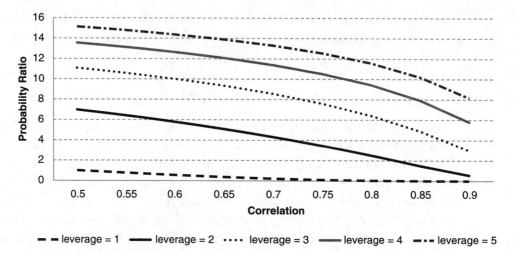

FIGURE 16.20 The probability of the relative value strategy returning -2σ or lower, as a ratio relative to the probability (2.3 percent) of a normal distribution returning -2σ or lower, at various leverage levels and correlations between the long and short portfolios.

For example, when the correlation is 0.9, n is 2.24. The net exposure for the relative value strategy is 33 percent but the gross exposure is 69 percent. This example shows how the gross risk exposure for a low-volatility relative value strategy can be much higher than the net exposure when using an equal risk approach. High gross risk exposure can lead to an increased chance for potentially disastrous left tail events.

When the long and short portfolios experience opposite and potentially detrimental moves simultaneously, the ensuing negative strategy return will be exacerbated by the leverage factor. It is important to examine how likely it is that the long-short portfolio experiences an adverse move. Under the assumption of a multivariate normal distribution in the long and short portfolios' returns, at various levels of leverage and correlation between the long and short portfolios, Figure 16.20 displays the probability of the relative value strategy having a return of -2σ or lower, relative to the probability (2.3 percent) of a normal distribution having a return of -2σ or lower. The ratio between the probabilities of returning -2σ or lower in both the relative value strategy and the normal distribution is called a **tail risk multiplier**. For example, when a relative value strategy has a correlation between the long and short portfolios of 0.75 and a leverage factor of 4, the resulting tail risk multiplier is 10. The tail risk multiplier indicates that the probability of the relative value strategy returning -2σ or lower is 10 times more likely than the normal distribution.

Further complications can arise when the correlation between the long and short portfolios changes significantly. When this correlation decreases, the volatility of the relative value strategy (σ_{RV}) will increase accordingly. Figure 16.21 shows the

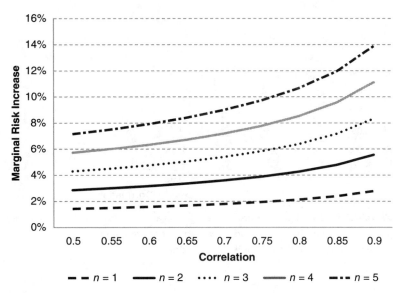

FIGURE 16.21 The increase in risk when the correlation decreases by 0.1 for different leverage levels (*n*) as a function of the original correlation.

volatility increase of the strategy when the correlation is decreased by 0.1 for various original correlation values with leverage varying from 1*x* to 5*x*.[9] When the original correlation is higher, the marginal increase in volatility due to the correlation decrease is larger. In addition, when leverage is higher, the marginal increase in volatility is also higher.

As correlations change, this has several implications for the risk of a combined portfolio. First, the original equal risk allocation between the portfolios is no longer equal. As such, the relative value strategy's risk allocation can be substantially higher than the original budget. Secondly, as shown in Figure 16.20, when the correlation between the long and short portfolios decreases, the probability of "going wrong," left tail events, or large adverse moves becomes higher.

High gross risk exposure can lead to potentially disastrous consequences. In the worst case, where both the long and short portfolios have a 0.5 standard deviation move in an unexpected, opposite direction, these moves of the long-short portfolio will be amplified at the total portfolio level due to leverage. For an unexpected, opposite *m*-standard deviation move for both the long and short portfolios, the corresponding move at the whole portfolio level can be written as:

$$\Delta P_{total} = \frac{2mn}{k}$$

---

[9] In this figure, the volatility of the long and short portfolios is set to 15 percent.

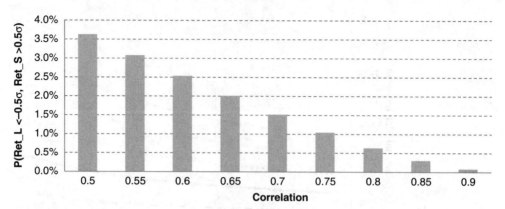

FIGURE 16.22 The joint probability of a negative 0.5-standard deviation move for the long portfolio and a positive 0.5-standard deviation move for the short portfolio as a function of the correlation between the long and short portfolios.

where (ΔP_{tot}) is the change in the total portfolio, (*n*) is the leverage factor and (*k*) is the multiplier for the whole portfolio's dollar risk relative to the individual portfolio's dollar risk. Depending on the correlations between the strategies, a 0.5 standard deviation move can cause roughly an *n*-standard deviation move for the whole portfolio.

When the long portfolio experiences a substantial negative move and the short portfolio experiences a substantial positive move simultaneously, the leverage factor will exacerbate the effects. It is important to consider how likely it is that a move will go in the wrong direction for a relative value strategy. Using the assumption of a multivariate normal distribution for the long and short portfolios' returns, the joint probability of negative 0.5-standard deviation move for the long portfolio and a positive 0.5-standard deviation move for the short portfolio simultaneously can be calculated as a function of the correlation between the long and short portfolios.

Figure 16.22 demonstrates that, even when correlation is high between the long and short portfolios within the relative value strategy, the probability for a long-short portfolio to go wrong is not negligible. Based on these probabilities at a leverage factor of 3 and correlation value of 0.7 between the long and short portfolios, the relative value strategy has a 1.5 percent chance of making a negative 3-standard deviation move. To put this move into perspective, for a normal distribution the chance of a negative 3-standard deviation move is only 0.1 percent.

The Impact of Variant Correlation

In reality, correlations are not constant across time. When correlation decreases between the long and short portfolios, the risk for the relative value strategy

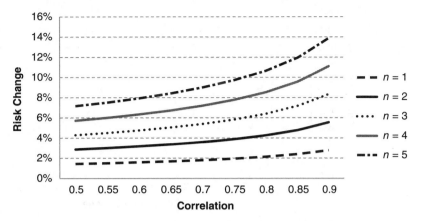

FIGURE 16.23 The increase in risk as correlation decreases for different leverage levels as a function of the original correlation.

increases. Figure 16.23 shows the risk increase when the correlation decreases by 0.1 for different leverage levels as a function of the original correlation.[10] When correlation is higher, the marginal increase in risk due to the correlation change is higher. When leverage is higher, the marginal increase in risk is also higher.

Correlation changes have several implications on risk. First, as correlations change, the original equal risk allocation between the three portfolios does not remain equal. The relative value strategy's risk allocation can be substantially higher than what it was set at the time of allocation. Second, as shown in Figure 16.22, the probability of going wrong becomes higher as the correlation between the long and short portfolios decreases.

The probability that the relative value strategy experiences a two-standard deviation adverse move for the entire portfolio can also be estimated.[11] Figure 16.24 displays the increased probability for the whole portfolio having a negative two-standard deviation move due to the correlation decrease between the long and short portfolios of the relative value strategy.[12] A change in correlation from 0.9 to 0.7 would increase the probability by 10 percent for the relative value strategy to experience a two-standard deviation or larger adverse move for the entire portfolio.

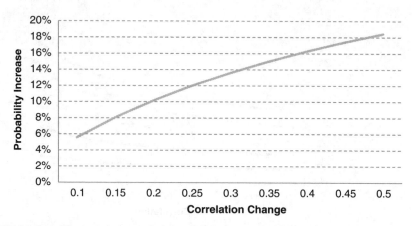

FIGURE 16.24 The increase in probability for the entire portfolio to have an adverse move of two-standard deviations or more as a function of the correlation decrease between the long and short portfolios in the relative value strategy.

Summary

Most investors cite diversification benefits as one of the key reasons for investing in trend following. Despite the appeal of a pure trend following approach, there is an increased trend from pure trend following to multistrategy. This chapter presents both a discussion of this move and the impact of a multistrategy approach on the diversification benefits of trend following. Multistrategy CTAs boast higher Sharpe ratios *on a standalone* basis but the move to multistrategy comes at the cost of less desirable correlation with traditional portfolios, less drawdown reduction, reduced crisis alpha, and less positive skewness. For both a 60/40 and a fund of funds (FoF) investor, the move to multistrategy reduces the diversification benefits of trend following across a wide range of trend following approaches. The results of this analysis are robust for shorter horizons and in the absence of fixed income. Because many multistrategy CTAs may consider adding convergent relative value strategies or low-volatility strategies as a general class, the final section of this chapter returned to the discussion of hidden risks for leveraging low-volatility strategies. The necessity to leverage for equal risk portfolios was used to demonstrate how adverse moves in relative value strategies are magnified by leverage at the portfolio level. This discussion provides a more detailed view into the hidden risks in leveraging low-volatility strategies from a total portfolio perspective.

Further Reading and References

Greyserman, A. "The Benefits of Pure Trend-Following: The Case against Diversifying the Diversifier." ISAM white paper, 2012.

Greyserman, A. "Hidden Risks of Leveraged Low Volatility." ISAM white paper, 2013.

CHAPTER 17

Dynamic Allocation to Trend Following

Trend following strategies take dynamic exposures across asset classes over time. The next logical question is whether market timing of trend following is possible. In other words, is it prudent for an investor to dynamically allocate to a dynamic trading strategy like trend following? During a significant drawdown, should an investor redeem, reduce, or increase an allocation? In the case where investors actively attempt to time an investment in trend following, their total performance will then be highly dependent on when they invest and divest. This chapter presents several simple approaches for dynamically allocating to trend following over time: momentum seeking, mean reversion, and buy-and-hold. The profitability of these approaches depends on the underlying distribution that governs trend following performance. To measure profitability empirically, the serial autocorrelation of trend following returns is shown to be negative. Negative serial autocorrelation implies that mean reversion or buy-and-hold are prudent approaches for allocating to trend following across time. This also means that momentum seeking approaches will reduce performance over time.

■ A Framework for Dynamic Allocation

In most cases, the allocation to a particular strategy can be considered passive or active. Dynamic allocation includes active decisions regarding investment and divestment. There are several approaches for dynamic investing: passive (buy-and-hold) and active (momentum seeking and mean reversion). A **buy-and-hold strategy** simply invests and maintains the position over time. The implementation of a buy-and-hold strategy requires an investor to simply invest and forget. For investors who consistently monitor fund performance, this approach can be difficult to follow especially during drawdowns.

Momentum seeking investment strategies seek to invest when the strategy starts to perform well and divest when it starts to lose money. Similar to trend following, a momentum seeking approach tries to profit from momentum, trends, or persistence in performance. Performance chasing is an example of a momentum seeking strategy. As with most hedge fund strategies, fund flows in managed futures are performance chasing. The highest fund flows occur following periods of performance; 2008 was a record year for trend following; 2009 was a year of high-strategy inflows: this demonstrates performance chasing. In the specific case where an investor seeks to perform trend following rules on trend following strategies, this approach can be called **trend following squared** (TF^2).

Mean reversion investment strategies seek to invest when a strategy has underperformed and to take profit when it has outperformed. Mean reversion strategies work well when performance mean reverts. For example, a **buying-at-the-dips** investment approach invests when the strategy is in a drawdown. This type of strategy will implicitly invest with the assumption that temporary underperformance will recover; mean reverting to its longer term average. Another example is a profit-taking strategy that is focused on outperformance. This approach locks in profits, cutting or reducing investment after a period of outperformance.

Despite the many approaches for dynamic allocation, the prudent method depends on the underlying performance of the strategy itself. If trend following returns are mean reverting, mean reversion approaches can be applied. If returns exhibit momentum or persistence, momentum-seeking approaches can be applied. If trend following returns follow a random walk, or if statistical evidence for either momentum or mean reversion is not compelling, it may be prudent to stick to buy and hold. To determine this, it is pertinent to analyze the underlying statistical properties of trend following returns. Serial autocorrelation in returns measures the amount that future returns are predicted by past returns. When serial correlation is positive (negative), this indicates momentum in returns (mean reversion). In the case of a random walk, serial autocorrelation is zero. Figure 17.1 plots a schematic for price processes, serial autocorrelation, and the corresponding appropriate dynamic investment strategies.

In addition to the level of persistence of mean reversion or momentum in returns, the underlying level of volatility can also determine whether risks outweigh any of the advantages of active investment allocation. By adjusting absolute performance by the relevant risk, the Sharpe ratio can also be used to compare across dynamic strategies. For example, an active strategy that requires infrequent underinvestment (an allocation of less than 100 percent) could possibly have both less return and less

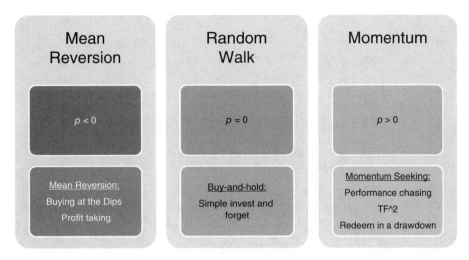

FIGURE 17.1 A schematic for price processes, serial autocorrelation (p), and the corresponding appropriate dynamic investment approaches.

risk. In this case, it is the ratio between risk and return that can give an indication of performance. As in any dynamic strategy, the properties of both serial autocorrelation and Sharpe ratios are time varying and not independent of each other. Sharpe ratios are impacted by the level of serial correlation in returns. Positive (negative) serial autocorrelation increases (decreases) Sharpe ratios.

■ Mean Reversion in Trend Following Return Series

The existence of mean reversion in a return series suggests that momentum-seeking approaches would be ineffective. If trend following returns are mean reverting, as many empirical studies suggest, buying-at-the-dips or even buy-and-hold may be more prudent. This also depends on the level of persistence of the serial correlation. It is important to point out that manager-based return series are plagued with survivorship bias. Survivorship bias may cast reasonable doubt on any empirical evidence related to estimates for mean reversion using indices of manager returns. It is easily argued that any track record that has survived large drawdowns can appear to be mean-reverting. Strategies that do not survive long drawdowns disappear from the sample set. A study by Cukurova and Martin (2011) discusses the Darwinian selection phenomenon related to drawdowns. They provide evidence that funds that have survived large relative drawdowns are managed by truly talented managers that can deliver future outstanding performance. In Chapter 9, negative serial correlation in trend following strategies was discussed briefly using manager-based indices. To revisit this issue, Figure 17.2 plots the serial autocorrelation estimates for several

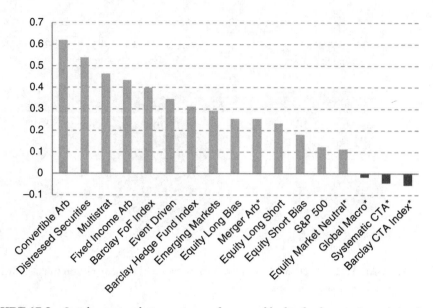

FIGURE 17.2 Serial autocorrelation estimates for several hedge fund strategies and trend following (Barclay CTA Index and Systematic CTA). The data sample period is monthly from 1993 to 2013. An asterisk (*) indicates that the estimate is statistically different from zero.
Data source: BarclayHedge.

hedge fund strategies and trend following (Barclay CTA Index and Systematic CTA). Strategies marked with (*) have serial autocorrelation, which is statistically different than zero. Using only monthly index returns, this figure demonstrates the unique negative serial correlation profile of trend following.

A Newedge whitepaper (2012) also finds serial autocorrelation in manager returns for lags of up to five months. An autocorrelation function (ACF) with (n) lags can be used to measure correlation effects from the past n returns for a time series. ACF-1 represents the correlation coefficient for the weight of the past month's return on the current return. ACF-5 represents the correlation coefficient for the weight of the return from five months prior on the current return. Autocorrelation coefficients can be estimated assuming a simple autoregressive model of order (n) or an AR (n). To demonstrate this, for a group of five large trend following managers (the Mini Sub Index) and each of them individually (Manager 1 to 5), Figure 17.3 plots a sum of the first five correlation coefficient estimates for lags 1 to 5 (ACF-1 to ACF-5). This example demonstrates how most trend followers seem to exhibit some negative serial autocorrelation. These effects remain somewhat negative for lags up to five months.

In the same autocorrelation study, they examine a comprehensive list of 793 CTAs. This large set of CTAs includes both trend followers and nontrend followers. For each CTA in the sample, the first five autocorrelation coefficient estimates are summed up. For each CTA, the correlation with the mini-trend index (including five well-established

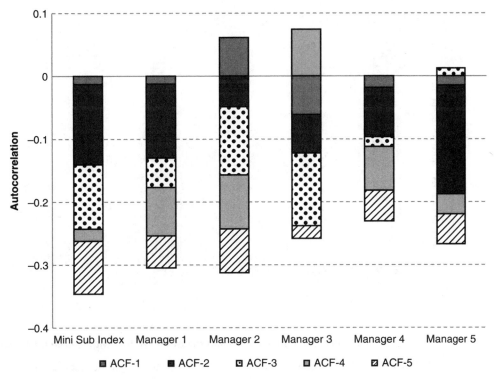

FIGURE 17.3 Autocorrelation coefficients 1 to 5 (ACF-1 to ACF-5) for the mini-trend index (Mini Sub Index) and the five managers in the index.
Source: Barclay Hedge and Newedge Investment Solutions.

trend following managers) is also estimated. Figure 17.4 first ranks the first five auto-correlation lags (a measure of negative serial autocorrelation) and compares this rank with the correlation to trend following (via the mini-trend index). Roughly the first 100 CTAs on the left-hand side have both high ranking for serial autocorrelation and high correlation with the mini-trend index. The main concept is that these managers are most likely trend following CTAs. The property of negative serial autocorrelation seems to be a general characteristic of trend following managers as a class.

The previous discussion of serial autocorrelation was based on actual track records. A theoretical view of serial autocorrelation may provide some confirmation or discussion. Fung and Hsieh (2001) demonstrate how trend following strategies can be replicated by a portfolio of lookback straddle options. If a lookback straddle option strategy is assumed to represent trend following performance over time, this strategy can be examined for mean reversion using a variance ratio test. The closed form expression for the lookback straddle option strategy allows for a closed form expression for the variance ratio statistic. A **variance ratio statistic** is the ratio between the variance of an n-time-unit ($n > 1$) aggregated change and n times of the

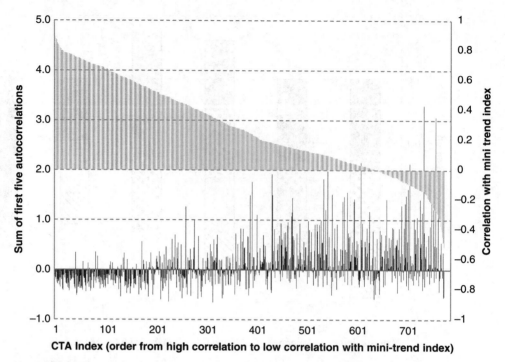

FIGURE 17.4 Upper panel: Serial autocorrelation effects (sum of the first five correlation coefficients for 793 CTAs). Lower panel: Correlation with the mini-trend index (a small index of five well-established trend following CTAs).
Source: Barclay Hedge, Newedge Alternative Investment Solutions.

variance of single-time-unit change. A variance ratio statistic of 1 indicates a random walk. When the variance ratio statistic is below 1, a time series is mean reverting. Under certain conditions in Greyserman (2012), the variance ratio statistic for the lookback straddle option strategy can be shown to be lower than 1, indicating that trend following return series may exhibit mean reversion. Given the highly technical nature of variance ratio statistics and lookback straddle options, details are discussed in the appendix of this chapter.

Performance of Momentum Seeking

If trend following returns are mean reverting, momentum seeking approaches for dynamic allocation to trend following should underperform. To examine an extreme case, trend following rules can be applied to dynamically allocate to a trend following program (the trend following squared approach). To demonstrate the performance of trend following a trend follower, trend following return series are fed back into a

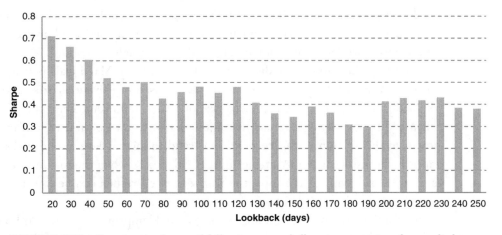

FIGURE 17.5 Sharpe ratios for trend following squared allocation strategies when applied to a representative trend following.

trend following system with a short-sales restriction. Unlike futures positions, it is only possible to invest in a trend follower. Short selling is not possible for funds. To examine the potential for using trend following squared as a method to dynamically allocate to trend following, a generic trend following system with a Sharpe ratio of 0.94 is examined.[1] It is important to remember that the Sharpe ratio of 0.94 comes from a buy-and-hold investment in trend following over the entire sample period. Trend following squared involves trying to find trends in trend following performance and allocating based on these trends. Figure 17.5 plots the Sharpe ratio for trend following squared as a function of the lookback window size for trend following a trend follower. Figure 17.3 demonstrates that, regardless of the chosen parameter (the lookback size), trend following squared (TF^2) never outperforms the buy-and-hold trend following portfolio with a Sharpe ratio of 0.94. The performance of a momentum seeking approach such as trend following squared demonstrates how improper dynamic allocation approaches can deteriorate performance.

Performance of Dynamic Allocation Strategies

Empirical evidence suggests that trend following return series exhibit negative serial autocorrelation. If this is the case, mean reversion strategies should potentially perform in line or possibly even better than a buy-and-hold strategy, and especially better than momentum seeking strategies. For a simple example, a buying-at-the-dips (or buying in a drawdown) approach might have some merit. A buying-at-the-dips approach increases allocation when the strategy is in a drawdown. On the other

---

[1] This trend following strategy is examined from 1993 to 2012.

hand, if return series are sufficiently noisy, it may be too difficult to determine when or if a true drawdown is occurring. In this situation, a buy-and-hold investment may still be more prudent than a buying-at-the-dips approach.

A strategy that buys at the dips is somewhat similar to Martingale betting. As discussed in Chapter 9, dynamic leveraging can be used to elevate Sharpe ratios while exposing an investor to the increased risk of a large tail event. This type of event is magnified by the higher leverage in conjunction with the continuation of the drawdown. In this section, mean reversion in trend following returns enhances Sharpe ratios for investors who buy-at-the-dips. For the cases when the maximum leverage is capped for buying-at-the-dips, the total expected return can be lower while the risk of extreme losses is held somewhat in check.

To examine if a buying-at-the-dips strategy would improve on a buy-and-hold portfolio, a simple experiment can be applied. Assume an investor buys and holds an allocation of x percent in trend following. For the remaining $(100 - x)$ percent, the investor increases investment in the trend following portfolio when the performance is down, buying-at-the-dips, and reduces investment when the performance is up, taking profits. Even more specifically, the change in investment is proportional to the strength of a trend signal based on cumulative trend following returns. The investor increases (reduces) allocation linearly to the portfolio when the downtrend becomes stronger (weaker). This means that when a drawdown is larger the allocation will be larger.

For allocations between 0 and 100 percent, Figure 17.6 plots the Sharpe ratios for the combined total portfolio return with x percent in buy-and-hold and

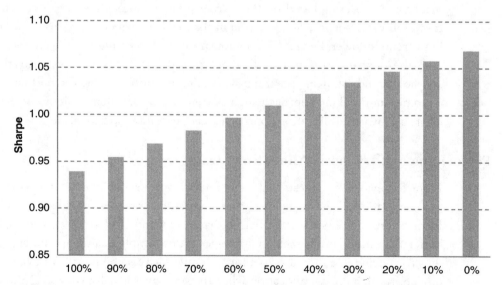

FIGURE 17.6 Sharpe ratios for a combined dynamic allocation trend following portfolio with x percent buy-and-hold (the horizontal axis) and $(100 - x)$ percent buying-at-the-dips. (x) ranges from 0 percent to 100 percent.

(100 − *x*) percent using a buying-at-the-dips approach. To demonstrate how this approach would work, assume that an investor wants to invest $200M to trend following with 50 percent of the allocation in a passive, buy-and-hold approach. The investor invests $100M in trend following buy-and-hold. When the trend signal for the cumulative trend following return becomes negative, the investor starts to add to the system from the remaining $100M budgeted for investment. When the negative signal reaches the maximum strength, the $100M will be completely invested in the system and the total investment becomes $200M. When the trend signal becomes positive, the total investment will be reduced back to the original $100M allocated. Using this mean reverting dynamic allocation scheme, the investor would achieve a Sharpe ratio of above 1.0. Despite the fact that this strategy allocates less than all of the capital, it performs with a Sharpe ratio above the buy-and-hold Sharpe ratio of 0.94. As the amount of capital allocated to the passive buy-and-hold approach decreases the overall Sharpe ratio increases somewhat linearly.[2]

Using Sharpe ratios as a measure for performance, an investor may be able to improve performance by timing allocations properly and buying-at-the-dips. When an investor combines a buy-and-hold allocation of *x* percent and a buying-at-the-dips allocation of (100 − *x*) percent, this is a form of dynamic leveraging. More importantly, in this case, the maximum leverage is restricted to the leverage employed by the buy-and-hold approach. This means that the leverage of the combined portfolio is often lower than, and *never* higher than the constant leverage employed by the buy-and-hold approach. It is also important to note that the buying-at-the-dips strategy is not always fully invested meaning that there are opportunity costs to underinvestment.

> Buying-at-the-dips is a dynamic leveraging approach. In this study, it is bounded to make sure that it does not allow maximum leverage to exceed the leverage of a buy-and-hold approach. This reduces the probability of extreme losses.

In this example, a cap on the total leverage avoids the risk of large losses for accelerated dynamic leveraging schemes (for example Martingale betting). To demonstrate this effect, if the total allocation was allowed to exceed 100 percent, this leveraging scheme may provide drastic improvements in Sharpe ratio but at the risk of extreme drawdowns when leverage accelerates too quickly during a drawdown.

---

[2] The return is based on the total maximum allocation. The uninvested capital is assumed to be in cash with zero return. Transaction costs as well as subscriptions and redemption costs are excluded from this analysis.

Given the need to cap leverage for a portfolio that buys at the dips, an investor may expect an improved risk-adjusted return (the Sharpe ratio) at the cost of a reduced total expected return. When serial autocorrelation in trend following returns is sufficiently negative, a buying-at-the-dips approach may be able to improve return. The analysis in this section has demonstrated that both the level of mean reversion and overall risk reward tradeoffs (as measured by Sharpe ratios) can impact when mean-reverting approaches for dynamic allocation may be appropriate. The following section discusses this in more detail.

■ Investigating Dynamic Allocation Strategies

In the first section of this chapter, both serial autocorrelation and Sharpe ratios represent two statistical properties of returns that may help to classify when dynamic allocation is appropriate. Serial autocorrelation provides some indication of when returns exhibit persistence or mean revert. When Sharpe ratios are lower, dynamic allocation may be more desirable as performance may tend to occur in certain periods. When Sharpe ratios are high and serial autocorrelation is low, a passive buy-and-hold investment strategy is appropriate. When returns mean revert and Sharpe ratios are low, a buying-at-the-dips approach can make sense. When returns exhibit momentum and Sharpe ratios are low, a momentum-seeking approach can make sense. Logically, these conclusions are intuitive but in practice estimates for serial autocorrelation and Sharpe ratios are point estimates and often noisy ones. Because both Sharpe ratios and serial autocorrelations interact, optimal allocation strategies can be discussed more explicitly by examining the joint distribution of serial autocorrelation and Sharpe ratios.

To examine the performance of dynamic allocation strategies, an autoregressive $AR(5)$ model can be used to generate return series. This model is selected to mimic the results from the Newedge whitepaper (2012), which demonstrates mean reversion for up to five months. The performance of dynamic allocation strategies can be estimated by Monte Carlo simulation. By ranging the serial autocorrelation and Sharpe ratio of returns in the $AR(5)$ model, a wide range of scenarios for trend following returns can be examined. Beginning with a buying-at-the-dips approach, Table 17.1 displays the average return difference between buying-at-the-dips and buy-and-hold. For example, if the correlation is −0.16 and the Sharpe ratio is 0.4 the average return difference is 3.14 percent. Consistent with intuition, when the serial autocorrelation is negative and the Sharpe ratio is low, buying-at-the-dips outperforms buy-and-hold. When the serial autocorrelation is positive, buying-at-the-dips underperforms buy-and-hold. The results for momentum seeking are also consistent;

TABLE 17.1 Average total return difference between buying-at-the-dips and buy-and-hold. Serial correlation ranges from –0.2 to 0.1 and the original Sharpe ratio is between 0.1 and 1.

	-0.2	-0.18	-0.16	-0.14	-0.12	-0.1	-0.08	-0.06	-0.04	-0.02	0	0.02	0.04	0.06	0.08	0.1
0.1	5.21	4.84	4.76	3.51	2.98	2.97	2.04	1.43	0.55	-0.12	-0.69	-2.18	-3.22	-4.68	-5.72	-6.69
0.2	4.81	4.30	3.80	3.21	2.68	2.20	1.54	1.07	0.20	-0.99	-1.55	-2.30	-3.91	-5.74	-6.39	-8.78
0.3	4.26	4.41	3.21	3.20	2.16	1.32	0.93	-0.03	-0.78	-1.52	-2.95	-4.17	-4.83	-7.43	-8.79	-11.53
0.4	3.84	3.72	3.14	1.91	1.73	0.96	-0.31	-0.69	-1.60	-2.20	-3.66	-4.60	-6.43	-8.37	-9.45	-12.29
0.5	3.50	2.56	2.46	1.44	0.92	0.26	-0.93	-1.57	-2.73	-3.85	-5.12	-5.47	-7.94	-10.29	-12.71	-14.22
0.6	3.15	2.08	1.66	0.72	0.24	-0.46	-1.38	-2.35	-2.91	-3.74	-5.54	-7.29	-9.09	-12.10	-13.22	-19.80
0.7	1.97	1.57	0.84	0.32	-0.52	-1.20	-1.65	-3.30	-4.21	-5.66	-6.79	-8.27	-11.04	-13.52	-15.31	-19.41
0.8	1.14	1.35	-0.05	-0.27	-1.66	-2.42	-3.27	-3.71	-5.77	-6.45	-8.79	-9.76	-11.37	-14.06	-17.87	-24.18
0.9	1.08	0.41	-0.72	-1.16	-2.18	-3.47	-4.40	-4.65	-6.31	-7.37	-9.33	-11.48	-13.34	-15.64	-20.86	-24.28
1	0.46	-0.81	-1.34	-1.99	-2.84	-3.99	-5.51	-6.16	-7.82	-9.20	-11.31	-13.08	-15.54	-19.53	-23.57	-28.00

when there is positive serial autocorrelation and a low Sharpe ratio, momentum seeking can outperform buy-and-hold.

For a range of combinations of Sharpe ratios and serial autocorrelation, Table 17.2 illustrates four scenarios for dynamic allocation (including buy-and-hold) and the corresponding favorable return profiles for their application. Based on simulation, and for the range of examples, the results from simulation mirror the intuition for both buying-at-the-dips and performance-chasing. Allocation approach D, redeeming-in-a-drawdown, is a specific type of momentum-seeking strategy that redeems in a drawdown; the mirror opposite of the buying-at-the dips approach, which allocates in a drawdown.

The most effective investment approach depends on the joint distribution of the return's Sharpe ratio and serial autocorrelation.

TABLE 17.2 Four scenarios for dynamic allocation and the corresponding favorable return profiles for their application.

	Allocation Approach	Sharpe Ratios	Serial Autocorrelation	Example
A	Buy-and-hold	High	Low	$Shp > 0.8, |\rho| < 0.1$
B	Buying-at-the-dips	Low	Negative	$Shp < 0.3, \rho < -0.1$
C	Performance-chasing	Low	Positive	$Shp < 0.3, \rho > 0.1$
D	Redeeming-in-a-drawdown	High	Positive	$Shp > 0.8, \rho > 0.1$

Returning again to the buying-at-the-dips allocation approach, a return profile similar to the point estimates for actual trend following return series can be examined more closely. Using a return generating process with a Sharpe ratio of 0.9 and slightly negative serial autocorrelation, the performance of the buying-at-the-dips strategy can be examined as a function of the amount x percent that remains buy-and-hold. For a given Sharpe ratio of 0.9 and slightly negative serial autocorrelation, Figure 17.7 plots the total return for a combined portfolio with x percent buy-and-hold and $(100 - x)$ percent buying-at-the-dips. Similar to the previous example with buying-at-the-dips, the total capital, or the maximum capital invested in the trend following program, is the same for all allocation percentages (x). Maximum leverage is capped at the same level for a 100 percent buy-and-hold portfolio. Figure 17.7 demonstrates Scenario A where a buy-and-hold allocation should be a favorable strategy. In the case where the serial autocorrelation is only slightly negative and the Sharpe ratio is high, buying-at-the-dips reduces the performance of a buy-and-hold strategy. More specifically, when the strategy has half of its capital in buy-and-hold ($x = 50$ percent), the total return is reduced from 13 percent to roughly 8 percent if the investor nothing.

On the other hand, for periods when the Sharpe ratio is sufficiently low and serial correlation is negative, the opposite may be true. This is a Type B scenario where buying-at-the-dips may outperform buy-and-hold. Using a return generating process

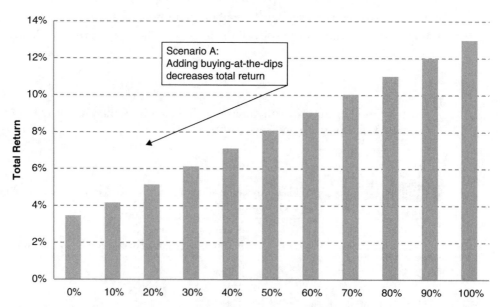

FIGURE 17.7 Scenario A: The total return of combining buy-and-hold x percent (the horizontal axis) and buying-at-the-dips $(100 - x)$ percent, with (x) varying from 0 to 100, to a representative trend following system.

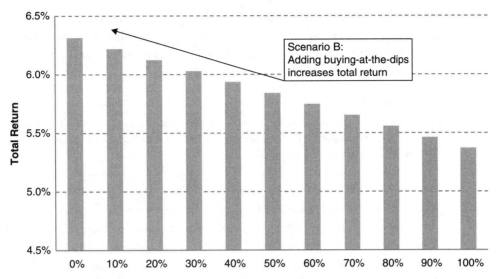

FIGURE 17.8   Scenario B: The total return of combining buy-and-hold *x* percent (the horizontal axis) and buying-at-the-dips (100 − *x*) percent, with (*x*) varying from 0 to 100, to a representative trend following system.

with a low Sharpe ratio and more negative serial autocorrelation, Figure 17.8 plots the total return for a combined portfolio with *x* percent buy-and-hold and (100 − *x*) percent buying-at-the-dips. Because Sharpe ratios are lower, overall returns are lower. In a Type B scenario, a reduction in the amount allocated to buy-and-hold in favor of buying-at-the-dips increases performance linearly.

Optimization with Uncertainty

Sharpe ratios and serial autocorrelation are not deterministic. Even more complicated, they are not independent of each other typically following a joint statistical distribution. The classifications for Type A and Type B scenarios are somewhat broad. From the investor's perspective, it would be ideal to have a method for determining (*x*), or the percentage that should remain in buy-and-hold. This problem is a classic problem of optimization under uncertainty. The objective is to maximize the total expected return using a penalty for uncertainty.[3] When an investor is relatively confident about the point estimates for the Sharpe ratio and serial correlation, the weight for the penalty item can be insignificant. In this case, the optimum solution will be either 100 percent Type A or Type B. On the other hand, when an investor is

[3] When the penalty item is the variance of the expected total return over the set of possible values for the Sharpe ratio and serial correlation, the optimization is similar to the classical mean variance optimization. In this case, the variance here is not the portfolio return variance.

less confident with the point estimates for the Sharpe ratio or serial autocorrelation, the uncertainty penalty should be large. The optimal solution is the x that makes the distribution of total expected return as uniform as possible across a range of possible values for the "true" Sharpe ratio and serial correlation.

> Because of the uncertainty related to the joint distribution of Sharpe ratio and serial correlation, the optimal approach is usually a combination of two investment approaches.

Optimization under uncertainty can be rather complex and heuristic solutions often provide rather robust solutions to these types of problems.[4] Intuitively, given uncertainty regarding the return distribution, the optimal solution can be estimated heuristically as the average value for x over a range of possible range of distributions for the Sharpe ratio and serial autocorrelation. For a specific example, a typical trend following program with serial autocorrelation of −0.1 and a Sharpe ratio distributed uniformly between 0.3 and 0.8 can be considered. In this case, the best solution is 50 percent buy-and-hold and 50 percent buying-at-the-dips. This result is based on the results in Table 7.1. As another example, imagine a scenario when an investor is more positive about the Sharpe ratio, perhaps between 0.5 and 0.8, and he/she estimates the serial autocorrelation between −0.12 and −0.08. The best solution would be 75 percent buy-and-hold and 25 percent buying-at-the-dips.

Reflections on Dynamic Allocation

For periods of mean reversion in performance, the buying-at-the-dips approach has been shown to increase the performance of buy-and-hold. This conclusion may raise the question of whether trend following managers themselves should consider incorporating this into their approach. There are several issues with this conclusion. First, trend following managers may consider it suboptimal to select a structured point of x percent. Second, the investors' and trend following managers' views on Sharpe ratios and serial autocorrelation may differ substantially creating a mismatch in expectations. Investors and managers may also have different objectives. For example, an investor interested in high crisis alpha may be less concerned with total return as an objective. Another investor who uses a risk parity approach may also have a completely different objective than total portfolio return.

---

[4] The field of robust optimization provides alternative methods for performing optimization when there is uncertainty in the distribution of underlying parameters. This section resorts to a heuristic method for estimating the optimal solution for such an optimization problem.

Despite many complications, there is one important message from this analysis. Dynamic allocation strategies should only be applied when there is sufficient evidence that trend following returns exhibit the proper return characteristics. The corresponding level of uncertainty regarding the underlying return characteristics for trend following returns point to either a buy-and-hold approach or buying-at-the-dips. An investor who is confident in long-term performance expectations (i.e., a Sharpe ratio close to 1) should size the initial investment according to expected drawdown risks and follow a buy-and-hold approach.[5] An investor, who is less confident about performance expectations, should maintain a significant level of baseline buy-and-hold investment (for example, 50 to 75 percent) and deploy the remaining capital buying-at-the-dips. This mean reversion strategy accumulates exposure during dips in performance and reduces exposure following a significant increase in performance. For one final point, this analysis also provides a word of caution for performance chasing. Performance chasing is not compatible with the mean reverting nature of trend following returns.

> Different investors may have a range of views on the distribution for the Sharpe ratio and serial correlation as well as different objectives. As a result, optimal allocation to buying-at-the-dips is investor specific.

■ Summary

Once an investor has decided to invest in trend following strategies, the next natural question is how and when. Dynamic allocation approaches can be divided into three types: buy-and-hold, momentum seeking, and mean reversion. The choice of dynamic allocation strategy should directly depend on the underlying statistical properties of trend following returns. Empirical evidence provides support for mean reversion in trend following performance. Despite this evidence, it is also necessary to take the level of risk in returns and Sharpe ratios into account. This chapter examined the buying-at-the-dips approach to dynamic allocation in comparison with a simple buy-and-hold. Using joint distributions for the Sharpe ratio and serial autocorrelation in returns, a number of scenarios for favorable environments for different allocation approaches can be summarized. Buy-and-hold strategies are the most favorable when the Sharpe ratio is high and absolute levels of serial autocorrelation are low. Mean reverting strategies, such as buying-at-the-dips, are the most favorable when Sharpe ratios are lower and serial autocorrelation is negative. Momentum strategies, such as performance chasing, are the most favorable when Sharpe ratios are lower and serial autocorrelation is positive. Given the empirical and theoretical

---

[5] For a comprehensive discussion of drawdown characteristics, see Chapter 8.

evidence for trend following returns, dependent on the investor's objectives and risk tolerance, the appropriate dynamic allocation approach varies between buy-and-hold and buying-at-the-dips. Given the analysis in this chapter, a word of caution is also extended for performance chasing trend following: dynamic allocation approaches of this type can reduce performance substantially.

■ Appendix: A Theoretical Analysis of Mean Reversion in Trend Following

Earlier in this chapter, mean reversion in trend following return series was a key factor in determining which dynamic allocation could be appropriate for an investor and when. This section turns to a theoretical analysis of serial autocorrelation properties and variance ratio statistics. Under the assumption that trend following returns are replicated by lookback straddle options from Fung and Hsieh (2001), it is possible to express the PnL as a function of the change in price of the lookback straddle price. Under certain simplifying assumptions, Greyserman (2012) demonstrates that the price change of a lookback straddle can be shown to be mean reverting using the variance ratio statistic (Lo and MacKinlay 1988). This appendix reviews the variance ratio statistic and the lookback straddle option for replicating trend following from Fung and Hsieh (2001).

Mean Reversion and the Variance Ratio Statistic

If a time series follows a random walk, the variance of the n-time-unit aggregated change is n times of the variance of single-time-unit change, as shown in the following equation:

$$V(n) \equiv \frac{\delta_n^2}{n \times \delta_1^2} = 1$$

where $V(n)$ is the variance ratio statistic between δ_n^2, the variance of the n-time-unit aggregated change ($n > 1$), and n times δ_1^2, the variance of single-time-unit change. The variance ratio test is one of the standard statistical tests for a random walk (Lo and MacKinlay 1988). This section is not focused on testing the statistical significance of a time series being a random walk. Instead this section is focused on the variance ratio's link to mean reversion. Negative serial correlation corresponds to a variance ratio statistic lower than 1.[6] Given this fact, return series can be loosely defined as

---

[6] The opposite case is that, when the serial correlation is positive, the variance ratio is larger than 1, indicating momentum in the time series.

FIGURE 17.9 A schematic for price processes, strategies, and variance ratio statistics.

mean-reverting when the variance ratio statistic is lower than 1. Figure 17.9 presents a schematic for price processes, strategies, and variance ratio statistics.

To demonstrate this empirically, Figure 17.10 plots two time series with a serial autocorrelation of 0.3 and −0.3 of per unit time change respectively. From this example, the time series with the negative serial autocorrelation appears to exhibit more mean reversion than the one with positive serial autocorrelation. In this example, the variance ratio statistic $V(2)$ for the time series with positive serial autocorrelation is 1.25, while $V(2)$ for the time series with negative serial autocorrelation is 0.70. This example demonstrates the link between serial autocorrelation and the variance ratio statistic.

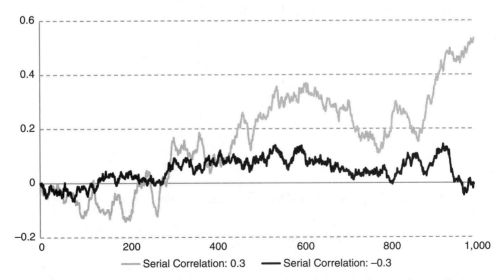

FIGURE 17.10 Sample time series for two series with serial autocorrelations of 0.3 and −0.3 respectively.

Trend Following and the Lookback Straddle Option

From a theoretical perspective, Fung and Hsieh (2001) established the equivalence of trend following and holding lookback straddle options. The performance of the lookback straddle option was discussed in Chapter 13. In this chapter, in comparison with other manager-based indices and price-based trend indices, the lookback straddle option seemed to exhibit the poorest fit in a return-based style analysis. This may demonstrate the subtle difference between position taking and option strategies. Due to the importance of the lookback straddle in the trend following literature, it is discussed further here. According to Goldman, Sosin, and Gatto (1979), the price of a lookback call option with time to maturity (T) at time t $(t < T)$, can be expressed using the following formula:

$$LC_t = S_t N(f_1(S_t, Q_t)) - Q_t e^{-r\tau} N(f_2(S_t, Q_t))$$

$$- \frac{S_t \sigma^2}{2r} \left(N(-f_1(S_t, Q_t)) - e^{-r\tau} \left(\frac{Q_t}{S_t} \right)^{\frac{2r}{\sigma^2}} N(-f_3(S_t, Q_t)) \right)$$

where $\tau = T - t$, r is the continuously compounded risk-free rate, S_t is the underlying market price at time t, σ is the underlying market volatility (assumed to be constant), Q_t is the lowest price for the underlying market up to time t, and $N(\cdot)$ is the standard normal cumulative distribution function. In addition, let

$$f_1(x, y) = \frac{\ln\left(\frac{x}{y} \right) + \left[r + \frac{1}{2} \sigma^2 \right] \tau}{\sigma \sqrt{\tau}}$$

$$f_2(x, y) = \frac{\ln\left(\frac{x}{y} \right) + \left[r - \frac{1}{2} \sigma^2 \right] \tau}{\sigma \sqrt{\tau}}$$

$$f_3(x, y) = \frac{\ln\left(\frac{x}{y} \right) - \left[r - \frac{1}{2} \sigma^2 \right] \tau}{\sigma \sqrt{\tau}}$$

Similarly, the price of a lookback put option at time t is expressed as follows:

$$LP_t = -S_t N(-f_1(S_t, M_t)) + M_t e^{-r\tau} N(-f_2(S_t, M_t))$$

$$+ \frac{S_t \sigma^2}{2r} \left(N(f_1(S_t, M_t)) - e^{-r\tau} \left(\frac{M_t}{S_t} \right)^{\frac{2r}{\sigma^2}} N(f_3(S_t, M)) \right)$$

where M_t is the highest price of the underlying market up to time t. The price of a lookback straddle at time t is then simply $LC_t + LP_t$. Correspondingly, the profit and loss (PnL) of a trend following portfolio is proportional to the change in $LC_t + LP_t$.

> The PnL of trend following in a given period can be expressed in the price change of a lookback straddle option.

■ Further Reading and References

Cukurova, S., and J. Martin. "On the Economics of Hedge Fund Drawdown Status: Performance, Insurance Selling and Darwinian Selection." Working paper, 2011.

Fung, W., and D. Hsieh. "The Risk in Hedge Fund Strategies: Theory and Evidence from Trend Followers." *Review of Financial Studies* 14, no. 2 (2001).

Greyserman, A. "The Fallacy of Trend Following Trend Following." ISAM white paper, November 2012.

Goldman, M., H. Sosin, and M. Gatto. "Path Dependent Options: 'Buy at the Low, Sell at the High.'" *Journal of Finance* 34, no. 5 (1979).

"It's the Autocorrelation, Stupid." Newedge white paper, November 2012.

Lo, A., and A. MacKinlay. "Stock Market Prices Do Not Follow Random Walks: Evidence from a Simple Specification Test." *Review of Financial Studies* 1, no. 1 (1988).

adaptation   an evolutionary process whereby a species, or group of market participants, is able to adapt to changes in the market environment.

adaptive markets hypothesis (AMH)   an approach to understanding how markets evolve, how opportunities occur, and how market players succeed or fail based on principles of evolutionary biology.

allocated dollar risk   the amount of dollar risk allocated to a particular futures market.

alpha decay   the speed at which performance degrades as you delay execution.

average holding period   the average amount of time a trade is held.

average PnL ratio   the ratio of wins and losses in the PnL ratio. This is a measure of the magnitude of wins, not simply the rate of wins.

average sector allocations   the average amount of capital allocated to a particular sector.

average trading range (ATR)   an average of the trading range over a given window of time.

average winning trade rate   the average overwinning trade rates.

backwardation   the opposite of contango where the futures price is below the expected spot price. In this situation, hedgers are willing to sell for prices below the expected spot prices.

bond crisis alpha   the return difference between an original return series and the return series with the monthly returns during crisis periods replaced by the risk-free rate. Crisis periods are defined by losses in a fixed income benchmark.

breakout strategy   takes a position when the price breaks out of a range of values, often called the resistance and support levels. A breakout strategy takes a long position when the price goes above the resistance level and a short position when the price goes below the support level.

buy-and-hold strategy   invests and maintains a position over time.

buying-at-the-dips   an investment approach that invests when the strategy is in a drawdown.

Calmar ratio   a comparison of the average annual compounded rate of return and the maximum drawdown risk.

capital allocation   an approach for allocating capital across markets.

channel breakout system   a breakout system that uses channels to determine when signals break out of a range.

coefficient of variation   (for margin to equity) measure of the normalized dispersion of margin to equity.

collateral yield   the return that is earned for collateralized positions via margin accounts.

commodity crisis alpha   the return difference between an original return series and the return series with the monthly returns replaced by the risk-free rate during crisis periods. Crisis periods are defined by losses for a commodity benchmark.

contango   when the futures price is above the expected spot price. In this situation, it is often suggested that hedgers are willing to pay more for something in the future as opposed to what they should expect to pay.

continuous price series   created by removing the gaps in futures price series. The rolling aspect of futures contracts will create gaps in price series requiring adjustments.

contract size   the notional size of one futures contract.

contrarian strategy   trades against the trend and seeks to profit from a price reversal.

convergent   a risk taking approach which is based on a particular view regarding the fair value of an underlying asset.

cost of carry   the costs associated with an investment position. These costs can include financial costs, interest costs, or convenience-related costs for the case of commodities.

counterparty risk   the risk that a counterparty will not fulfill the terms of an agreement.

credit risk   the risk associated with counterparties not being able to repay their obligation or fulfill their side of a contract or position. Credit risk relies on the behavior of individual counterparties.

crisis alpha   performance during periods of market crisis.

crisis alpha opportunities   profits that are gained by exploiting the persistent trends that occur across markets during times of crisis.

crisis beta   an alternative beta related to the traditional beta. The key difference is that crisis beta is constructed to take into account conditional correlation. More negative crisis beta indicates greater diversification benefits.

crisis period   a period of time defined by crisis. Many alternative definitions may be used to define a crisis period. Crisis can be defined by past returns, increases in volatility, or by other measures.

directional strategies   take long or short positions in financial securities in hopes to profit from directional moves. Common examples of these include managed futures (CTAs), equity long bias, equity short bias, and global macro.

discretionary   strategies that use some level of manager discretion.

dislocation   prices move away from no arbitrage relationships.

divergence   the process that market participants and groups of market species evolve and adapt to new market conditions creating trends in prices.

divergent   a risk taking approach which is based on no particular view regarding the fair value of an underlying asset.

divergent trend following index (DI)   a basket of divergent trend following strategies that represent a wide range of loss tolerances.

divergent trend following strategy   a basic trend following strategy that includes a basic entry decision, uses a trailing stop for exit decisions, and employs equal risk allocation across markets.

diversification ratio   a measure of diversification in a portfolio. This ratio is measured by the sum of individual market value-at-risk divided by the total portfolio value-at-risk.

downside risk   measures the variability of underperformance below a minimum target rate. The minimum target rate can be zero, the risk-free rate or any other fixed threshold. All returns above the threshold are included as zero in the calculation of the downside risk.

drawdown   measures the loss from an investor's peak net asset value (NAV).

drawdown length   the length of time spent in a drawdown.

dynamic leveraging   a situation where the amount of leverage depends on the past profits and losses (PnL) in a portfolio.

entry decision   the decision of when to enter a position.

equal dollar risk allocation (EDR)   a strategy that allocates the same amount of dollar risk to each market. This approach does not consider the correlation between markets. It is similar to the $1/N$ approach, but at the dollar risk level.

equal risk contribution (ERC)   a strategy that allocates risk based on the risk contribution of each market, taking correlation into account. This approach is similar to risk parity.

equity bias factor   a style factor that is the difference between a portfolio strategy with an explicit equity long bias and a portfolio with explicit equity short bias.

equity crisis alpha   the return difference between an original return series and the return series with the monthly returns during crisis periods replaced by the risk-free rate. Crisis periods are defined according to an equity benchmark.

exit decision   the decision of when to exit a position.

expected drawdown length   the expected length of a typical drawdown.

expected longest drawdown length   the expected value of the maximum length of time spent in a drawdown.

expected maximum drawdown   the expected value of the maximum drawdown for a return series given a specific distribution for the return-generating process.

expected recovery time   an indication of the length of time needed to wait for recovery from a drawdown.

explained volatility   the amount of volatility that can be ascribed to fair value and fundamental models. Explained volatility represents the level of risk that is "knowable" or model-able using fundamental models.

forward contract   an agreement between two counterparties (the buyer and seller) to exchange a certain good or commodity (the underlying) for a determined price (the forward price) agreed on at the beginning of the contract (agreement time) and delivered and settled at maturity (settlement date).

futures contract   a forward-like contract with a value that depends on the future value of a good or commodity (the underlying). Futures contracts are standardized, transferable, and exchange traded. Contracts are traded in standard units where the current contract value is contingent on the future value of the specific underlying.

futures contract dollar risk   the dollar risk for one particular futures contract defined by the dollar risk per contract times the point value (or contract value).

futures curve   a plot of futures prices over time.

futurization   the migration of traditional dealer-based bilateral contracts into multilateral standardized "futures-style" contracts that are centrally cleared and exchange traded.

good volatility the type of volatility where higher volatility is associated with higher positive skewness.

hedger a market participant who attempts to take positions counter to protect against adverse price moves.

hedging premium a premium that is earned for taking the other side of a hedging position. When there is excess demand for hedging, a premium can be earned for taking the other side of the trade.

individual market correlation correlation with other markets for a specific future market.

individual market volatility price volatility for an individual futures market.

information ratio the ratio of the annualized excess return relative to a specific benchmark to the corresponding annualized tracking error. Tracking error is defined as the standard deviation of the excess return relative to a benchmark.

interquartile range (IQR) the edges of a box plot that represent the 25th and 75th percentiles for a given distribution.

intrastrategy or **interstrategy** intrastrategy are differences internal to a strategy and interstrategy are differences between external strategies.

invested capital the total capital invested in a strategy.

leverage risk the risks associated with taking exposures based on the use of leverage or on borrowed funds.

limit orders orders that are filled when the market price hits a specific limit or price. As soon as a limit order has been hit, the order is marked to be executed immediately at the best available price.

liquidity risk stems from a lack of marketability or that an investment cannot be bought or sold quickly enough to prevent or minimize a loss.

lookahead window a length of time used to look ahead in an observation period.

lookback window the length of time used for calculations in signal generation.

loss tolerance the level of losses a strategy or individual can tolerate.

maintenance margin the amount of margin required to maintain a futures position. When collateral in a margin account falls below the maintenance margin, a margin call is issued.

margin account a buffer fund that protects the clearinghouse against fluctuations in prices.

margin call a call for a market participant to supply additional capital or variation margin to a margin account. If a margin call is not responded to, the futures position will be closed.

margin to equity ratio a measure of the amount of traded capital that is being held as margin at any particular time divided by the total equity.

mark-to-market   the process of marking the value of positions to settlement prices. This process is done on a daily basis in most futures markets. Accounts are marked to settlement prices and the market is cleared to restart again the following trading day.

market allocation   the process with which capital is allocated across various futures markets.

market capacity weighting (MCW)   an approach where capital is allocated as a function of individual market capacity.

market correlation   the correlation of buy-and-hold returns across individual markets.

market divergence   divergence in market prices. *See also* **divergence**.

market divergence index (MDI)   a metric at the portfolio level, which is used as a measure of the market trendiness. It can be measured by the average signal to noise ratio across markets.

market diversification benefit (MDB)   the ratio of average strategy volatility for each individual market divided by portfolio volatility.

market order   an order that is marked to be carried out immediately at the best available price.

market size factor   a style factor that represents the difference between a strategy that allocates more risk to smaller markets minus one that allocates more to only bigger (larger capacity) markets based on market capacity weightings.

market volatility   total market volatility for a buy-and-hold portfolio.

Martingale betting   an explicit type of dynamic leveraging. Martingale betting works in the following way: a long position is increased until the first day of positive PnL. Bets are increased when they are losing (a form of doubling down).

maximum drawdown   represents the biggest loss an investor could have suffered by buying at the highest point and selling at the lowest. This measurement often gauges the worst case scenario for an investor.

mean reversion   the act of reverting to the average. In statistical terms, mean reversion can be measured by negative serial autocorrelation.

momentum   prices moving in one direction continue to do so for some period of time.

momentum seeking   (investment strategies) seek to invest when a strategy starts to perform well and divest when it starts to lose money.

moving average crossover strategy   uses moving averages across different windows coupled with crossover rules to determine when to go long or short.

moving average crossover system   a trading system which is built using moving average crossover strategies.

moving average strategy   uses moving averages across different windows to determine when to go long or short.

negative convexity   a function that has a negative second derivative. In practical terms, events on the extreme have much lower value than a linear extrapolation. Negative convexity is often a situation where the input can be a scalar larger than one times the output.

net convenience yield   a yield included in futures prices (particularly commodities), which account for the net benefits over time based on both storage costs and convenience.

nondirectional strategies   focus on taking relative value positions where the positions are both long and short (often) in the same asset class at the same time. Convertible arbitrage, fixed income arbitrage, merger arbitrage, equity long/short, and several others are often classified as nondirectional strategies.

Omega ratio   a ratio that compares the amount of weighted gains to weighted losses. This ratio does not make any assumptions about the distribution of returns. This allows the ratio to take into account the information in higher moments of return distributions.

percentage of winning markets   the percentage of markets that have winning positions for a trend following program.

portfolio correlation   correlation across a portfolio.

portfolio volatility   the total volatility for a portfolio.

position selectivity   the act of selecting certain positions in favor of others.

positive convexity   a function that has a positive second derivative. In practical terms, events on the extreme have a higher value than a linear extrapolation. Positive convexity is often a situation where the input can be a scalar larger than one times the output.

positive skewness   a situation where the distribution of returns has larger gains and less large losses.

price risk   (often called market risk) the risk that the price of a security or portfolio will move in an unfavorable direction in the future. In practice, price risk is often proxied by volatility.

probability matching   a behavioral heuristic whereby individuals select between two choices at the same frequency as the estimated frequency of occurrence for the two choices.

punctured equilibrium   a theory in evolutionary biology proposing that species exhibit stasis, a situation with minimal evolutionary change, these moments are sometimes hit with significant evolutionary change, which punctures the previous equilibrium. Following these significant events, there are rapid changes that occur in species.

pure trend following system   the most agnostic system that can be constructed. A pure trend following system is a trading system designed with no particular bias in liquidity, risk allocation, or sector.

random entry system   an "agnostic" divergent risk-taking system that enters a long or short position with equal probability and exits from an existing position only when a trailing stop is reached. Such a system does not depend on any entry signal, and provides a unique platform to evaluate the market environment from the aspect of position management of a trend following system. The tightness of the trailing stop is the only parameter to characterize the system.

recovery period   the amount of time it takes to recover from the specific drawdown.

resistance and support levels   defined by many different techniques including past prices, trading range, and other indicators. A breakout position takes a long position when the price goes above the resistance level and a short position when the price goes below the support level.

risk   the chance that things will not turn out as expected.

risk target   (level of leverage use) the total amount of risk allocated to a trend following strategy in aggregate.

risk to uncertainty ratio   a measure of the amount of uncertainty in total risk. The ratio is explained volatility divided by unexplained volatility. When this ratio is low, volatility is governed more by uncertainty than fundamental models.

roll yield   the price difference between the near and far contracts (near minus far) normalized by the number of days between the expiration dates for a pair of contracts.

sector bias   occurs when a particular sector is overweighted relative to other sectors.

sector directional bias   when a trading system is specifically designed to have a slant toward long or short positions in a particular market sector. The most common example is an equity long bias.

sector specific crisis alpha   the return difference between the return series and the return series with the monthly returns replaced by the three-month T-bill rate when the months meet a sector-crisis definition.

Sharpe ratio   a simple measure of risk-adjusted performance. The risk-free rate is subtracted from total return and divided by the associated portfolio volatility.

signal to noise ratio   the ratio between the trend and individual price changes for a specific period.

sizing function   a number between −1 and 1 that indicates the size and direction of a position for a particular market. The sizing function often integrates trend strength into position sizing.

skewness   the level of asymmetry in a distribution. It is the degree to which the distribution is not balanced around the mean.

speculative opportunities   opportunities that occur for speculative capital when there are price discrepancies in supply and demand.

speculative risk premium   a premium that is earned by speculative strategies during moments when supply and demand takes time to correct prices.

speculator   a market participant that attempts to take positions to speculate on the direction of market prices.

Sterling ratio   a performance ratio that measures compounded annual return divided by the maximum loss minus a threshold.

stop loss orders   orders to sell at a prespecified price. A stop loss limit order is a stop loss order that becomes a limit order as soon as a certain limit has been reached.

strategy category   the category in which a strategy can be classified.

strategy correlation   correlation between returns from different strategies on an array of individual markets.

strategy returns   returns from a strategy on an individual market.

strategy volatility   volatility of the returns of a strategy on an individual market.

success rates   the rate of successful trades.

swap futures   (or futurized swaps) new, exchange-traded variants of swap contracts that are meant to mimic swaps.

systematic   means that a manager uses technical signals and a trading system to implement positions in a systematic fashion. Systematic trading systems are fully automated.

tail risk multiplier   the ratio between the probability of returning a value two standard deviations or lower to the probability of the normal distribution returning a value two standard deviations or lower. For a particular returns series, if the probability is 10 times the normal distribution, the tail risk multiplier is 10.

tightness of the trailing stop   defined by the number of rolling standard deviations of daily price change for setting a trailing stop.

time to recovery   (of a drawdown) amount of time a strategy requires to recover from a drawdown.

total adjusted dollar risk   the total amount of risk allocated to a market after adjusting for the dollar risk for contracts in that particular market.

tradability   the ability to capture trends in actual positions.

trading range   an estimate in the range that an individual market trades over in a given day. It is defined as the maximum of the high for a day or the previous closing price minus the minimum of the low for the day or the previous closing price.

trading signal   a signal that defines the position in a particular market long or short. Trading signals may be directly trend signals or they may also be filtered or aggregated versions of trend signals.

trading speed factor   a style factor that is the difference between a portfolio of slower (high loss tolerance) strategies and a portfolio of faster (low loss tolerance) strategies.

trailing stop   a stopping rule that depends on the recent path of the price such that the stop "trails" the price.

trailing stop indicator   an indicator that determines when the position should be exited due to the hitting of a trailing stop level.

trailing stop loss tolerance   the amount of loss tolerated by a divergent risk-taking strategy defined by the tightness of trailing stops.

trend beta   the beta coefficient for the relationship between a trend index and an underlying strategy.

trend following squared   an investment approach where an investor seeks to perform trend following on trend following.

trend following system   a system that takes data inputs, processes the information in these data sequences, and systematizes trading decisions.

trend leakage   the rate at which trends leak out into trend signals. This is typically measured by the difference in percentage of positions that are the same sign as the future trend minus the percentage that are a different sign.

trend signal   a signal generated to measure a trend. Common examples use moving average crossover rules or breakout rules. Trend signals are typically but not necessarily binary.

trend size   the magnitude of a trend measured by total price change.

trend strength   the measured strength of a trend. This is a quantitative measure of the level of conviction of a trend. Trend strength is typically measured at the total signal level by aggregating trend signals across various lookback windows.

uncertainty   the situation where the consequences, extent, or magnitude of circumstances, conditions, or events is unknown.

unexplained volatility   the amount of volatility that is attributed to unexplainable factors.

variance ratio statistic   the ratio between the variance of an n-time unit ($n > 1$) aggregated change and n times the variance of single-time-unit change. The variance ratio statistic can be used to test for deviations from a random walk.

variation margin   the additional cash added to offset adverse price moves. This is often added as the result of a margin call.

volatility cyclicality   the relative speed of cycles in volatility for a particular trading strategy. This can be measured by examining frequencies in the spectral representation of a time series.

win/loss ratio (of trade PnL)   the ratio of trades that have a winning PnL to the trades that have a losing PnL.

winning ratio   (of trades) the ratio of trades that are winners to the number that are currently losers. This ratio gives some sense of if there are more winners or losers. It does not take into account the size of a win or loss.

Alex Greyserman, PhD, holds the position of chief scientist at ISAM, a specialist managed futures fund manager. With more than 25 years of experience in the hedge fund industry, Alex initially began his tenure serving as research director of Mint Investment Management, the world's first managed futures advisor managing more than $1 billion in assets. At Mint, Alex was responsible for research and development of trading strategies as well as overall portfolio risk management. From 2001 to 2010 Alex held the position of chief investment officer, working alongside Larry Hite, at Hite Capital Management, a family office operation specializing in systematic strategies. Hite Capital Management merged with ISAM in 2010. Prior to entering the hedge fund industry, Alex held several positions in the engineering field; his last role was in the field of signal processing at RCA Labs.

Alex holds a BA in mathematics from Rutgers University, an MS in electrical engineering from Columbia University, and a PhD in statistics and management science from Rutgers University. His dissertation focused on empirical data analysis and application of Bayesian statistics to portfolio selection. Since 2001 Alex has served as an adjunct professor in the graduate program in mathematical finance at Columbia

University, teaching various courses and seminars in the field of quantitative investment management.

Kathryn Kaminski, PhD, holds the position of deputy managing director of the Institute for Financial Research (SIFR) and affiliated faculty at the Stockholm School of Economics in the department of finance. She has previously been a senior lecturer at MIT Sloan School of Management and visiting professor at the Swedish Royal Institute of Technology (KTH). Kathryn has been an external market commentator for the CME Group and she is the featured writer for Institutional Insights for Eurex Group Clearing/Exchange. Kathryn's work has been published in a range of industry publications as well as academic journals. From 2008 to 2012, Kathryn was a senior investment research analyst for the CTA fund of funds, Risk and Portfolio Management (RPM). She also has experience as a quant analyst in fixed income and credit.

Kathryn's areas of interest are behavioral finance, trend following, managed futures, systematic trading, asset allocation, derivatives, and portfolio management. Kathryn holds a BS in electrical engineering from MIT (2001) and a PhD in operations research from MIT Sloan School of Management (2007). Her dissertation was supervised by Professor Andrew Lo and it focused on stopping strategies and financial heuristics. Kathryn holds the CAIA designation as a 100 Women in Hedge Funds PAAMCO CAIA Scholar.

D